HABITUATION
Perspectives from Child Development, Animal Behavior, and Neurophysiology

HABITUATION
Perspectives from
Child Development,
Animal Behavior,
and Neurophysiology

EDITED BY
THOMAS J. TIGHE
ROBERT N. LEATON
DARTMOUTH COLLEGE

   LAWRENCE ERLBAUM ASSOCIATES, PUBLISHERS
1976   Hillsdale, New Jersey

DISTRIBUTED BY THE HALSTED PRESS DIVISION OF

JOHN WILEY & SONS

New York   Toronto   London   Sydney

Lawrence Erlbaum Associates, Inc., Publishers
62 Maria Drive
Hillsdale, New Jersey 07642

Distributed solely by Halsted Press Division
John Wiley & Sons, Inc., New York

Library of Congress Cataloging in Publication Data

Main entry under title:

Habituation.

    Papers from a conference held at Dartmouth College's
Minary Conference Center in Holderness, N. H., Sept. 12–
17, 1974.
    Includes bibliographical references and index.
    1. Habituation (Neuropsychology) –Congresses.
2. Developmental psychobiology–Congresses.   3. Infant
psychology–Congresses.   4. Neurophysiology–Congresses.
I. Tighe, Thomas J. II. Leaton, R. N.
QP374.H3   156'.2'33   76-47506
ISBN 0-470-99008-2 (Halsted)

Printed in the United States of America

Contents

Preface

This volume is based on a conference on habituation held at Dartmouth College's Minary Conference Center in Holderness, New Hampshire, September 12–17, 1974. The purpose of the conference was to foster communication between those researchers studying habituation or closely related processes in children and those studying habituation at the level of neurophysiology and animal behavior. Within each of these groups there is burgeoning interest in habituation, yet there has been little, if any, interaction between them. Despite differences in subject populations, levels of analysis, and specific research goals, it is clear that these separate research endeavors are addressed to fundamentally the same behavioral process—response decrement resulting from repeated stimulation. The experimental procedures used with human infants, intact rats, and single neurons in simplified invertebrate preparations are at least superficially the same. A stimulus is repeatedly presented (a complex visual pattern in the infant, direct stimulation of a neuron in the invertebrate) and a decrement in a response (a visual orienting response in the infant, a postsynaptic potential in the invertebrate) is recorded. Of course, operational parallels at different levels of analysis may be seriously misleading, but it seems reasonable to make the working assumption that the experiments encompassed within these areas involve the same or highly similar processes.

Thus, it appeared to be an appropriate time to encourage an exchange of information between researchers working in animal behavior and neurophysiology and those working with human development. The careful analysis available to the animal-neurophysiological researcher could provide the human developmentalist with parametric relationships and theoretical foundations that are difficult to secure when dealing with the less easily controlled behavior of the young child and the neonate. On the other hand, the complexities of the human organism and human behavior should alert the animal neurophysiologist to the complexities that his theories and cellular analyses must ultimately handle. At the least, an exchange of basic information between these approaches should identify points of agreement and disagreement, and should reveal gaps in specific matters of data and methodology. In this way critical directions for research within each area may be suggested.

With these ideas in mind we applied to the Long Range Planning Committee of the Society for Research in Child Development. This Committee, with funds provided by the Grant Foundation, sponsors interdisciplinary study groups on basic problems of development. The Committee's response was positive and generous. Through the Society, the Grant Foundation provided funds to cover the cost of the conference. We are most grateful for this support.

Our belief in the timeliness and value of this interdisciplinary venture was reinforced by the enthusiasm with which the idea was greeted by the participants. We were fortunate in securing leading investigators in all of the areas selected for representation.

The content and organization of this text reflect quite directly the content and organization of the conference. Participants were chosen to represent levels of analysis ranging from the molecular to the molar and to reflect concern not only with the nature of habituation per se but also with the relation of habituation to other behaviors. In the text, this organization is seen both in the presentation of the animal-neurophysiological studies prior to the developmental studies and by the ordering of chapters within each research area.

We begin with Castellucci and Kandel's review of their work on the cellular basis of habituation in invertebrates. Thompson and Glanzman pursue a molecular analysis with vertebrate and simplified vertebrate preparations, and consider the implications of this and more molar analyses for the dual-process theory of habituation. Wagner presents a new theoretical position on habituation that uses the language of information-processing models of human memory to integrate conceptualizations of habituation and animal learning. The animal-neurophysiological studies end with Campbell and Coulter's review of research on the development of memory. This chapter should have significant heuristic value for consideration of possible developmental processes in habituation. The child development studies begin with Clifton and Nelson's analysis of the methodological problems involved in studying habituation in neonates. Cohen then describes the development of research on visual attention in children and presents his own theoretical perspective on the habituation of visual attention. Olson applies the perspective of human cognitive psychology to the literature on infant habituation. Jeffrey's chapter focuses on the possible influences of habituation on human development, with particular emphasis on perceptual development. The developmental studies end with Zeaman's illustrations of the significance of habituation for understanding developmental phenomena of learning. In the final chapter we attempt to compare the two research areas on dimensions of data and procedure as well as to define more general issues of mutual concern.

Overall, then, this volume provides a medium for cross-fertilization between animal-neurophysiological and developmental research on habituation, highlighting some of the current empirical and theoretical concerns within each area. While other volumes (notably Horn & Hinde, 1970; Peeke & Herz, 1973) may provide more comprehensive and detailed reviews of aspects of habituation, the juxtaposition of developmental and animal-neurophysiological research provided in this text is unique in the literature. We hope that this treatment will promote further interactions between these areas and, more significantly, that it will lead to a greater awareness of the truly ubiquitous and fundamental nature of habituation.

Finally, we would like to acknowledge the contribution of two conference participants who do not appear in this volume. Dr. Stanley C. Ratner attended the conference under severe time pressures and provided a valuable comparative perspective on habituation. Dr. Harriet L. Rheingold attended the conference in her capacity as a liason between the study group and the Society for Research in Child Development and contributed importantly to the working sessions.

THOMAS J. TIGHE
ROBERT N. LEATON

1

An Invertebrate System
for the Cellular Study
of Habituation and Sensitization

Vincent Castellucci
Eric R. Kandel

College of Physicians and Surgeons
Columbia University

INTRODUCTION

The mechanisms of behavior have traditionally interested psychologists, but in recent years the analysis of behavior has also attracted a number of neurobiologists. One reason for the neurobiologists' interest is that the study of behavior has advanced dramatically during the last decades. Another reason is that recent progress in the analysis of nerve cells and of synaptic transmission has encouraged neurobiologists to look beyond cellular function, which they are beginning to understand, to the analysis of systems of cells. Among the most interesting neural systems for study are those that control complete behavioral acts. Here one can examine how an interconnected group of cells mediates behavior and how simple forms of learning, such as habituation and sensitization, produce alterations in cellular function.

At first glance, the idea of studying behavioral acts and their modification on the cellular level seems staggering. The mammalian brain is made up of 10^{12} cells and the interconnections between these cells are many times more numerous still. To specify the complete neural circuit mediating a behavior in such a complex brain seems difficult. Fortunately this task can be simplified in a number of ways. A major simplification—and the one on which we will focus in this chapter—is provided by the use of the nervous system of invertebrate animals such as the leech, crayfish, lobsters, insects, and snails (Kandel & Kupfermann, 1970). The nervous system of these animals contains only about

10^5 cells. Some ganglia contain only 1000 to 2000 neurons, yet they are capable of mediating several behavioral responses. In these instances the total number of cells mediating a single behavior act may be only several hundred or even less. As a result, the task of analyzing the neural network mediating a given behavior is significantly reduced. In addition to fewer cells, invertebrate ganglia have identifiable neurons that can be reliably recognized in every member of the species. Using identified nerve cells, one can relate the functions of unique cells to behavior and thereby develop, for example, a cellular approach to habituation and sensitization.

Once a combined cellular and behavioral approach can be achieved, it is possible to address oneself to a variety of biological and behavioral questions. From a biological perspective it would be interesting to know the cellular mechanisms of habituation and sensitization. Does the laying down of the memory produced by these processes involve the growth of new cells or new connections, or does it result from functional changes in preexisting connections? From a behavioral perspective it would be interesting to know the relationships between habituation and dishabituation, between dishabituation and sensitization, and between the short-term memory of these processes and their long-term form. These interrelationships have, until recently, only been described behaviorally; with cellular techniques it is now possible to examine their biological basis.

We submit that these questions are not only important to psychology and biology, but that they are also central to psychiatry. Broadly defined, psychiatry is concerned with human behavior and its abnormalities. It will be difficult to have a meaningful analysis of abnormal behavior before we have at least a crude understanding, on a cellular level, of how experiential and genetic factors interact in determining normal behavior. One may question whether the study of invertebrates is the best place to begin this analysis. But it is difficult to argue against the premise that better animal models of behavioral modifications and behavioral abnormalities are much needed in psychiatric research.

In this chapter we will illustrate how a simple system can be used to analyze cellular mechanisms and interrelationships of simple behavioral modifications such as short- and long-term habituation, dishabituation, and sensitization.

THE NERVOUS SYSTEM OF *Aplysia*

We have used for our studies the large marine gastropod mollusc *Aplysia californica* (Figure 3). The central nervous system of this animal contains about 15,000 neurons which are grouped into 9 major ganglia (Eales, 1921). The abdominal ganglion that controls the behavioral responses we will consider contains about 2000 neurons (Coggeshall, 1967). This ganglion first came to the attention

of neurophysiologists because its neurons are exceptionally large (Arvanitaki &
Tchou, 1941). The largest cells are gigantic and can reach up to 1 mm in
diameter (Figure 1). Half of the cells have been categorized into different
functional clusters, and more than 50 large cells have been identified as unique
individuals that can be recognized reliably in every animal by their position,
color, and physiological properties (Frazier *et al.*, 1967; Koester & Kandel,

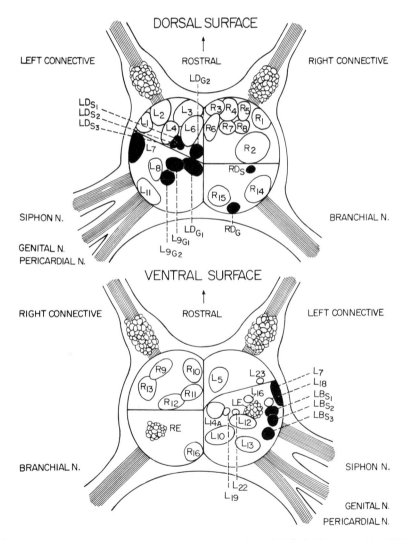

FIG. 1   Dorsal and ventral views of the abdominal ganglion of *Aplysia* illustrating identified
cells (modified from Frazier *et al.*, 1967). The motor neurons for siphon and gill have been
darkened. LE and RE indicate two sensory clusters (Byrne *et al.*, 1974a).

1976). The abdominal ganglion and other ganglia have proved very useful for a variety of neurobiological studies. For example, biochemical and pharmacological studies have been carried out on the synthesis, packaging, axonal transport, and release of transmitter substances in individual cells (Eisenstadt & Schwartz, 1975; Eisenstadt *et al.*, 1974; Goldman & Schwartz, 1974; Koike *et al.*, 1974; Schwartz *et al.*, 1975). Similarly, the distribution and properties of the receptors to various transmitters have been studied in identified cells (Ascher, 1972; Blankenship *et al.*, 1971; Kandel & Gardner, 1972; Kandel *et al.*, 1967; Kehoe, 1972a, 1972b, 1972c; Tauc & Gerschenfeld, 1962). The technical advantage most important for the purpose of our discussion is the ability to map, electroanatomically, the connections between individual cells on a cell-to-cell basis (Fig. 2) as well as the connections between a cell and the sensory or

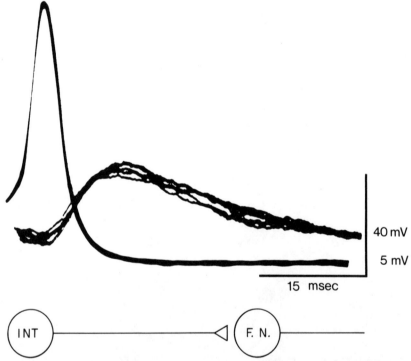

FIG. 2 Electroanatomical mapping of direct excitatory connection. Upper part: simultaneous recording from a presynaptic interneuron (upper trace) and a follower neuron (lower trace). Each action potential in the presynaptic neuron is associated with an EPSP in the follower neuron. The EPSP is constant in latency and appears in an all–or–none fashion. Lower part: schematic diagram illustrating postulated monosynaptic connection assumed to subserve direct electrophysiological connection between an interneuron (INT) and its follower neuron (F.N.). For schematic purpose the connections terminate on the cell body. Actually all synapses in the ganglion end on the axon of the postsynaptic cell. (From Kandel *et al.*, 1967.)

motor structures to which it is connected (Byrne *et al.*, 1974a; Carew *et al.*, 1974; Kandel & Gardner, 1972; Kandel *et al.*, 1967; Kehoe, 1972a; Koester *et al.*, 1974; Kupfermann *et al.*, 1974; Liebeswar *et al.*, 1975; Mayeri *et al.*, 1974). As a result specific identified cells can be related to specific behavioral function.

We have used these advantages to carry out a series of studies designed to analyze the cellular mechanisms of habituation and sensitization.

HABITUATION AND DISHABITUATION OF THE GILL- AND SIPHON-WITHDRAWAL REFLEX IN *Aplysia*

The mollusc *Aplysia* has a respiratory cavity, the mantle cavity, that contains the gill, the respiratory organ. The gill is in part covered by the mantle shelf, a protective skin that forms the roof of the mantle cavity. The posterior edge of the mantle shelf forms a respiratory funnel called the siphon. When a weak tactile stimulus is applied to the siphon, or the mantle shelf, the siphon and the mantle shelf contract, and the gill withdraws further into the mantle cavity (Figure 3). Each of the two main components of the total reflex response, the siphon (and mantle shelf) contraction and the gill contraction, has a short latency and its amplitude is graded depending on the intensity of the tactile stimulus. This reflex is analogous to defensive withdrawal responses found in invertebrates and, as is the case with those reflexes, this reflex readily undergoes both short-term habituation and dishabituation (Carew *et al.*, 1972; Pinsker *et al.*, 1970, 1973).

Habituation—often considered the most elementary form of learning—is a decrease in a behavioral response that occurs when an initially novel stimulus is repeatedly presented (Figure 4a) (Thorpe, 1956). Once habituated, two processes can lead to the restoration of the gill-withdrawal response: *spontaneous recovery*, which occurs when the stimulus to which the animal has habituated is withheld for several minutes or hours; and *dishabituation*, which restores the habituated response immediately when a strong stimulus is applied to another site such as the head (Figure 4b). Habituation and dishabituation of the gill-withdrawal reflex are parametrically similar to the comparable behavioral modifications described in higher vertebrates (Thompson & Spencer, 1966). For example, habituation tends to occur more rapidly to weak than to strong stimuli (Figure 5), and the rate of habituation increases if the frequency of stimulation is increased. Whereas many responses show these parametric features characteristic of elementary forms of habituation, some responses also show certain higher order features of habituation.

For example, in studies of habituation of the flexion reflex in spinal cat, Spencer, Thompson, and Nielson (1966a, 1966b, 1966c) presented the first evidence for the important idea that dishabituation of this reflex response is not due to a removal of habituation, but to a special case of sensitization, the

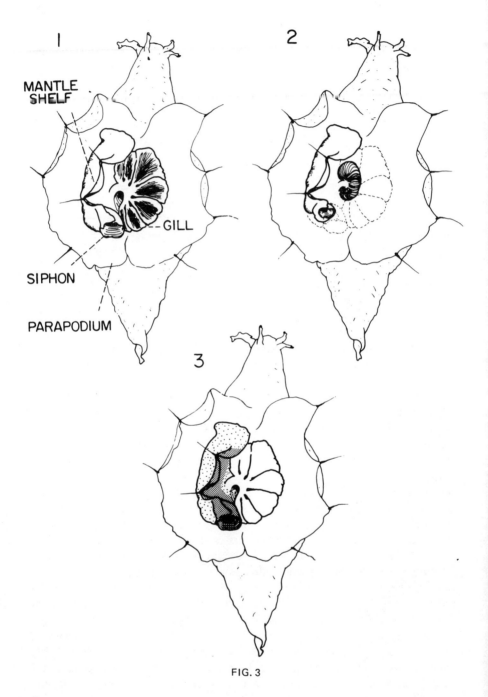

MANTLE SHELF

GILL

SIPHON

PARAPODIUM

FIG. 3

6

Fig. 3 Gill-withdrawal reflex in *Aplysia*. Part 1. Dorsal view of an intact animal. The parapodia and mantle shelf have been retracted to reveal the gill and the position of the organs in the unstimulated relaxed position. Part 2. Position of organs during withdrawal reflex following tactile stimulation within the receptive field. In addition to the gill contraction, the withdrawal response includes also movements of the siphon and parapodia. Part 3. Tactile receptive field for withdrawal reflex. The area which produces strong effects is heavily stippled and includes the siphon and mantle shelf. The surrounding area (dotted) produces weaker effects. Weak contractions were obtained by strong stimulation outside of the main receptive field. (From Kupfermann & Kandel, 1969. Copyright 1969 by the American Association for the Advancement of Science.)

---

process whereby a strong stimulus enhances the responsiveness of a variety of reflexes. Carew, Castellucci, and Kandel (1971) therefore examined the relationship between dishabituation and sensitization in *Aplysia* by comparing the effects of a common dishabituating stimulus on habituated and nonhabituated responses (Figure 6). If dishabituation is a removal of habituation, then a dishabituating stimulus should facilitate only a habituated response and restore it to its original value. But if dishabituation is a special case of sensitization, one would predict that a dishabituating stimulus might facilitate an unhabituated response as well as a habituated one, and the habituated response might be facilitated beyond its control value. Carew *et al.* (1971) used two independent

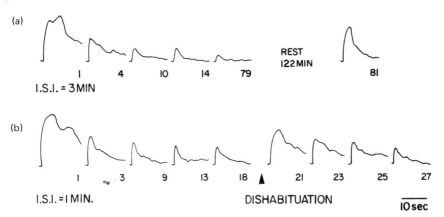

FIG. 4 Habituation, spontaneous recovery, and dishabituation of the gill-withdrawal reflex. Photocell record from 2 response habituations in a single preparation (see Figure 10a for the experimental setup). The interval between stimuli (ISI) and total number of habituatory stimuli are indicated. Part a shows decrement of the response with repetition of the tactile stimulus. Following a 122-min rest the response was almost fully recovered. Part b shows a later experiment from the same preparation. After rehabituation of the response a stimulus consisting of a strong and prolonged tactile stimulus to the neck region was presented at the arrow. Successive test responses were facilitated for several minutes. (From Pinsker *et al.*, 1970. Copyright 1970 by the American Association for the Advancement of Science.)

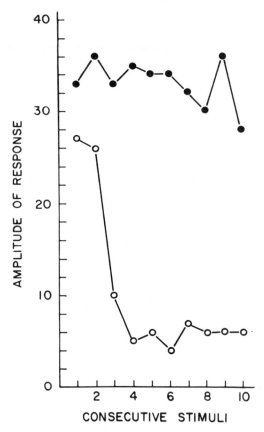

FIG. 5 Habituation of gill-withdrawal reflex with weak and strong tactile stimuli. Responses to the stronger stimulus (filled circles) are initially larger and show less decrement with repetition than responses to the weaker stimulus (open circles). (From Pinsker *et al.*, 1970. Copyright 1970 by the American Association for the Advancement of Science.)

afferent pathways for eliciting the reflex: the siphon and the mantle shelf. Repeated elicitation of the gill-withdrawal reflex following stimulation of the siphon led to habituation of the reflex to siphon stimulation but did not alter the reflex responsiveness to stimulation of the mantle shelf. However, a common dishabituatory stimulus facilitated both habituated and unhabituated responses. Moreover the habituated responses could be facilitated above their control level (Figure 6). Thus, in the gill-withdrawal reflex in *Aplysia,* as in the flexion reflex of vertebrates, dishabituation is a special case of sensitization. This feature is

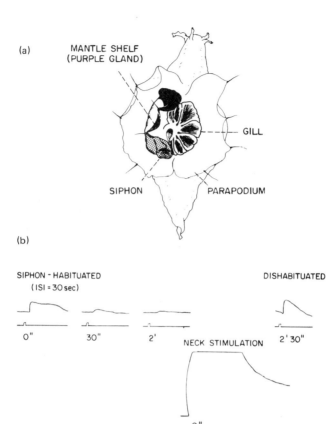

Fig. 6 Facilitation of both habituated and nonhabituated gill-withdrawal responses by presentation of a single dishabituatory stimulus. (a) Dorsal view of an intact *Aplysia*. The parapodia and mantle shelf have been retracted to reveal the gill. The anterior part of the mantle shelf and its edge, the purple gland, are indicated in solid black. This area of the receptive field for the gill-withdrawal reflex was used and called purple gland. The siphon and the posterior part of the mantle shelf and of the purple gland are stippled; in our experiments they are called siphon. (b) after a single test stimulus to the purple gland (0″) repetitive stimuli were delivered to the siphon, producing habituation of gill withdrawal. After a second test to the purple gland (2′ 20″) (indicating that no generalization of habituation had occurred) a series of vigorous brush strokes were presented to the neck region, producing a gill contraction. Subsequent presentation of a stimulus first to the purple gland and then to the siphon revealed facilitation of both nonhabituated responses (sensitization) and habituated responses (dishabituation). (From Carew *et al.*, 1971.)

9

perhaps the most interesting parametric aspect of the habituation because the ability to dishabituate a response by stimulating another pathway tends to distinguish simple forms of the habituation paradigm from more complex forms.

A second feature for distinguishing simple forms of habituation from complex ones is the time course. The behavioral modifications we have so far discussed last minutes or hours. Yet, the more interesting behavioral modifications characteristic of higher animals last days, and may even be permanent. In an attempt to explore the usefulness of the gill-withdrawal reflex for the study of long-term processes, Carew, Pinsker, and Kandel (1972) examined whether habituation and sensitization (Pinsker et al., 1973) in Aplysia could also be prolonged.

In these experiments unrestrained animals were used and the siphon component of the defensive reflex was monitored. The two components of the reflex (withdrawal of the gill and of the siphon) parallel each other so that observing one component provides an index of the other (Carew et al., 1972; Pinsker et al., 1973). Because the siphon normally protrudes from the mantle cavity, this component of the reflex can be readily studied in freely moving animals and is particularly useful for studying long-term behavioral modifications. When habituation training (10 trials a day) was repeated daily for 4 days, habituation of the reflex response built up progressively across days so that on the fourth day the sum of trials 1–10 was only 20% of the first day (Figure 7). Long-term habituation persisted unchanged for a week, and was only partially recovered after 3 weeks. The same training procedure also produces long-term habituation of the gill-withdrawal component as examined in restrained animals.

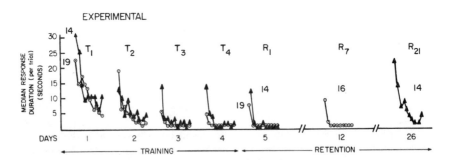

FIG. 7 Long-term habituation of siphon withdrawal. Build-up of habituation during 4 days of training (T_1 to T_4) and retention of 1 day (R_1), 1 week (R_7), and 3 weeks (R_{21}) after training. Data from 3 experiments are presented: 2 independent, identical replications in which retention was tested 1 day and 1 week after training have been pooled (⊙); in the third experiment, retention was tested at 1 day and 3 weeks (▲). Each data point for each trial is the median duration of siphon withdrawal for the entire group. The number of animals contributing scores for each curve is indicated. Experimental animals showed significantly greater habituation than the control group (not shown) on all the testing week sessions. A Mann–Whitney U Test was used for intergroup comparisons. (From Carew et al., 1972. Copyright 1972 by the American Association for the Advancement of Science.)

A third feature that distinguishes simple from more complex forms of habitua-tion is pattern of stimulation. In a variety of motor-learning tasks in vertebrates temporally spaced training produced better long-term retention than massed training. The same applies for the siphon- and gill-withdrawal reflex. Training sessions of 10 trials a day spaced over 4 days produced much better retention of habituation than 40 trials massed in 1 day (Figure 8a, b). Even when training sessions are separated by as little as 90 min they produced significantly longer lasting habituation than uninterrupted massed training (Figure 8c; Carew *et al.,* 1972; Carew & Kandel, 1973).

Similarly, 4 days of sensitization training (4 noxious stimuli a day) led to long-term reflex enhancement that also lasted 3 weeks (Figure 9) and spaced training was again more effective than massed training (Pinsker *et al.,* 1973).

Thus habituation and sensitization of the gill and the siphon component of the withdrawal reflex have some interesting higher order features of habituation. The reflex can be depressed as well as enhanced by training and these behavioral modifications can have both short-term and long-term forms. In this chapter we consider mainly the short-term behavioral modifications. We focus on the gill-withdrawal component of the defensive reflex, since its detailed neural circuit is understood.

NEURONAL NETWORK UNDERLYING THE GILL-AND SIPHON-WITHDRAWAL REFLEX IN *Aplysia*

In order to relate individual cells to behavior and to analyze the mechanisms underlying habituation and sensitization, we use two different preparations (Figure 10). The first preparation consists of an intact animal restrained in a small aquarium, containing cooled circulating seawater, in which gill responses to tactile stimuli can be measured by means of a photocell. For a more detailed and qualitative analysis, motion pictures can also be taken. Quantifiable tactile stimuli are provided by jets of seawater from a Water Pik. A slit is produced in the animal's neck, through which the abdominal ganglion is externalized so that the intracellular responses from nerve cells can be monitored, while gill or other mantle organ movements are simultaneously recorded. The second preparation consists of the isolated abdominal ganglion with or without the siphon skin and gill. This preparation can be used as a test system of the behavior for more detailed cellular studies.

In an attempt to delineate the neural circuit of this reflex, Kupfermann and Kandel (1969) and Kupfermann, Carew, and Kandel (1974) first investigated the motor components of the reflex in the intact preparation. One or more nerve cells were impaled with microelectrodes and stimulated with intracellular current pulses while the movements of the different external organs of the mantle cavity were monitored (Figure 11). Thirteen motor neurons in the abdominal ganglion

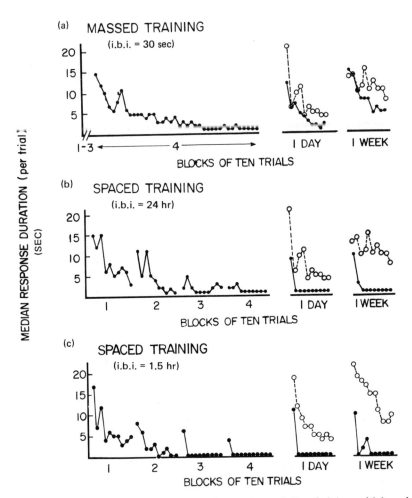

FIG. 8 Comparison of massed and spaced habituation training of siphon withdrawal in *Aplysia*. (a) Experimental massed animals [$n = 15$, (●)] received no stimulation for 3 days. On Day 4 they were given 40 consecutive training trials (intertrial interval = 30 sec). The controls [$n = 5$, (○)] received no training. Retention was tested 1 day and 1 week after training. (b) Experimental spaced animals [$n = 5$, (●)] were given 4 blocks (10 trials/block) of habituation training, with each block separated by 1 day. Studies illustrated in Figures 8a and 8b were carried out concurrently and used the same control population. The spaced-training group was significantly lower than the massed-training group at both 24 hr ($p < 0.01$) and 1 week ($p < 0.01$) retention test. The massed-training group was not significantly different from controls in either retention test. (c) Experimental spaced animals [$n = 9$, (●)] were given 4 blocks of training separated by 1.5 hr. Controls [$n = 9$, (○)] received no training. Retention was tested 1 day and 1 week after training. Experimentals exhibited significantly greater habituation than control in retention testing ($p < .001$ for both tests). (Mann–Whitney U Tests have been used for intergroup comparisons (8a) and (8b) are from Carew *et al.*, 1972; (8c) from Carew & Kandel, 1973. Copyright 1972, 1973 by the American Association for the Advancement of Science.)

12

were found: five neurons moved only the gill, seven moved only the siphon, and one moved gill, siphon, and mantle shelf (Figure 15). Each motor neuron was characterized by its location, its electrophysiological properties, and by the type of movement it produced (Kupfermann *et al.*, 1974).

The relative importance of individual cells in mediating the behavior can be assessed by means of a reversible lesion technique (Figure 12). The reflex is evoked with a given motor cell hyperpolarized and removed from the reflex on alternate trials (Kupfermann *et al.*, 1971; Kupfermann *et al.*, 1974). It is thus possible to compare the amplitude of the reflex with and without the contribution of a single motor neuron. Each of the two major gill neurons, L7 and LDG_1, were found to contribute between 30 and 40% of the gill reflex. The individual

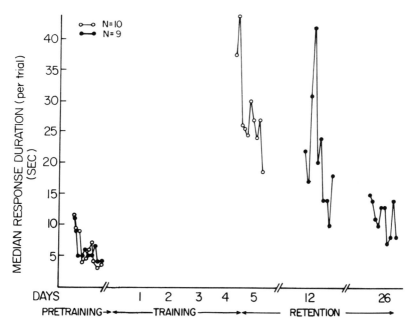

FIG. 9 Long-term sensitization of siphon withdrawal. Thirteen days after matching, the experimental animals were given 4 electrical shocks per day for 4 days whereas the controls received no shocks. The median duration of siphon withdrawal is shown for each trial of a 10-trial block. Minimum intertrial interval is 30 seconds. Experiment 1 (o) subjects tested 24 hours after training, experiment 2 (●) subjects tested 1 week and 3 weeks after training. Twenty-four hours and 1 week after the end of training the experimental animals showed significantly longer siphon withdrawal as compared to both their pretraining scores and that of the controls (not shown) (Mann–Whitney U tests for intergroup comparisons). In the 3 week retention test there was no longer a significant difference between the experimental and control groups, but the responses of the experimental animals were still significantly prolonged compared to their own pretraining controls (Wilcoxon matched pairs signed-ranks test; $p < 0.005$) whereas the control animals were unchanged. (Based on Pinsker *et al.*, 1973.)

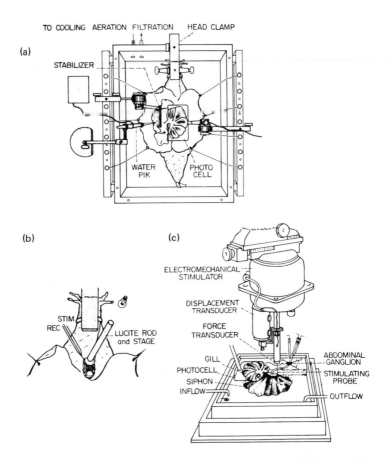

Fig. 10 Different preparations used to study gill- and siphon-withdrawal reflexes. (a) Experimental setup for behavioral studies of gill withdrawal in the intact restrained animal. *Aplysia* immobilized in a small aquarium containing cooled, filtered and aerated circulating seawater. The edge of the mantle shelf is pinned to a substage and a constant and quantifiable tactile stimulus is delivered by brief jets of sea water from a commercially available Water Pik. The behavioral responses were monitored with a photocell placed under the gill or by means of 16 mm movies (modified from Pinsker *et al.*, 1970. Copyright 1970 by the American Association for the Advancement of Science.) (b) Preparation for simultaneous study of cellular and behavioral responses. Intact animal immobilized as in (a). A small slit is made in the neck of the animal, and the abdominal ganglion with its peripheral nerves and connectives intact is externalized and pinned to a lucite stage. Identified motor cells are impaled with double-barrelled microelectrodes for intracellular stimulation and recording. Gill movements are recorded with photocell and camera (from Kupfermann *et al.*, 1970). (c) Test system of gill-withdrawal reflex. The abdominal ganglion remains connected to the gill via the branchial and pericardial-genital nerves and to the siphon via the siphon nerve. Intracellular recordings are obtained from motor neurons and mechanoreceptor neurons; tactile stimuli are applied to the siphon skin by means of an electromechanical stimulator (Byrne, 1975) that can deliver stimuli using feedback control for displacement or force.

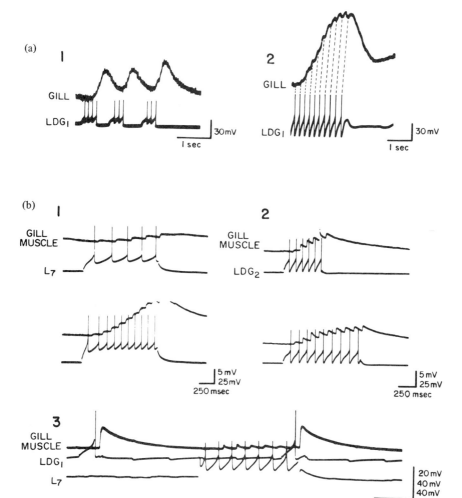

FIG. 11 Responses of gill and individual gill muscle fibers to stimulation of identified motor cells. (a) Response of the gill. Upper traces represent the output of a photocell placed under the gill, lower traces intracellular recordings from a motor neuron causing gill contraction. (a1) Smooth contraction produced by small number of spikes in cell LDG_1. (a2) Individual twitches produced by LDG_1 after it was first stimulated at high frequency to potentiate its effects (from Kupfermann and Kandel, 1969). (b) Intracellular recordings of excitatory junctional potentials (EJP'S) in gill muscle fibers (top trace) due to intracellular stimulation of L7 or LDG_2 (bottom traces). (b1) Spikes in L7 were elicited by depolarizing pulses of different intensities. The EJP's in the gill followed L7 spikes one for one with a fixed latency at both low frequencies (5/sec) and higher frequencies (10/sec). At the higher frequency the EJP's potentiate. (b2) Response of gill muscle fiber to intracellular stimulation of LDG_2. (b3) Intracellular recording from LDG_2, L7, and a single muscle fiber showing 2 types of EJP's, 1 from LDG_1 and the other from L7. (From Carew et al., 1974.)

15

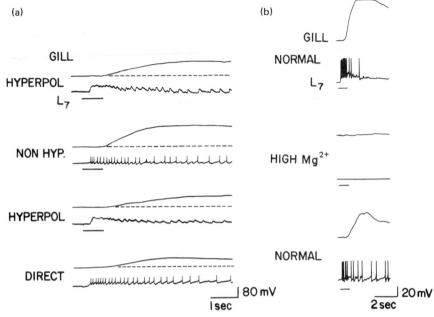

FIG. 12 Contribution of the central motor cells to total gill-withdrawal reflex. (a) Contri-bution of motor neuron L7. The gill-withdrawal reflex was elicited every 5 min by a jet of seawater (indicated by solid line, under L7 record) applied to the siphon and, on alternate trials, L7 was hyperpolarized (Hyp.) so that the excitatory input could not discharge it. Comparisons of hyperpolarized to nonhyperpolarized (Nonhyp.) trials showed that the gill contraction was reduced by about 40%. This reduction was approxi-mately equal to the size of the gill contraction produced by L7 when it was directly fired by a long depolarizing pulse (last pair of traces) that caused L7 to fire in a pattern comparable to that produced by the normal excitatory input. (b) Contribution of the total central pathway. With the abdominal ganglion in normal seawater a jet of seawater applied to the siphon produced a large excitatory input to L7, and a large gill contraction. With the abdominal ganglion bathed in high magnesium solution, and with all synaptic input elimi-nated to L7 and presumably to other cells in the ganglion, the gill-withdrawal reflex was totally abolished. When the ganglion was returned to normal seawater, synaptic input and the gill contraction partially recovered. In (a) and (b) the lower traces are the intracellular records from L7, and the upper traces are the output of a photocell placed under the gill to monitor contraction. (from Kupfermann *et al.*, 1971. Copyright 1971 by the American Association for the Advancement of Science.)

contribution of the other four gill motor cells was considerably less. If one blocks synaptic transmission by bathing the abdominal ganglion in a solution of high magnesium content, the gill contraction to weak stimulation is reversibly blocked, illustrating that the neural circuit is restricted to this ganglion (Kupfer-mann *et al.*, 1971; Peretz *et al.*, 1976). With moderate intensity stimulation a peripheral pathway which contributes 5 to 10% is recruited (Kupfermann *et al.*, 1971, 1974). Using these same techniques Perlman (1975) found that the siphon reflex can be shown to be partially (55%) mediated by motor neurons in the abdominal ganglion and partially (45%) by peripheral motor neurons (see also Lukowiak & Jacklet, 1972, 1975). Bailey *et al.* (1975) have located along the course of the siphon nerve motor neurons that mediate part of the siphon contraction.

When the reflex is evoked by stimulating the siphon skin, the sensory component of the reflex is mediated by both direct (monosynaptic) and indirect (polysynaptic) synaptic convergence onto the motor neurons. The monosynaptic contribution is mediated by a cluster of about 24 mechanoreceptor (LE of Figure 1) neurons located in the abdominal ganglion (Byrne, Castellucci, & Kandel, 1974a). Each of the sensory cells has about the same threshold to mechanical stimulation. The cells differ from each other, however, in the size and the location of their receptive fields (Figure 13).

The mechanoreceptor sensory neurons make direct connections to the gill motor cells, to the central and peripheral siphon motor cells, and to at least two excitatory interneurons that in turn synapse on motor cells. Finally, the sensory neurons connect directly to an inhibitory interneuron that feeds back on the sensory neurons and feeds forward to the excitatory interneurons (Figures 14, 15).

The monosynapticity of these connections can be shown by several criteria: (1) one-for-one following; i.e., each presynaptic spike produces a discrete postsynaptic potential in the follower cell; (2) the synaptic potential has a short and constant latency, even in solutions containing high concentrations of divalent cations that increase the threshold of all neurons and reduce the likelihood of an interneuron being fired; (3) the latency stays constant when the transmitter release is reduced by a high magnesium solution or is increased by injecting tetraethylammonium chloride in the presynaptic element (Castellucci & Kandel, 1974). On the basis of these data one can describe a neural circuit of both the gill and siphon components of the defensive reflex (Figure 15). Below we mainly consider the gill component of the withdrawal reflex.

LOCUS AND NATURE OF THE FUNCTIONAL CHANGES UNDERLYING SHORT-TERM HABITUATION AND DISHABITUATION

The neural circuit of the gill component of the withdrawal reflex is characterized by two features: simplicity and invariance. The circuit consists of only about 40 cells, each of which seems to be invariant and to make specific connections with other invariant elements and with peripheral sensory and motor structures. How then are behavioral modifications achieved in this circuit? As Figure 15 illustrates, despite the small number of elements, there are numerous possible sites for plasticity, even in a simple circuit. For example, the physiological and

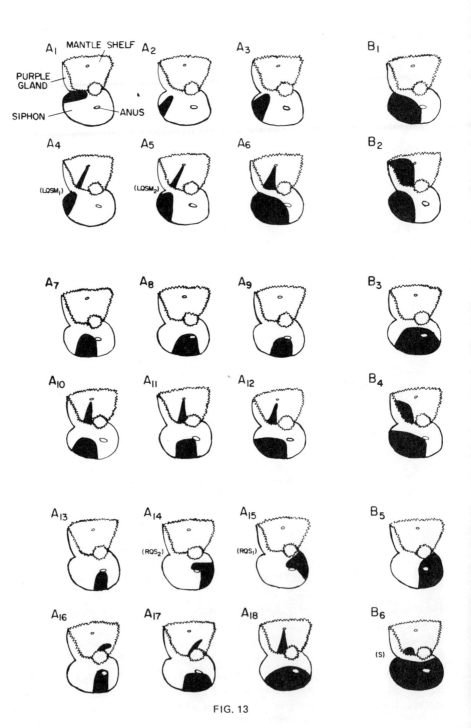

FIG. 13

FIG. 13 Sensory neurons' receptive fields. Reconstruction of 24 mechanoreceptor fields which are typical of the sensory cells innervating the tip of the siphon skin (LE cluster). There is a wide distribution of field sizes and extensive field overlap. Some fields are so characteristic that they could be repeatedly identified from preparation to preparation (see A_4, A_5, A_{14}, A_{15}, and B_6). The ventral surface of the siphon skin is schematized in each case. The jagged lines indicate the sites of cut from the rest of the animal. (From Byrne *et al.*, 1974a.)

---

decremental changes underlying habituation could occur peripherally, either as receptor adaptation or motor fatigue. Alternatively they could occur centrally, either as alterations of synaptic input (such as recruitment of inhibitory drive or a decrease of excitatory drive) or as an alteration of the biophysical properties of the membrane of the motor neurons or a change in the responsiveness of the postsynaptic receptor molecules.

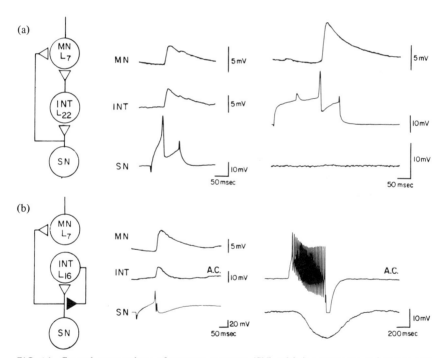

FIG. 14 Central connections of sensory neurons (SN) with interneurons and motor neurons. (a) Intracellular stimulation of sensory neuron produces an EPSP in an excitatory interneuron (L22) (middle) and in the motor cell (L7). An action potential in the excitatory interneuron, in turn, causes an excitatory potential in the motor neuron L7 (right). These connections are summarized in the drawing on the left. (b) Intracellular stimulation of a sensory neuron produces an EPSP in inhibitory interneuron L16 (middle column) and in the motor cell L7. Repetitive discharge of the interneuron produce an hyperpolarization in the sensory neuron (right). These connections are summarized in the drawing on the left. (From Castellucci *et al.*, in preparation.)

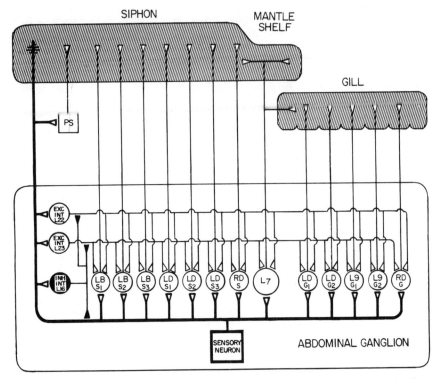

FIG. 15 Schematic diagram of the neural network controlling defensive withdrawal reflex. Dark triangles indicate inhibition; light triangles, excitation. The sensory input from the siphon is mediated directly and via interneurons (Sensory Neuron represents a class of sensory cells, LE cluster). Motor neurons and interneurons are identified cells (modified from Kupfermann & Kandel, 1969; Kupfermann, *et al.,* 1974). PS represents a group of peripheral siphon motor cells (Bailey *et al.,* 1975).

As a first step Byrne *et al.* (1974a, b) stimulated the skin in an isolated preparation at intervals that produced habituation (once every 10 sec to once every 2 min) and found no evidence for receptor adaptation. Similarly, stimulating the motor neurons intracellularly, at intervals that produced habituation, also did not produce motor fatigue (Carew *et al.,* 1974). Dishabituation also did not alter the properties of the sensory receptor organs or the nerve muscle functions. These results suggest that both habituation and dishabituation result from changes within the central nervous system.

To determine the nature of these changes Kupfermann *et al.* (1970) recorded from the major gill motor neurons in the intact animal during the course of habituation and dishabituation. They found that in the rested state, tactile stimulation of the siphon produced large and effective excitatory synaptic potentials that caused repetitive discharges in the motor neurons, leading to a

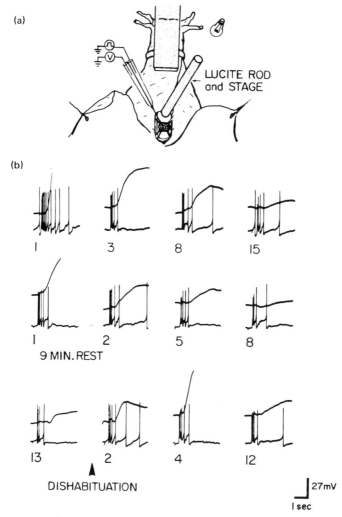

(a)

(b)

| 1 | 3 | 8 | 15 |

| 1 | 2 | 5 | 8 |

9 MIN. REST

| 13 | 2 | 4 | 12 |

▲ DISHABITUATION

⎤ 27mV
⎦ 1 sec

FIG. 16 Correlation of contraction of the gill and responses of motor neuron (L7) during habituation and sensitization. (a) Top view of anterior portion of an intact preparation. The abdominal ganglion was externalized through a small slit made in the skin above the ganglion (see also Figure 10b). (b) Gill contractions (top traces of each pair) and simultaneous intracellular recordings from an identified motor neuron, L7 (bottom traces). Sample records are all from the same preparation. Tactile stimuli in jets of seawater (500 msec in duration) were presented to the mantle shelf every 90 sec. Stimulus number are indicated below each pair of traces. Habituation stimuli (first line) were presented over a period of 21 min. Number of spikes in the 1-sec interval following the first evoked spike in each trace: 9, 6, 6, 4. Partial recovery (after a 9-min rest) and subsequent rehabituation of the reflex. Number of spikes: 7, 6, 5, 3. Following the last habituation trial shown in the first trace, (13), of the third line a strong stimulus was applied to the siphon. The discharge of the motor neuron and the amplitude of the gill contraction progressively increased during the first three stimuli following the dishabituatory stimulus and remained elevated for several minutes. Number of spikes: 4, 5, 7, 4. (From Kupfermann *et al.*, 1970. Copyright 1970 by the American Association for the Advancement of Science.)

(a)

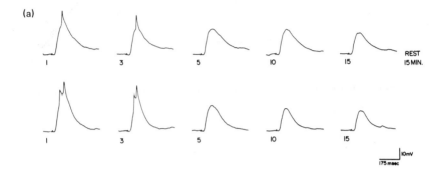

(b)

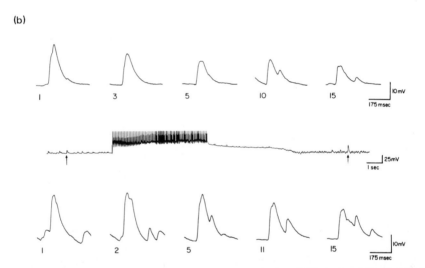

FIG. 17 Depression and facilitation of the evoked complex EPSP produced by electrical stimulation of afferent fibers in the isolated ganglion test system. Complex evoked EPSP in cell L7 were produced by electrical stimulation of the siphon nerve. (17a) The EPSP produced showed decrement (habituation) with repetition of the stimulus every 10 sec. Recovery of the amplitude was obtained after a 15-min rest, after which a new decrement was produced. Stimulus numbers are indicated below each trace. (b) A decremented EPSP could be facilitated (dishabituation) following a train of electrical stimuli to the left connective (6 Hz for 6 sec). The cell was hyperpolarized at a constant level of resting membrane potential to prevent spiking. First line is the first decremental run. Middle trace is a continuous record at lower gain and slower time scale indicating the facilitating stimulus effect on the motor neuron and showing at the two arrows PSP15 of the first line and PSP1 of the bottom line. In the botton traces facilitated PSP's following the extrastimulus are illustrated.

full reflex response (Figure 16) (Kupfermann *et al.*, 1970). When the tactile stimulus was repeated the number and frequency of evoked spikes decreased and the reflex response habituated. Restoration of reflex responsiveness produced either by rest or by a dishabituatory stimulus was associated with an increase in the number and frequency of spikes in the gill motor neurons.

To determine the cellular changes underlying the alterations in firing frequency of the motor neurons, the motor cells were hyperpolarized and the changes in the underlying synaptic potentials were examined. For these studies the simplified test system (Figure 10c) consisting of the siphon and the gill connected to the abdominal ganglion was used. As in the intact animal, a tactile stimulus applied to siphon in this preparation produced a complex excitatory postsynaptic potential (EPSP) recorded in a motor neuron. A similar complex EPSP can also be produced by electrically stimulating the siphon nerve that contains the axon of the sensory neurons (Figure 1) (Castellucci *et al.*, 1970; Carew *et al.*, 1971).

Paralleling the habituation, the complex EPSP's evoked by tactile stimulation of the siphon or electrical stimulation of the siphon nerve decreased in amplitude when the stimulus was repeated (Figure 17). Rest or stimulation of a pathway from the head (which simulates the application of a dishabituatory stimulus to the head of the intact animal) produced a restoration of the EPSP amplitude.

Such changes in the complex EPSP could be produced by changes in input resistance of the motor cells, or by changes in the synaptic input onto the motor cells. We first examined the input resistance of the motor neurons and found it unchanged during either decrement or facilitation of the EPSP. These results ruled out a gross change in input resistance near the cell body and suggested that synaptic alterations are more likely due to changes in the synaptic convergence to the motor neurons.

A change in the synaptic convergence on the motor neurons could be caused either by a recruitment in central inhibition (that decreases the number or the firing frequency of the active sensory neurons contributing to the complex EPSP) or by a change in the synaptic efficacy of individual excitatory elements. These alternatives can be distinguished by examining the monosynaptic excitatory connection made by single sensory cells onto motor cells (Castellucci *et al.*, 1970; Castellucci & Kandel, 1974). This EPSP is found to decrease when stimulation is repeated at a rate that produces habituation (Figure 18) and to recover with rest. Similar changes occur in the monosynaptic EPSP's produced by the sensory neurons on the interneurons as well. These results indicate that the major loci of habituation of the reflex are the synapses made by branches of the sensory neurons on their follower cells.

Does dishabituation also occur at the same site? To answer this question we examined the monosynaptic EPSP produced by a single mechanoreceptor neuron while stimulating the pathway from the head (Figure 19). The stimulus

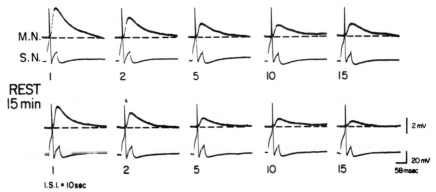

FIG. 18 Synaptic depression of the monosynaptic EPSP produced in motor cell L7 (M.N.) by stimulation of a single sensory neuron (S.N.) in high divalent cation solution (138 mM Mg^{2+}, 62 mM Ca^{2+}). Interstimulus interval (ISI) 10 sec. Two series of 15 stimuli each were presented with a rest of 15-min in between. The rest led to partial recovery, but a slight buildup of the depression is evident in the second run. (from Castellucci & Kandel, 1974.)

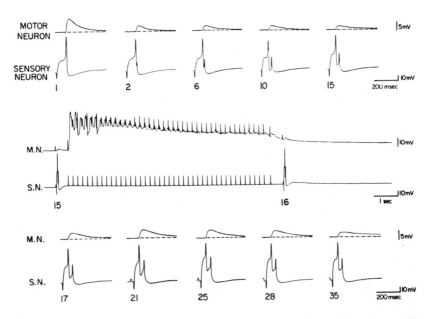

FIG. 19 Synaptic depression and facilitation at the synapse between mechanoreceptor neurons and motor neurons. Fifteen intracellular stimuli applied to 1 sensory cell at 10 sec intervals produced depression of the EPSP (number of stimuli 15). After the 15th stimulus a train of stimuli was applied to the left connective (6 Hz for 10 sec). The stimulation produces EPSP and action potentials in the motor neuron (top trace) of middle set but it does not fire the sensory neuron (bottom trace) of middle set. Stimulus 15 and 16 are illustrated in the middle traces. Note the stimulus artifacts in the middle traces. The follower cell is illustrated at lower gain and slower time scale. Facilitation of the EPSP following connective stimulation lasted for several minutes (Stimuli 17 to 35).

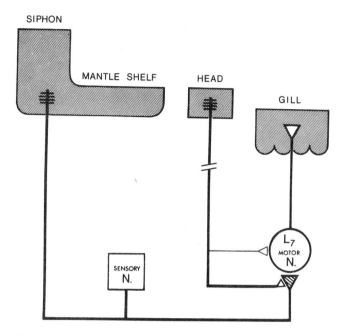

FIG. 20 Simplified schematic wiring diagram to indicate the locus of the postulated plastic changes underlying habituation and dishabituation (sensitization) of the gill-withdrawal reflex. Only one sensory neuron and one motor neuron are represented. Habituation is due to a decrement in excitatory transmission at the synapse (cross-hatched) between the mechanoreceptor neurons and the motor neurons. Dishabituation (sensitization) is due to heterosynaptic facilitation at the same synapse. An hypothetical pathway which synapses on the presynaptic terminals of the sensory fibers and mediates the proposed presynaptic facilitation is indicated. The dishabituatory stimulus also produces an excitatory input to the motor neuron. Dishabituation can be produced by a strong stimulus to most parts of the animal's body surface although only the head is indicated in the diagram. The exact neural pathway from the head, indicated by the interrupted line, has not yet been worked out. (From Castellucci *et al.*, 1970. Copyright 1970 by the American Association for the Advancement of Science.)

produced synaptic facilitation that paralleled the dishabituation. This facilitation did not involve a change in the frequency of firing of the sensory neuron, thereby excluding posttetanic potentiation as a mechanism for facilitation. These data suggest that habituation and dishabituation thus occur at the same set of synapses, those between the sensory neurons of the reflex and their central target cells (Figure 20). Habituation involves a homosynaptic depression, and dishabituation involves a heterosynaptic facilitation.

THE SYNAPTIC MECHANISMS UNDERLYING
SHORT-TERM HABITUATION AND DISHABITUATION

What mechanisms underlie the synaptic changes that mediate habituation and dishabituation? Are the changes in synaptic efficacy presynaptic, involving alterations in transmitter release, or are they postsynaptic, involving changes in receptor responsiveness? These two possibilities can be distinguished by means of a quantal analysis (del Castillo & Katz, 1954). We therefore applied quantal analysis to synaptic transmission between the sensory cells and their follower cells.

According to the quantal hypothesis, transmitter release is not graded but quantized (for review see Katz, 1964; Martin, 1966). Each quantum contains about 1,000–10,000 transmitter molecules. The number of quanta released by an action potential is given by $m = n \times p$, where m is the mean quantal content, p is the mean probability of a quantum being released, and n is the available population of quanta. The average amplitude $(\bar{E})$ of an evoked EPSPs is therefore given by

$$\bar{E} = m \times \bar{q}$$

$$(1)$$

FIG. 21 Quantal release at the synapse between mechanoreceptor neurons and motor neurons. (a) Comparison of normal release and low release of transmitter. (a1) Normal release. When a sensory neuron (S.N.) is repeatedly stimulated intracellularly there is only small fluctuation in the amplitude of the evoked EPSPs (ISI = 10 sec). (a2) Low release. When release is reduced by increasing external Mg^{++} (165 mM) and reducing Ca^{2+} (8 mM) stimulation of the sensory neuron produces marked fluctuation in the amplitude of the EPSP's; and some stimuli produce failures (arrow) (ISI = 10 sec). 21(b) Computer averages of unitary EPSP's and failures during synaptic depression. (b1) The first 5 EPSP's of a series were averaged to determine average EPSP (AV EPSP). Failures (AV failure, $N = 21$) and unit EPSPs (AV unit, $N = 21$) were averaged separately. The background noise ($N = 21$) was averaged 2 sec before the occurrence of a presynaptic spike. The failure average resembles the background noise average; there was not a time locked depolarization. (b2) Time course of average EPSP and average unit. The averaged EPSP and the unit average (AV unit) of (b1) were matched for amplitude and superimposed photographically to illustrate the similarity in their time course. (c1) Amplitude histogram of successive EPSPs. The peak of failure (dark bar) is followed by the first response peak (I), assumed to be the amplitude of a unitary EPSP $(\bar{q}_1)$. The successive peaks occur at voltage levels that are roughly integral multiples of the level of the initial peak (I). Roman numerals and vertical arrows refer to the successive multiples of the estimated unit potential. From the value of m_1 obtained from these amplitude histograms a predicted curve (broken line) was generated assuming a Poisson distribution and a coefficient of variation for $\bar{q}_1$ of 30%. Arrow on the ordinate refers to the predicted number of failures. N = number of stimuli. (c2) Correlation between estimates of m from the histogram method (m_1) and estimates of m from the method of failures (m_2) derived from the Poisson equation. (from Castellucci & Kandel, 1974)

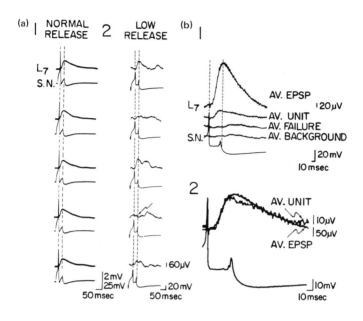

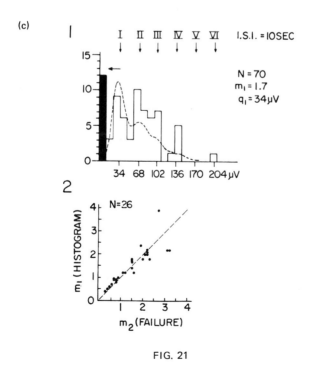

FIG. 21

where $\bar{q}$ is the mean size of the unit EPSP or the potential produced by a single quantum or transmitter packet. Changing estimates of m thus provide a measure of alteration in the number of transmitter quanta released by the presynaptic terminals, whereas constant estimates of $\bar{q}$ indicate an unvarying response of the postsynaptic receptor.

The first evidence that transmission at the synapse of sensory cells on follower motor cells is quantized came from experiments carried out at low levels of transmitter release. Under conditions of normal release repetitive stimulation of the sensory neuron produced only small fluctuations in the amplitude of the evoked EPSP. But when the transmitter output was reduced by increasing the Mg^{2+} content and by reducing the Ca^{2+} content in the bathing solution, repetitive stimulation of the sensory neuron produced marked fluctuation in the amplitude of the EPSP, in an apparently quantal fashion (Figure 21a) and one can observe failures to generate an EPSP. We made amplitude histograms of 30 to 100 consecutive responses obtained in regions of stability where the mean EPSP decreased by less than 15%. These histograms revealed a peak of failures followed by *multimodal distributions,* with the mean voltage value of each subsequent peak being an integral multiple of the value of the first (unit) peak (Figure 21c1). These results were consistent with the idea that transmitter is released in packets (quanta) that are integral multiples of a unit quantum.

We assumed that the first peak is the amplitude of q, the unit EPSP, and we called this estimate q_1. Knowing q_1 we could use Eq. (1) to compute m_1, the mean quantal content obtained from the histogram. In 16 experiments the mean estimates of the quantal size derived from these histograms were small (33.8 μV $\pm$ 13.8 μV SD). But these values were similar to those found by Miledi (1967) at another molluscan synapse, the giant synapse of the squid.

To determine if the evoked quantal units and observed failures were properly recognized, we averaged all putative failures in a run so as to determine whether a smaller, occult unit EPSP had gone unrecognized. The averaged failures were indistinguishable from the averaged background when no response was elicited (Figure 21b). There were no occult EPSPs. We also averaged the unit EPSP and found that its configuration was similar to the average of the large evoked EPSP's when many quanta were released (Castellucci & Kandel, 1974). This gave us confidence that we could recognize both evoked unit quanta and failures.

We have shown elsewhere that release at these synapses can roughly be approximated by a Poisson distribution (Castellucci & Kandel, 1974; Kandel *et al.,* 1976). Using this distribution one can obtain a second and independent estimate of m (m_2) at low levels of release (del Castillo & Katz, 1954) by examining the ratio of failures (n_0) to the total number of trials (N) where

$$m_2 = \ln N/n_0. \tag{2}$$

The estimates of m (m_2) obtained by the failure analysis and those (m_1) obtained from the amplitude histograms proved highly correlated (Figure 21c2), indicating a fair degree of internal consistency in the data. This consistency strengthened the assumption that Poisson statistics can approximate the EPSP distribution in our experiments.

Using both the amplitude histogram and the failure analysis we attempted to estimate, in two independent ways, quantal size (q) and quantal content (m) during synaptic depression and during facilitation. First we considered the amplitude histograms obtained during depression. We obtained 150–300 consecutive responses using 3 interstimulus intervals that produced habituation in the intact animal: 10, 30, and 60 sec. The responses were separated into three successive regions of stability, each consisting of 30–100 responses (Figures 22, 23a). Because of the need for stability required for a Poisson analysis we could not analyze the first few EPSPs in each run. A comparison of the amplitude histograms of the successive regions illustrated that with repeated stimulation the relative incidence of failures increased progressively. The position of the unit peak and, where evident, the later peaks, did not change, indicating that the quantal size was not changing. Thus, in the example illustrated in Figure 23a, the 30 stimuli in the first region produced 2 failures (or 7%), the next 70 stimuli produced 12 failures (or 17%), and the last region produced 14 failures for 35 stimuli (or 40%). Thus, incidence of failures increased sixfold from the first to the third region. These findings suggested that the EPSP depression during continued stimulation is due to a decrease in quantal output (in Figure 23a m decreased from 3.9 to 0.9) while quantal size (q_1), as estimated by the location of the first peak or its multiples remains relatively unaltered.

We next examined synaptic facilitation. As before, we first produced synaptic decrement with 100–300 consecutive stimuli to the sensory neuron. To produce facilitation we stimulated the pleuroabdominal connectives that carry the fibers from the head ganglia. There were again a large number (26%) of failures (Figure 23b). In the first region following the facilitating stimulus, there are no more failures. In the second region after the facilitating stimulus the relative number of failures is still markedly reduced (14%). Throughout the facilitation the position of the unit peak or its multiples again remained the same. Thus, during facilitation, quantal output increased while the size of a quantal unit did not seem to change (Castellucci & Kandel, 1976).

We found similar trends using the failure analysis (Eq. 2). Eight experiments on synaptic depression were normalized to the first region where failures were encountered (Figure 24a). A second group of six experiments on synaptic facilitation were normalized to the regions preceding the facilitation (Figure 24b). In both conditions the estimated values of $\bar{q}_2$ remained constant during successive regions while $\bar{E}$, the average EPSP amplitude, and m_2, the quantal output, decreased by 50% during the depression and increased by 100% in

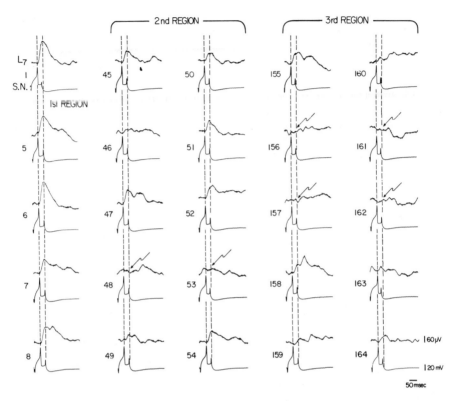

FIG. 22 Quantal fluctuations accompanying synaptic depression at a low level of release (165 m*M* Mg^{2+}, 8 m*M* Ca^{2+}). Samples of successive EPSP's evoked in L7 by a series of 200 consecutive intracellular stimuli to the sensory neuron at 10-sec intervals. Total membrane potential shift during the series was less than 1 mV. Samples are taken from consecutive responses in three different plateau regions defined in the text. The first region (5–8) shows marked amplitude fluctuations and no failures. In Regions 2 and 3 there is a progressive increase in the number of failures (arrows). Number beside each pair of traces refers to the stimulus number in the series. The amplitude histograms of the EPSP's were obtained by measuring the magnitude of the response in time intervals (window) between the peak of the presynaptic spike and the peak of the first EPSP (1). (From Castellucci & Kandel, 1974.)

relation to the control region during facilitation. Finally, we estimated $\bar{q}$ and m at normal levels of release by assuming a Poisson distribution and by using a coefficient of variation analysis. We again observed similar trends.

In summary, the analysis of habituation and dishabituation of the gill-withdrawal reflex indicates that these behavioral modifications result from plastic changes in the excitatory transmission of previously existing connections.

The mechanisms share a common locus, the presynaptic terminals of the sensory neurons projecting on their central target cells (Figure 20). Habituation involves a homosynaptic depression of the terminals due to repeated activity of the sensory neurons. Dishabituation involves presynaptic facilitation of the synaptic action of the sensory neuron, we postulate, as a result of a pathway that

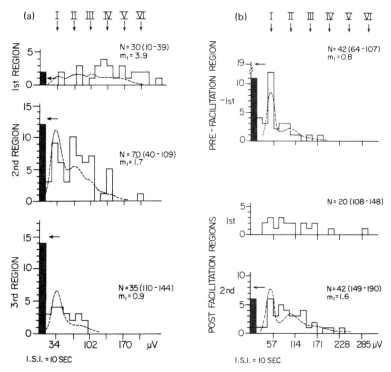

FIG.23 Amplitude histograms of EPSPs and failures evoked by stimulation of sensory neuron during synaptic depression and facilitation. The two values in parentheses next to each histogram refer to the first and last EPSP of a stable region as defined in the text. (a) Synaptic depression: histograms from the successive regions. With repeated stimulation at interstimulus intervals of 10 sec successive regions show proportionately more failures. The position of the unit peak or, when evident, the positions of the later peaks do not change, indicating that q has not changed while m decreases. (From Castellucci & Kandel, 1974.) (b) Synaptic facilitation: histograms from the region preceding the facilitating stimulation and from two subsequent regions following the stimulus. Prior to facilitation there are many failures. The region following the facilitating stimulus has proportionately fewer failures but the unit peak position or its multiples are not altered, indicating that the estimate of m increases but $\bar{q}$ does not change. With continued stimulation (second region) the number of failures is still proportionately reduced but the unit peak remains the same. Interstimulus intervals 10 sec. In Parts a and b the dotted lines illustrate theoretical curves based upon the Poisson distribution obtained by assuming a coefficient of variation of 30% for the unit EPSPs.

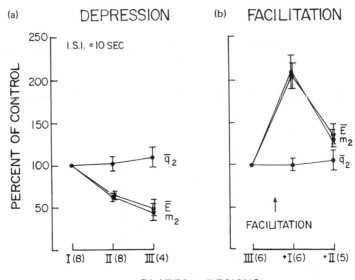

FIG. 24   Comparison of results on synaptic depression and synaptic facilitation underlying habituation and sensitization. The data are based on estimates of m_2 and $\bar{q}_2$ values which are derived by the failure method (see text for details). (a) Synaptic depression: data from 8 experiments were normalized in relation to the region (I) where failures were first observed. During successive regions (I and II) the estimated values of $\bar{q}_2$ did not change significantly while the average EPSP amplitude ($\bar{E}$) and estimates of m decreased by 50%. (b) Synaptic facilitation: data from 6 experiments were normalized in relation to the last region preceding the facilitating stimulus (III). During the successive region (+I), the estimates of $\bar{q}_2$ did not change significantly, while $\bar{E}$ the average EPSP amplitude and m_2 the quantal content increased by 100%. Number in parentheses after each region indicates number of preparations. In both (24a) and (24b) t test of correlated pairs was performed on the nonnormalized values of $\bar{q}_2$, m_2 and $\bar{E}$. Only m_2 and $\bar{E}$ values were found to be significantly different. A: Regions I and II; m_2, $p < 0.005$, $\bar{E}$, $p < 0.01$. B: Regions III and +I; m_2, $p < 0.005$, E, $p < 0.001$.

synapses on the sensory neuron terminals. In each case, there is an alteration in transmitter release and, in both cases, receptor sensitivity seems to be unaffected.

BIOCHEMICAL STUDIES OF SHORT-TERM
HABITUATION AND DISHABITUATION

How are these alterations in transmitter release underlying habituation and dishabituation produced? As a start toward a biochemical understanding of these processes, we have examined the effect of protein synthesis inhibition on them.

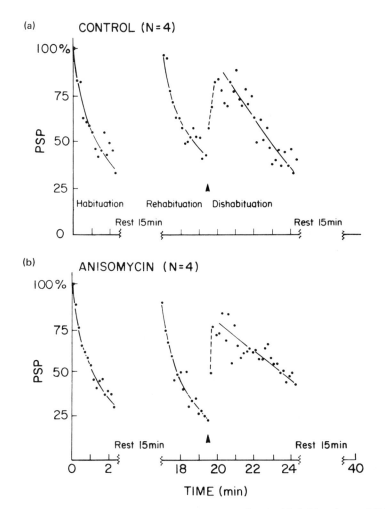

FIG. 25 Summary of changes in synaptic potential correlated with habituation and dishabituation of the gill-withdrawal reflex in the absence (control) and in the presence of 18 μM anisomycin. Isolated ganglia were incubated for 30–50 min. The strength of the stimulus to the siphon nerve was adjusted so that the initial EPSP amplitudes (normalized to 100%) were similar. No difference in threshold was observed between the control and the experimental groups. Fifteen stimuli were applied (ISI = 10 sec); these produced a decrease in the amplitude of the EPSP to about 30% of the initial control. A rest of 15 min resulted in almost complete recovery. Fifteen stimuli were then applied and again produced a decrement in the amplitude of the EPSP. Stimulation of the left connective produced facilitation lasting several minutes. After a second 15-min period of rest, 1 stimulus was given to test recovery. Each point on the curves is the mean of 4 experiments. (From Schwartz, Castellucci, & Kandel, 1971.)

Schwartz, Castellucci, & Kandel (1971) have used three antibiotics (anisomycin, sparsomycin, and pactamycin) that inhibit protein synthesis in the abdominal ganglion by more than 95%; they repeatedly stimulated the siphon nerve and monitored the EPSP decrement and facilitation in the absence or in the presence of the drugs in the isolated ganglion test system (Figures 10c and 25). They found that the changes in synaptic efficacy associated with habituation and dishabituation were unaffected by prior incubation with anisomycin for up to 6 hr. Thus short-term habituation and dishabituation of this reflex do not depend on new protein synthesis. This result is consistent with experiments in vertebrates that indicate that new protein synthesis is not required for short-term learning (Glassman, 1969). It will be important to determine, however, if long-term habituation (Squire & Becker, 1975) and dishabituation depend on the synthesis of new protein and, if so, at what stage in the conversion from short- to long-term memory the need for new protein synthesis occurs.

THE CELLULAR RELATIONSHIPS
OF THE MECHANISMS MEDIATING
DISHABITUATION AND SENSITIZATION

As we have seen earlier, a common dishabituatory stimulus can facilitate habituated and nonhabituated behavioral responses (Figure 6). This would suggest that dishabituation and sensitization share a common cellular mechanism. Carew *et al.* (1971) examined this question in the test system of the isolated ganglion (Figure 10c), taking advantage of the fact that the mechanoreceptors that innervate the mantle shelf send their axons through the branchial nerve while those that innervate the siphon send their axons through the siphon nerve (Byrne *et al.,* 1974a). Stimulation of one of these two nerves leads to depression of the EPSP produced in the motor neuron by that nerve, but leaves unaltered the EPSP produced by the other nerve. Carew *et al.* (1971) found, paralleling the behavioral studies, that a common stimulus applied to the connectives from the head ganglia facilitates both the depressed and the nondepressed EPSPs (Figure 26).

These neurophysiological experiments and the others reviewed above support the notion that dishabituation is not simply the removal of habituation, but is an independent superimposed facilitation (Spencer *et al.,* 1966a, b, c). In the gill-withdrawal system the neuronal correlates of habituation and dishabituation (sensitization) are not mirror-image processes, but reflect two separate presynaptic mechanisms acting on a common set of synapses. Whereas habituation is limited to the stimulated pathway (Figure 27), sensitization has a more widespread distribution involving both stimulated and unstimulated pathways.

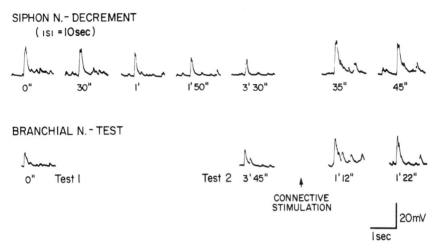

FIG. 26   Facilitation of both decremented and nondecremented EPSP's by presentation of a single train of stimuli to the connective. A single test stimulus was delivered to the branchial nerve (Test 1), and produced an EPSP in L7. Repetitive stimulation was then applied to the siphon nerve to produce EPSP decrement. After a second test to the branchial nerve (Test 2) which revealed that no generalization of EPSP decrement had occurred from the siphon nerve to the branchial nerve, a single train of stimuli (6 Hz for 6 sec) was delivered to the left connective. Subsequent presentation of a stimulus, first to the siphon nerve and then to the branchial nerve revealed facilitation of both decremented and nondecremented EPSP's. (From Carew *et al.,* 1971.)

THE CELLULAR RELATIONSHIPS OF SHORT-TERM
HABITUATION TO LONG-TERM HABITUATION

Another relationship that can be explored on the cellular level is that between short- and long-term habituation. Carew and Kandel (1973) have initiated research in this direction by examining the acquisition and retention of a long-term synaptic decrement in the test system of the isolated abdominal ganglion. They used a shortened training procedure (Figures 8c, 28a) of 4 training sessions (10 trials each) separated by 1.5-hr intervals. They found that the synaptic depression of the complex EPSP built up within each training session and across the 4 training sessions (Figure 28b). Thus, stimulation of an afferent nerve with the same temporal patterning as in the behavior experiments produced a progressive decrease in the complex EPSP, which persisted for at least 24 hr. In view of the evidence that the complex EPSP is primarily due to the monosynaptic connections made by the sensory fibers on the motor neurons (Byrne *et al.,* 1974b), this finding suggests that the crucial change for long-term

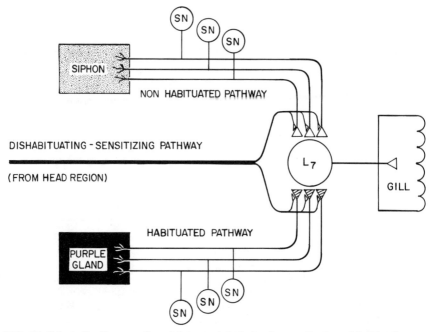

FIG. 27 Schematic diagram of model to explain lack of generalization of habituation as well as the evident generalization of sensitization (dishabituation). The model postulates that the sensitizing pathway mediates presynaptic facilitation on the synapse between the primary sensory neurons (SN) and the motor neuron L7 (chosen as a representative motor neuron for the reflex). The model deals only with the monosynaptic components of the reflex. The polysynaptic components apparently do not contribute significantly to generalization. Habituation is limited to the stimulated pathway (shaded synapses) while sensitization involves both habituated and nonhabituated pathways. (From Carew *et al.*, 1971.)

habituation also occurs at the synapse between the sensory and the motor neurons.

TRANSMITTER RELEASE AND THE ACQUISITION OF LONG-TERM SYNAPTIC DEPRESSION

The finding that short- and long-term habituation share a common locus permits one to examine further the mechanisms for the acquisition of the long-term process. Is repeated transmitter release that accompanies short-term habituation a necessary prerequisite for the acquisition of the synaptic changes that accompany long-term habituation? Or is acquisition due to an independent and parallel process that depends only on impulse activity and the concomitant ion movements (Na entry and K efflux) in the presynaptic terminals? To examine

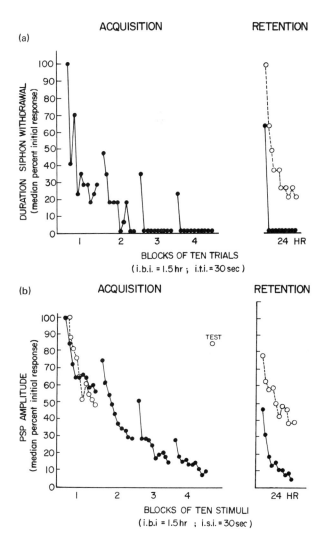

FIG 28 Acquisition and retention of habituation: correlation of behavioral and cellular processes. (a) Acquisition and retention of long-term habituation of siphon withdrawal. Data are expressed as percentage of the median of each group initial response (Block 1, Trial 1), which was 17 sec for the experimentals and 19 sec for the controls. For statistical analysis, the duration of siphon withdrawal for each animal was summed for Trials 1–10; this measures the total time an animal spent responding in the habituation session. After 4 blocks of siphon-habituation training (acquisition), experimentals exhibited significantly greater habituation than controls in retention testing after 24 hr ($p < .001$) Mann–Whitney U Tests (see also Figure 8c). Interblock intervals, (IBI) = 1.5 hr. (b) Acquisition and retention of long-term synaptic decrement. The amplitudes of excitatory synaptic potential produced by stimulating experimental (●) and control (○) nerves are expressed as a percentage of the initial amplitude. In acquisition, 2 afferent nerves, the branchial and siphon were used, serving either as experimental (6 siphon, 4 branchial), or control. In Block

(caption continued bottom page 38)

37

these questions we again used the shortened training schedule described above for the acquisition of long-term habituation and presented 4 sets of 10 stimuli each to 1 experimental nerve, with a 1.5-hr interval between training sessions (Figure 29b). During the first session the control nerve also received a set of 10 stimuli. After this training session (applied to experimental and control nerves) the ganglion was bathed in a high-Mg solution so that transmitter release was blocked. The second and third training sessions were then only applied to the experimental nerve, with 1.5 hr between each session. But this time no transmitter substance was released by the stimulated neurons. During these 2 sessions the control nerve was not stimulated. Following the third session the high-Mg solution was removed and normal seawater was reintroduced, so that transmitter release was restored. During the fourth session both experimental and control nerves received a set of 10 stimuli.

If the profound synaptic depression that accompanies the acquisition of long-term habituation had only resulted from Na entry into the terminal (or K efflux) and did not require transmitter release, then the response of the experimental nerve (which received 3 training sessions separated by 1.5 hr) to the fourth training session should have resembled that normally found with acquisition of long-term habituation (Figure 29a). The responses would therefore be different from those to the control nerve, which received only 2 training sessions separated by 4.5 hr. This proved not to be the case. The synaptic responses to the experimental nerve during the fourth session did not differ from control and failed to show the profound buildup of depression characteristic of the acquisition of long-term habituation (Figure 28). These experiments (although indirect) suggest that Na entry or K efflux are insufficient to produce long-term synaptic depression. One or more steps in transmitter release are essential for the long-term process.

A large component of the complex EPSP produced in the motor neurons by stimulation of the siphon nerve is produced by the monosynaptic connections of

---

(Figure 28 caption continued)

1, 10 stimuli, intertrial interval (ITI) = 30 sec, were first applied to the experimental nerve and then 10 to the control nerve. Stimuli to each nerve produced comparable synaptic decrement in L7. Repeated blocks of stimuli (IBI = interblock intervals = 1.5 hr) to the experimental nerve produced a progressive increase in synaptic decrement. A single stimulus to the control nerve after Block 4 produced a synaptic potential substantially recovered from the last control potential of Block 1, and was significantly greater than the first experimental synaptic potential of block 4 ($p < .001$). In retention testing, the cell was reimpaled 24 hr-later and repolarized to the same membrane potential maintained during acquisition. The retention ordinate is redrawn to indicate that the repolarization was not exact, although it could be closely approximated. The first experimental synaptic potential was significantly less than the first control potential ($p < .01$), and the overall synaptic responsiveness from repeated stimulation of the experimental nerve (sum of synaptic potential amplitudes for trials 1 to 10) was significantly less than from the same number of stimuli to the control nerve ($p < .001$). (From Carew & Kandel, 1973.)

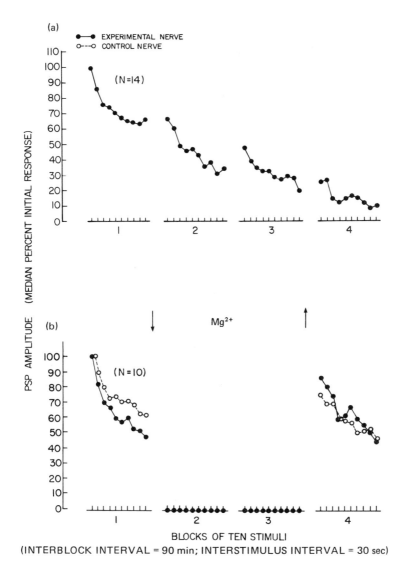

FIG. 29 Transmitter release and acquisition of long-term synaptic depression. (a) In normal seawater 4 training sessions of 10 stimuli each applied to the siphon nerve (as in Figure 28b) produce a progressive buildup of the depression of the complex EPSP in motor neuron L7 (interstimulus interval 30 sec, interblock interval 90 min). (b) Experimental (•) and control (○) nerves are both stimulated 10 times during the first training session. Synaptic transmission is then blocked with high-Mg solutions (220 mM Mg^{2+} and 10 mM Ca^{2+}) and 2 more sets of stimuli are applied to the experimental nerve only but now they do not lead to transmitter release. Normal seawater is then reintroduced and both the experimental and control nerves are stimulated during the fourth training session. When transmitter release is blocked at some time during training the expected build-up of EPSP depression does not occur.

the sensory neurons (Byrne *et al.,* 1974b). Short- and long-term habituation therefore seems to share a common neural locus, that is the synapses that the sensory neurons make on the motor neurons and interneurons. It is also likely that short- and long-term habituation share aspects of a common cellular mechanism, homosynaptic depression. By these criteria alone, the neural mechamisms of long-term habituation of the gill-withdrawal reflex seem to be an extension of the short-term process. However, by using better criteria, finer distinctions may emerge. For example, whereas short-term synaptic depression is presynaptic, involving a decrease in the number of quanta released per impulse, the factors underlying long-term synaptic depression are not yet known. If long-term depression proves also to be presynaptic, it would support the behavioral notion that a *single trace* memory can be entertained. However, the kinetics of the two types of habituation are different and this may imply two different processes in the presynaptic terminals. Thus the short-term process may represent the depletion of the releasable store of transmitter by inadequate mobilization, whereas the long-term process may be a depletion of the storage pool of transmitter by an inhibition of transmitter synthesis or transmitter export from the cell body.

On the bases of these speculations one can consider a simple model, as illustrated in Figure 30. In this model short- and long-term memory can be regarded as one process on the cellular level or synaptic level, that is, synaptic depression at the terminals of the sensory neurons. But on a more fundamental or subcellular level memory can be considered as two interrelated processes: a short-term process consisting of depletion of the releasable pool of transmitter substance and a long-term process consisting of depletion of storage pool (perhaps by inhibition of transmitter synthesis or transmitter export).

We have illustrated this model in relation to that developed by Bower (1967) and Atkinson and Shiffrin (1968) for human learning (see also Wagner, Chapter 3, this volume). We would emphasize, however, the speculative nature of our model and the even more speculative nature of the comparison to the human-learning model. Different learning processes of the sort we are comparing here are very likely to involve different cellular mechanisms of memory.

PERSPECTIVES

Habituation has now been analyzed in several other reflex systems. The work of Krasne (1969), Kennedy, Selverston, and Remler (1969), and Zucker (1972) indicates that the critical change underlying habituation of the tail-flip escape response in crayfish involves a similar locus and perhaps even a similar mechanism to that of the gill-withdrawal reflex in *Aplysia.* In the crayfish habituation is also due to a decrease in the excitatory synaptic efficacy in the synaptic connections made by the mechanoreceptor neurons. Preliminary experiments by

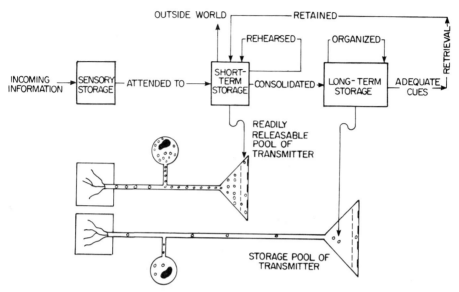

FIG. 30 Multistage model of human verbal learning (after Bower, 1967) and a speculative cellular model, illustrating a two-stage memory trace involving a single cellular locus and a common plastic mechanism, synaptic depression. Short-term storage involves mobilization of transmitter substance from a storage pool to a readily releasable pool. Habituation produces an interference with mobilization of transmitter substance to the release site. In the short-term case this leads to a depletion of the readily releasable pool of transmitter (short-term habituation). In the long-term case prolonged mobilization failure leads to reduced synthesis or reduced transport of transmitter substance, thus resulting in a depletion of the storage pool of vesicles as well (long-term habituation). These findings suggest that the mechanisms underlying short- and long-term depression are in series. Transmitter release accompanying the short-term depression is a necessary prerequisite for the acquisition of the long-term depression. (From Kandel, 1976.)

Zucker (1972) suggest that this change is presynaptic. A similar locus seems also to be involved in certain instances of habituation in insects (Callec et al., 1971). In the mammalian flexion reflex the site for habituation is more central, lying at the level of the interneuronal chains that are interposed between sensory and motor cells (Spencer et al., 1966a, b, c). But the available evidence is consistent with a decrease in excitatory synaptic efficacy (see Thompson and Glanzman, Chapter 2, this volume). In the frog the primary sensory neurons also do not mediate habituation of the flexion response, but Farel, Glanzman, and Thompson (1973) have defined a monosynaptic system that may be critically involved in a habituating pathway. This system also shows homosynaptic depression (Farel et al., 1973; Thompson & Glanzman, Chapter 2, this volume).

Thus homosynaptic depression at specific synapses in the afferent pathway may be a common mechanism for mediating habituation in defensive reflex systems in vertebrates and invertebrates. Too few cases have been examined, however, to indicate whether this is the only mechanism. Indeed the various forms and time courses of habituation make it unlikely that all forms of habituation are mediated by a single mechanism. Nonetheless it is reassuring that one form of habituation and sensitization can now be analyzed at the synaptic level. Unfortunately we are not as close to a comparable understanding of more complex forms of learning. It therefore becomes of interest to extend studies of habituation and sensitization in the direction of molecular mechanisms, and in the direction of behavioral complexity.

Molecular Mechanisms

The finding that the synaptic mechanisms underlying short-term habituation and sensitization are presynaptic makes it interesting to analyze the terminals of the sensory neurons morphologically for changes in the number and distribution of the synaptic vesicles (the likely storage sites of transmitter quanta). Techniques for marking the presynaptic terminals of identified neurons for electronmicroscopic examination have recently been developed and could permit a subcellular analysis of the synaptic changes accompanying short- and long-term habituation and sensitization and particularly the transition from a short-term process to a long-term process (Thompson, Schwartz, & Kandel, 1976).

In addition, it will be important to examine the biochemical mechanism involved in short- and long-term sensitization. Brunelli, Castellucci, & Kandel (1976) have recently found that serotonin simulates the effects of heterosynaptic facilitation, and that a serotonin antagonist (cinanserin) blocks presynaptic facilitation. Moreover, stimulating the sensitizing pathway from the head or incubating the ganglion with serotonin leads to an increase in cyclic AMP in the ganglion (Cedar, Kandel, & Schwartz, 1972). Finally, intracellular injection of cyclic AMP in the sensory neurons facilitates the EPSP simulating presynaptic facilitation. These findings suggest that presynaptic facilitation may be mediated by serotonin and that serotonin may act to increase cyclic AMP in the terminals of the sensory neuron. Cyclic AMP in turn could increase the free Ca in the terminal and thereby mobilize transmitter from one compartment (storage pool) to another (releasable pool). In future work on this system one might therefore be in a position to seek a molecular explanation of the neural mechanism underlying sensitization.

Behavioral Complexity

Because of its simplicity, there has been a long-standing controversy among students of behavior as to whether habituation can be considered learning, even in its most elementary form (Kling, 1971; Miller, 1967). Often not appreciated in these discussions is that there are restricted and extended forms of the habituation paradigm. In its restricted form, habituation consists of a short-term response decrement lasting minutes or hours. The decremented response recovers spontaneously but cannot be dishabituated or shows dishabituation only if the same pathway is stimulated. In its extended form, the habituation paradigm can be prolonged to last days and weeks, and its duration is dependent upon the pattern of stimulation. In addition, the response can be dishabituated for hours or days by stimulating an entirely different site or pathway.

Independent of one's definition of learning, what intuitively separates the more interesting forms of learning from the less interesting ones are three features: (1) time course or duration of the memory; (2) specificity to pattern of stimulation; and (3) the ability of the response to be manipulated to cause both an increase and a decrease in response strength. Thus what distinguishes the extended form of the habituation paradigm from its restricted form are features that generally distinguish more interesting forms of learning from less interesting forms. As a result, an effective argument can be made that the extended form of the habituation paradigm blends, almost imperceptibly, with other learning paradigms. These arguments are consistent with Wagner's theoretical position, presented in this volume, and with data suggesting that habituation is context-specific. In general, Wagner's findings indicate that in vertebrates habituation and sensitization can also be used to study how associative learning is generated. It therefore becomes interesting to see to what degree context-specific habituation (or other forms of associational specificities) can be demonstrated in the gill-withdrawal reflex of *Aplysia*. If such specificity could be demonstrated then the advantages of this system could also be brought to bear on the analysis of several forms of complex learning.

ACKNOWLEDGMENTS

This research was supported by Research Career Development Award 5K04-NS-70346-03 to Vincent Castellucci; Research Scientist Award MH 18-558 to Eric Kandel; and National Institute of Health Grants MH-262102-01 and NS-09361-05.

REFERENCES

Arvanitaki, A., & Tchou, S. H. Les Lois de la croissance relative individuelle des cellules nerveuses chez *l'Aplysie. Bulletin D'Histologie et de Technique Microscopique,* 1941, *19,* 244–256.

Ascher, P. Inhibitory and excitatory effects of dopamine on *Aplysia* neurons. *Journal of Physiology (London),* 1972, *225,* 173–209.

Atkinson, R. C., & Shiffrin, R. M. Human memory: A proposed system and its control processes. In K. W. Spence & J. T. Spence (Eds.), *The psychology of learning and motivation* (Vol. 2). New York: Academic Press, 1968.

Bailey, C., Castellucci, V., Koester, J., & Kandel, E. R. Central mechanoreceptor neurons in

Aplysia connect to peripheral siphon motor neurons: A simple system for the morphological study of the synaptic mechanism underlying habituation. *Neuroscience Abstracts* 1975, *1*, 588.

Blankenship, J. E., Wachtel, H., & Kandel, E. R. Ionic mechanisms of excitatory inhibitory and dual synaptic actions mediated by an identified interneuron in abdominal ganglion of *Aplysia. Journal of Neurophysiology*, 1971, *34*, 76–92.

Bower, G. H. A multi-component theory of the memory trace. In K. W. Spence & J. T. Spence (Eds.), *The psychology of learning and motivation* (Vol. 1). New York: Academic Press, 1967.

Brunelli, M., Castellucci, V., & Kandel, E. R. A possible role for serotonin and cyclic AMP in the synaptic facilitation accompanying behavioral sensitization in *Aplysia. Science*, 1976, in press.

Byrne, J. A feedback controlled stimulator that delivers controlled displacements or forces to cutaneous mechanoreceptors. *Institute of Electrical and Electronics Engineers Transactions of Bio-Medical Engineering*, 1975, 66–69.

Byrne, J., Castellucci, V., & Kandel, E. R. Receptive fields and response properties of mechanoreceptor neurons innervating siphon skin and mantle shelf in *Aplysia. Journal of Neurophysiology*, 1974, *37*, 1041–1064. (a)

Byrne, J., Castellucci, V., & Kandel, E. R. Quantitative aspects of the sensory component of the gill-withdrawal reflex in *Aplysia. Neuroscience Abstracts*, 1974, *104*, 106. (b)

Callec, J. J., & Guillet, J. C., Pichon, Y., & Boistel, J. Further studies on synaptic transmission in insects. II. Relations between sensory information and its synaptic integration at the level of a single giant axon in the cockroach. *Journal of Experimental Biology*, 1971, *55*, 123–149.

Carew, T. J., & Kandel, E. R. A cellular analysis of acquisition and retention of long-term habituation in *Aplysia. Science*, 1973, *182*, 1158–1160.

Carew, T. J., Castellucci, V. F., & Kandel, E. R. An analysis of dishabituation and sensitization of the gill-withdrawal reflex in *Aplysia. International Journal of Neuroscience*, 1971, *2*, 79–98.

Carew, T. J., Pinsker, H. M., & Kandel, E. R. Long-term habituation of a defensive withdrawal reflex in *Aplysia. Science*, 1972, *175*, 451–454.

Carew, T. J., Pinsker, H., Rubinson, K., & Kandel, E. R. Physiological and biochemical properties of neuromuscular transmission between identified motoneurons and gill muscle in *Aplysia. Journal of Neurophysiology*, 1974, *37*, 1020–1040.

Castellucci, V. F., & Kandel, E. R. A quantal analysis of the synaptic depression underlying habituation of the gill-withdrawal reflex in *Aplysia. Proceedings of the National Academy of Science (U.S.A.)*, 1974, *71*, 5004–5008.

Castellucci, V. F., & Kandel, E. R. Presynaptic facilitation as a mechanism for behavioral sensitization in *Aplysia. Science*, 1976, in press.

Castellucci, V., Pinsker, H., Kupfermann, I., & Kandel, E. R. Neuronal mechanisms of habituation and dishabituation of the gill-withdrawal reflex in *Aplysia. Science*, 1970, *167*, 1745–1748.

del Castillo, J., & Katz, B. Quantal components of the endplate potential. *Journal of Physiology (London)*, 1954, *124*, 560–573.

Cedar, H., Kandel, E. R., & Schwartz, J. H. Cyclic adenosine monophosphate in the nervous system of *Aplysia californica*. I. Increased synthesis in response to synaptic stimulation. *Journal of General Physiology*, 1972, *60*, 558–569.

Coggeshall, R. E. A light and electronmicroscope study of the abdominal ganglion of *Aplysia californica. Journal of Neurophysiology*, 1967, *30*, 1263–1287.

Eales, N. B. *Aplysia. Proceedings of the Liverpool Biological Society*, 1921, *35*, 183–266.

Eisenstadt, M. L., & Schwartz, J. H. Metabolism of acetylcholine in the nervous system of

Aplysia californica. III. Studies of an identified cholinergic neuron. *Journal of General Physiology,* 1975, *65*(3), 293–313.

Eisenstadt, M. L., Goldman, J. E., Kandel, E. R., Koike, H., Koester, J., & Schwartz, J. H. Intrasomatic injection of radioactive precursors for studying transmitter synthesis in identified neurons of *Aplysia californica. Proceedings of the National Academy of Science USA,* 1974, *70,* 3371–3375.

Farel, P. B., Glanzman, D. L., & Thompson, R. F. Habituation of a monosynaptic response in vertebrate central nervous system: Lateral column–motor neuron pathway in isolated frog spinal cord. *Journal of Neurophysiology,* 1973, *36,* 1117–1130.

Frazier, W. T., Kandel, E. R., Kupfermann, I., Waziri, R., & Coggeshall, R. Morphological and functional properties of identified neurons in the abdominal ganglion of *Aplysia californica. Journal of Neurophysiology,* 1967, *30,* 1288–1351.

Glassman, E. The biochemistry of learning: An evaluation of the role of RNA and protein. *Annual Review of Biochemistry,* 1969, *38,* 605–646.

Goldman, J. E., & Schwartz, J. H. Cellular specificity of serotonin storage and axonal transport in identified neurons of *Aplysia californica. Journal of Physiology (London),* 1974, *242,* 61–72.

Kandel, E. R. *Cellular basis of behavior. An introduction to invertebrate neurobiology.* San Francisco: Freeman, 1976.

Kandel, E. R., & Kupfermann, I. The functional organization of invertebrate ganglia. *Annual Review of Physiology,* 1970, *32,* 193–258.

Kandel, E. R., & Gardner, D. The synaptic actions mediated by the different branches of a single neuron. In *Neurotransmitters Research Publications of Association for Research in Nervous and Mental Disease,* 1972, *50,* 91–146.

Kandel, E. R., Frazier, W. T., Waziri, R., & Coggeshall, R. E. Direct and common connections among identified neurons in *Aplysia. Journal of Neurophysiology,* 1967, *30,* 1352–1376.

Kandel, E. R., Brunelli, M., Byrne, J., & Castellucci, V. A common presynaptic locus for the synaptic changes underlying short-term habituation and sensitization of the gill-withdrawal reflex in *Aplysia.* In *The synapse XL Cold Spring Harbor Symposium.* Cold Spring Harbor, N.Y.: Biological Laboratory, 1976. Pp. 465–482.

Katz, B. *The release of neural transmitter substances.* Charles C Thomas Publ.: Springfield, Illinois. 1964.

Kehoe, J. Ionic mechanisms of a two-component cholinergic inhibition in *Aplysia* neurons. *Journal of Physiology (London),* 1972, *225,* 85–114.   (a)

Kehoe, J. Three acetylcholine receptors in *Aplysia* neurons. *Journal of Physiology (London),* 1972, *225,* 115–146.   (b)

Kehoe, J. The physiological role of three acetylcholine receptors in synaptic transmission in *Aplysia. Journal of Physiology (London),* 1972, *225,* 147–172.   (c)

Kennedy, D., Selverston, A. I., & Remler, M. P. Analysis of restricted neural networks. *Science,* 1969, *164,* 1488–1496.

Kling, J. W. Learning: Introductory survey. In J. W. Kling & L. A. Riggs (Eds.), *Woodworth and Schlosberg's experimental psychology* (3rd ed.). New York: Holt, Rinehart and Winston, 1971. Pp. 551–613.

Koester, J., & Kandel, E. Further identification of neurons in the abdominal ganglion of *Aplysia californica* using behavioral criteria. *Brain Research,* 1976, in press.

Koester, J., Mayeri, E., Liebeswar, G., & Kandel, E. R. Neural control of circulation in *Aplysia.* II. Interneurons. *Journal of Neurophysiology,* 1974, *37,* 476–496.

Koike, H., Kandel, E. R., & Schwartz, J. H. Synaptic release of radioactivity after intra-somatic injection of choline–[3]H into an identified cholinergic interneuron in abdominal ganglion of *Aplysia californica. Journal of Neurophysiology,* 1974, *37,* 815–827.

Krasne, F. B. Excitation and habituation of the crayfish escape reflex: The depolarizing response in lateral giant fibers of the isolated abdomen. *Journal of Experimental Biology*, 1969, *50*, 29–46.

Kupfermann, I., & Kandel, E. R. Neuronal controls of a behavioral response mediated by the abdominal ganglion of *Aplysia*. *Science*, 1969, *164*, 847–850.

Kupfermann, I., Castellucci, V., Pinsker, H., & Kandel, E. R. Neuronal correlates of habituation and dishabituation of the gill-withdrawal reflex in *Aplysia*. *Science*, 1970, *167*, 1743–1745.

Kupfermann, I., Pinsker, H., Castellucci, V. F., & Kandel, E. R. Central and peripheral control of gill movements in *Aplysia*. *Science*, 1971, *174*, 1252–1256.

Kupfermann, I., Carew, T. J., & Kandel, E. R. Local, reflex, and central commands controlling gill and siphon movements in *Aplysia*. *Journal of Neurophysiology*, 1974, *37*, 996–1019.

Liebeswar, G., Goldman, J. E., Koester, J., & Mayeri, E. Neural control of circulation in *Aplysia*. III. Neurotransmitters. *Journal of Neurophysiology*, 1975, *38*, 767–779.

Lukowiak, K., & Jacklet, J. W. Habituation and dishabituation: Interactions between peripheral and central nervous systems in *Aplysia*. *Science*, 1972, *178*, 1306–1308.

Lukowiak, K., & Jacklet, J. Habituation and dishabituation mediated by the peripheral and central neural circuits of the siphon of *Aplysia*. *Journal of Neurobiology*, 1975, *6*, 183–200.

Martin, A. R. Quantal nature of synaptic transmission. *Physiological Reviews*, 1966, *46*, 51–65.

Mayeri, E., Koester, J., Kupfermann, I., Liebeswar, G., & Kandel, E. R. Neural control of circulation in *Aplysia*. I. Motor neurons. *Journal of Neurophysiology*, 1974, *37*, 458–475.

Miledi, R. Spontaneous synaptic potentials and quantal release of transmitter in the stellate ganglion of the squid. *Journal of Physiology*, 1967, *192*, 379–406.

Miller, N. E. Certain facts of learning relevant to the search for its physical basis. In G. C. Quarton, T. Melnechuk, & F. O. Schmitt (Eds.), *The neurosciences: A study program*. Rockefeller University Press, New York, 1967.

Peretz, B., Jacklet, J. W., & Lukowiak, K. Habituation of reflexes in *Aplysia*: Contribution of the peripheral and central nervous system. *Science*, 1976, *191*, 396–399.

Perlman, A. Neural control of the siphon in *Aplysia*. Unpublished doctoral dissertation, New York University School of Medicine, 1975.

Pinsker, H., Kupfermann, I., Castellucci, V., & Kandel, E. R. Habituation and dishabituation of the gill-withdrawal reflex in *Aplysia*. *Science*, 1970, *167*, 1740–1742.

Pinsker, H., Hening, W., Carew, T., & Kandel, E. R. Long-term sensitization of a defensive withdrawal reflex in *Aplysia*. *Science*, 1973, *182*, 1039–1042.

Schwartz, J. H., Castellucci, V., & Kandel, E. R. Functioning of identified neurons and synapses in abdominal ganglion of *Aplysia* in absence of protein synthesis. *Journal of Neurophysiology*, 1971, *34*, 939–953.

Schwartz, J. H., Eisenstadt, M. L., & Cedar, H. Metabolism of acetylcholine in the nervous system of *Aplysia californica*. I. Source of choline and its uptake by intact nervous tissue. *Journal of General Physiology*, 1975, *65*, 255–274.

Spencer, W. A., Thompson, R. F., & Neilson, D. R., Jr. Response decrement of the flexion reflex in the acute spinal cat and transient restoration by strong stimuli. *Journal of Neurophysiology*, 1966, *29*, 221–239. (a)

Spencer, W. A., Thompson, R. F., & Neilson, D. R., Jr. Alterations in responsiveness of ascending and reflex pathways activated by iterated cutaneous afferent volleys. *Journal of Neurophysiology*, 1966, *29*, 240–252. (b)

Spencer, W. A., Thompson, R. F., & Neilson, D. R., Jr. Decrement of ventral root electrotonus and intracellularly recorded PSPs produced by iterated cutaneous afferent volleys. *Journal of Neurophysiology,* 1966, *29,* 253–274. (c)

Squire, L., & Becker, C. K. Inhibition of cerebral protein synthesis impairs long-term habituation. *Brain Research,* 1975, *97,* 367–372.

Tauc, L., & Gerschenfeld, H. M. A cholinergic mechanism of inhibitory synaptic transmission in a molluscan nervous system. *Journal of Neurophysiology,* 1962, *25,* 236–262.

Thompson, E. B., Schwartz, J. H., & Kandel, E. R. A radioautographic analysis in the light and electronmicroscope of identified *Aplysia* neurons and their processes after intrasomatic injection of ³H-*l*-fucose. *Brain Research,* 1976, *112,* 251–281.

Thompson, R. F., & Spencer, W. A. Habituation: A model phenomenon for the study of neuronal substrate of behavior. *Psychological Reviews,* 1966, *73,* 16–43.

Thorpe, W. H. *Learning and instinct in animals.* Cambridge, Mass.: Harvard University Press, 1956.

Zucker, R. S. Crayfish escape behavior and central synapses. II. Physiological mechanisms underlying behavioral habituation. *Journal of Neurophysiology,* 1972, *35,* 621–637.

2

Neural and Behavioral Mechanisms of Habituation and Sensitization

Richard F. Thompson
Dennis L. Glanzman
University of California, Irvine

It has become increasingly clear in recent years that habituation is a fundamental and elementary form of behavioral plasticity, both phylogenetically and onto-genetically. Historically, Humphrey (1933) and Harris (1943) were among the first to emphasize the importance of habituation in behavior. However, the important work of the Soviet scientist, Sokolov (1963), is perhaps most responsible for the current widespread interest in phenomena of habituation in humans. Sharpless and Jasper (1956), Hernández-Peón (1960), and Sokolov (1963) all emphasized the importance of the phenomenon in neurophysiology.

Those of us working on habituation at the levels of animal behavior and neurophysiology are gratified to encounter such enthusiastic interest in habituation among scientists working at the much more immediate and important level of the development of the human infant. Several chapters in this volume provide us a rich context of data on habituation in the infant human.

Habituation is appealing in large part because it is so simple. If a moderate stimulus to which an organism initially responds is repeated, the organism ceases to respond. It is perhaps the simplest form of learning—learning not to respond. It can be very adaptive for humans, as Glass and Singer (1972) have persuasively argued in their book, *Urban Stress.* Habituation is also ubiquitious—invertebrates do it, humans do it, and the human infant does it very well indeed.

Before plunging into the complexities of habituation (even though habituation is very simple to define, detailed analysis of even the behavior, let alone the neurophysiology, rapidly becomes complex), we would like to sketch very briefly the origins of our own interest. Some 12 years ago, W. A. Spencer and R. F. Thompson joined forces at the University of Oregon Medical School in a collaborative project on the neural basis of learning. Initially it was planned to

49

study spinal conditioning as a simplified neuronal model of learning. A series of pilot studies was begun using flexor muscle response with hindlimb skin and cutaneous nerve stimuli as the CS and US in the classical conditioning paradigm in acute spinal cats. However, habituation kept getting in the way. The flexor muscle response to repeated cutaneous stimulation almost invariably decremented. The decrement is a very clear and robust phenomenon in spinal reflexes. Indeed, Sherrington studied it (he termed it "reflex fatigue") at length in classic experiments (1906). Because spinal flexor reflex habituation is robust and simple it was focused on as a simplified neuronal model of a simplified form of learning.

There are really two major issues in the use of a simplified neuronal model for analysis of a behavioral phenomenon: whether it is amenable to analysis, and; whether it is a good model. The answer to the first question is yes to some degree for most simplified preparations. The second question is the key issue of generality. It was approached by reviewing the behavioral literature on habituation and abstracting the common parametric features. This led to the nine "criteria" of habituation that have come to serve as the detailed operational definition of the phenomenon (Thompson & Spencer, 1966). If a neuronal model shows all or most of these criteria, it may be considered a good model of habituation. At the very least, the criteria have heuristic value. The ultimate verdict on generality is, of course, not yet in—do the mechanisms of habituation in simplified models (such as our spinal studies and the work of Kandel and Tauc (1965) and Kandel and Spencer (1968) on *Aplysia* in fact operate in the intact mammalian brain? We will deal with both issues, analysis of mechanisms and generality in this chapter.

When Spencer and Thompson began their work, one of the defining properties of habituation was "dishabituation," the disruption of habituation by an extra, usually strong, stimulus. In the course of these studies it became clear that dishabituation is not a specific disruption of habituation, but rather a superimposed and rather more generalized facilitation or sensitization, at least in spinal reflexes (Spencer, Thompson, & Nielson, 1966a, b, c; Thompson & Spencer, 1966). This observation formed the basis of the dual-process theory (Groves & Thompson, 1970). The notion of two independent inferred processes, habituation and sensitization resulting from repeated stimulation, was simply generalized to the intact behaving organism. This dual-process approach has provided a useful framework for analysis of the phenomena of habituation. Kandel and associates (see Kandel & Tauc, 1965) have identified a phenomenon comparable to sensitization that they have termed "heterosynaptic facilitation" in their work on *Aplysia*. With the possible exception of the most interesting observations by Wagner in his chapter in this volume, all earlier examples of dishabituation that have been appropriately tested are in fact examples of sensitization. In any event, the dual-process theory of habituation has stimulated considerable research and discussion (Peeke & Herz, 1973).

Perhaps the most useful contribution the dual-process theory can make to those interested in child development is to emphasize the importance of sensitization as a phenomenon of behavioral plasticity in the infant. All too often sensitization is viewed as an unwanted stepchild or contaminating variable in studies of learning. There are many more experiments designed with controls for sensitization than there are experiments designed to study it. As will hopefully become more evident in this chapter, sensitization is an elementary form of behavioral plasticity, perhaps equal in importance to habituation and apparently generated by somewhat different neuronal mechanisms.

HABITUATION AND SENSITIZATION AS SIMPLIFIED MODELS OF LEARNING

To many of us, the most fundamental and challenging problem in psychology and the neurosciences is the nature of the "engram," the set of physical processes and changes in the brain that form the basis of learning. Karl Lashley was the first to conceptualize the issue clearly. He ended his brilliant lifelong search for the engram with the somewhat ironic suggestion that learning is impossible.

Experimental analysis of the location and nature of the engram is extraordinarily difficult. Given the limitation of present techniques, a paradox of sorts exists. All forms of learning must involve alterations somewhere between the input and the output of the central nervous system. The known forms of specific interaction between neurons occur at synapses. Consequently, learning may be assumed to involve changes at synapses. In order to analyze the synaptic mechanisms underlying learning, the critical synapses where learned changes occur must be identified. Present techniques permit identification and analysis of synapses only in systems involving one set of synaptic junctions: monosynaptic pathways. However, monosynaptic pathways do not, by definition, form new associations.

The two general research strategies currently employed to study the neurology of learning, whether the manipulations and/or measures involve lesions, anatomy, chemistry or electrophysiology, are the use of "model" biological systems and the use of more or less intact, behaving animals. The objective is description of the physical–chemical processes of the nervous system that form the basis of learning. Learning is obviously not a unitary phenomenon. Broadly construed, it is reflected in changes in behavior as a result of experience. A simple dichotomy can be made between habituation and sensitization on the one hand, which imply decreases or increases in already existing responses to particular stimuli, and "associative" learning on the other, which involves development of response to a previously neutral stimulus as a result of temporal association, for example, classical and instrumental conditioning.

The model–systems approach has been particularly successful for study of habituation and sensitization. A consensus seems to be developing from studies on such diverse preparations as crayfish central reflexes (Zucker, 1972), *Aplysia* monosynaptic pathways (Castellucci *et al.*, 1970), polysynaptic and mono-synaptic pathways of isolated frog spinal cord (Farel, Glanzman, & Thompson, 1973), polysynaptic pathways of mammalian spinal cord (Thompson & Spencer, 1966; Spencer *et al.*, 1966a, b, c) and many forms of behavior in intact, be-having animals (Groves & Thompson, 1970) that habituation reflects some form of synaptic depression. Similarly, the view is growing that sensitization reflects some form of superimposed or heterosynaptic facilitation (Thompson & Spen-cer, 1966; Kandel & Spencer, 1968). It is, of course, not yet known whether the detailed synaptic mechanisms of habituation are similar or different in these many preparations and systems, and whether mechanisms in simple systems can be applied to habituation in higher animals or man. However, the fact that the parametric relations for stimulus and training variables in habituation are vir-tually identical from monosynaptic systems of *Aplysia* abdominal ganglion and isolated frog spinal cord to human behavior suggests that the issue is, at least in principle, admissible of solution. We will explore this in detail below.

Impressive advances have been made in analysis of the neural control of behavioral responses and response sequences in invertebrates (e.g., Davis & Kennedy, 1972a, b, c; Kandel, 1975; Willows, 1967; Willows & Hoyle, 1969). In most instances, analysis has been possible because the efferent (and afferent) neurons controlling the behavior can be identified and are few in number, relative to brain control systems in higher animals. Further, the behavior se-quences are often relatively inflexible (Abraham & Willows, 1971). To over-simplify greatly, it might be argued that two general strategies have evolved for adaptation of behavior to environment. One is to develop relatively simple "fixed action patterns" elicited by external and internal stimuli and then to rely on evolution to change these action patterns when the environment changes. This can be done with economy of neurons. Many invertebrates (with, of course, a number of exceptions) exemplify this strategy. The alternative strategy is to add to simpler fixed actions by developing the capacity for behavioral adapta-tion within the individual. Higher vertebrates have greatly developed capabilities for adaptation, which find their ultimate expression in human learning. Con-comitantly (perhaps because, but that is an assumption) they have developed brains with a great many more neurons, making analysis more difficult.

Analysis of the neural bases of the more complex phenomena of associative learning has not progressed very far (Thompson, Patterson, & Teyler, 1972). Simplified model biological systems do not, for the most part, exhibit very robust classical or instrumental conditioning. No phenomena that could be called associative learning have been described for monosynaptic pathways. Some simplified models appear to offer considerable promise (Eisenstein & Cohen, 1965; Patterson, Cegavske, & Thompson, 1973). However, the problem of generalization from simple systems to associative learning in intact, behaving animals, particularly higher animals and man, is severe. In this instance we know far more about the parametric features of behavioral learning in higher verte-brates than is known for any simplified systems.

A VERTEBRATE POLYSYNAPTIC
MODEL OF HABITUATION

Even to approach neurophysiological analysis of relatively long-time course events such as habituation requires the development of simplified neuronal systems of biological "models" where neuronal events can be analyzed. Thomp-son and Spencer (1966) reviewed the habituation literature and identified some nine parametric features or properties that define habituation in the intact, behaving animal, that is, effects of stimulus frequency, intensity, repeated series, etc. These criteria were applied to a simplified model—habituation of hindlimb flexion reflex in acute spinal cat—and showed that this system indeed exhibited the properties of habituation. It was then demonstrated that this decrease in flexion response to repeated cutaneous stimulation was not due to changes in afferent information to the spinal cord, did not involve changes at the level of the motoneuron, or feedback via the gamma system, and hence must be the result of changes in the activity of interneurons in the polysnaptic flexor pathway in the spinal gray.

Figure 1 shows a typical example of habituation to repeated cutaneous shock stimulation of the flexor response from the hindlimb of an acute spinal cat. The stimulus (a 2-msec shock to the hindfoot) was given twice per sec for 100 sec (i.e., 200 trials). Test stimuli were then given 15 and 30 sec following the 200 trials and at one min intervals thereafter until the response had recovered in amplitude. Note that the decrease in response is a relatively smooth exponential function which reaches an approximate asymptote. The recovery may then take a number of minutes. The time course of this habituation is, of course, much faster than general human habituation to repeated stimuli or stressors, or, for that matter, habituation of a reflex orienting response in an intact behaving cat. However, it shows the same properties of these more long lasting and general aspects of habituation exhibited by behaving animals.

Figure 2, taken from the paper by Thompson and Spencer (1966), illustrates some of these parametric relations. In the first graph (Figure 2a), the flexor response shows the typical exponential habituation with a long-time course of recovery. In Figure 2b, a rather important aspect of habituation is shown. If a habituation series is given, and the response allowed to recover, the second series shows a more pronounced habituation. In Figure 2c, the effect of stimulus frequency is shown. The more rapid the frequency of stimulation, the more rapid and pronounced is the degree of habituation. The effect of stimulus

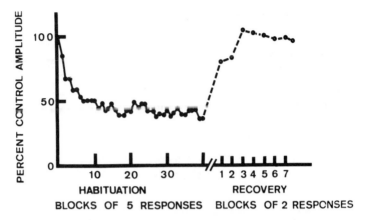

FIG. 1 Habituation and spontaneous recovery of the reflex contraction of the tibialis anterior muscle to iterated cutaneous stimulation. Shock stimuli were delivered to hindlimb skin at a rate of 2 per second. Intermittent probe stimuli were then delivered to monitor spontaneous recovery. Habituation is expressed by consecutive averages of blocks of five responses. Spontaneous recovery is expressed by blocks of two responses. Response amplitude is expressed in terms of percent of control amplitude. (From Groves, Lee, & Thompson, 1969. Copyright 1969 by Pergamon Press.)

intensity is shown in Figure 2d. The weaker the stimulus, the more pronounced is the habituation.[1] With a very strong stimulus there may be no habituation. Indeed, with a very strong stimulus, there may be an increased response initially, rather than a decrement. Finally, in Figure 2e, stimulus generalization of habituation is shown. Two separate inputs, two branches of a cutaneous nerve, are stimulated. One is given habituation training and the other is tested infrequently. There is pronounced flexor habituation to the habituating input. Infrequent tests given to the other input reveal the development of a significant degree of transfer of habituation. This generalization of habituation must be a central event since separate input fibers are being stimulated.

These are some of the general properties that serve to define the phenomenon of central habituation. They are exhibited by all varieties of organisms in response to repeated stimulation. They characterize what is undoubtedly the simplest form of learning.

[1] Reference here is to *relative* habituation, that is, response decrement with repeated application of a constant intensity stimulus relative to response to the same stimulus in initial infrequent control tests. As noted later in this paper, when different intensities are used for training and testing (as in Davis & Wagner, 1968), the situation is far more complex and involves generalization of habituation along the intensity dimension (see also Thompson *et al.*, 1973).

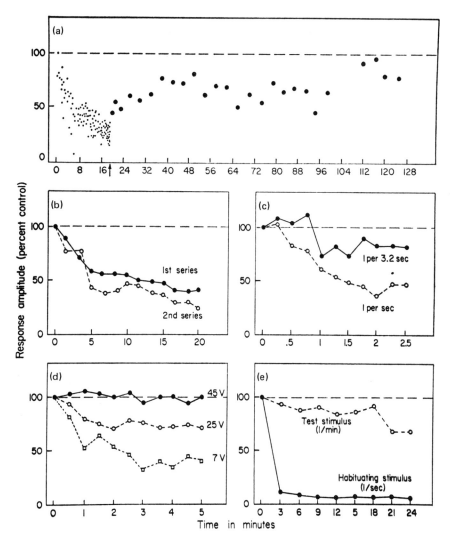

FIG. 2 (a) Habituation (zero minutes to arrow) and spontaneous recovery (arrow to 128 minutes) of the hindlimb flexion reflex of the spinal cat in response to repeated skin shocks. Stimuli were brief trains of shocks—5 in 50 msec—delivered every 10 sec during habituation and every 3 min during spontaneous recovery, except for a 12-min period of no stimuli at about 100 min. In this and all subsequent graphs, the response measured is tension developed by contraction of the tibialis anterior muscle, expressed as a percentage of mean initial-control response amplitude. (b) Effect of repeated habituation and spontaneous recovery series on degree of habituation. Response recovered to control level following first habituation series and was then rehabituated—second series. Conditions are as in 2(a). Data are averages of 10-trial blocks. (c) Effect of stimulus frequency on habituation. Single shocks given one per 3.2 seconds in one habituation series and 1 per second in the other to

(caption continued on page 56)

Figure 3, again from experiments on a spinal cat, demonstrates absence of change in excitability of spinal motorneuron during habituation to repeated cutaneous nerve stimulation. The tracings are superimposed intracellular recordings from deep peroneal motoneurons, identified antidromically, in a spinal cat anesthetized with Nembutal. In the upper series of tracings is shown the postsynaptic potential (PSP) to the polysynaptic cutaneous input: (a) in the control condition at once per 30 sec (no decrement was seen at this stimulation rate); (b) at once per second after habituation developed; and (c) after recovery at once per 30 sec. Note that there is pronounced decrement in the polysynaptic PSP from (a) to (b). The second line of tracings shows interpolated monosynaptic responses of the same motoneuron to stimulation of the deep peroneal nerve given every 30 sec during the corresponding periods above. Note that there is no decrease in the monosynaptic response in e during the period of pronounced decrement in the polysynaptic response of the same motoneuron; similarly, there is no change during recovery in f. Consequently the motoneuron exhibits no change in excitability to monosynaptic test volleys during pronounced habituation to the polysynaptic input. The lowest line of response tracings, g, h, and i, illustrate control, habituation, and recovery of the polysynaptic PSP's in another deep peroneal motoneuron. In this cell, the spike threshold was determined by delivering a brief current pulse, shown in l. The approximate 50% spike threshold level of current was identical in the control level (g) and after habituation (h), as shown by records j and k. Consequently, the motoneuron shows no change in general excitability to an intracellular current pulse during the course of habituation. On these grounds one may conclude that the general excitability of the motoneuron does not change during habituation. This in turn means that the change must occur prior to the motoneurons in the spinal gray.

In another study (Groves *et al.,* 1970) the possibility was explored that alterations of excitability in afferent terminals to the spinal cord could account for habituation. One of the major theories of habituation is that centrifugal activity acts back on the afferent terminals in a negative feedback manner as a result of repeated stimulation. This feedback action could induce primary

---

(caption of FIG. 2 continued from page 55)
the saphenous nerve. Data are averages of 10-trial blocks. (d) Effect of stimulus intensity on habituation. Brief trains of shocks, as in (a), were delivered every 10 sec to the saphenous nerve with spontaneous recovery allowed after each series. Voltages refer to output of stimulator and were attenuated, but in the same ratios, when delivered to the nerve. Data averaged over 3-trial blocks. (e) Stimulus generalization of habituation. Single shocks to two separate branches of the saphenous nerve. The habituating stimulus to one branch was given one per second, and the test stimulus to the other branch was given one per minute. Data are averaged over 3-trial blocks for response to the test stimulus and averages over the same periods of time for response to the habituating stimulus. (From Thompson & Spencer, 1966. Copyright 1966 by the American Psychological Association. Reproduced by permission.)

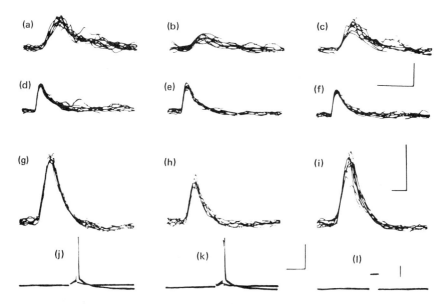

FIG. 3 Demonstration of constant amplitude of interpolated monosynaptic PSP's and stability of threshold to applied depolarizing currents during period of polysynaptic PSP decrement in deep peroneal motoneurons. (a–c) Polysynaptic PSP's to single shock stimuli delivered to posterior femoral cutaneous nerve. (a) Control period established by stimulating at 30-sec intervals. (b) Period of decrement during stimulation at 1-sec intervals. (c) Period of recovery, stimuli at 30-second intervals. (d–f) Monosynaptic PSP's to stimuli delivered to deep peroneal nerve at 30-sec intervals during periods corresponding to those in a, b, and c, respectively. Note constancy of monosynaptic responses during period of polysynaptic PSP decrement. g, h, and i are identical to a, b, and c, but from a different motoneuron in the deep peroneal group. j and k show responses to depolarizing current pulses of shape shown in l during control and decrement periods corresponding to g and h. Note that pulse continues to be of threshold-straddling intensity. Calibrations: (a–f) time = 10 msec, voltage = 2mV; (g–i) time = 10 msec, voltage = 10 mV; (j and k) time = 5 msec, voltage = 50 mV; (l) vertical bar represents 1×10^{-8} A. (From Spencer, Thompson, & Nielson, 1966c.)

afferent depolarization on the afferent terminals, which would then decrease the effective input volley from a constant stimulus (see, e.g., Hernández-Peón, 1960). In these experiments the flexor reflex was recorded (shown in the lower curve in Figure 4) for a series of stimuli producing habituation. A brief, higher intensity train of shocks was then given to produce sensitization, followed by rehabituation and spontaneous recovery. As indicated in Figure 4, there is pronounced habituation, dishabituation, and spontaneous recovery of the reflex response to repeated cutaneous stimulation. At the same time, afferent terminals were electrically stimulated through a microelectrode in the dorsal spinal gray, and the antidromic response from the cutaneous afferent nerve being used as the

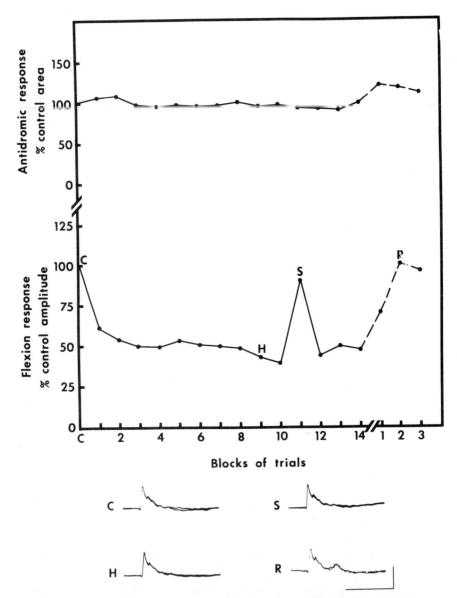

FIG. 4 Area under antidromic volley evoked by microelectrode stimulation (upper graph) recorded in the superficial peroneal nerve during control (C), habituation (H), sensitization (S), and spontaneous recovery (R) periods of the flexor twitch of the tibialis anterior muscle (lower graph) to repetitive stimulation of the same nerve. Data points represent successive means of 10 responses. Sample oscilloscope tracings of the antidromic response during various periods are shown in inserts. Calibration: 10 msec and 50 μV. (From Groves *et al.*, 1970)

stimulating nerve was recorded. The antidromic response provides an index of the excitability of the afferent terminals of the cutaneous nerve during the course of habituation. The excitability of these terminals is shown in the upper curve. Note that there is essentially no change whatever in the excitability of the afferent terminals during pronounced habituation, sensitization, and spontaneous recovery. Other control experiments demonstrated that this particular technique was quite sensitive to the development of primary afferent depolarization. Consequently, alterations in excitability of afferent terminals are ruled out as the mechanism of habituation. This leads to the conclusion that the general mechanisms of habituation must involve interneuron processes rather than alterations at the afferent input level or at the level of the motoneuron.

As indicated above, strong stimulation often leads to increases in responsiveness, so-called "sensitization." This is not a disruption of the process of habituation, but rather a superimposed process of sensitization or facilitation. It is commonly observed in habituation experiments where the stimulus is moderately strong. The response shows an increase above control level on the first few trials prior to the development of the pronounced habituation that will subsequently occur. An experiment on the spinal cat illustrates this phenomenon and also demonstrates the independence of the processes of sensitization and habituation (Figure 5). A moderately strong cutaneous shock stimulus was used and the flexor response was first habituated, and a brief strong shock train was applied elsewhere on the skin to produce pronounced sensitization, as shown in the upper tracing (Figure 5a). The habituating stimulus was continued and the response rehabituated rapidly. Note also that there was an initial increase in the first few trials of the habituated response. In Figure 5b, the same response system was used. However, following the interpolated shock train to produce sensitization, the habituating stimulus was discontinued until that point (5 sec) when the response had recovered to the habituated level. Note that the control response in Figure 5b is also at the habituated level. In other words, sensitization is a superimposed independent process with an intrinsic decay time. When a strong additional stimulus is given, the habituated response increases, and then rapidly decays back to the habituated level whether or not the habituating stimulus is continued. This demonstrates that sensitization, or dishabituation, does not disrupt permanently the process of habituation, but merely causes a transitory increase in excitability of response.

Experiments described above were done on a spinal cat. One would like to extend generality by replicating the same observations on intact, behaving organisms. In Figure 6 is shown an experiment in which startle responses of rats to a very loud sound, a typical stressor, are plotted. Two groups of animals were run, 8 animals in each group. The results of the 2 groups are averaged for the first 14 trials of the experiment. They did not differ significantly. They were all given loud tones once every minute and the amplitude of startle response to the tone was measured. Note that again there is a marked initial increase in the

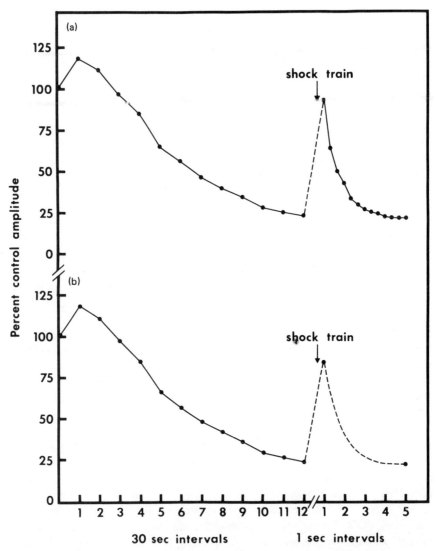

FIG. 5 The independence of habituation and sensitization for the hindlimb flexion reflex of acute spinal cat. In the upper graph, single shocks were delivered at two per second until pronounced habituation had developed. A brief shock train was then delivered to nearby skin electrodes, but the habituation stimulus was continued. Note the rapid decay of response sensitization. In the lower graph, the identical procedure was carried out except that the habituation stimulus was discontinued following the shock train. After five seconds, however, a single test shock revealed that response amplitude had spontaneously decayed to its previously habituated level. (From Groves & Thompson, 1970. Copyright 1970 by the American Psychological Association. Reproduced by permission.)

60

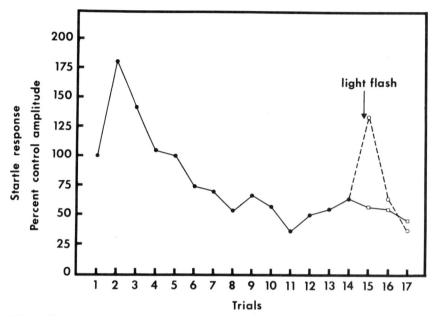

FIG. 6 The independence of habituation and sensitization for habituation of acoustic startle in intact rat. Following habituation, one group received a flashing light prior to Trial 15 (dashed line), whereas the other group did not (solid line). Although the experimental group showed dishabituation to the tone stimulus on Trial 15, response amplitude decayed spontaneously to its previously habituated level within one minute, as shown by the similar responses of both groups on Trials 16 and 17. (From Groves & Thompson, 1970. Copyright 1970 by the American Psychological Association. Reproduced by permission.)

response in the first 2 trials. Subsequently, habituation of response to the repeated stress becomes pronounced. On Trial 14 a flashing light was interpolated for 1 group of 8 animals only. Note that the subsequent response on Trial 15 to the loud tone was above the control level, but by the 16th trial the response had decayed back to the habituated level of the other group. The control group was not given the interpolated light stimulus. Consequently, this experiment, like the experiment on spinal cat shown above, argues that "dishabituation" or "disruption" of habituation is not in fact a disruption of the habituation process that develops, but is rather a superimposed process of sensitization or facilitation that causes a brief transitory increase in responsiveness. Furthermore, it has an intrinsic decay time to the *habituated* level. Habituation and sensitization are separate, superimposed processes.

These experiments led to the notion that the net behavioral output of response to a repeated stimulus or stress is really the result of two processes. A process of habituation invariably develops, and a process of sensitization may also develop

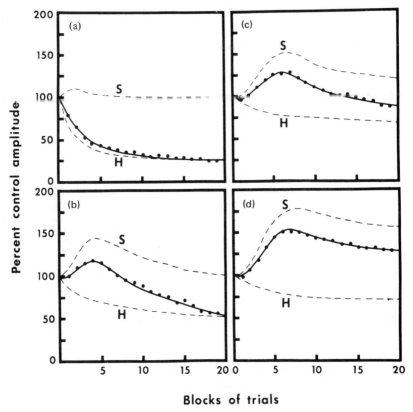

Blocks of trials

FIG. 7 Dual-process theory of habituation. Dashed lines represent two hypothetical processes which result in plasticity of response to repeated stimulation. Dots are actual data points obtained for hindlimb flexion reflex in acute spinal cat. In trial a shocks to hindpaw were presented at low intensity (near response threshold) at four per second frequency. Note pronounced response habituation. In trials b and c, as intensity is increased, hypothetical sensitization process (S) increases, while habituation process (H) becomes less pronounced. In trial d, at high intensity, sensitization is most pronounced, resulting in response sensitization. (From Groves & Thompson, 1970. Copyright 1970 by the American Psychological Association. Reproduced by permission.)

if the stressor is sufficiently strong. These two phenomena interact to yield a net behavioral outcome. Examples of this notion are shown in Figure 7 in which four outcomes from experiments on the spinal cat are shown (dots and solid lines). Responses to repeated stimulation vary as a function of stimulus intensity. Note that all of these graphs show some degree of decrement. However, the degree of increment is a function of stimulus intensity. It is easy to reconstruct all four of these behavioral outcomes by assuming two processes within the central nervous system: a process of habituation, symbolized by H; and a process of sensitization, symbolized by S. Both habituation and sensitization occur to varying degrees with every series of repeated stress stimulation. The interaction of these two inferred phenomena of sensitization and habituation leads to the net behavioral outcome, a decrement, or an increment followed by a decrement, in response.

Figure 8 shows our attempt to make the argument more convincing by illustrating the striking degree of comparability in response to repeated shocks in the flexion reflex of the acute spinal cat and in the response of intact behaving man, in the latter case the measure being skin resistance level for weak, moderate, and intense stimuli. In the human study, taken from Raskin, Kotses, and Bever (1969), the stimulus was a tone varied in loudness for the three different curves. Note that, as in the cat, the human response to a weak tone is an immediate habituation. When the tone is moderately loud, there is an initial increase in response followed by a pronounced decrement. Finally, with a very loud tone, there is a pronounced increment in the response with a subsequent partial decrement. These results parallel very closely the results of habituation in spinal cat and argue that in the intact human, as well as in the cat and rat, the response to repeated stimulation or stress is the result of two processes, one incremental and one decremental that add together to produce the net behavioral outcome.

These observations and the fact that in the case of the acute spinal cat, at least, the mechanisms of habituation appear to be a property of interneurons in the spinal gray, led us to explore the behavior of spinal interneurons in response to repeated stimulation. An example of an interneuron responsive to repeated cutaneous stimulation is shown in Figure 9. In these experiments the flexion response to the repeated cutaneous stimulation is recorded simultaneously with recordings of the interneuron responses. The upper graph shows the actual response of the muscle. A moderately strong cutaneous stimulus was used, so that the muscle response showed an initial increment followed by decrement to about 50% response amplitude, and subsequent spontaneous recovery. The discharges of the interneuron are shown in the tracings and in the lower graph, and the anatomical location of the interneuron is shown in the insert. Note that the number of spikes per stimulus of the interneuron follows very closely the actual course of response of the flexion reflex. This interneuron parallels closely the behavior of the response itself. However, it shows even more pronounced sensitization than the behavioral response; it is a strongly sensitizing interneuron (type S interneuron).

Figure 10 illustrates a different type of interneuron, the so-called type H interneuron. The upper graph again shows the muscle response with a very strong stimulus producing pronounced sensitization of the flexor response, followed by habituation and spontaneous recovery. The lower graph illustrates the discharge of the interneuron. Note that the interneuron shows only habituation. It shows marked and pronounced habituation followed by spontaneous recovery, but no sensitization. The location of this interneuron in the spinal gray

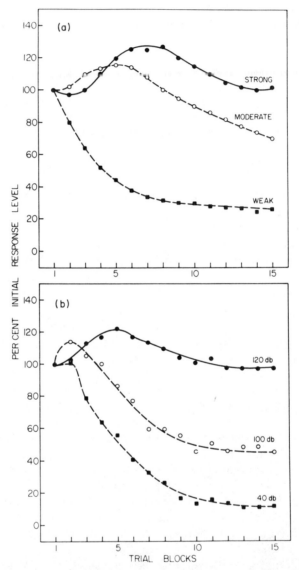

FIG. 8 Habituation and sensitization of amplitude of response to repeated stimulation as a function of stimulus intensity for two quite different response systems: (a) hindlimb flexor reflex of acute spinal cat to skin shock (From Groves & Thompson, 1970); and (b) intact human skin potential base level to sound. (From Raskin *et al.*, 1969. Copyright 1969 by the American Psychological Association. Reproduced by permission.)

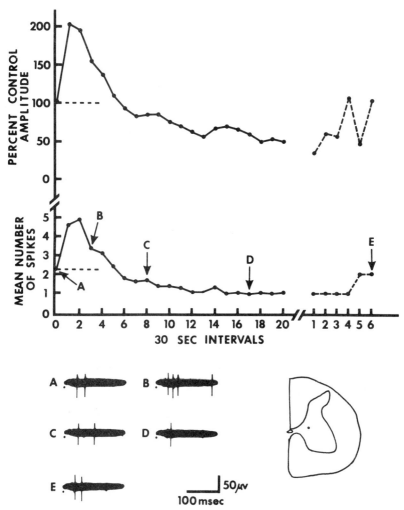

FIG. 9 Simultaneous recording of flexor muscle response (upper graph) and activity of spinal interneuron (lower graph) to repeated cutaneous shocks given 2 per second during habituation and 1 per 30 sec during recovery. Examples of neuron responses and location of neuron indicated below. The neuron shows marked sensitization followed by habituation and parallels response of muscle closely. (From Groves & Thompson, 1973.)

is shown in the insert. A number of such spinal interneurons that exhibit plasticity of response to repeated stress were studied, and all of those that show increments followed by decrements are localized in Rexed Layers 5–7 of the spinal gray. In contrast, the type H interneurons that show only initial decrements are located in Layers 1–5 of the spinal gray. There appears to be virtually complete anatomical separation of the two functional categories of interneurons.

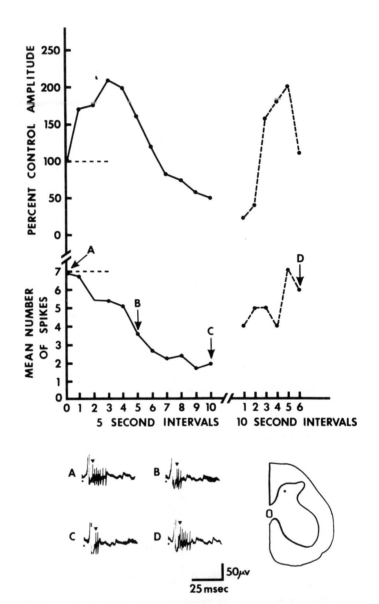

FIG. 10 Simultaneous recording of flexor muscle response (upper graph) and activity of spinal interneuron (lower graph) to repeated cutaneous shocks given 2 per second during habituation and 1 per 10 sec during recovery. Examples of neuron responses and location of neuron given below. The neuron shows only habituation even though the muscle shows marked sensitization (Groves & Thompson, unpublished observations).

Figure 11 illustrates the manner in which the responses of the type H and type S interneurons can be schematized as a general model of central habituation. If one assumes that the type H interneurons are located in the most direct reflex paths then they will always show a decrement. However, external to the type H interneurons are "state systems" or type S interneurons that show increased activity with repeated stimulation, if sufficiently intense. These interneurons build up activity and act back on either the type H interneurons or the final

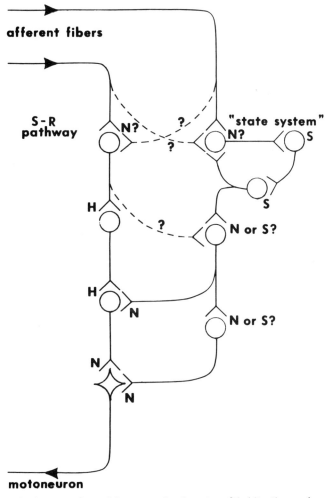

FIG. 11 Schematic diagram of possible neuronal substrates of habituation and sensitization. N indicates nonplastic synapses, H indicates habituating synapses, and S indicates sensitizing synapses. (From Groves & Thompson, 1970. Copyright 1970 by the American Psychological Association. Reproduced by permission.)

common path motoneuron to add sensitization to the process of decrement. This argument assumes that there may be several different types of interneurons, or at least synapses on interneurons, which are specialized in their responses to repeated stimulation. In short, different forms of behavioral plasticity may be coded by different specialized forms of synapses in the central nervous system.

The dual-process theory is sufficiently simple and specific that testable behavioral predictions can be made. Indeed, Kilmer and his associates at the University of Massachusetts, Amherst, have abstracted the most elementary formal properties of the schema given in Figure 11 and developed a computer simulation model which is amazingly accurate in predicting the behavioral outcomes for the spinal flexion reflex to repeated stimulation, varying intensity and frequency parameters (Kilmer, personal communication).

Thanks largely to the elegant behavioral studies of Allan Wagner, Michael Davis, and their associates at Yale, it has been possible to test several predictions developed from the dual-process theory about behavioral response habituation. Perhaps the most satisfying example concerns their study of the incremental stimulus intensity effect in the startle response of the intact rat (Davis & Wagner, 1969). In brief, they compared the amount of habituation of the startle response as evidenced by the number of startle responses during a final block of test trials to the same loud auditory stimulus in a group given the same stimulus in previous trials, a group given a constant tone of intermediate intensity in previous trials, and a group given a tone that began at a lower level and increased gradually during previous trials to a final level just below the test intensity. The results for the three groups are shown in Figure 12a. On the test trial the gradually increasing intensity group showed the greatest amount of habituation, the constant loud intensity group showed significantly less habituation, and the constant intermediate intensity group showed the least habituation, exhibiting a marked rebound effect in the test trials. As Davis and Wagner note, these results have important implications for theories of habituation. In particular, it is difficult to see how a single-process theory can account for the effect.

The dual-process theory would account for their results in the following way. The constant intense stimulus would yield pronounced sensitization (inferred) and a small degree of relative habituation (inferred). The incremental series results in marked habituation and little sensitization, which may decay within each block. Both habituation and sensitization generalize to each new series of stimuli. The result is a summation of habituation occurring within all blocks of trials, with a consequent marked response decrement at the end of the incremental series. The rebound seen in the group given a constant intermediate stimulus would be due to the absence of substantial generalization of habituation, coupled with the fact that sensitization to the final intense stimulus is maximal (due to the absence of generalization of prior decay of sensitization to the intermediate stimulus). We put these notions to the critical test and replicated Davis and Wagner's experiment on the hindlimb flexion reflex of the acute spinal

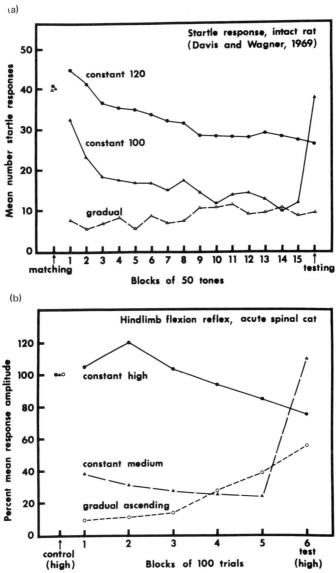

FIG. 12 The incremental stimulus intensity effect for intact rat (a) and acute spinal cat (b). Habituation to a series of stimuli of gradually increasing intensity is more pronounced than to a series of constantly intense or moderately intense stimuli, even though groups are matched initially and the final test trials use the same high intensity stimulus in all cases. (Upper figure reprinted from an article by M. Davis and A. R. Wagner published in the April 1969 *Journal of Comparative and Physiological Psychology.* (Copyright 1969 by the American Psychological Association. Reproduced by permission.) (From Groves & Thompson, 1970. Copyright 1970 by the American Psychological Association. Reproduced by permission.)

cat. The results are shown in Figure 12b. The incremental stimulus intensity effect holds both for the intact rat and spinal cat.

Perhaps the key assumption in this analysis of incremental stimulus intensity is the notion of stimulus generalization (of habituation and sensitization) across intensity. If an animal is given habituation training at one stimulus intensity and tested at another, it must be construed in terms of generalization, just as in the more obvious case of stimulus quality (i.e., tone frequency). We have analyzed this issue in detail in an earlier discussion (Thompson *et al.*, 1973).

In brief, adopting a "common elements approach" (Hull, 1920), when an animal is habituated to a stimulus one of intensity and tested to another intensity, incomplete generalization of habituation will occur. The generalization will be asymmetrical—if testing is to two stimuli equally stronger or weaker than the habituating stimulus, then there will be a greater increase in responding to the stronger stimulus than to the weaker stimulus. Such a finding was reported by James and Hughes (1969) for human GSR. This result, consistent with our dual-process view, may pose problems for Sokolov's theory. A more complicated set of predictions can be made from the dual-process theory about habituation in studies where different groups of animals are trained and tested at different intensities (e.g., Davis & Wagner, 1968). In brief, a set of six predictions can be made concerning generalization of habituation. The most interesting is the nonintuitive result that relative generalization of relative habituation will be greater than 100% for animals trained at a stronger stimulus and tested at a weaker stimulus. The reader may consult Thompson *et al.* (1973), for further details.

In the past few years there have been a gratifyingly large number of studies concerned with the dual-process theory of habituation. These have been largely basic behavioral and/or physiological studies with animals. It would not be appropriate here even to begin to cite them all, except to say that among the most elegant are the recent papers of Michael Davis at Yale (Davis, 1972, in press; Davis & Sheard, 1974). To date, most studies have supported the dual-process theory and none have provided strong negative evidence. See, however, Graham (1973) for a rather critical review in the context of complex human autonomic responses.

A major heuristic purpose of the admittedly simplistic dual-process theory is to permit inferences from simple neuronal models (spinal reflexes) to neuronal substrates of habituation and sensitization in the intact mammalian brain.

Results of a number of interneuron studies are consistent with the theory (see Groves & Thompson, 1970). The recent work of Groves and associates on neuronal mechanisms of habituation of the startle response in intact rat provides a good example (Groves *et al.*, in press). Of particular interest is the current work of Barry Peterson and associates at Rockefeller University on neuron responses in reticular formation to repetitive stimulation of cutaneous vestibular, cortical, and tectal pathways (Peterson, personal communication). Results to date are beautifully consistent with the dual-process theory.

To return to the notion of synapses specialized for habituation and sensitization (see Figure 11), it would provide considerable economy of function if different categories or classes of synapses were so specialized to respond to repeated afferent stimulation in these different manners. This would be particularly true in the case of stressful stimuli. A stressor leads to increased response in some systems of interneurons, and in behavior, so that the organism can attempt to increase or vary his response to avoid stress. If another system responds by developing marked habituation, the animal can adapt to the stress by simply not responding to it, if he cannot avoid it. It makes a great deal of evolutionary sense to devise the system with both options for response to strong or stressful stimulation. The organism first increases response and tries to avoid the stimulus. If unable to do so, he learns to deal with the stimulus by adapting to it. Viewed in this manner, habituatory decrement in response to repeated stress is a simple but important form of adaptive learning. It is the principle manner in shich organisms deal with unavoidable stress.

The dual-process theory of habituation provides a theoretical framework in which to interpret adaptation to repeated stimulation. Unfortunately, it is not possible to analyze the synaptic mechanisms underlying this process of adaptation, even in polysynaptic systems as simple as the cat spinal flexion reflex. There is a good deal of indirect evidence arguing against postsynaptic inhibition acting on interneurons as the mechanism. It appears to be some form of synaptic depression. However, what is really needed is a central vertebrate system in which one can identify decrement at a single synapse, a decrement to repeated stimulation showing the properties of habituation in a monosynaptic pathway.

A VERTEBRATE MONOSYNAPTIC
MODEL OF HABITUATION

Several model systems have been developed in invertebrates. Particularly productive has been the work of Kandel and associates on a monosynaptic system in *Aplysia* abdominal ganglion that exhibits a reduced excitatory postsynaptic potential to repeated stimulation at slow rates, without alteration in postsynaptic membrane properties (Castellucci *et al.*, 1970; Kandel, 1975; Castellucci & Kandel, Chapter 1, this volume; Kupfermann *et al.*, 1970; Pinsker *et al.*, 1970). Similarly, an afferent synapse on an interneuron in the crayfish involved in the escape reflex appears to be a locus of habituation; the decrement again appears to be a form of synaptic depression rather than any kind of postsynaptic or presynaptic inhibitions superimposed from outside the synaptic system (Zucker, 1972). These invertebrate models are promising.

We have recently utilized a vertebrate model system in which habituation can be demonstrated to occur in a single monosynaptic pathway. The preparation is the isolated frog spinal cord (see Farel, Glanzman, & Thompson, 1973). The cord is removed from the frog and maintained in an oxygenated bathing solution circulated through a chamber from a reservoir maintained at about 15°C. A photograph of the preparation, with stimulating and recording electrodes in place, is shown in Figure 13. A schematic diagram of several pathways in the frog spinal cord is shown in Figure 14, together with recording and stimulating electrodes indicating some of the experimental maneuvers possible with this simplified preparation. The monosynaptic pathway formed by the lateral column fibers (LC in Figure 14) projecting to the lumbosacral motoneurons exhibits marked decrement or habituation to repeated stimulation of the lateral column at relatively slow rates. Habituation of the population monosynaptic response of the motoneurons can easily be measured by recording from the ventral root (VR in Figure 14) and habituation of individual motoneuron responses can be measured with intracellular recording microelectrodes.

Examples of habituation and spontaneous recovery of this monosynaptic lateral column-ventral root pathway are shown in Figure 15. A stimulus (single shock to lateral column) is given once every 5 sec in 3 different series: 10 trials, 30 trials, or 50 trials in the different series. Note that the response even at this slow stimulation rate shows rapid and pronounced habituation to approximately 50% of initial control response level. Examples are shown in Figure 15a—d of progressive habituation of the ventral root response to lateral column stimulation and Figure 15e shows spontaneous recovery. Also illustrated in the figure is that the longer the train of stimuli given, the longer habituation requires to recover. This is characteristic of habituation in other systems. Examples of habituation of intracellularly recorded PSP's from a motoneuron in this monosynaptic pathway to repeated stimulation are shown in Figure 16. The motoneuron initially shows a spike discharge, the spike fails after a few stimuli in Figure 16b, and the PSP subsequently decreases further in Figure 16c. Recovery after one and two minutes is shown in Figure 16d and e.

Perhaps most important, this simplified monosynaptic system in the isolated frog spinal cord exhibits retention or "memory" of habituation, the critical parameter distinguishing habituation as a simple form of behavioral plasticity or learning from neuronal refractory phenomena. This retention of habituation is shown in Figure 17. The lateral column was stimulated .2/sec for 10 stimuli. The first and tenth responses are shown in Figure 17a and b; the tenth response shows marked habituation. The preparation was then allowed to recover for a period of 2 minutes and the series of 10 stimuli repeated. The first and tenth responses of the second series are shown in Figure 17c and d. Note that the system fully recovered between series, in that the first response of the second series is identical in amplitude to the first response of the first series. However, the response to the tenth stimulus of the second series is substantially lower than

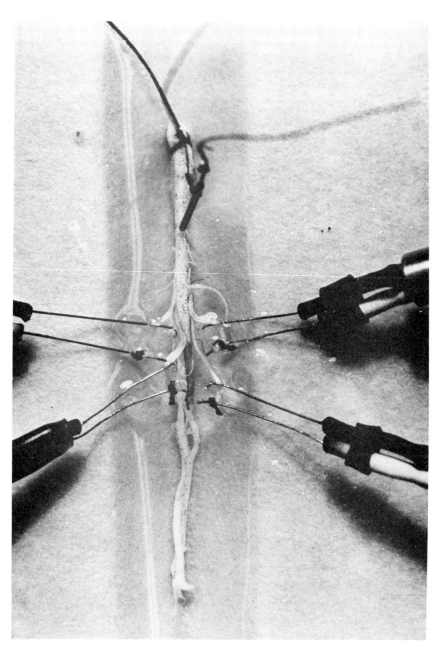

FIG. 13 Photograph of the isolated frog spinal cord "model" system for neuronal analysis of habituation. Electrodes are shown on the dorsal and ventral roots (below) and penetrating into the lateral column (above). The spinal cord is about 1 inch long.

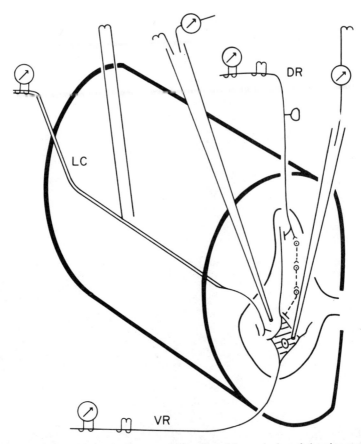

FIG. 14 Simplified schematic diagram of a section of frog spinal cord showing some of the inferred neuronal pathways and possible experimental maneuvers. The lateral column (LC) motoneuron monosynaptic pathway response can be recorded from the ventral root (VR) or from the motoneuron directly (pipette penetrating motoneuron). Field potentials and antidromic stimuli can be obtained from the pipette on the left placed outside the motoneuron. Dorsal root (DR) stimulation can be used as a test of motoneuron excitability.

the tenth response from the first series. This effect was found reliable in identical tests on 9 separate preparations: The mean percentage of initial control response was 69.4% for the last trial of the first series and was 53.4% for the last trial of the second series. This difference is statistically significant ($t = 2.74$, 7 df, $p < .05$, two-tailed test).

The effects of the first series of stimuli thus persist or are retained by the synapse for a substantial period of time. Further, this retention does not show itself with single test stimuli, but rather as an increased rate and degree of

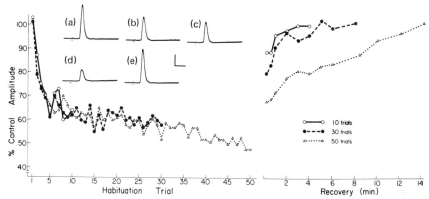

FIG. 15 Habituation and recovery of ventral root response in isolated frog spinal cord to 10, 30, and 50 lateral column stimuli presented 1 per 5 sec. The graph represents means drawn from 3 preparations each of which was run in each stimulus condition. Note the exponential decline in response amplitude and the inverse relation between number of stimulus presentations and recovery rate. (Inset) Example of decrement of ventral root response to repeated lateral column stimulation. Responses are shown to the first (a), second (b), third (c), and tenth (d) stimuli of a train of 10 stimuli presented to lateral column. Recovery 2 min later (e) is also shown. (From Farel, Glanzman, & Thompson, 1973.)

habituation to a subsequent "training" series of stimuli. It is in many ways analogous to the improvement in performance over repeated practice sessions in much more complex human learning.

To summarize, the decrement of this monosynaptic response of motoneurons to repeated lateral column stimulation exhibits essentially all the properties of

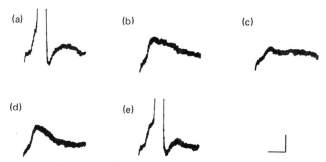

FIG. 16 Decrement and recovery of intracellularly recorded responses of a motoneuron to repeated lateral column (LC) stimulation. Ten stimuli at a rate of 1 per 2 sec: (a) first stimulus; (b) second stimulus; (c) tenth stimulus; (d) recovery test after 1 min; (e) recovery test after 2 minutes. Calibration: 10 msec and 4 μV. (From Farel, Glanzman, & Thompson, 1973)

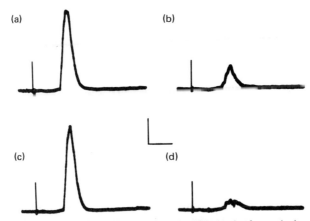

FIG. 17 Long term retention or "memory" of habituation in the frog spinal cord mono-synaptic pathway. Two trains of 10 stimuli at .2/sec were separated by a 2-min recovery period: (a) Response to first stimulus; (b) Response to tenth stimulus; (c) Response to first stimulus of second series; and (d) Response to tenth stimulus of second series. Note that, although response amplitudes at the beginning of each series are comparable, more decrement was produced by the second stimulus series. Calibration: 4 mV, 4 msec. (From Farel, Glanzman, & Thompson, 1973.)

behavioral response habituation and hence may be considered a legitimate synaptic model of the process of habituation, the simplest form of learning.

In an elegant series of experiments, Brookhart and associates (Brookhart & Fadiga, 1960; Brookhart, Machne, & Fadiga, 1959; Fadiga & Brookhart, 1960; Machne, Fadiga, & Brookhart, 1959) demonstrated that this lateral column system projects monosynaptically on the soma and proximal dendrites of motor neurons in the frog spinal cord. Consequently, the frog spinal cord has a strong direct monosynaptic system from lateral column to soma of motor neuron which exhibits pronounced behavioral plasticity. It is a type of "plastic" synapse that agrees remarkably in its behavioral properties with the plastic interneurons described above for the cat spinal cord.

In a series of experiments (see Farel, Glanzman, & Thompson, 1973), it was demonstrated that the decrement in this monosynaptic pathway in the frog occurs at the synapses on motoneurons activated by the lateral column stimulus and does not involve processes of postsynaptic inhibition, presynaptic inhibition, or other actions of interneurons. The decrement is homosynaptic—limited to the synapses in question.

The great advantage of dealing with plasticity in a monosynaptic pathway is, of course, that strong inference can be used. Various alternative hypotheses can be disproved directly and rather simply in "crucial" experiments. Our analysis is indicated briefly here. In terms of known synaptic mechanisms, there are only five possible ways that a monosynaptic system could exhibit decrement to repeated stimulation. These are shown in Figure 18. A and b involve activation of an interneuron pool (indicated by a single interneuron, but it could involve as many interneurons as one wishes) via recurrent axon collaterals from motoneuron axons. If these are the mechanisms, they will be activated equally by stimulation of LC (orthodromic stimulation), which yields habituation, and by stimulation of the ventral root, VR (antidromic stimulation). The experiment is very simple. A test stimulus is given to LC and the VR response measured. The VR is then repeatedly stimulated and the LC–VR again tested. When such stimulation is given to VR, no habituation develops in the LC–VR pathway. Consequently, mechanisms A and B are ruled out.

Mechanism C would involve activation of interneurons by LC fibers which act to develop tonic presynaptic inhibition on the LC terminals. The critical test uses Wall's method (1958) for detecting primary afferent depolarization (see Figure 14). A stimulating electrode is inserted in the vincinity of the LC terminals and the antidromic response of the LC pathway measured. Habituation training of the LC–VR pathway is then given until marked habituation develops. The antidromic test of LC terminals is then given again. If presynaptic inhibition has developed on the LC terminals, the antidromic LC response will be increased. There is in fact no increase. Consequently, mechanism C is ruled out.

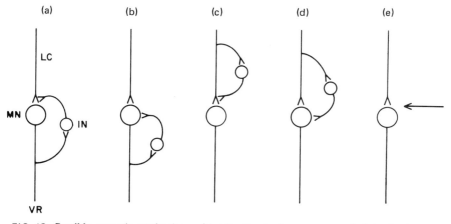

FIG. 18 Possible synaptic mechanisms of habituation in the monosynaptic lateral column (LC)–ventral root (VR) pathway in isolated frog spinal cord. MN = motoneuron, IN = interneuron and could represent a complex pool of interconnected interneurons: (a) Recurrent collateral from motoneuron axon acts back through interneurons to induce tonic presynaptic inhibition on lateral column fiber terminals; (b) Recurrent collateral acts back through interneurons to induce tonic postsynaptic inhibition on motoneuron; (c) Lateral column fibers act through interneurons to induce tonic presynaptic inhibition on lateral column terminals; (d) Lateral column fibers act through interneurons to produce tonic postsynaptic inhibition on motoneurons; (e) Synaptic depression–decrement is localized to synapses activated by repeated stimulation of LC. Possibilities (a–d) can be ruled out in "critical" experiments (see text for details). (Modified from Farel, Glanzman, & Thompson, 1973.)

Mechanism D would involve activation of interneurons by LC fibers which would build up tonic postsynaptic inhibition on motoneurons. This can be tested very simply by using the polysynaptic dorsal root input to the same motoneuron pool (see Figure 14). The VR response to DR stimulation is measured, habituation training is given to the LC–VR pathway and the DR–VR test given again. If tonic inhibition has built up on motoneurons, the test DR–VR response will be reduced. It is in fact unchanged, both in terms of the VR population measure of the motoneuron pool response and in terms of intracellular recordings from the same motoneuron. Consequently, mechanism D is ruled out. This leaves only mechanism E, some form of synaptic depression limited to the synapses being activated by the habituating stimulus (arrow).

Current work by a former colleague, Paul Farel, has shown that this lateral column–motoneuron pathway also exhibits a very pronounced and prolonged sensitization-like process. Thus, stimulation of LC at 500 per second for 500 msec produces a marked increase in the test VR response to a single LC stimulus that persists in excess of 2 hr (Farel, 1974a). "Strong inference" tests ruled out changes in motoneuron excitability and presynaptic terminal excitability. Consequently, this sensitization effect appears to be localized to the same set of synapses that show habituation at slow stimulus rates. Even more striking is Farel's demonstration (1974b) that both habituation and sensitization effects can occur simultaneously and independently at the same group of LC–MN synapses. Even at the monosynaptic level, the process of sensitization can occur as a strong and prolonged process of behavioral plasticity independent of habituation.

We have recently undertaken a quantal analysis of possible alterations in transmitter release along similar lines to those of Kandel and associates in their work on *Aplysia* (see Castellucci & Kandel, Chapter 1, this volume). There are two major possible categories of mechanisms that might underlie habituation in monosynaptic pathways, given that the general process is a form of synaptic depression. One is a decrease in release of the chemical transmitter substance and the other is a decrease in the sensitivity of the postsynaptic receptor sites. Granting a few assumptions, quantal analysis permits localization of the process to presynaptic release or postsynaptic receptors (see Kuno, 1971). In brief, assuming that transmitter is released in quantal packages, e.g., from presynaptic vesicles, (see Figures 25 and 26), then habituation would be due to a decrease in the number of vesicles released or a decrease in the response of the postsynaptic receptors to the transmitter quanta. To oversimplify greatly, the potential synaptic mechanisms underlying habituation may be divided into two categories—pre- versus postsynaptic events. Presynaptic events may be (1) a decrease in the number of quanta available for release within the axon terminal or varicosity, (2) a decrease in the probability of release of available quanta, or (3) a decrease in the amount of transmitter packaged into each vesicle. The first possibility may be tested indirectly in the following way. Intracellular recordings of spontaneous miniature potentials (mini's) are made before and after habituating the LC–MN pathway. A mini is usually accepted as being the recorded electrophysiological response of a receptor membrane to the action of a single quantum or packet of transmitter material released spontaneously from presynaptic terminals in the absence of externally applied stimulation. If a decrease in the number of quanta available for release as a result of habituation brings about a concomitant decrease in the number of quanta available for spontaneous release, then a decrease in the frequency of spontaneously occurring mini's may occur. The possibility of incomplete vesicle filling remains, however, but appears unlikely. At least in the Mauthner cell, relatively long periods of high frequency stimulation are needed to produce identifiable incompletely filled vesicles (e.g., 70 per second for 10-min stimulation; see Bennett, 1975). If, on the other hand, the mechanism is a decrease in postsynaptic receptor sensitivity, there will be a decrease in the amplitude of the recorded unit mini's, but no change in their frequency.

A typical intracellular recording from a motoneuron in isolated frog spinal cord of spontaneous mini's is shown in Figure 19. The postsynaptic response of the impingement of single quanta of transmitter is a depolarization of 200–800 μV, with a half-height width of about 20 msec, the magnitude of depolarization being dependent upon the resting membrane potential of the impaled cell (see Kuno & Miyahara, 1969a, b). There are also occasional "doublets" and "triplets" of transmitter release, believed to be the simultaneous release of more than one quantum. Examples of typical multiple miniature responses appear in the third column of Figure 19. Normally, we record these potentials at a much slower sweep speed, as in Figure 20. Analyses of the number and amplitude of the potentials are performed both by hand and by computer (from magnetic tape) with essentially identical results. An example of the amplitude–frequency distribution of spontaneous mini's recorded from the soma of a frog spinal motoneuron is shown in Figure 21. These potentials and distributions are in excellent agreement with those reported by other investigators (Colomo & Erulkar, 1968; Katz & Miledi, 1963).

We have adapted a method of iron deposit marking developed by Sokolov, Arakelov, and Levinson (1966) to label cells from which these recordings are made (personal communication). An example is shown in Figure 22. Because the deposit (solid black spot in motoneuron) remains localized, it is possible to visualize the locus of penetration of the recording micropipette; in this instance in the motoneuron soma.

Although our quantal analysis is still in process and our data are not yet conclusive, results are consistent with the hypothesis that habituation is due to decreased probability of release of transmitter quanta from LC terminals as a result of repeated stimulation. Preliminary analysis of spontaneous miniature potentials as a function of habituation training indicates that the frequency of mini's is transiently increased following the application of moderate intensity

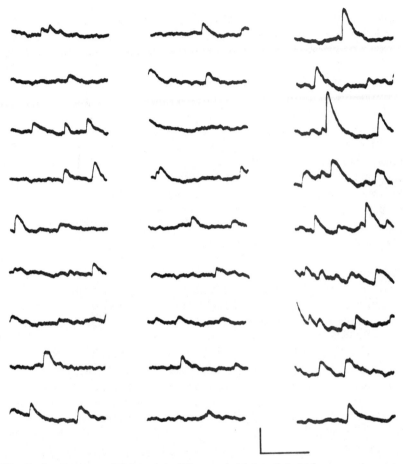

FIG. 19 Spontaneous miniature potentials recorded intracellularly from a motoneuron of isolated frog spinal cord. Filters set at 1 Hz and 1 kHz. Calibration: 1 mV and 100 msec.

stimuli (see Figure 23). This is in agreement with other published accounts of increases in the frequency of spontaneous miniature potentials following either a single stimulus or a brief train of stimuli to presynaptic fibers, for example, in cells of the stellate ganglion of the squid (Miledi, 1966) and in cells of the ciliary ganglion of the chick (Martin & Pilar, 1964a, b). In addition, there regularly appears a marked increase in the relative number of "doublets" and "triplets" of mini's following habituation of the LC–MN pathway.

We have preliminary data on the occurrence of "unitary" potentials, that is, the minimum potentials evoked by LC stimulation that closely resemble spontaneous miniature potentials both in amplitude and duration, as a function of habituation training. These minimum unitary potentials are presumably evoked by an action potential at one or a few synapses. In our experiments, an extremely weak test lateral column stimulus is presented to the LC. A stimulus level is chosen so that an appreciable number of "failures" of response occur, and this weak stimulus is presented at 10-sec intervals for several minutes before habituating training is begun (see Figure 24). From data collected in this way, we can calculate the mean number of transmitter quanta released from the lateral column terminals per weak stimulus. The preparation is then habituated to a more intense stimulus to LC until response to the intense stimulus habituates to less than 70% of control level. The weak test stimulus is then repeated. Preliminary results indicate that the mean number of transmitter quanta released

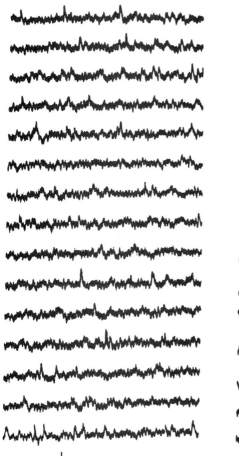
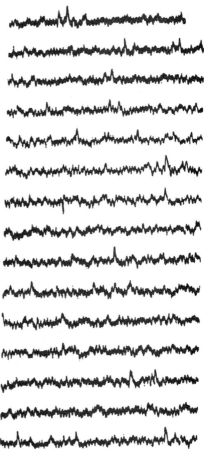

FIG. 20 Spontaneous miniature potentials recorded from a motoneuron of isolated frog spinal cord. Calibration: 1 mV and 200 msec. (We normally record at this slower time base so more data can be displayed.) Every "hump" in the baseline is a miniature potential.

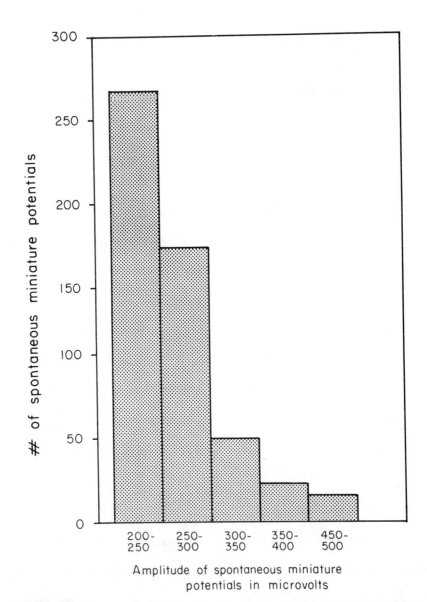

FIG. 21 Amplitude–frequency histogram of the data sampled in Figure 20. This distribution is in close agreement with results of Katz and Miledi (1963) and Colomo and Erulkar (1968).

decreases following habituation training. It is important to note that the amplitude of the unitary evoked responses remains constant before and after habituation; only the mean number of quanta released declines. This implies no alterations in postsynaptic receptor sensitiviey but rather a decrease in probability of release from presynaptic terminals. This observation supports the hypothesis that a decrease in probability of release of neurotransmitter substance with repeated stimulation is the mechanism underlying habituation in this preparation.

The possibility of desensitization of the postsynaptic receptors to the transmitter molecules must still be considered as a potential synaptic mechanism

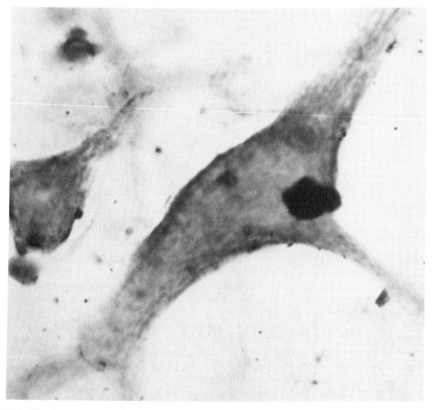

FIG. 22 A motoneuron from frog spinal cord marked with iron deposit (large solid black spot that protrudes just outside cell membrane). Spontaneous miniature potentials were recorded and the cell marked by iontophoretic injection of ferric chloride. The cell continued to function normally (by our measures) following injection. The iron deposit was developed with potassium ferrocyanide and the tissue counterstained with Safranin-O. Note how localized the iron mark remains. One can visualize the penetration of the cell by the micropipette. × 3120.

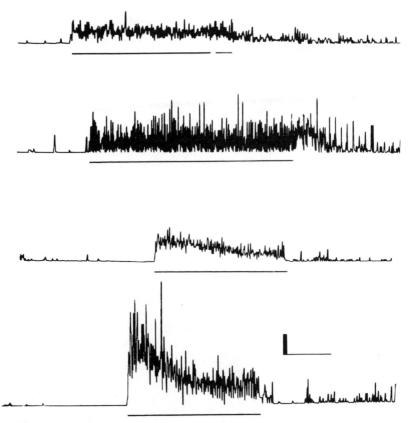

FIG. 23 Frequency histogram of the number of spontaneously occurring miniature synaptic potentials as influenced by repetitive stimuli presented to LC fibers. Responses were recorded intracellularly from three motoneurons in a single preparation. Habituation training stimuli were delivered where the solid horizontal bar appears beneath each histogram. Two points should be noted: (1) the *increase* in mini frequency following the termination of each habituation series (compare the period immediately preceeding presentation of habituation stimuli with the poststimulus period); (2) the net lessened effect of successive stimuli as habituation progresses within a given series, especially in the lower two histograms. During the period of stimulation, the records are contaminated with stimulus artifacts and with an overwhelming evoked response; hence, the decreases in evoked activity during a given habituation run may be taken as one measure of habituation. Histograms three and four are data from a single cell during a single habituation run; the differences are due to using two trigger levels for the pulse counter. Different stimulation and analysis modes were used for each histogram. TOP: stimulus frequency 1/sec; trigger level 300 μV; 85 stimulu presented; SECOND: stimulus frequency 2/sec; trigger level 600 μV; 200 stimuli presented; THIRD: stimulus frequency 4/sec; trigger level 750 μV; 280 stimuli presented; LOWER: stimulus frequency 4/sec; trigger level 600 μV; 280 stimuli presented. Calibration: 30 counts (sum of mini's, evoked activity and stimulus artifacts) per each 200-msec time bin; 33 sec.

84

underlying habituation in some systems. Membrane desensitization may be produced in many preparations by administering excitatory (Nastuk & Parsons, 1970; Rang & Ritter, 1970) and/or inhibitory (Epstein & Grundfest, 1970) substances on a regular schedule. Most long-term effects are slowly developed over several days when such substances are applied directly to the membrane several times per day. Such a mechanism may indeed play a role in long term habituation (Sharpless, 1964), but appears not to be involved in short-term

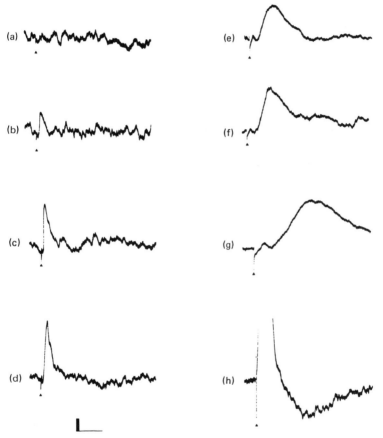

FIG. 24 Intracellularly recorded responses from motoneuron of isolated spinal cord of the frog, to weak lateral column stimulation: (a) LC stimulus failed to evoke any discernable depolarization of the motoneuron; (b) unitary evoked potential; (c, d) double and triple unitary potentials, respectively; (e, f, g) double unitary responses recorded at faster sweep speeds to demonstrate smoothly rising onset of response; (h) the response of the same motoneuron to a more intense LC stimulus of the type used to habituate the LC–MN synapse. Amplifier filter settings are .1 and 10 kHz. Calibration: 100 μV all traces; (a–d, h) 40 msec; (e, f) 10 msec; (g) 4 msec.

habituation, since the sensitivity of receptor membranes appears to remain stable over the course of at least several hours. This stability persists over the time course of short-term habituation and its complete recovery, at least in our preparation.

We have also begun an examination of the morphology of lateral column synapses on motoneurons, using light microscopy—classical lesion techniques with standard silver stains—and electron microscopy to map LC terminals on motoneuron somata. The LC terminals appear to be large (1–3 microns diameter) and relatively evenly distributed over the motoneuron soma and proximal dendrites (Mensah, 1974), in agreement with electrophysiological data (Brookhart & Fadiga, 1960).

In preliminary experiments we have evidence suggesting that the lateral column fibers may have structurally characteristic form of synapse on motoneuron soma. Examples of the kind of synapse believed to be involved are shown in the electron microscope pictures in Figures 25 and 26. Note that the presynaptic terminal bouton is large (about 3 microns) and has several large dense-core vesicles, as well as the common smaller clear vesicles (each presumably containing a quantum of transmitter). There is also an additional membrane (termed a subsynaptic cistern) underlying the postsynaptic membrane of the motoneuron. These two characteristics appear common to all such synapses. Whenever large dense-core vesicles are found in the presynaptic terminal, the additional membrane is found postsynaptically. In a series of serial reconstructions of synaptic terminations on motoneuron somas, more than a third of all of the synaptic terminals are of this form on the soma.

In preliminary studies currently in progress, 10 days following sectioning of the lateral column on one side, many of the large synaptic terminals containing the large dense-core vesicles appear to have degenerated on the side of the lesion. These data are tentative. It will be remembered that lateral column synapses with the motoneuron somas have been shown to be the site of habituation. If it is in fact true that lateral column fiber terminals have this characteristic synaptic form, then it will provide a convenient means of identifying morphologically a synapse showing marked habituation. It has been suggested that this type of synaptic terminal containing large dense-core vesicles may involve biogenic amines, for example, serotonin and norepinephrine, as transmitters (Cooper, Bloom, & Roth, 1974). Indeed, very indirect evidence implicates serotonin in brain substrates of startle habituation in the rat (Aghajanian & Sheard, 1968; Conner et al., 1970).

Following upon this tentative possibility, we completed an experiment that was rather a shot in the dark. Frogs were pretreated with varying doses of 5,6-dihydroxytryptamine (5,6-DHT) injected intracisternally, sacrificed four days later, and the spinal cord assayed for degeneration using silver stains (Mensah et al., 1974). This substance (5,6-DHT) has been reported to produce selective degeneration of serotonin containing nerve terminals (Baumgarten et

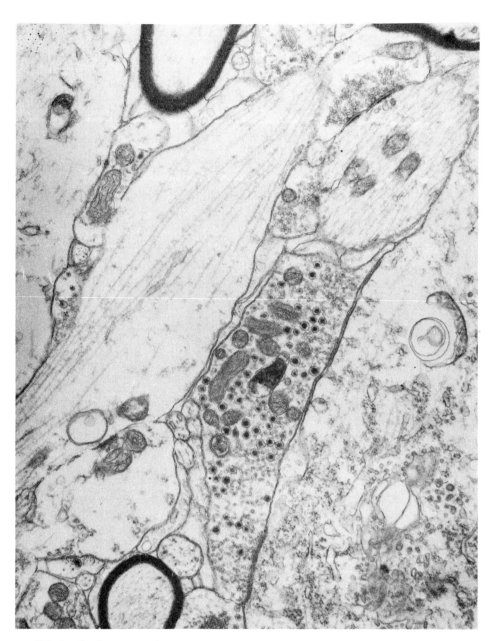

FIG. 25 In the center of the picture is a large terminal containing several dense core vesicles. Pleomorphic, clear vesicles are also present. To the right below is the cell body of a motoneuron. A subsynaptic cistern is closely apposed to the plasma membrane of the motoneuron. The subsynaptic cistern and aggregations of endoplasmic reticulum extend the entire length of the synaptic contact. × 17,640.

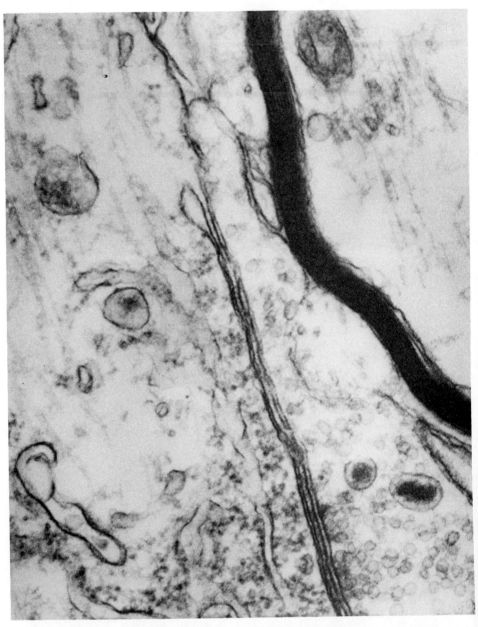

FIG. 26 The axosomatic contact made by a terminal (lower right) on motoneuron soma (left part of figure). This terminal, containing large dense core vesicles, is shown in greater detail here. Notice the length and position of the subsynaptic cistern. ×60,760.

al., 1972a, b; Baumgarten, Lackenmyer, & Schlossberger, 1972). Results were striking. The pattern of terminal degeneration in the lumbosacral spinal cord is virtually identical to that produced by bilateral lesions of the lateral columns. Thus, at low doses the large terminals on motoneuron somata degenerate. Higher doses actually cause degeneration in the lateral columns themselves, although not in dorsal columns: the pattern of degeneration remains selective. Although these data are of course not conclusive, they raise the interesting possibility that the "habituating synapse" may be a serotonin synapse.

It is not completely improbable that particular forms of synapses and associated transmitters are specialized to code or subserve particular forms of plasticity in the central nervous system. Thus, norepinephrine, serotonin, or some related substance, may be the "habituating" transmitter. Other types of synapses and transmitters might be specialized to code more complex associative learning, for example, classical and instrumental conditioning. This general hypothesis, "a specialized transmitter for each form of learning," is obviously highly oversimplified and vulnerable to both neurobiological and behavioral objections. However, nature has a way of evolving the simplest solutions to the most complex problems.

HABITUATION AND DEVELOPMENTAL PSYCHOLOGY

The major purpose of this conference has been to bring together experts in habituation working at the levels of animal behavior, neurophysiology, and developmental psychology in the hope that some cross stimulation will result. The extent to which animal data, neurophysiological findings, and more general theories such as Sokolov's "model comparator" and our "dual process" theory may be of use to those studying the development of plasticity in the human infant was one of the questions that motivated this conference.

In comparing current theories of habituation (e.g., Sokolov's and our own), it must be emphasized that one fundamental distinction lies partly in how the word "model" is defined. Many interpret Sokolov's hypothesized "formation of the model of the stimulus" as an active process. If the development of synaptic depression is admitted the status of a model of the stimulus, then we do not really disagree. Our emphasis has been on the nature of the mechanistic processes, both incremental and decremental, in the nervous system that underlie behavioral habituation and sensitization. Our approach does differ from Sokolov's in that we stress the importance of sensitization as an independent process.

Perhaps the most significant contribution we may have made to this conference is the suggestion that sensitization is an extremely important process in its own right, and one that can serve as a basic mechanism of behavioral plasticity in the human infant. Sensitization is all too often viewed as a confounding process in studies of learning. In fact, it may well be that sensitization is the necessary substrate process for the development of more complex learning. In animal studies of aversive conditioning, sensitization commonly develops early in training. It may be the "glue" that facilitates the formation of associative bonds. In any event, it appears to be a ubiquitous form of behavioral plasticity in response even to moderately intense stimuli and may have extremely important adaptive benefits, not only for the human neonate, but for all organisms. If a stimulus threatens harm, what more adaptive response can be made than to increase all responses to the point where the threat can be avoided. Specific learning about particular threats can develop more slowly. The initial imperative is simply to escape.

ACKNOWLEDGMENTS

Supported in part by Research Grant MH19314 and Research Scientist Award MH06650 from the National Institute of Mental Health, Research Grant NS07661 from the National Institutes of Health, and Research Grants GB14665 and GB40147 from the National Science Foundation to RFT and NIMH fellowship #55997 to DLG. We gratefully acknowledge the technical assistance of Shirley Adams, Sarah Beydler, and Fé Glanzman.

REFERENCES

Abraham, F. D., & Willows, A. O. D. Plasticity of a fixed action pattern in the sea slug, *Tritonia diomedia. Communications in Behavioral Biology*, 1971, *6*, 271–280.

Aghajanian, G. K., & Sheard, M. H. Behavioral effects of raphe stimulation-dependence upon serotonin. *Communications in Behavioral Biology*, 1968, *1*, 37–41.

Baumgarten, H. G., Evetts, K. D., Holman, R. B., Iverson, L. L., Vogt, M., & Wilson, G. Effect of 5,6-Dihydroxytryptamine on monoaminergic neurons in the central nervous system of the rat. *Journal of Neurochemistry*, 1972, *19*, 1587–1597. (a)

Baumgarten, H. G., Göthert, M., Holstein, A. F., & Schlossberger, H. G. Chemical sympathectomy induced by 5,6-Dihydroxytryptamine. *Zeitschrift für Zellforschung*, 1972, *128*, 115–134. (b)

Baumgarten, H. G., Lackenmayer, L., & Schlossberger, H. G. Evidence for a degeneration of Indoleamine containing nerve terminals in rat brain, induced by 5,6-dihydroxytryptamine. *Zeitschrift für Zellforschung*, 1972, *125*, 553–569.

Bennett, M. V. L. Presynaptic vesicles and postsynaptic potentials: short term and long term changes in Hatchet fish. Paper presented at a Conference on Plasticity in Simple Systems, Laguna Beach, California, 1975.

Brookhart, J. M., & Fadiga, E. Potential fields initiated during monosynaptic activation of frog motoneurons. *Journal of Physiology*, 1960, *150*, 633–655.

Brookhart, J. M., Machne, X., & Fadiga, E. Patterns of motor neuron discharge in the frog. *Arch. Ital. Biol.*, 1959, *97*, 53–67.

Castellucci, V., Pinsker, H., Kupfermann, I., & Kandel, E. R. Neuronal mechanisms of habituation and dishabituation of the gill withdrawal reflex in *Aplysia. Science*, 1970, *167*, 1745–1748.

Colomo, F., & Erulkar, S. D. Miniature synaptic potentials at frog spinal neurones in the presence of tetrodotoxin. *Journal of Physiology,* 1968, *199,* 205–221.

Conner, R. L., Stolk, J. M., Barchas, J. D., & Levine, S. Parachlorophenylalanine and habituation to repetitive auditory startle stimuli in rats. *Physiology and Behavior,* 1970, *5,* 1215–1219.

Cooper, J. R., Bloom, F. E., & Roth, R. H. *The biochemical basis of neuropharmacology.* (2nd ed.) New York: Oxford University Press, 1974.

Davis, M. Sensitization of the rat startle response by noise. *Journal of Comparative and Physiological Psychology,* in press.

Davis, M. Differential retention of sensitization and habituation of the startle response in the rat. *Journal of Comparative and Physiological Psychology,* 1972, *78*(2), 260–267.

Davis, M., & Sheard, M. H. Habituation and sensitization of the rat startle response: Effects of raphe lesions. *Physiology and Behavior,* 1974, *12,* 425–431.

Davis, M., & Wagner, A. R. Startle responsiveness after habituation to different intensities of tone. *Psychonomic Science,* 1968, *12,* 337–338.

Davis, M., & Wagner, A. R. Habituation of startle response under incremental sequence of stimulus intensities. *Journal of Comparative and Physiological Psychology,* 1969, *67,* 486–492.

Davis, W. J., & Kennedy, D. Command interneurons controlling swimmeret movements in the lobster. I. Types of effects on motoneurons. *Journal of Neurophysiology,* 1972, *35,* 1–12. (a)

Davis, W. J., & Kennedy, D. Command interneurons controlling swimmeret movements in the lobster. II. Interaction of effects of motoneurons. *Journal of Neurophysiology,* 1972, *35,* 13–19. (b)

Davis, W. J., & Kennedy, D. Command interneurons controlling swimmeret movements in the lobster. III. Temporal relationships among bursts in different motoneurons. *Journal of Neurophysiology,* 1972, *35,* 20–29. (c)

Eisenstein, E. M., & Cohen, M. J. Learning in an isolated prothoracic insect ganglion. *Animal Behavior,* 1965, *13,* 104–108.

Epstein, R., & Grundfest, H. Desensitization of gamma aminobutyric acid (GABA) receptors in muscle fibers of the crab, *Cancer borealis. Journal of General Physiology,* 1970, *56,* 33–45.

Fadiga, E., & Brookhart, J. M. Monosynaptic activation of different portions of the motor neuron membrane. *American Journal of Physiology,* 1960, *198,* 693–703.

Farel, P. B. Persistent increase in synaptic efficacy following a brief tetanus in isolated frog spinal cord. *Brain Research,* 1974, *66,* 113–120. (a)

Farel, P. B. Dual processes control response habituation across a single synapse. *Brain Research,* 1974, *72,* 323–327. (b)

Farel, P. B., Glanzman, D. L., & Thompson, R. F. Habituation of a monosynaptic response in the vertebrate central nervous system: Lateral column–motoneuron pathway in isolated frog spinal cord. *Journal of Neurophysiology,* 1973, *36,* 1117–1130.

Glass, D. C., & Singer, J. F. *Urban stress.* New York: Academic Press, 1972.

Graham, F. K. Habituation and dishabituation of responses innervated by the autonomic nervous system. In H. V. S. Peeke & M. J. Herz (Eds.), *Habituation: Behavioral studies* (Vol. I). New York: Academic Press, 1973.

Groves, P. M., Glanzman, D. L., Patterson, M. M., & Thompson, R. F. Excitability of cutaneous afferent terminals during habituation and sensitization in acute spinal cat. *Brain Research,* 1970, *18,* 388–392.

Groves, P. M., Lee, D., & Thompson, R. F. Effects of stimulus frequency and intensity on habituation and sensitization in acute spinal cat. *Physiology and Behavior,* 1969, *4,* 383–388.

Groves, P. M., & Thompson, R. F. Habituation: A dual-process theory. *Psychological Review,* 1970, *77,* 419–450.

Groves, P. M., & Thompson, R. F. Dual-process theory of habituation: Neural mechanisms. In H. V. S. Peeke & M. J. Herz (Eds.), *Habituation: Physiological substrates* (Vol. II). New York: Academic Press, 1973.

Groves, P. M., Wilson, C. J., & Miller, S. W. Habituation of the acoustic startle response: A neural systems analysis of habituation in the intact animal. In A. H. Riesen & R. F. Thompson (Eds.), *Advances in psychobiology* (Vol. III). New York: Wiley, in press.

Harris, J. D. Habituatory response decrement in the intact organism. *Psychological Bulletin,* 1943, *40,* 385–422.

Hernández-Peón, R. Neurophysiological correlates of habituation and other manifestations of plastic inhibition. *Electroencephalography and Clinical Neurophysiology* (Suppl.), 1960, *13,* 101–114.

Hull, C. L. Quantitative aspects of the evolution of concepts. *Psychological Monographs,* 1920, *28,* No. 123.

Humphrey, G. *The nature of learning.* New York: Harcourt, 1933.

James, J. P., & Hughes, G. R. Generalization of habituation of the GSR to white noise of varying intensities. *Psychonomic Science,* 1969, *14,* 463–464.

Kandel, E. R. *The cellular basis of behavior.* San Francisco: Freeman Press, 1975.

Kandel, E. R., & Spencer, W. A. Cellular neurophysiological approaches in the study of learning. *Physiological Review,* 1968, *48,* 65–134.

Kandel, E. R., & Tauc, L. Heterosynaptic facilitation in neurons of the abdominal ganglion of *Aplysia depilans. Journal of Physiology,* 1965, *181,* 1–27.

Katz, B., & Miledi, R. A study of spontaneous miniature potentials in spinal motoneurones. *Journal of Physiology,* 1963, *168,* 389–422.

Kuno, M., & Miyahara, J. T. Non-linear summation of unit synaptic potentials in spinal motoneurones of the cat. *Journal of Physiology,* 1969, *201,* 465–477.   (a)

Kuno, M., & Miyahara, J. T. Analysis of synaptic efficacy in spinal motoneurones from "quantum" aspects. *Journal of Physiology,* 1969, *201,* 479–493.   (b)

Kuno, M. Quantal aspects of central and ganglionic synaptic transmission in vertebrates. *Physiological Review,* 1971, *51*(4), 647–678.

Kupfermann, I., Castellucci, V., Pinsker, H., & Kandel, E. R. Neuronal correlates of habituation and dishabituation of the gill withdrawal reflex in *Aplysia. Science,* 1970, *167,* 1743–1745.

Machne, X., Fadiga, E., & Brookhart, J. M. Antidromic and synaptic activation of frog motor neurons. *Journal of Neurophysiology,* 1959, *22,* 483–503.

Martin, A. R., & Pilar, G. Quantal components of the synaptic potential in the ciliary ganglion of the chick. *Journal of Physiology,* 1964, *175,* 1–16.   (a)

Martin, A. R., & Pilar, G. Presynaptic and post synaptic events during post-tetanic potentiation and facilitation in avian ciliary ganglion. *Journal of Physiology,* 1964, *175,* 17–30.   (b)

Mensah, P. L. The lateral funiculus of the amphibian spinal cord. Unpublished doctoral dissertation, University of California, Irvine, 1974.

Mensah, P. L., Glanzman, D. L., Levy, W. B., & Thompson, R. F. The effects of 5,6-dihydroxytryptamine in the amphibian spinal cord using silver staining techniques. *Brain Research,* 1974, *78,* 255–261.

Miledi, R. Miniature synaptic potentials in squid nerve cells. *Nature,* 1966, *212,* 1240–1242.

Nastuk, W. L., & Parsons, R. L. Factors in the inactivation of postjunctional membrane receptors of frog skeletal muscle. *Journal of General Physiology,* 1970, *56,* 218–249.

Patterson, M. M., Cegavske, C. F., & Thompson, R. F. Effects of a classical conditioning paradigm on hindlimb flexor nerve response in immobilized spinal cat. *Journal of Comparative and Physiological Psychology*, 1973, *84*, 88–97.

Peeke, H. V. S., & Herz, M. J. (Eds.), *Habituation*. New York: Academic Press, 1973. (2 vols.)

Pinsker, H., Kupfermann, I., Castellucci, V., & Kandel, E. R. Habituation and dishabituation of the gill withdrawal reflex in *Aplysia. Science*, 1970, *167*, 1740–1742.

Rang, H. P., & Ritter, J. M. On the mechanism of desensitization at cholinergic receptors. *Molecular Pharmacology*, 1970, *6*, 357–382.

Raskin, D. C., Kotses, H., & Bever, J. Autonomic indicators of orienting and defensive reflexes. *Journal of Experimental Psychology*, 1969, *80*, 423–433.

Sharpless, S. Reorganization of function in the nervous system—Use and disuse. *Annual Review of Physiology*, 1964, *26*, 357–388.

Sharpless, S., & Jasper, H. Habituation of the arousal reaction. *Brain*, 1956, *79*, 655–680.

Sherrington, C. S. *The integrative action of the nervous system*. New Haven, Conn.: Yale University Press, 1906.

Sokolov, E. N. *Perception and the conditioned reflex*. (S. W. Waydenfeld, translator.) Oxford: Pergamon, 1963.

Sokolov, E. N., Arakelov, G. G., & Levinson, L. V. Marking the microelectrode position within a single nerve cell. *Tsitologia*, 1966, *8*, 567–569.

Spencer, W. A., Thompson, R. F., & Neilson, D. R., Jr. Response decrement of the flexion reflex in the acute spinal cat and transient restoration by strong stimuli. *Journal of Neurophysiology*, 1966, *29*, 221–239. (a)

Spencer, W. A., Thompson, R. F., & Neilson, D. R., Jr. Alterations in responsiveness of ascending and reflex pathways activated by iterated cutaneous afferent volleys. *Journal of Neurophysiology*, 1966, *29*, 240–252. (b)

Spencer, W. A., Thompson, R. F., & Neilson, D. R., Jr. Decrement of ventral root electrotonic and intracellularly recorded PSPs produced by iterated cutaneous afferent volleys. *Journal of Neurophysiology*, 1966, *29*, 253–274. (c)

Thompson, R. F., Groves, P. M., Teyler, T. J., & Roemer, R. A. Dual-process of theory of habituation: Theory and behavior. In H. V. S. Peeke and M. J. Herz (Eds.), *Habituation: Behavioral studies* (Vol. I). New York: Academic Press, 1973.

Thompson, R. F., Patterson, M. M., & Teyler, T. J. Neurophysiology of learning. *Annual Review of Psychology*, 1972, *23*, 73–104.

Thompson, R. F., & Spencer, W. A. Habituation: A model phenomenon for the study of neuronal substrates of behavior. *Psychological Review*, 1966, *173*, 16–43.

Wall, P. D. Excitability changes in afferent fibre terminations and their relation to slow potentials. *Journal of Physiology*, 1958, *142*, 1–21.

Willows, A. O. D. Behavioral acts elicited by stimulation of single, identifiable brain cells. *Science*, 1967, *157*, 570–574.

Willows, A. O. D., & Hoyle, G. Neuronal network triggering a fixed action pattern. *Science*, 1969, *166*, 1549–1551.

Zucker, R. S. Crayfish escape behavior and central synapses. II. Physiological mechanisms underlying behavioral habituation. *Journal of Neurophysiology*, 1972, *35*, 621–637.

3

Priming in STM:
An Information-Processing Mechanism
for Self-Generated or
Retrieval-Generated Depression
in Performance

Allan R. Wagner

Yale University

That this volume joins two recent and important collections of papers (Horne & Hinde, 1970; Peeke & Herz, 1973) on the topic of habituation, with contributions from a diverse assemblage of investigators, leads one to surmise that the phenomenon is enjoying increased research attention. From the point of view of animal learning theory this attention has been long overdue as habituation has been left largely outside the scope of the major theories and their preoccupation with Pavlovian and Thorndikian conditioning. Attempts to provide some theoretical integration of habituation with other learning phenomena have been rare and then have typically expressed the biases of prevailing conditioning theory, for example, the occasional proposal that habituation may be due solely to hidden Pavlovian contingencies (e.g., Stein, 1966) or that it may bear uncertain similarities to the response decrement that occurs in experimental extinction of a conditioned response (see Kling & Stevenson, 1970).

It is unlikely that habituation is to be understood simply in terms of the laws of the conditioning laboratory any more than conditioning is to be understood in terms of a concatenation of the principles of habituation. Yet at the level of theory one would hope to integrate the regularities observed in the two cases along with other phenomena of learning and performance. It is the position of this chapter that a useful synthesis may be accomplished within the language of information-processing models now familiar to treatments of human memory (e.g., Atkinson & Shiffrin, 1968). Such models distinguish between a Short-Term

Long-Term Memory (LTM) and acknowledge variability in
sing in STM via differential "rehearsal." With the addition
ssumptions concerning the effects of "priming" of STM it
for a variety of behavioral phenomena, including certain
and Pavlovian conditioning with infrahuman subjects as
have been under investigation in our laboratory.

The essential notion concerning *priming* can be stated succinctly. Stimulus presentation is proposed to be differentially effective in provoking processing steps, as may lead to the elicitation of an unconditioned response or to poststimulation rehearsal, depending on whether or not the stimulus on such occasion is prerepresented (primed) in STM: When an event is already represented in STM further corresponding stimulation may be rendered less effective than it otherwise would be. The interesting implications of this proposal, in fact, depend upon a number of conventional information-processing assumptions that must be detailed. However, much of the workings of the formulation can be anticipated if it is further acknowledged that there are two ways in which a stimulus can come to be represented in STM, either as a result of the recent presentation of that same stimulus, or as a result of a retrieval from LTM initiated by other cues with which the stimulus has been associated. We can thus distinguish between a "self-generated" and a "retrieval-generated" priming of STM, but each with a common final consequence in altered processing of subsequent stimulation.

In outline the following chapter will first show how a specialized form of the general thesis was developed to handle recent data on variations in the effectiveness of an Unconditioned Stimulus (US) in Pavlovian conditioning, depending upon the "expectedness" versus "surprisingness" of the event. Then it will attempt to indicate how the thesis may be naturally extended so as to account for a number of additional phenomena, including decrements in processing of iterated stimulation. While the approach to habituation is still in need of evaluation, the opportunity will be taken to present recent findings from our laboratory, particularly in investigations of vasomotor habituation in the rabbit, that lend it provisional support.

PROCESSING OF "EXPECTED" VERSUS "SURPRISING" USs IN PAVLOVIAN CONDITIONING

In the immediate background of the work to be discussed is the research of Kamin (e.g. 1968) and his suggestion that in Pavlovian conditioning a "surprising" US may be processed differently than an "expected" US. There are now *three* distinctly different ways in which we have shown that this appears to be the case. As is generally true, the different observations can be appreciated as converging only if one is willing to accept certain arguments about what ties them together. Thus, an examination of the several studies will necessarily provide an introduction to our theoretical view and how it developed.

Certain of the experiments to be described have been replicated in a variety of Pavlovian conditioning situations. However, for convenience of exposition, initial discussion will be restricted to our studies that have involved eyelid conditioning in the rabbit. In this case it may be assumed that a Conditioned Stimulus (CS) was 1100 msec in duration and, when reinforced, overlapped and terminated with a 100-msec, 4.5-mA shock US applied to the area surrounding the eye. An important feature of all of the experiments is that they involved a number of CSs, presented in isolation or in compound. For example, a common occurrence in the several studies was the call for 3 CSs. It may then be assumed that these involved a 20 per second flashing light, an 11 per second train of clicks or 3-kHz tone, and a vibratory stimulus in contact with the animal's chest. It may also be assumed that the experimental designs were such as to counterbalance the identification of the different cues within any experimental treatment when appropriate. Training and testing were typically carried out over a number of daily sessions, although different studies involved relatively massed (e.g., 132 trials per session at a 2-min intertrial interval) or more distributed (e.g., 5 trials per session at an 18-min intertrial interval) experience, according to the experimental interests. In each case eyelid deflections were monitored and scored as Conditioned Responses (CRs) when occurring during the first 1000 msec of CS presentation.

Blocking

The first class of study has as its prototype Kamin's (1968) original investigation of the so-called "blocking" phenomenon. In the general case, a target CS, X, is reinforced or nonreinforced in compound with a second CS, A, that has been experimentally treated so as to yield different US-signaling values of the AX compound at the time of this training. The principal observation from such studies is that, in testing, there is systematic variation in the conditioned responding to X alone with different pretreatments of A, even though the reinforcement schedule in the presence of X is held constant. For example, it is well documented (Kamin, 1968; Wagner, 1969) that the greater is the prior acquisition training to A, the less will be the increment in conditioned responding to X as a result of an AX reinforcement, and the greater will be the decrement in conditioned responding to X as a result of an AX nonreinforcement. Two studies conducted in collaboration with Maria Saavadra will illustrate the essential phenomenon.

In the first, unpublished study 36 rabbits were initially conditioned to 2 CSs, A and B. The intent was to highly train cue A and only weakly train cue B. This was done by administering a total of 448 reinforcements to A and only 28 to B in a quasi-random sequence. At the end of this first phase, the subjects were separated into 2 matched groups of 18 and a new cue, X, was then reinforced in compound with one of the two pretrained cues, that is, either in an AX or BX compound. The third, and final, phase evaluated the degree of learning to respond to X as a result of the compound training. This was done by presenting a series of nonreinforced test trials to X alone. Figure 1a depicts the results from

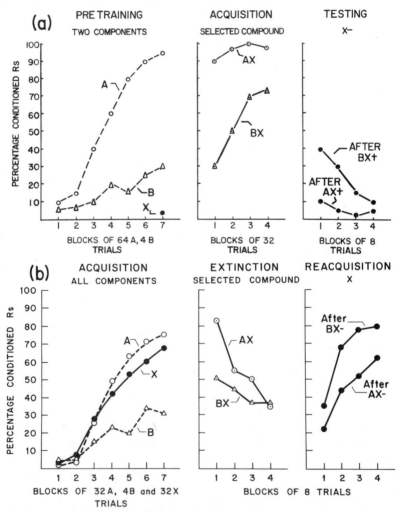

FIG. 1 Mean percentage of conditioned eyeblink responses during three stages of two separate "blocking" experiments. The top panels, (a), summarize the results when a novel cue, X, was reinforced in compound with differentially pretrained, A or B, cues, prior to nonreinforced testing alone. The bottom panels, (b), summarize the results when a reinforced cue, X, was nonreinforced in compound with differentially pretrained, A or B, cues prior to reacquisition testing alone. (From Wagner, 1969.)

the several stages of this experiment. Notice in phase 1 the differential acquisition to A and B and in phase 2 the correspondingly higher level of responding to AX than to BX, as both groups received exactly the same number of reinforcements of X in one of these compounds. The important result was that there was less responding to X alone following the AX reinforcements than following the BX reinforcements. The difference in this study is not as dramatic as in some of Kamin's (1968) studies, but the effect is still substantial. Two test trials were included at the end of phase 1 to X alone. Comparing X responding immediately before and after compound training, there was a 5% increase in Group AX and a 35% increase in Group BX.

In the next experiment (reported in Wagner, 1969) the procedure of the preceding experiment was only slightly modified to arrive at the following paradigm: Cues A and B were again arranged during stage 1 to acquire different signal values as a result of different numbers of reinforced trials. In this case, however, all animals were also well trained to respond to X alone. In phase 2 the CS, X, was then *nonreinforced* in compound with either cue A for half of the subjects or cue B for the remaining subjects. After 32 nonreinforced compound trials, X was tested alone over a series of reinforced trials to evaluate the degree of extinction that had occurred in each group. Figure 1b illustrates the percentage of conditioned responding over the three phases of this experiment in a manner similar to the preceding experiment. The important observation to be noted is that there was more extinction of responding to X as a result of nonreinforcing X in compound with the stronger A cue than as a result of nonreinforcing X in compound with the weaker B cue.

These two experiments are meant only to exemplify a rich pattern of findings from Pavlovian conditioning with compound CSs (see Rescorla & Wagner, 1972; Wagner & Rescorla, 1972). It is the pattern that first suggested to Kamin that an expected US may have little influence in relationship to a surprising US, where the terms "expected" and "surprising" can be objectified in terms of the degree to which the US is *predicted by the total aggregation of cues that precede it.* We added the observation that nonreinforcement, or US failure, is similarly more or less effective depending upon the signal value of the *total aggregation of cues.*

In two related theoretical papers by Rescorla and Wagner (1972) and Wagner and Rescorla (1972) we attempted to state the variation involved in a general fashion as a minor modification of conventional linear operator models. We proposed that the change in the signal value (V) of a component CS_i that results from any training trial can be expressed as

$$\Delta V_i = \alpha\beta(\lambda - \overline{V}),$$

where α and β are rate parameters, λ is the asymptotic (or fixed-point) signal value supported by any US or its absence (e.g., it might be assumed to be zero in the case of nonreinforcement and be larger the greater the US intensity), and, finally, $\overline{V}$ is the summed signal value of *all of the cues that occurred on such trial.* This model has held up rather well thus far in relationship to a considerable body of data. The point is that in doing so it incorporates the notion that a surprising US or absence of a US (involving a discrepancy between λ and $\overline{V}$) is more effective than an expected US or absence of a US (involving little or no discrepancy between λ and $\overline{V}$).

Posttrial Interference

The second class of studies began from asking: What is the *process* whereby a surprising US or failure of a US is more effective in Pavlovian conditioning than is a similar expected event? Again, Kamin (1968) provided the seminal suggestion in proposing that an expected US does not instigate the necessary "mental work" of "retrospective contemplation."

We read this proposal of Kamin's, as did Atkinson and Wickens (1971), as suggesting an interesting assumption that might be added to those memory models which distinguish between a short-term memory (STM) and a long-term memory (LTM). It is characteristically assumed that transfer of information to LTM occurs only while that information is resident in STM, but that information may be variably retained in STM by virtue of the duration of *rehearsal.* The important new assumption would be that information concerning surprising episodes is more likely to be rehearsed and hence entered into LTM. The notion is congenial to accounts like that of Atkinson and Shiffrin (1968) which would assume that CS presentation promotes the retrieval from LTM of the representation of events previously associated with that CS, such as a given US. Then it is only necessary to assume that when events occur whose representations match those already in STM (so-called "expected events") little if anything occurs, and the episode decays rapidly from STM. When events occur for which there is not already a representation in STM (so-called "surprising events") rehearsal is engaged so that the episode representation is retained longer in STM.

This speculation leads to a rich set of testable predictions. Consider the implications of the common assumption that the subject has a finite STM, that is, a limited rehearsal capacity. Given this assumption, it should be anticipated that rehearsing one episode would decrease the likelihood of rehearsing some other temporally adjacent episode. Then, if a surprising CS–US episode is assumed to be especially rehearsed, such episode should not only be especially learned about, as the above blocking studies presumably show, but also should especially *interfere* with the learning about other temporally adjacent episodes as it deprives these episodes of rehearsal.

This reasoning was evaluated in a series of experiments (Wagner, Rudy, & Whitlow, 1973) all of which had the same general characteristics. In phase 1, rabbits were trained in eyelid conditioning with a CS_A reinforced and CS_B nonreinforced. Figure 2a shows the results of this training in four separate groups in one experiment. This phase was necessary only to develop what could

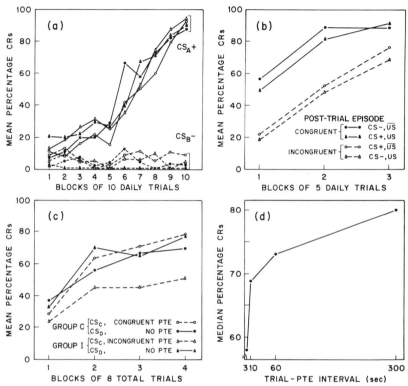

FIG. 2 Percentage of conditioned eyeblink responses in investigations of the interference effects of different Post-Trial Episodes (PTE's). (a) Initial discrimination learning of four separate groups as common to the several experiments. (b) Subsequent acquisition of responding to CS_C when the PTE was congruent or incongruent with the initial discrimination training, in the manner indicated. (c) Concurrent acquisition of responding to CS_C and CS_D in two groups, when CS_D was never followed by a PTE whereas CS_C was followed by a PTE that was either congruent or incongruent with initial discrimination training. (d) Median total percentage responses over 10 acquisition trials to CS_C in 4 groups receiving incongruent PTE's at different intervals following the CS_C trials. (From Wagner, Rudy, & Whitlow, 1973. Copyright 1973 by the American Psychological Association. Reproduced by permission.)

be subsequently viewed as surprising or expected Pavlovian episodes: CS_A-US and $CS_B-\overline{US}$ (congruent with original training) could be considered expected; $CS_A-\overline{US}$ and CS_B-US (incongruent with original training) could be considered surprising. In phase 2 all animals received a series of *reinforced* trials with a new cue, CS_C, in a different modality than CS_A and CS_B, at very distributed intervals and in some cases separated by buffer trials involving the phase 1 training trials. The important manipulation was that a short interval after each CS_C-US trial (usually 10 sec) different groups of subjects received different posttrial episodes (PTEs) involving CS_A and CS_B either reinforced or nonreinforced in a manner either congruent or incongruent with phase 1 training.

Figure 2b depicts the acquisition of conditioned responding to CS_C in the four groups of Figure 2a. Each group received as the PTE one of the four episodes, CS_A–US, CS_B–$\overline{US}$, CS_A–$\overline{US}$, or CS_B–US. The important observation is that when the PTE's were incongruent with original training, that is, surprising, acquisition to CS_C was depressed in relationship to the case in which the PTE's were congruent with original training, that is, expected. It made no reliable difference overall whether the PTE included CS_A or CS_B, or the US or $\overline{US}$. All that mattered was whether the pairing of CS and US events was congruent or incongruent with the animal's prior experience.

The remaining experiments in the series reported by Wagner, Rudy, and Whitlow (1973) add appropriate details. The above study does not uniquely indicate that an incongruent PTE interferes with conditioning. Perhaps a congruent PTE facilitates conditioning. Furthermore, there are a considerable number of ways in which an experimental event might interfere with performance, for example, via some general processing disturbance, or via proactive transfer effects, as well as by interfering with rehearsal. The basic experimental phenomenon seen in Figure 2b does not distinguish among these. If an incongruent PTE interferes with rehearsal in a manner that a congruent PTE does not, one should observe a decrement in acquisition that is specific to just those trial CS's with which the incongruent PTE was temporally adjacent during training, and a greater decrement the shorter the trial-PTE interval.

In one of the further experiments each of two groups of rabbits was trained in phase 1 identically to the above experiment, but then was trained with *two* new cues, CS_C and CS_D, each separately reinforced in phase 2. Each CS_C trial was shortly followed by a PTE, each CS_D trial was not, in an ordering that equated the frequency with which each cue was preceded by a PTE. The two groups differed only in the nature of the PTE that occurred following CS_C trials. In Group C it was always congruent with phase 1 training, involving either CS_A–US or CS_B–$\overline{US}$. In Group I it was always incongruent with phase 1 training, involving either CS_A–$\overline{US}$, or CS_B–US. The principal results are depicted in Figure 2c. In Group C there was no difference in acquisition to CS_C and CS_D. A congruent PTE had no differential effect upon adjacent as compared to more temporally separated training stimuli. In contrast, in Group I, CS_C was considerably slower to produce conditioned responding than was CS_D and was similarly retarded in relationship to either CS_C or CS_D in Group C. An incongruent PTE had a decremental effect upon performance that was specific to the temporally adjacent training stimulus, CS_C.

In the final experiments in this series Wagner, Rudy, and Whitlow (1973) systematically investigated the effects of placing an incongruent PTE at different intervals following CS_C trials. In brief, it was observed that the shorter the trial–PTE interval, over the range of 3–300 sec, the poorer the acquisition of responding to CS_C. Figure 2d summarizes this tendency by indicating the percentage conditioned responding over five sessions of phase 2 training for groups with different trial-PTE intervals.

In all, the Wagner, Rudy, and Whitlow (1973) studies offer abundant evidence that surprising and expected USs (or absence of USs) are differententially effective. The manner of difference, in interfering with the learning that results from contemporaneous training episodes, lends consistent support to the view that surprising events operate to command rehearsal.

Assessment of STM

What is still missing in this pattern of data is any relatively direct assessment of a subject's posttrial processing of information. If surprising and expected USs are assumed to promote differences in LTM due to differential commanding of rehearsal, they should also be differentially available in STM during the presumed rehearsal interval. The third class of study to be described thus sought to answer a very simple question: Does the rabbit better remember that it has just experienced a US when the US was preceded by a CS which otherwise had reliably signaled the absence of a US (that is, when the US was surprising) than when the US was preceded by a CS which otherwise had reliably signaled the occurrence of a US (that is, when the US was expected)?

Unfortunately, to ask this simple question in the confines of Pavlovian conditioning requires a relatively complex sequence of training and testing. Terry and Wagner (1975) used a variation upon the "preparatory-releaser" technique discussed by Konorski and Lawicka (1959). The experimental strategy was first to train subjects to respond in a distinctive fashion to a designated CS whenever a US had occurred within the past few seconds so as presumably to be available in short-term memory. In each of two groups CS_R (the releasing stimulus) was sometimes reinforced and sometimes nonreinforced according to an irregular sequence with the only reliable cue available to a subject during training being the occurrence versus nonoccurrence of a shock US (the preparatory stimulus) 2, 4, 8, or 16 sec prior to the time that CS_R might be reinforced. In Group 1, when the preparatory stimulus was presented at any one of the four intervals prior to CS_R (designated as P episodes) CS_R was reinforced. When the preparatory stimulus was not presented prior to CS_R (designated as $\bar{P}$ episodes) CS_R was nonreinforced. In Group 2 just the opposite contingency was arranged: when the preparatory US was presented CS_R was nonreinforced, whereas when the preparatory US was not presented CS_R was reinforced.

As a result of this training the subjects learned to respond differentially to CS_R depending upon the prior occurrence versus nonoccurrence of the preparatory US. Figure 3a depicts the mean percentage responding to CS_R in each of the two groups on $\bar{P}$ episodes and on P episodes at each of the scheduled preparatory-releaser intervals, over the 12th through 15th sessions of training. As

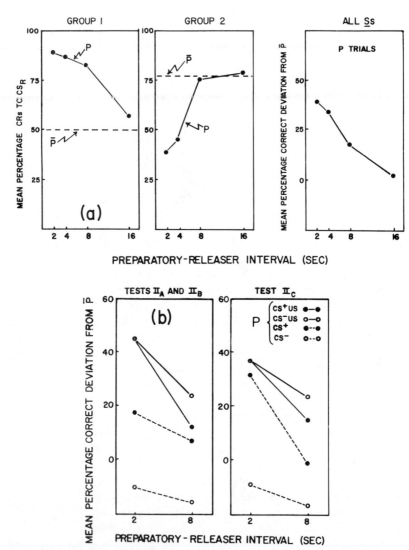

FIG. 3 Mean percentage of conditioned eyeblink responding to a releasing stimulus, CS_R, when preceded by a preparatory stimulus, P, at different intervals. The top panels (a) depict the levels of performance attained under the training conditions, where P was a US signaling the reinforcement or nonreinforcement of CS_R. The left and middle sections indicate the percentages in comparison to the percentage responding on $\bar{P}$ episodes in different contingency groups, whereas the right section summarizes the same percentages collapsed across the two groups as "correct" deviations from the percentages on $\bar{P}$ episodes (see text). The bottom panels (b) depict the mean correct deviation of responding to CS_R on P versus $\bar{P}$ episodes during test sessions in which the preparatory US was made expected (CS^+US) or surprising (CS^-US), or was replaced by a CS^+ of CS^- alone. (From Terry & Wagner, 1975. Copyright 1975 by the American Psychological Association. Reproduced by permission.)

may be seen, Group 1 learned to respond more to CS_R on P than on $\overline{P}$ occasions, while Group 2 learned to respond less to CS_R on P than on $\overline{P}$ occasions, consistent with the significance of the preparatory stimulus for the reinforcement of CS_R. Furthermore, it is important to note that in both groups, as the preparatory-releaser interval was lengthened from 2 to 16 sec, the characteristic manner of responding to CS_R on P episodes became more and more like that on $\overline{P}$ episodes, that is, as though the preparatory US was less available in memory at the time of CS_R. This tendency on P episodes is conveniently summarized over all subjects in the right-hand panel of Figure 3a, in terms of "correct," meaning here contingency appropriate, deviation from the subjects' $\overline{P}$ responding. At this point it could be assumed that the subjects were differentially likely to respond to CS_R depending upon whether or not the US was on that occasion represented in STM. This set the stage for asking whether a US presented some interval before CS_R was more likely to still evidence representation in STM if it had been surprising than if it had been expected.

In order to manipulate the surprisingness of a US, all subjects were further trained in a simple Pavlovian discrimination with two additional CS's orthogonal to CS_R, CS^+ being consistently reinforced with the US, while CS^- was consistently nonreinforced. This training, which was conducted in separate discrimination sessions and never involved a preparatory US, culminated in consistent conditioned responding to CS^+ and negligible responding to CS^-. Thus it might be assumed that a US which was preceded by CS^+ would be expected while a US preceded by CS^- would be surprising.

The eventual test was provided by running all subjects in the preparatory-releaser paradigm, as during training, in which CS_R was sometimes preceded by a preparatory US and sometimes not. Now, however, the preparatory US was either announced by CS^+, as was the same US during discrimination training, or was announced by CS^-, as was never the case for a US during discrimination training. Figure 3b presents the results from two series of test sessions over all subjects in the manner of the right panel in Figure 3a. The panel labeled II_A and II_B summarizes the data from separate sessions in which the preparatory-releaser interval was either 2 or 8 sec. The panel labeled II_C summarizes similar data from later sessions in which the same 2- and 8-sec preparatory-releaser intervals were intermingled within the same session. The essential findings were reproducible. Subjects acted more toward CS_R as they had been trained to act following a preparatory US when the US had been surprising, that is, was part of the sequence CS^-US than when the US had been expected, that is, was part of the sequence CS^+US. In these test sessions the difference was not detectable with a 2-sec preparatory-releaser interval, but was apparent with an 8-sec interval. Since the distinctive responding to CS_R was necessarily dependent upon the immediate memory of the preparatory US, we are left with the reasonable conclusion that a surprising US is more likely to be retained in STM than is an expected US.

Additional data reported by Terry and Wagner (1975) confirm the central observation, but go little further in adding more particular conclusions. One concern that was addressed, however, was that the differential preparatory effects of CS⁻US versus CS⁺US may have been due only to the differential preparatory effects of the separate CS's rather than to their modulating influence upon the effectiveness of the US commonly included. This possibility can be rejected by observing what happens if CS^+ and CS^- are presented *alone* as preparatory signals following the training outlined.

Within each of the test series summarized in Figure 3b were included P episodes in which CS^+ or CS^- were presented alone prior to CS_R. The data from these test episodes are included in Figure 3b. As may be seen, CS^+ alone acted quite effectively as a substitute for the preparatory US, while CS^- alone acted to depress the distinctive mode of responding to CS_R below what was observed in the absence of a preparatory stimulus in P episodes. It would thus be difficult to argue that the differential responding to CS_R following CS⁻US and CS⁺US is due simply to the differential additive contributions by the separate CS's.

The observations concerning CS^+ and CS^- in themselves may be of more than passing interest. To suggest that a US is expected when preceded by a CS with which it has been repeatedly paired has been taken to mean that the CS has initiated the retrieval from LTM of a representation of the US prior to the latter's occurrence (e.g., Atkinson & Wickens, 1971). The present findings that CS^+ acts as an effective substitute for a preparatory US could then be taken to provide objective support for such a retrieval process; that is, a US may appear to be represented in STM at the time of presentation of CS_R either as a result of the immediately prior exposure to the US or as a result of a similar exposure to a CS which can retrieve the US representation from LTM. To be consistent one would thereby be led to argue that whatever CS^- retrieved from LTM, it acted to diminish the representation of the US in immediate memory. This could be due to the displacement of US representation in STM that may have otherwise been retrieved by situational cues. Or, it could be due to CS^- retrieving a "$\overline{US}$," or "safety" representation as would be implied in another theoretical language by the assumption that CS^- was an "inhibitory" cue. But we should not lose sight of the essential point of the study: A surprising US appears to be better retained in STM than does an expected US.

Recapitulation

The three classes of studies that have been described are offered as confirmation of Kamin's suggestion concerning the differential effectiveness of expected versus surprising USs in Pavlovian conditioning. A surprising US (a) is more likely to be learned about; (b) is more likely to interfere with the learning about temporally adjacent events; and (c) is more likely to act as though it continued in immediate memory, available to control discriminative responding.

We can tie these separate observations together if we assume a conventional dual-memory-trace schema and certain propositions about the differential processing of events in STM. If a US is already represented in STM as a result of the retrieval action of a preceding CS, that US will be less likely to be rehearsed, that is, to be retained in STM. This in turn should influence: (a) the degree of consolidated transfer of the episode information to LTM; (b) the degree of availability of STM for learning about other surrounding episodes; and (c) the degree of continued control of responding by the US after it has been removed from experience.

DEVELOPMENT OF A MORE GENERAL
STIMULUS-PROCESSING ACCOUNT

The theory that has been outlined can be seen as substantially more powerful if we acknowledge that what has been said about surprising and expected USs has been but suited to a special set of stimuli and circumstances. What has been asserted is that a US is less likely to be rehearsed or continue to be processed in STM after its presentation if, at the time of presentation, it is already represented in STM as a result of the retrievel action of the aggregation of antecedent cues. Consider then the following possibilities for relaxing this wording.

If the critical ingredient underlying the differential effects of an expected versus surprising US is whether the stimulus is or is not already represented in STM at the time of its occurrence, such need not be viewed as uniquely dependent upon a CS-initiated retrieval process. It may rather be useful to acknowledge that any manner of manipulating the prior representation of a US in STM before its presentation will similarly influence the likelihood of consequent rehearsal. The principal method of prerepresenting a stimulus in STM other than via the retrieval action of another cue should be, of course, via the prior presentation of the stimulus itself. Speaking of "expected" versus "surprising" events is suited to cases where a representation of the event has or has not been called into STM, in anticipation of the occurrence of the event, by the retrieval action of an associated cue. To allow for the more general possibility it will be preferable to speak of "primed" versus "nonprimed" events, that is, events that are or are not prerepresented in STM by whatever route, and to distinguish, when appropriate, between different manners of prerepresentation, for example, between a retrieval-generated priming and a self-generated priming.

Furthermore, there is no reason to suppose that what has been said about US's is peculiar to just those stimuli, such as electric shock and food, that are commonly employed as US's in Pavlovian conditioning. It may rather be the case that what has been said about US's is true of any stimulus. That is, it may be useful to assume that any stimulus that is prerepresented in STM will be less likely to be rehearsed than will be an equivalent stimulus that is not prerepresented. In Pavlovian conditioning a principal implication of this reasoning is that CSs as well as USs may be differentially rehearsed under different conditions of priming. But the assumption then need not be restricted in application to Pavlovian conditioning. It may equally apply to the stimuli encountered in a variety of learning and performance tasks.

Finally, it is no doubt a simplification to characterize the differential, post-stimulation processing of primed versus nonprimed stimuli as only involving differences in likelihood or duration of rehearsal. Stimulation presumably initiates a sequence of processing steps to culminate in performance in different situations. The most cautious general assertion would be that a primed stimulus is processed *differently* than a nonprimed stimulus, allowing for all possible variations in the control routines that might be called forth in specific situations to influence behavior beyond what would be expected simply from differences in likelihood or duration of rehearsal. But without more empirical guidance it may be provisionally adequate to assume that when differences in rehearsal appear to occur, they are likely to be part of a larger complex, corresponding to a more or less general variation in the functional impact of the stimulus. In the present context the proposition that we wish to entertain is that the same basic assumptions that have been made with respect to variations in the theoretical process of rehearsal being initiated by a stimulus can also be made with respect to variations in an objective unconditioned response being elicited by that stimulus. That is, whether or not a stimulus will evoke an unconditioned response such as startle, orientation, withdrawal, etc., will vary with whether or not the stimulus involved is prerepresented in STM at the time. When the stimulus is not prerepresented it will more likely evoke the measured response; when the stimulus is prerepresented it will less likely evoke the response.

APPLICATION TO HABITUATION

How the above formulation comes in general contact with the waning of responsiveness to iterated stimulation that is known as "habituation" should be apparent. Still there are a number of ancillary assumptions that must be made. The extended theory can be explicated by indicating how it would approach certain findings from our laboratory on the effects of interstimulus interval upon habituation that predated the present formulation. Then we can turn to the consideration of more recent studies of habituation specifically addressed to its evaluation.

Interstimulus Interval

A series of studies reported by Davis and Wagner (Davis, 1970a, b; Davis & Wagner, 1968, 1969) on habituation of the startle response in the rat indicate the desirability of distinguishing between two historical influences in habituation. That is, the likelihood of a response on Trial n of an habituation sequence appears to be depressed by a short-term refractory-like effect generated by recent trial events, and to be separably reduced by the more persistently detectable effects of the overall sequence of prior stimulation. The pressures for this view can be well seen in the Davis (1970a) dissertation on interstimulus interval.

Davis employed a stabilimeter device to measure the startle response of the rat to 50-msec, 4000-Hz tones that increased the sound pressure level from 80 to 120 dB (re. 20 $\mu N/m^2$). In an initial prehabituation test and an identical post-habituation test all subjects were exposed to a series of 300 tones during which the interstimulus interval was varied among 2, 4, 8, and 16 sec, in an order that equated the first, second, and third order sequential probabilities. Between these two tests all subjects received an habituation series of 1000 tone stimulations, half of the subjects with a constant 2-sec interstimulus interval, the remainder with a constant 16-sec interval.

Figure 4a presents a summary of percentage startle responses during each of the three experimental phases for two groups of 16 animals which received the posthabituation test series beginning 1 minute after the habituation sequence. It should be noted that in each of the pre- and posthabituation test series the probability of startle on any Trial n was an increasing function of the interval separating Trial n from Trial $n - 1$; a subject was less likely to startle the shorter the interval on that occasion. Likewise during the habituation sequence with a constant 2- or 16-sec interstimulus interval in the separate groups, a similar pattern was quite evident; when the stimuli were consistently separated by 2-sec intervals there was a lower level of responding than when the stimuli were consistently separated by 16-sec intervals. The striking finding, in relationship to this pattern, is that when the two habituation groups were subsequently tested again at all interstimulus intervals, the group that had received habituation exposures at 16-sec intervals was much less responsive than the group that had received habituation exposures at 2-sec intervals, and this difference was apparent at all interstimulus intervals during the posttest, for example, whether at 2 sec or 16 sec after the immediately preceding trial. Figure 4b shows the same pattern in another pair of groups treated identically to the groups represented in Figure 4a except that the posthabituation test was delayed for 24 hr after habituation. While there was some recovery of responding over the longer retention interval in this case and less subsequent difference between the two groups in the posthabituation test, the overall picture is otherwise the same: A subject is *less* likely to respond on Trial n of the post test the shorter the interval since Trial $n - 1$, but *more* likely to respond the shorter the similar intervals more remotely involved in the preceding habituation sequence, for example, between Trials $n - 100$ and $n - 99$.

Thompson and Spencer (1966) offer as one of the parametric characteristics of habituation that "the more rapid the frequency of stimulation, the more rapid

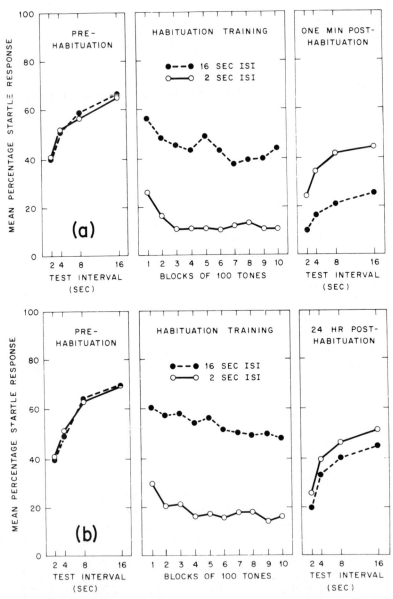

FIG. 4 Mean percentage of startle responses for subjects commonly tested pre- and post-habituation at each of 4 interstimulus intervals (ISIs) but segregated into separate groups for intervening habituation at either a constant 2- or 16-sec ISI. The top panels (a) present the percentages from groups receiving the posthabituation test 1 min following habituation. The bottom panels (b) present similar percentages from groups receiving the posthabituation test 24 hr after habituation. (From Davis, 1970. Copyright 1970 by the American Psychological Association. Reproduced by permission.)

3. PRIMING IN STM 111

and/or pronounced is habituation" (p. 18). The data presented in the middle

and/or pronounced is habituation" (p. 18). The data presented in the middle
panels of Figures 4a and 4b would offer further support for this assertion. On
trial 1 of the habituation training (not shown) there was no difference in
responding by the comparison groups. Over the subsequent course of habituation training, as shown, the groups receiving the more rapid, 2-sec stimulation
evidenced a more pronounced response decrement than the groups receiving the
less rapid, 16-sec stimulation. However, it can be pointed out that the difference
between the 2- and 16-sec groups appeared in full on the second trial of
habituation training (see Davis, 1970a) to be maintained over the remaining 998
trials in which the interval separating each trial from the immediately preceding
trial was consistently 2 or 16 sec. It is thus likely that the more pronounced
decrement seen with the more rapid frequency of stimulation during habituation
training was a function of the same local effect observed in the pre- and
posthabituation sessions, where responding varied with the immediately preceding interstimulus interval. The assertion, that habituation is more pronounced
the more rapid the stimulation, is certainly not consistent with the results from
the separate groups during the posthabituation test, as the 16-sec groups were
more depressed in responding than were the 2-sec groups. It appears that there is
some local refractory-like effect that operates to reduce responding more the
shorter the interval since the preceding trial, but that apart from this effect there
is a separable tendency for habituation to be more pronounced the more
distributed the prior stimulation.

Davis (1970a) considered several interpretations of his findings, among which
was a dual-memory-store approach. Basically it might be assumed that the
responding to a stimulus on Trial n of an habituation sequence is inversely
related to the memory for that event. The more recently the stimulus has been
presented over relatively brief intervals of time the more likely it should be
available in STM. The more distributed the sequence of prior stimulation the
better the opportunity for consolidated storage and the more likely it should be
available in LTM. We can now expand upon this manner of interpretation to
account for the Davis findings in terms of the set of assumptions involving
differential processing of primed versus nonprimed stimuli.

Whether or not an unconditioned response will occur to a stimulus during an
habituation sequence, or on a more remote test, can be assumed to vary with
whether or not the stimulus on such occasions is prerepresented in STM: When
the stimulus is primed in STM it will less likely evoke the measured response
than when it is not primed in STM. This can be taken to be the basic mechanism
producing variations in response probability or vigor properly attributable to
"habituation" (as opposed to effector fatigue, sensitization, etc.). The effects of
interstimulus interval, as seen in the Davis study, are especially instructive in that
they reflect upon two different manners in which priming may occur.

Given that a stimulus can be prerepresented in STM as a result of a recent
presentation of that stimulus, we should anticipate a short-term, refractory-like

effect to show through in the influence of the proximity of Trial $n - 1$ on Trial n responding. That is, we would anticipate that the integrity of event representation placed in STM on Trial $n - 1$ will decrease with time (or opportunity for displacement by other events) so that responding will increase, within limits, the longer the interval separating Trials n and $n - 1$, as seen in the test session data of Figures 4a and 4b.

More persistent, remotely detectable, habituation effects can be attributed to a retrieval-generated priming of STM. Using the language of the earlier studies in Pavlovian conditioning, a habituated stimulus should come to be "expected." As a result of repeated stimulation in the experimental environment, other stimuli in that environment can be assumed to become retrieval cues for the test stimulus, serving to prime the latter stimulus in STM, apart from any opportunities for self-generated priming. To carry this through in the case of the Davis findings, it needs to be argued that with the longer interstimulus intervals of 16 rather than 2 sec during the habituation sequence there was more of an association developed between other environmental cues and the test stimulus. There are 2 separable reasons why this should be the case. The most obvious is that longer interstimulus intervals throughout the sequence should allow greater opportunity for rehearsal in STM after each stimulation. The other reason is that just as a short interval between Trial $n - 1$ and n would be expected to lead to little response on Trial n, as the stimulus is primed in STM, it should, pari passu, lead to little poststimulation rehearsal of the Trial n events regardless of the length of the interval allowed after Trial n. The greater likelihood that the environmental cues would subsequently act to retrieve a representation of the startle stimulus into STM prior to stimulation in the 16-sec groups than in the 2-sec groups was presumably made apparent when the groups were evaluated under common test intervals in the posthabituation sequences as summarized in Figure 4a and b.

Evaluation

The foregoing treatment of habituation has recognizable similarities to other available accounts. It is also unique in several ways. It distinguishes, as do many theories (e.g., Groves & Thompson, 1970) between a refractory-like response decrement and a more persistent habituation effect. However, it suggests that at least in some instances the former as well as the latter effect may be due to memorial processing, where the common mechanism involves the priming of the stimulus representation in STM. It implicates an association process as do the treatments of Stein (1966) and Ratner (1970). However, it does not appeal to the acquisition of response tendencies to the habituating stimulus, but rather to the acquisition of tendencies by other stimuli in the environment to retrieve a representation of the habituating stimulus from LTM. In this respect the formulation is most similar to the theorizing of Sokolov (e.g. 1963, 1969) who has suggested (1969) that as a result of iterated stimulation the subject develops "impulses signaling the operation of an expected stimulus" (so-called "impulses of extrapolation") which are then compared to consequent afferent stimulation to determine the immediate response and subsequent stimulus processing. Sokolov is explicit in locating the impulses of extrapolation in "operative memory" (STM) and treating them as a restricted subset of the hypotheses that could be retrieved from "more permanent memory" (LTM) to be tested against the occurring stimulation. And, he makes use of the assumption that the contents of operative memory may be induced to change with recent stimulation, but then revert to reflect the most established neuronal model in subsequent impulses of extrapolation. Sokolov's discussion (1969), however, is primarily addressed to instances of habituating stimuli that are sequentially patterned so that one component can serve to activate the "impulses of extrapolation" relevant to later components (and hence the terminology). The present formulation, while not denying such possibilities in appropriate instances, emphasizes the role of other environmental cues in provoking the representational process.

We lack the kinds of observations that would assuredly comment on the usefulness of this theory of habituation in relationship to alternatives. We have begun, however, a research program investigating the habituation of auditorily evoked vasomotor activity in the rabbit that has resulted in a number of encouraging findings. The studies that have been conducted may be segregated into those which are principally concerned with the short-term refractory-like decrement presumed to be attributable to self-generated priming, and those which are principally concerned with the more remotely detectable decrement in performance presumed to be attributable to retrieval-generated priming.

Short-term effects. An immediate question that must be asked with respect to the kind of short-term refractory-like effect seen in the Davis (1970a) study is whether or not it is a memorial effect. A transient decrement in responsiveness could equally be due to effector fatigue or to sensory adaptation. In a recent dissertation Whitlow (1975) arranged a number of comparisons that could comment on the appropriateness of the latter interpretations in contrast to the notion of self-generated priming of STM. A decrement in response attributable to the priming of STM should occur only when stimulus input matches the contents of STM. Thus, considering the transient storage characteristics of STM, one should observe a transient decrement specific to recent presentation of the evoking stimulus. Alternatively, if effector fatigue is responsible for the transient decrement in responding, the decrement should not be stimulus specific, that is, it should be observed equally in the responding to any stimulus normally capable of evoking the same response. Furthermore, considering the limited capacity of STM and the assumed susceptibility of stimulus representation to displacement by other events, one should observe not only a stimulus-specific decrement, but a lability in such decrement, whereby it could be removed by other temporally adjacent, interfering stimuli. Alternatively, if sensory adaptation is responsible for the transient stimulus-specific decrement in responding, there would be no basis for anticipating a stimulation-induced recovery in responding.

The choice of preparation for this research, evoked peripheral vasomotor activity in rabbits, was determined by several factors. Since the vasoconstriction response is elicited by a broad range of stimuli in different modalities, it seemed plausible that discriminable stimuli could be selected for the necessary manipulations and comparisons. The response is easy to record via a photoplethysmograph from the ear of the rabbit under conditions of restraint as used in the previously described studies of Pavlovian eyelid conditioning (e.g., Wagner, 1969; Wagner, Rudy, & Whitlow, 1973; Terry & Wagner, 1975). And finally, the rabbit has, in the latter studies, otherwise shown evidence of differential processing of primed versus nonprimed stimuli.

In order to assess the possibility of a stimulus-specific decrement in responding produced by recent stimulation, Whitlow (1975) presented his subjects with a series of 1-sec tones, equally often 530 Hz and 4000 Hz. The series was arranged with successive pairs of tones being separated by 150 sec, and the members within each pair (designated as S_1 and S_2) separated by 30, 60, or 150 sec in an irregular counterbalanced order. It was expected that the refractory-like response decrement would be observed in variation in responding to S_2 as a function of the S_1-S_2 interval. However, it was arranged that on half of the S_1-S_2 pairs, involving each interstimulus interval, the two stimuli were the same (equally often 530 Hz or 4000 Hz) while on the remaining pairs the two stimuli were different (equally 530 Hz followed by 4000 Hz, or 4000 Hz followed by 530 Hz). It was thus possible to evaluate the degree to which any decremental effect of the input stimulus (S_1) was specific to the occasions in which it matched the test stimulus (S_2).

The study was run over two 2-hr sessions and involved 48 S_1-S_2 pairs. There was an overall decrease in response to the respective stimuli in the pairs with repetitive stimulation (Whitlow, 1975). But the major data of interest can be seen in Figure 5 which plots the averaged evoked vasoconstriction response to S_1 and S_2, at successive 5-sec intervals, over all pairs in which the interstimulus interval was either 30, 60, or 150 sec, and separately for those pairs in which the stimuli were the same versus different tones. The principal finding is obvious and highly reliable. When S_2 followed S_1 by 30 sec there was a substantial depression in the vasoconstriction evoked by the same as compared to the different tone. When S_2 followed S_1 by 60 sec this difference was smaller, although still quite apparent. However, when S_2 followed S_1 by 150 sec there was no longer a detectable depression in responding to S_2, as the subjects responded equivalently when S_2 was the same or different from the preceding stimulus. There is, in this preparation, evidence of a stimulus-specific response decrement that dissipates

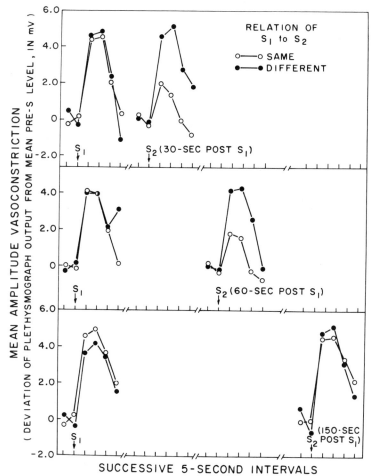

FIG. 5 Mean average evoked responses to successive auditory stimuli, S_1 and S_2, when the two were the same or different frequencies. Plotted separately in the top, middle, and bottom panels, respectively, are the responses to those stimuli separated by 30, 60, and 150 sec. (Reprinted from Whitlow, 1975. Copyright 1975 by the American Psychological Society. Reproduced by permission.)

over the tested intervals in a manner congruent with conventional assumptions concerning a transient representation in STM.

Granted this finding, it was then possible for Whitlow to ask whether or not an extraneous stimulus that should compete for occupancy of STM would act to remove the stimulus-specific response decrement. The experiment was closely patterned after the previous study with the exceptions that (a) the S_1–S_2 interval was consistently 60 sec, and that (b) on half of each of the occasions in which S_2 was the same tone as S_1 or was different from S_1, the interval embraced a "displacement stimulus" 20 sec after S_1 and thus 40 sec prior to S_2. From the data presented in Figure 5 it could be expected that in the absence of the displacement stimulus there would be ample stimulus-specific response decrement to S_2 at this S_1–S_2 interval. The question was whether or not the displacement stimulus (which was a sequential compound of 1-sec flashing light and 1-sec electrotactile stimulation of the cheek) would remove the decrement in the same manner as extending the duration of the S_1–S_2 interval to 150 sec had been found to do.

Figure 6 summarizes the relevant data in the same manner as Figure 5. When there was no intervening stimulation (see top panel of figure) the response to S_2 was reduced on occasions in which S_1 was the same stimulus, relative to occasions on which S_1 was a different stimulus. When the displacement stimulus was presented between S_1 and S_2 (see bottom panel of figure) it produced an evoked response itself, but more importantly, it removed any differential effect upon S_2 responding of the same versus different S_1 events. These findings are what one would expect if the refractory-like response decrement were dependent upon a perseverating representation of the test stimulus in STM, and the displacement stimulus acted to remove such representation.

The above studies by Whitlow argue against an effector fatigue or sensory adaptation interpretation of the transient response decrement in this preparation. The last study also comments on the manner in which a "dishabituator" can be effective. What we have referred to as a "displacement stimulus" is, of course, what is usually termed a "dishabituator." And, it is not unusual to find that such stimulation produces an increase in subsequent responding to an habituated stimulus. When the effects of dishabituators have been investigated, however, they have generally been found to have equivalent incremental influence on the responding to nonhabituated stimuli (e.g., Thompson & Spencer, 1966) indicating that they may have acted as nonspecific response potentiators. On this basis it has become common to challenge whether "dishabituation" literally occurs, and to conclude that nonspecific "sensitization" better characterizes the effects involved (e.g., Humphrey, 1933; Groves & Thompson, 1970; Sharpless & Jasper, 1956; Thompson & Spencer, 1966). In this context, it is particularly noteworthy that the displacement stimulus in the Whitlow study had the effect of removing a stimulus-specific response decrement, and did not appear to have a more general sensitizing influence. In short, it appeared to act as a dishabituator of the short-term habituation effect. It may be that previous failures to see dishabituation effects that could be distinguished from nonspecific sensitization has been due to the typical employment of strong and noxious stimuli (e.g., Humphrey, 1933; Lehner, 1941; Thompson & Spencer, 1966) that have such profound sensitizing effects as to obscure more subtle memorial influences.

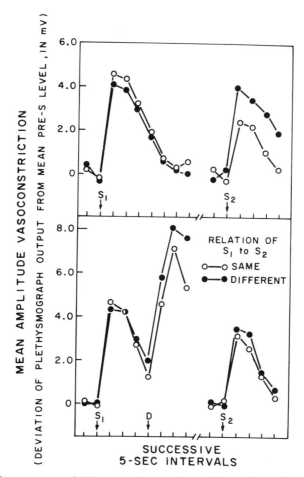

FIG. 6   Mean average evoked response to successive auditory stimuli, S_1 and S_2, when the two were the same or different frequencies. Plotted separately are the responses to those pairs involving no intervening stimulation (top panel) and those pairs separated by a displacement stimulus, D, as indicated (bottom panel). (From Whitlow, 1975. Copyright 1975 by the American Psychological Association. Reproduced by permission.)

The Whitlow studies may also be seen as opening the way to the kinds of investigations that may ultimately allow a richer detailing of the relevant operating characteristics of STM, with implications for what gets stored in LTM. We have only assumed that a distractor stimulus, or dishabituator, will more likely remove a prior stimulus representation than will no explicit stimulation. But how do the quality, intensity, and temporal relationship among the stimuli determine what is retained? As a first step toward evaluating such questions Whitlow (1975) ran a further study following the same general procedures as in the preceding investigations. In this case, however, S_1 was always presented in the context of distractor stimuli, prior to S_2. That is, S_1 was always embedded in a list containing four additional stimuli, with the successive items separated by 5-sec intervals.

S_1 was again a tonal stimulus, while the remaining items were a flashing light, an electrotactile stimulus to the cheek, a vibratory stimulus to the chest, and a thermal stimulus to the subject's side, the latter items being presented in varied orders from occasion to occasion. On one third of the list presentations the tonal S_1 was presented as the first member of the list, on one third as the middle member of the list, and finally, on one third as the last member of the list. S_2 was then consistently presented 40 sec after the last stimulus in the list, on half of the occasions being the same frequency and on half a different frequency than S_1. The data may be summarized very simply: There was a substantially lower level of responding to the same S_2 than to the different S_2 when S_1 was last in the list, a similar but reduced such tendency when S_1 was in the middle of the list, but little difference when S_1 was first in the list. There was a recency effect whereby the stimulus-specific decrement in responding to S_2 was progressively less detectable as the number of items intervening between S_1 and S_2 was increased from 0 to 2 to 4.

It is notable that, in this study, Whitlow found no evidence of a *primacy* effect, for example, with S_1 more effective when in the first than when in the middle position in the list, as is frequently observed in investigations of human memory (see, e.g., Kintsch, 1970). If, as we have assumed to be the case, the stimulus-specific decrement in responding to S_2 reflects the likelihood that S_1 representation is entered into STM and persists until the occasion of S_2, there is thus no reason to conclude that the first member of the list had preferential access to STM or was preferentially maintained, in relationship to later stimuli. This may have occurred, of course, but not have been detectable by the time of S_2. Alternatively, it is possible that a primacy effect may result only from the further involvement of LTM effects, that is when the test is such as to be sensitive to the degree to which the several list stimuli have become associated with contextual cues, beyond their immediate perseveration in STM. Decisions on such matters are as important to our understanding of habituation as to our theories of human memory, in which latter context they are frequently encountered (e.g., Glanzer & Cunitz, 1966; Waugh & Norman, 1965).

Long term effects.   According to our interpretation, an habituation decrement that is more persistent than the short-term refractory-like effect is closely akin to the loss in processing of an expected US, as demonstrated in the previously summarized studies in Pavlovian conditioning (e.g., Wagner, 1969; Wagner, Rudy & Whitlow, 1973; Terry & Wagner, 1975). The habituation stimulus is presumably less reacted to because it is, on the measurement occasion, primed in STM, not by recent instances of the same stimulus, but by the retrieval action of the aggregation of antecedent cues. If this is the case we should be able to see that habituation, when assessed on tests remote from the habituating sequence, is dependent upon the integrity of the presumed retrieval cues and dependent upon the opportunity which has been afforded for such cues to be associated with the test stimulus.

The kind of experiment to which one might be led by this reasoning would be one in which each instance of a to-be-habituated target stimulus is consistently announced by some other cue. In this way one could arrange to make the latter stimulus an effective retrieval cue for the target stimulus and thereby favor observing an habituation decrement when response to the target stimulus is tested following that cue. At the same time one could assess whether or not the habituation decrement thus seen to the target stimulus is dependent upon the integrity of the preceding retrieval cue by presenting test occasions with the target stimulus alone. Under such test conditions the habituation decrement should be less apparent. To determine whether or not any habituation decrement that is observed to be more pronounced in the presence than in the absence of the retrieval cue is due to the signaling properties of the latter cue, one could manipulate the presumed association between the retrieval and target cues. For example, repeatedly presenting the retrieval cue alone should extinguish its association with the target stimulus and lead to a subsequent recovery of responding to the target stimulus on paired test occasions.

This kind of experiment might be called a "cued habituation experiment" except that the procedure, of regularly preceding a target stimulus that evokes an unconditioned response with some distinct cue, is otherwise known as Pavlovian conditioning. And, interestingly enough, there are relevant data on the changes in the UR during Pavlovian conditioning. There is frequently observed a "conditioned diminution of the UR" (Kimble & Ost, 1961; Kimmel, 1966). What this term refers to is a decrease in amplitude of the response to the US on successive exposures to the CS–US pair that can be shown to be due to the integrity and signaling properties of the CS. Thus the UR "recovers" on test trials with the US alone or on CS–US trials which are preceded by CS-alone extinction trials. The "conditioned diminution" terminology has been meant to convey that the decrease in responding to the US is due to the CS–US association and is thus not simply a function of US habituation. The present interpretation is that habituation (at least what we have distinguished as long-term habituation) is attributable to the same factors as are well illuminated in the "conditioned diminution of the UR" phenomenon. The stimulus is less likely to provoke a response when it is primed in STM by associated retrieval cues.

An obvious challenge to this reasoning is that an habituation sequence does not typically involve an explicit signaling of each occasion of the habituating stimulus, that is, does not involve a stimulus arrangement as in the studies of Pavlovian conditioning wherein there is an identifiable CS that can be assumed to prime US representation. As a first response to this challenge it may be noted

that even in treatments of Pavlovian conditioning it has frequently been necessary to assume that stimuli other than the explicit CS's, so-called "situational
cues," can come to have the same signaling function as the nominal CS
(Asratyan, 1961; Dweck & Wagner, 1970; Kremer, 1974; Rescorla & Wagner,
1972; Sheafor, 1975; Welker et al., 1974) and that, indeed, the nominal CS
frequently must compete with situational cues, becoming more effective only to
the degree that it is more reliably followed by the US (Dweck & Wagner, 1970;
Rescorla & Wagner, 1972). A similar assumption would need to be made in
reference to habituation, i.e. that situational, or contextual, cues are important
where explicit priming stimuli are not arranged.

More direct response can be made, but as yet only on the basis of minimal
data. For example, if the long-term response decrement in habituation is dependent upon the retrieval action of situational cues, we should clearly expect that
it would be *context specific.* Curiously enough, this has rarely been evaluated in
studies of habituation. Peeke and Veno (1973) reported a relevant observation.
They recorded the aggressive behavior of male stickle-backs toward presentation
of a male stimulus in 2 separate exposure sessions. What they observed was that
there was more aggressive behavior (less evidence of habituation) in the second
session if it were conducted in a different location in the aquarium than if it
were conducted in the same location as the first session. Leaton (1974),
however, reported no effects of changing the chamber illumination and floor
texture from training to test in an investigation of the habituation of drinking
suppression by auditory stimuli in the rat. It may be remarked that Leaton's
measure of habituation may have been skewed to detect minimal degrees of
habituation (all response changes generally took place with two stimulus exposures) and may have been relatively insensitive to variations beyond this. One
may note, for example, that following 40 stimulations no loss of habituation was
detectable over a 21-day retention interval, and that the shift in context was
evaluated following yet more protracted training. It is clear, however, that
investigations like this, involving a range of response systems and varieties of
contextual change, need be further pursued to determine the degree to which
the habituation decrement is dependent upon the integrity of contextual cues.
We must also examine the possibility that contextual change, when effective,
may have a sensitizing effect, as discussed above in relationship to the Whitlow
(1975) dishabituation studies, and thus act less specifically than to remove the
retrieval cues for a particular habituated stimulus.

The most encouraging observation that we have made involves the effects of
degrading the signal value of the contextual cues following habituation. It was
noted above that the "conditioned diminution of the UR" can be removed by
repeated exposures to the CS alone. By this manipulation it is presumably
possible to extinguish the CS—US association so that on subsequent CS—US tests
the CS has diminished tendency to prime US representation into STM. The same
manipulation should be effective with contextual cues when they are presumed
to function as the retrieval stimuli. That is, following habituation training in

some context it should be possible to promote a recovery of the habituated response in that context by intervening exposure to the contextual stimuli alone. This is a theoretically powerful prediction in that no other interpretation of habituation, including those which appeal to some associative mechanism (e.g., Stein, 1966; Ratner, 1970) seem prepared to anticipate a similar *extinction* of habituation.

The relevant study was conducted in collaboration with Jesse W. Whitlow and Penn L. Pfautz, using the same vasomotor preparation employed by Whitlow (1975). In initial training, 2 groups of 8 rabbits were subjected to a 2-hr habituation session during which a 1-sec tonal stimulus was presented on 32 occasions with a 150 sec interstimulus interval. The frequency of the habituation stimulus was for half of each group 530 Hz and for the remainder 4000 Hz. All subjects were returned for a retention test 2 days later. The only difference in treatment of the 2 groups was that on the intervening day 1 group (Control) was simply left in their home cages, while the other group (Extinguished) was placed in the experimental chamber, had the recording apparatus attached, and was treated identically as in the previous habituation session except that no tones were presented. On the retention day all subjects received a series of 32 exposures to the previously habituated tone, as in session 1, and then received 2 test exposures to the alternate frequency tone.

Figure 7 summarizes the essential data from this experiment. In each panel is presented the averaged evoked response, at 5-sec intervals preceding and following the test stimulus, for each group. The left panel indicates the initial level of responding to the to-be-habituated stimulus (designated A) as it shows the averaged response to the first 2-tone presentations in the training session for each of the 2 groups. The middle panel indicates the responding of the 2 groups to the comparable 2-tone presentations at the beginning of the retention test session. The major effect is obvious in these data. Both groups evidenced an habituation decrement in their responding on the retention day as compared to the initial stimulation. However, whereas there was a very sizable habituation decrement (an 85% reduction in response magnitude) seen in the case of the Control Group, there was a much smaller habituation decrement (a 34% reduction in response magnitude) seen in the case of the Extinguished Group, which difference was highly reliable, $U = 7.5, p < .005$.

The test trials to the nonhabituated tonal stimulus (designated B) were included in the retention session as a gross check that the extinction manipulation had not been effective by producing some general change in vasomotor responsivity. The right panel of Figure 7 presents the evoked response to the novel tone. It is apparent that the two groups did not differ in their response to this stimulus whereas they did differ in their response to the previously habituated tone.

If contextual cues have acquired an association with the habituated stimulus, so as to act to prime representation of the latter stimulus in STM, it should be possible to extinguish the relevant association and thus promote recovery of the

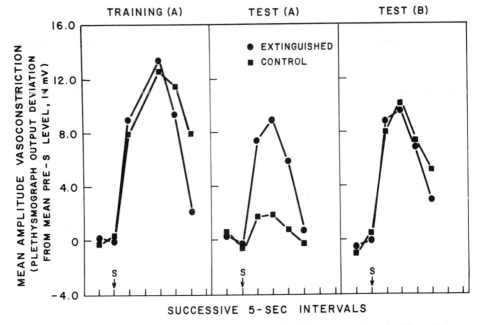

FIG. 7 Mean averaged evoked response to auditory stimuli in two groups of subjects. The successive panels present the response to the first 2 presentations of the habituated tone, *A*, the first 2 exposures to the same tone on a retention test, and finally 2 exposures to a novel tone, *B*. Between training and testing one group (Extinguished) was exposed to the experimental environment in the absence of the habituated stimulus, and the other group (Control) was not.

habituated response. We view this experimental test as a relatively critical way to evaluate our interpretation of the long-term habituation decrement. That the results of our initial study, as summarized above, are in agreement with the predicted outcome is certainly encouraging. But our confidence in the interpretation will depend upon the reproducibility of the extinction phenomenon over a variety of situations involving different stimuli and responses that can be shown to suffer more than transient habituation.

The Davis (1970a) dissertation on interstimulus interval led us to the view that there are separable short-term and long-term habituation effects. The theory which has presently been outlined is an attempt to offer a plausible mechanism for such effects, encouraged by the usefulness of a related set of propositions concerning the interaction of STM and LTM in Pavlovian conditioning. To conclude this section describing the available data that stand in evaluation of the theory, we can cite one further unpublished investigation from our laboratory that is particularly relevant to our present approach to the Davis findings.

Davis (1970a), it should be recalled, observed that the longer the interval between Trial $n - 1$ and Trial n in an habituation sequence the more likely there would be a response on Trial n, but the less likely there would be a response on a more remote testing occasion. We have interpreted these effects by suggesting that the longer the intertrial interval the greater is the likelihood that the self-generated representation of the test stimulus will have been cleared from STM prior to Trial n, but also the greater is the opportunity for the representation to run its full course in STM and become associated with contextual cues, to be retrieved on later test occasions. If this reasoning is correct, along with the interpretation of the Whitlow (1975) studies, that a poststimulation dishabituator can act to clear STM of the perseverating stimulus representation, then it should be possible to employ distractor events to influence the long-term as well as the short-term habituation decrement. That is, suppose that each stimulus presentation during an habituation sequence is closely followed by a distractor that effectively terminates the residence of the stimulus in STM. Less association should thereby be allowed between the contextual cues and the habituating stimulus, and less long-term habituation should be observed on a remote test.

Whitlow and Wagner tested this expectation using the same vasomotor preparation as in the previous experiments. Eight rabbits were run in a single 2.5-hr session segregated into 3 periods designated, respectively, as Pretest, Training, and Posttest, and separated by 15-min intervals. In the Pretest all subjects were administered three exposures to each of two 1-sec tonal stimuli, one 530 Hz, the other 4000 Hz, in different counterbalanced orders, at 150-sec interstimulus intervals. During the Training period subjects received 32 habituation trials, 16 with each tonal stimulus, again at 150-sec intervals. Trials with one stimulus, A, which for half of the subjects was 530 Hz and the remainder 4000 Hz, were always followed, after a 20-sec interval, by presentation of the visual–tactile compound displacement stimulus employed in the Whitlow study (1975). Trials with the alternate stimulus, B, were never followed by the distractor. The order in which A and B occurred was determined by different pseudorandom sequences designed so that the first order transitional probabilities were equated. Thus, only A trials were consistently *followed* by the distractor, but A and B were equally often *preceded* by a distractor occasion. The Posttest was identical to the Pretest, involving three assessments of responding to each of the cues that were differentially treated during training. No distractor stimuli were scheduled outside of the Training period.

Figure 8 displays the mean, across all subjects, average evoked vasoconstriction response to the A and B stimuli during the Pretest and Posttest periods. As may be seen, there was no difference in response to the stimuli prior to differential habituation training. In the Posttest, both stimuli evoked smaller responses than in the Pretest. The major observation of interest, however, is that the diminution in response was less in the case of the A tone that had been followed by the distractor stimulus than in the case of the B tone that had not been followed by the distractor stimulus. This pattern, as summarized in Figure 8, was seen in 7 of the 8 individual subjects (sign test, $p < .05$). It is the pattern that would be expected if the distractor stimulus occupies STM to reduce the rehearsal and

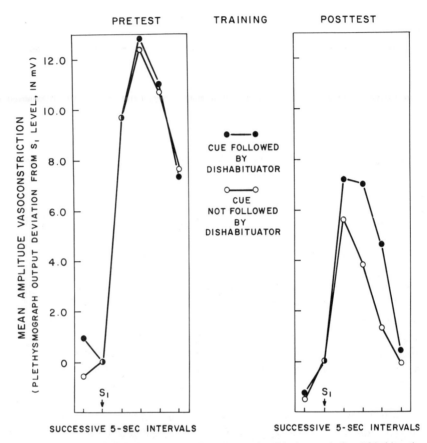

FIG. 8   Mean average evoked response to 2 auditory stimuli before and after 16 habituation exposures to each stimulus. During habituation training 1 cue was consistently followed by a distractor (dishabituator), the other was not.

consolidated association allowed between the preceding stimulus and contextual cues.

CONCLUDING REMARKS

The thrust of this chapter has been directed to the theoretical interpretation of the waning of responsiveness that is known as "habituation." Prerepresentation of a stimulus in short-term memory, via recent presentation of that stimulus (self-generated priming) or via exposure to stimuli previously associated with that stimulus (retrieval-generated priming), has been suggested as a possible common factor in the refractory-like, short-term response decrement and the more remotely detectable, long-term diminution in responding that results from repetitive stimulation.

As has been duly emphasized, however, the essential propositions have not been uniquely shaped to account for habituation phenomena. The general conceptual framework is most familiar in treatments of human memory, while the priming thesis itself was first developed in more specialized form to deal with facts of Pavlovian conditioning. The attractive possibility is that findings in each of these otherwise disparate areas of research may be integrated in terms of related information processing mechanisms.

Hopefully, certain of the integrative possibilities have been made evident. To recognize further concrete instances where the formulation may have utility, considered the fact that the same procedures of stimulus exposure that result in a diminution in an evoked response also result in the "latent inhibition effect" in Pavlovian conditioning (see, e.g., Lubow, 1973; Reiss & Wagner, 1972) and the "stimulus familiarization effect" in human reaction time experiments (e.g., Cantor, 1969). The "latent inhibition effect" refers to a decreased associability of a preexposed stimulus with a US when the stimulus is subsequently employed as a CS in CS–US pairings, while the "stimulus familiarization effect" refers to an increased reaction time to a preexposed stimulus when subjects are instructed to respond to stimulus occurrence as quickly as possible. As others (e.g., Lantz, 1973; Lubow, Alek, & Arzy, 1975) have recognized, there is presumptive reason to suspect that these two effects are related to each other and to the phenomenon of habituation.

It is instructive then to see that some of the experimental manipulations that were proposed as particularly relevant to evaluation of the present treatment of habituation have been employed in investigations of latent inhibition and the stimulus familiarization effect with encouraging results. For example, if a latently inhibited CS suffers a processing decrement in part because of a retrieval-generated priming of short-term memory by situational cues, that decrement should be context specific. Consistent with this expectation, Anderson and his colleagues (Anderson, O'Farrell, Formica, & Caponegri, 1969; Anderson, Wolf, & Sullivan, 1969) have found that the loss of associability of a preexposed CS is more demonstrable when the preexposure takes place in the conditioning apparatus than within a different environment. A study by Lantz (1973) could be similarly interpreted. Within a single session subjects were preexposed to a series of tones and then administered a terminal pairing of the tone with electric shock. If the illumination of the training chamber was changed between the tone preexposures and the tone–shock pairing, the conditioning observed to the tone was enhanced, that is, the degree of latent inhibition was reduced. As a further example, suppose that the stimulus familiarization effect upon reaction time is likewise dependent in part upon the association of the test stimulus with contextual cues. Then it should be possible to reduce the effect by presenting a distractor stimulus after each instance of the test stimulus during preexposure so as to deprive the test stimulus of rehearsal in STM, in the same manner as in the previously summarized study of vasomotor habituation by Whitlow and Wagner. Lubow, Alek and Arzy (1975) have reported just such an observation.

There is encouragement to believe that the present formulation can be applied as comfortably to a variety of learning and performance tasks involving different measures of behavior. How adequate it will ultimately be judged to be depends upon the answers to some very researchable questions. For example, can the stimulus familiarization effect be extinguished by exposure to situational cues in the absence of the preexposed stimulus? Can the effectiveness of a CS or US in a Pavlovian pairing be reduced not only by rendering the stimulus "expected" in its context, but, more temporarily, by recent isolated exposure to the event? The proposed mechanisms of self-generated and retrieval-generated priming of STM suggest affirmative answers.

ACKNOWLEDGMENTS

The research reported was supported by National Science Foundation Grants GB-14384, GB-30299X, and BMS 74-20521. It was conceived and conducted in collaboration with a number of students, Michael Davis, Penn L. Pfautz, Jerry W. Rudy, Maria A. Saavedra, William S. Terry, and Jesse W. Whitlow, whose contributions extended beyond the specific studies for which they are cited.

REFERENCES

Anderson, D. C., O'Farrell, T., Formica, R., & Caponegri, V. Preconditioning CS exposure: Variation in place of conditioning and presentation. *Psychonomic Science,* 1969, *15,* 54–55.

Anderson, D. C., Wolf, D., & Sullivan, P. Preconditioning exposure to the CS: Variation in place of testing. *Psychonomic Science,* 1969, *14,* 233–235.

Asratyan, E. A. The initiation and localization of cortical inhibition in the conditioned reflex arc. *Annals of the New York Academy of Sciences,* 1961, *92,* 1141–1159.

Atkinson, R. C., & Shiffrin, R. M. Human memory: A proposed system and its control processes. In K. W. Spence & J. T. Spence (Eds.), *The psychology of learning and motivation.* (Vol. 2). New York: Academic Press, 1968.

Atkinson, R. C., & Wickens, T. D. Human memory and the concept of reinforcement. In R. Glaser (Ed.), *The nature of reinforcement.* New York: Academic Press, 1971.

Cantor, G. N. Stimulus familiarization effect and the change effect in children's motor task behavior. *Psychological Bulletin,* 1969, *71,* 144–160.

Davis, M. Effects of interstimulus interval length and variability on startle-response habituation in the rat. *Journal of Comparative and Physiological Psychology,* 1970, *72,* 177–192. (a)

Davis, M. Interstimulus interval and startle response habituation with a "control" for total time during training. *Psychonomic Science,* 1970, *20,* 39–41. (b)

Davis, M., & Wagner, A. R. Startle responsiveness after habituation to different intensities of tone. *Psychonomic Science,* 1968, *12,* 337–338.

Davis, M., & Wagner, A. R. Habituation of startle response under incremental sequence of stimulus intensities. *Journal of Comparative and Physiological Psychology,* 1969, *67,* 486–492.

Dweck, C. S., & Wagner, A. R. Situational cues and correlation between CS and US as determinants of the conditioned emotional response. *Psychonomic Science,* 1970, *18,* 145–147.

Glanzer, M., & Cunitz, A. R. Two stage mechanisms in free recall. *Journal of Verbal Learning and Verbal Behavior,* 1966, *5,* 351–360.

Groves, P. M., & Thompson, R. F. Habituation: A dual process theory. *Psychological Review,* 1970, *77,* 419–450.

Horn, G., & Hinde, R. A. *Short-term changes in neural activity and behavior.* Cambridge, England: Cambridge University Press, 1970.

Humphrey, G. *The nature of learning.* New York: Harcourt, Brace & Company, 1933.

Kamin, L. J. Attention-like processes in classical conditioning. In M. R. Jones (Ed.), *Miami symposium on the prediction of behavior: Aversive stimulation.* Miami: University of Miami Press, 1968.

Kimble, G. A., & Ost, J. W. P. A conditioned inhibitory process in eyelid conditioning. *Journal of Experimental Psychology,* 1961, *61,* 150–156.

Kimmel, H. D. Inhibition of the unconditioned response in classical conditioning. *Psychological Review,* 1966, *73,* 232–240.

Kintsch, W. *Learning, memory and conceptual processes.* New York: Wiley, 1970.

Kling, J. W., & Stevenson, J. G. Habituation and extinction. In G. Horn & R. A. Hinde (Eds.), *Short term changes in neural activity and behavior.* Cambridge, England: Cambridge University Press, 1970. Pp. 41–61.

Konorski, J., & Lawicka, W. Physiological mechanisms of delayed reactions: I. The analysis and classification of delayed reactions. *Acta Biologiae Experimentalis,* 1959, *19,* 175–197.

Kremer, E. F. The truly random control procedure: Conditioning to the static cues. *Journal of Comparative and Physiological Psychology,* 1974, *86,* 700–707.

Lantz, A. Effect of number of trials, interstimulus interval and dishabituation during CS habituation on subsequent conditioning in a CER paradigm. *Animal Learning & Behavior,* 1973, *4,* 273–278.

Leaton, R. N. Long term retention of the habituation of lick suppression in rats. *Journal of Comparative and Physiological Psychology,* 1974, *87,* 1157–1164.

Lehner, G. F. J. A study of the extinction of unconditioned reflexes. *Journal of Experimental Psychology,* 1941, *29,* 435–456.

Lubow, R. E. Latent inhibition. *Psychological Bulletin,* 1973, *79,* 398–407.

Lubow, R. E., Alek, M., & Arzy, J. Behavioral decrement following stimulus pre-exposure: Effects of number of pre-exposures, presence of a second stimulus, and the interstimulus interval in children and adults. *Journal of Experimental Psychology: Animal Behavior Processes,* 1975, *1,* 178–188.

Peeke, H. V. S., & Herz, M. F. *Habituation* (Volume I): *Behavioral studies.* New York: Academic Press, 1973.

Peeke, H. V. S., & Veno, G. Stimulus specificity of habituated aggression in three-spined sticklebacks (*Gasterosteus aculeatus*). *Behavioral Biology,* 1973, *8,* 427–432.

Ratner, S. C. Habituation: Research and theory. In J. Reynierse (Ed.), *Current issues in animal learning.* Lincoln: University of Nebraska Press, 1970.

Reiss, S., & Wagner, A. R. CS habituation produces a "latent inhibition effect" but no active "conditioned inhibition." *Learning & Motivation,* 1972, *3,* 237–245.

Rescorla, R. A., & Wagner, A. R. A theory of Pavlovian conditioning: Variations in the

128   ALLAN R. WAGNER

effectiveness of reinforcement and nonreinforcement. In A. H. Black & W. F. Prokasy (Eds.), *Classical conditioning II.* New York: Appleton-Century-Crofts, 1972. Pp. 64–99.

Sharpless, S., & Jasper, H. Habituation of the arousal reaction. *Brain,* 1956, *79,* 655–680.

Sheafor, P. J. "Pseudoconditioned" jaw movements of the rabbit reflect associations conditioned to contextual background cues. *Journal of Experimental Psychology: Animal Behavior Processes,* 1975, *1,* 245–260.

Sokolov, E. N. *Perception and the conditioned reflex.* New York: Pergamon, 1963.

Sokolov, E. N. Modeling properties of the nervous system. In I. Maltzman & M. Cole (Eds.), *Handbook of contemporary Soviet psychology.* New York: Basic Books, 1969.

Stein, L. Habituation and stimulus novelty: A model based on classical conditioning. *Psychological Review,* 1966, *73,* 352–356.

Terry, W. S., & Wagner, A. R. Short-term memory for "surprising" vs. "expected" unconditioned stimuli in Pavlovian conditioning. *Journal of Experimental Psychology: Animal Behavior Processes,* 1975, *1,* 122–133.

Thompson, R. F., & Spencer, W. A. Habituation: A model phenomenon for the study of neuronal substrates of behavior. *Psychological Review,* 1966, *197,* 16–43.

Wagner, A. R. Stimulus selection and a "modified continuity theory." In G. H. Bower & J. T. Spence (Eds.), *The psychology of learning and motivation* (Vol. 3). New York: Academic Press, 1969.

Wagner, A. R., & Rescorla, R. A. Inhibition in Pavlovian conditioning: Application of a theory. In R. A. Boakes & M. S. Halliday (Eds.), *Inhibition and learning.* London: Academic Press, 1972. Pp. 301–335.

Wagner, A. R., Rudy, J. W., & Whitlow, J. W. Rehearsal in animal conditioning. *Journal of Experimental Psychology Monograph,* 1973, *97,* 407–426.

Waugh, N. C., & Norman, D. A. Primary memory. *Psychological Review,* 1965, *72,* 89–104.

Welker, R. L., Thomie, A., Davitt, G. A., & Thomas, D. R. Contextual stimulus control over operant responding in pigeons. *Journal of Comparative and Physiological Psychology,* 1974, *86,* 549–562.

Whitlow, J. W. Short-term memory in habituation and dishabituation. *Journal of Experimental Psychology: Animal Behavior Processes,* 1975, *1,* 189–206.

4
Neural and Psychological Processes Underlying the Development of Learning and Memory

Byron A. Campbell

Princeton University

Xenia Coulter

State University of New York, Stony Brook

Our work has not dealt directly with the process of habituation, but rather with developmental processes in learning and memory. However, if one assumes as some have (e.g., Thorpe, 1956) that habituation is a relatively permanent change in behavior, an elementary form of learning, then one must assume that developmental processes underlying learning and memory may be significantly involved in habituation. Clearly we need direct experimental work on developmental processes in habituation that would parallel that on the development of learning and memory. Developmental work in children has not often dealt directly with the process of habituation. Infrahuman work has dealt specifically with habituation as a process but has rarely been developmental. It is hoped that the material treated here will suggest some bridges between these areas.

In a recent paper (Campbell & Coulter, 1976) we have provided a detailed review and analysis of research on the development of learning and memory. We concluded that the young organism shows relatively poor retention in a variety of basic learning tasks yet does not appear to differ from adults in the original learning of those tasks. Our purpose in the first part of this chapter is to summarize the major features of the data supporting this conclusion as a background to a more detailed consideration of the underlying psychological and neurological processes.

LEARNING AND DEVELOPMENT

Learning Capacity: Neonatal Studies

An increasing number of reports over the past decade provide evidence for the view that the immature organism, including the neonate, has the capacity to learn. For example, Rosenblatt (1972) presents evidence that newborn kittens locate the mother and a particular nipple through the learning of various olfactory, tactile, and thermal discriminations in the earliest days of life. Fox (1971) provides similar observations for puppies. Caldwell and Werboff (1962), working with the albino rat, established a conditioned aversive response to a vibrotactile conditioned stimulus (CS) on the first day of life. Stanley and his colleagues have demonstrated a variety of conditioned responses in puppies over the first two weeks of life, including classical conditioning to taste cues, avoidance conditioning to a cold air unconditioned stimulus (UCS), and an appetitive discrimination reversal (Bacon & Stanley, 1970a, b; Stanley, Bacon, & Fehr, 1970; Stanley et al., 1963). Similarly, Bacon (1973) has reported observations of instrumental avoidance in kittens by the third day of life. Other reports of behavior change in neonates include anticipatory eating responses in tube-fed pups by the third day (Thoman, Wetzel, & Levine, 1968), habituation and conditioning to odor cues in puppies within five postnatal days (Fox, 1971), and classical conditioning in newborn monkeys (Harlow, 1959; Mason & Harlow, 1958a). At the human level, Lipsitt's studies (1969) provide perhaps the most dramatic evidence that newborn infants can be habituated and conditioned by both classical and instrumental procedures. Similarly dramatic evidence is available for neonatal learning in other altricial species.

While there have been some failures to obtain conditioning in newborn organisms, particularly in early studies (Cornwall & Fuller, 1961; Fuller, Easler, & Banks, 1950; James & Cannon, 1952), Campbell and Coulter (1976) argue that such outcomes may reflect failure to insure that the task demands are appropriate to the neonatal state. In any event, the current literature appears to fully warrant the conclusion that learning can take place in neurologically undeveloped organisms. In the context of this chapter, the point to be noted is that the relatively poor retention of the immature organism can not be attributed to any fundamental deficiency in capacity to learn.

Learning Rate: Juvenile Studies

Even if capacity is present, young organisms may learn less efficiently than adults and this in turn may result in a less permanent form of learning. This question has been studied by comparing animals of different ages on rate of learning particular tasks.

Simple approach and escape. These tasks involve the learning of a simple response—reinforcement contingency, such as to approach a particular place to find food or to make a particular response to escape a noxious stimulus. Tasks of this type were employed by Stone (1929a, b) in an early developmental study of learning distinguished by the adequacy of its control procedures. He found that rats ranging in age from 30 to 700 days did not differ either in learning to escape shock or in learning to approach food. In one of the few recent studies of development of approach learning, McGaugh and Cole (1965) compared 30- and 150-day-old maze-bright and maze-dull rats in learning of a Lashley III maze at two intertrial intervals. There were no age differences in learning rate in maze-bright rats at either interval, but young maze-dull animals learned more slowly than adults at the longer (30 min) interval. Mason and Harlow (1958b) found that 15- and 45-day-old monkeys did not differ in the rate of learning to approach the correct arm of a Y maze.

Developmental studies of escape tasks are more numerous. Crockett and Nobel (1963) found that 21- and 90-day-old rats learned to escape light with equal facility. Working with 6 different strains of mice, Meier (1964) trained groups ranging from 21 to 147 days of age to escape from a 3-choice water maze. Overall, the younger mice learned at optimal rates, with lower rates always occurring in older subjects. Similar observations were reported by Smith (1968) for 25-, 100-, and 175-day-old rats trained in a four-choice shock—escape situation. Campbell *et al.* (1974) in studying rats ranging from 15 to 35 days of age noted that 15-day-old rats appeared to learn shock—escape in a simple T-maze somewhat more slowly than 17-, 20-, and 25-day-olds. The difference, however, was very small and the learning rate of the 15-day-olds resembled that of the 35-day-old group.

Dealing with considerably younger ages, Nagy and Murphy (1974) report that mice pups learned to escape shock at 9 days of age but not at 5 or 7 days. But since these investigators defined escape learning as a reduction in turning in response to shock, it is possible that the deficit observed in younger animals simply reflects an age-dependent change in reactivity to shock rather than inability to acquire an escape contingency per se. Another report of an early deficiency in escape learning (James & Binks, 1963) is open to a similar interpretation. While James and Binks found that chickens could not learn to escape shock until the second day after hatching, Peters and Isaacson (1963) found that newborn chickens are as capable of escape learning as 10-day-olds when cold water is used as the aversive stimulus.

In sum, the evidence permits the tentative conclusion that the immature organism is not necessarily inferior in rate of learning simple approach and escape tasks.

Spatial avoidance and CER. These tasks require the animal to learn a contingency between a stimulus and a reinforcer, with learning assessed in terms of an altered level of responding to the stimulus. Thus in the CER paradigm the effect of a number of CS–shock pairings is measured by the power of the CS alone to later suppress some previously established ongoing activity. Brunner, Roth, and Rossi (1970) presented one CS–UCS pairing and Wilson and Riccio (1973) 3 stimulus pairings and found that 25- and 23-day-old rats, respectively, suppressed less than older rats. But these observations are in contrast to a number of studies with rats that found no difference in CER learning between comparable age levels when many (12 or more) CS–UCS pairings are used (Campbell & Campbell, 1962; Snedden, Spevack, & Thompson, 1971). Moreover, Frieman, Frieman, Wright and Hegberg (1971) found that 18-day-old pups required somewhat fewer trials (7.7) than adults (8.8) to attain 90% suppression to three successive CS presentations. And Green (1962) showed that a few CS–UCS pairings had equal suppressive effects on 1-, 30-, and 300-day-old monkeys.

Another variable which may influence CER acquisition in the young organism is intertrial interval. Thus, Frieman, Warner, and Riccio (1970) found that young rats did not acquire as much suppression as adults under CER training that involved an apparently adequate number of CS–UCS presentations but a relatively rapid rate of UCS presentation. In this regard it is interesting to note that Caldwell and Werboff (1962) report that newborn rats appear to condition quite rapidly in a stimulus-contingent task with longer interstimulus intervals than are optimal with adults, an effect they attributed to slow rates of memory consolidation in young organisms (see also Thompson, 1957; Doty & Doty, 1964; Doty, 1966; Dye, 1969 for further discussion of the age–memory consolidation hypothesis). Finally, Coulter and Collier (unpublished data) found that one CS–UCS pairing each on days 23, 30, and 37 culminated in complete suppression of bar pressing at 44 days, whereas three such pairings separated by minutes usually results in slight suppression even with adults (Coulter, 1974).

Studies of spatial avoidance, to which we now turn, are less informative on the development of stimulus-contingency learning since none of these studies have examined the effects of variation in number of trials or intertrial interval. In spatial avoidance the animal suppresses its normal tendency to approach a place following association of that location with an aversive stimulus. While Rohrbaugh and Riccio (1968) found that 18-day-olds showed somewhat less avoidance of a compartment in which they had been shocked than did adults, this difference was very small, and the conditions of this study were highly similar to those of a later experiment in which no age differences obtained (Frieman, Rohrbaugh, & Riccio, 1969). Similarly, Campbell and Campbell (1962) found that young animals learned spatial avoidance as well as adults.

To sum up this section, under most circumstances young rats learn simple stimulus contingencies as readily as adults. In those cases when they do not, it is not clear whether it is because young rats require more trials or longer intertrial intervals than adults.

Active avoidance. Here the animal must learn to respond appropriately in the presence of a particular stimulus in order to avoid an aversive stimulus. Hence the task can be said to involve both response-reinforcement learning and stimulus-contingency learning. The history of research on this problem is instructive. Of 6 studies involving rats reported between 1958 and 1966, none of which involved subjects younger than 25 days, all but one (Kirby, 1963) found that the youngest age group took longer to learn avoidance than adults (Denenberg & Kline, 1958; Denenberg & Smith, 1963; Doty, 1966; Doty & Doty, 1964; Thompson, Koenigsberg, & Tennison, 1965). In contrast, none of the 9 studies reported since 1967 has replicated this deficit at comparable age levels (Brennan & Riccio, 1972; Feigley & Spear, 1970; Goldman & Tobach, 1967; Klein & Spear, 1969; Parsons & Spear, 1972; Porter & Thompson, 1967; Riccio & Marrazo, 1972; Riccio, Rohrbaugh & Hodges, 1968). Three studies in the latter category included groups younger than 20 days and each reported deficits in those groups. Overall, it appears that experimenters are becoming more proficient at arranging conditions appropriate for learning at younger age levels.

In regard to the deficits currently observed at very young age levels, it is possible that the running response demanded for avoidance in all these studies undergoes developmental changes that facilitate learning by older animals. In addition, Bacon's (1973) data indicate that the appropriateness of the CS as well as the avoidance response, should be considered with young organisms. Specifically, Bacon found that neonatal kittens could not learn to avoid a cloth-lined compartment but could learn to avoid a compartment of plastic mesh.

In sum, the trend of research in this area suggests that young organisms can readily learn to actively avoid and that deficits in such learning are more likely to reflect the use of stimuli and responses inappropriate to the age level studied than a true deficit in learning.

Discriminations. There is evidence that visual discrimination performance improves with age. This has been clearly shown for the monkey during the first month of life (Harlow *et al.*, 1960; Zimmerman, 1961; Zimmerman & Torrey, 1965), and suggestive evidence in this direction has been provided for dogs (Fox, 1971) and for rats (Roberts, 1966). Such age differences can be interpreted as resulting from changes in perceptual sensitivity rather than in learning ability. In general, evaluation of developmental differences in task performance should always consider the possible contributions of differences in sensitivity to both task relevant and irrelevant cues. In this regard, it is interesting but puzzling that studies comparing young and adult animals on stimulus generalization, which can be regarded as a test for stimulus control, show less stimulus control, that is greater generalization, in older animals (Frieman *et al.*, 1969; Frieman *et al.*, 1970; Rohrbaugh & Riccio, 1968). Although a more recent study of auditory frequency generalization in the chick by Ruble and Rosenthal (1975) presents compelling evidence demonstrating greater generalization in the 1-day-old chick than in the 10-day-old chick.

Given the capacity to discriminate the relevant stimuli, the literature indicates that young and adult rats will learn discriminative contingencies at the same rate, whether in the context of avoidance tasks, for example, avoid shock only by moving to a lit rather than an unlit compartment (Dye, 1969; Thompson, 1957) or in the context of appetitive tasks (Campbell, Jaynes, & Misanin, 1968; D'Amato & Jagoda, 1960; Fields, 1953; Kay & Sime, 1962). However, even if rate of discrimination learning is the same across developmental levels, there could be differences in *how* the discrimination is learned. For example, on generalization tests two-week-old puppies showed no evidence of control by the negative stimulus of a previously learned tactile discrimination (Bacon, 1971). Paré (1969) found that during acquisition of a discriminated CER older animals generalized more from CS^+ to CS^- than younger animals.

Overall, then, while discriminative abilities develop with age, there is considerable evidence that young animals are not particularly deficient in ability to learn the discriminative contingencies imposed by various tasks. However, the degree and/or nature of discriminative control may differ at different ages, although the data in this regard are scanty.

Passive avoidance and delayed responding.   In passive avoidance, animals must learn *not* to make a particular response in order to avoid an aversive stimulus. Experiments have consistently found this problem to be significantly more difficult for the young rat (10–25 days of age) than for the mature animal (Brunner, 1969; Feigley & Spear, 1970; Riccio & Marrazo, 1972; Riccio, Rohrbaugh, & Hodges, 1968; Riccio & Schulenberg, 1969; Schulenberg, Riccio, & Stikes, 1971). In the delayed response task, the animal is shown the location of a reward that is then hidden for a given amount of time before the animal is permitted to seek it. Successful performance on this task (correctly "remembering" the reward location) is generally thought to require the animal to cease normal activity and orient itself toward the reward location throughout the delay. The length of the delay that can be tolerated has been found to increase markedly over the early months of life in both monkeys (Harlow *et al.,* 1960) and in dogs (Fox, 1971).

Since both passive avoidance and delayed responding apparently require the animal to refrain from responding, the observed performance deficits of the young animal in these tasks have been taken to support the long-standing view that immature organisms are deficient in ability to inhibit behavior. Campbell and Coulter (1976) have evaluated this interpretation of the passive avoidance and delayed response data in some detail and conclude that the supporting evidence is not particularly compelling. Briefly, they note that inhibitory deficits are in fact not always seen in young organisms (Fox, 1971; Grote & Brown,

1971; Lipsitt, 1971) and that the few existing measures of passive avoidance and delayed response in the same species do not show positive correlation (Doty, 1966; Fox, 1971).

Another explanation sometimes applied to the passive avoidance and delayed response studies is that younger organisms bring to the task a strong tendency to make the to-be-inhibited response. Thus, Moorcroft, Lytle and Campbell (1971) have shown that young rats are dramatically more active than adults at the ages when they also show marked deficits in passive avoidance. However, pretests of crossing between the two compartments of the passive avoidance apparatus have not found differences between young and adult animals (e.g., Riccio *et al.,* 1968).

Still another explanation for passive avoidance deficits in young animals is that they may be truly deficient in ability to learn an association between their behavior and consequent punishment. This hypothesis is suggested by comparison of passive avoidance and spatial avoidance which, as we have seen, is readily learned by the young animal. The essential difference between these procedures is not the required response (in each case the animal must avoid a particular compartment) but the contingency that must be learned. Spatial avoidance imposes a stimulus contingency, i.e., a particular location is associated with an aversive stimulus, while in passive avoidance the animal must learn that a particular response results in punishment. In this regard, it is notable that the two studies which failed to find deficits in passive avoidance by young animals (Fox, 1971; Grote & Brown, 1971) are open to interpretation in terms of stimulus-contingency learning (Campbell & Coulter, 1976).

In a study relevant to this issue, Riccio and Marrazo (1972) examined the effects of delaying onset of the punishing stimulus during passive avoidance learning by young (18–20-day-old) and adult rats. They found that as the delay between entering the unsafe compartment and shock increased, adult performance declined as would be expected (Kamin, 1959) but the performance of the younger animals did not. In fact, there was some indication that increasing delays facilitated avoidance learning by the pups. Note that with increases in the interval between running into the unsafe compartment and shock, the task becomes increasingly like that of spatial avoidance. The implication is that young animals may not have learned the response–punishment contingency, but rather may have solved the problem as a stimulus contingent task, at least at the longer delay.

To sum up this section, young animals find passive avoidance considerably more difficult than do adults, and it is possible that this difference reflects a true developmental difference in ability to learn response–punishment contingencies. There is also some evidence that young organisms are quite limited in delayed response ability relative to adults, but no compelling explanation of this difference has appeared.

Ontogeny of learning: Recapitulation. As our review progressed through tasks of increasing complexity we were more likely to encounter evidence of developmental differences in learning. But it should be pointed out that increasing complexity usually increases the perceptual—motor demands of the task and makes more difficult the control of task-related variables such as motivation. Therefore, the meaning of reported age differences in "learning" within complex tasks is not always clear, and as we have seen, simple changes in task parameters may be sufficient to eliminate such differences.

Thus, the major conclusion we draw from the existing data is that where the contingencies and task requirements are relatively easy to specify, young organisms seem to show no difficulty in learning, except possibly those contingencies involving punishment. As long as the perceptual—motor requirements are appropriate to the age level studied, there seems to be no major underlying deficit in the ability of young organisms to learn these simple but fundamental tasks.

MEMORY AND DEVELOPMENT

Our concern in this section is with the relative permanance of early versus later learning; more specifically, our focus will be developmental studies of long-term memory for the types of learning we have considered to this point.

Neonatal Studies

The ontogeny of memory is clearly a neglected area of study. To our knowledge there are no experiments on long-term retention in human infants, and the few neonatal studies with animals are at best suggestive.

Mason and Harlow (1958a) gave monkeys tone—shock pairings for 30 days starting on the 3rd day of life. The monkeys were then trained to approach food in a runway for 12 days, during the last 6 days of which the tone was presented and found to have no effect on approach behavior. The following day the monkeys were tested for retention of the CS in the original training situation and showed no memory of conditioning. It is possible, of course, that the lack of response to the CS on the retention test could be due to extinction resulting from tone presentations during runway training. Green (1962) found that although young monkeys acquire responses to the CS as well as older monkeys, they do extinguish more rapidly. Green also found poorer retention by the youngest age group, but again after much experience with the tone alone.

Juvenile Studies

Escape and approach. An important consideration in developmental study of retention is to insure that the animal is still immature when the acquisition period ends, a condition that generally has not obtained in studies of simple approach and escape learning (Crockett & Nobel, 1963; Goodrich, 1968; Stone, 1929a, b). This criterion can best be met if the task can be learned rapidly, as with escape training. Two such studies have been reported. Smith (1968) trained 25- and 100-day-old rats to escape shock to a common criterion, using only 3 days of training, and then measured relearning of the task 75 days later. While the 2 groups did not differ on initial acquisition, the young rats took significantly more trials to relearn. Extending this study to younger animals and to shorter retention intervals, Campbell, Misanin, White, and Lytle (1974) trained rat pups to escape shock at 15-, 17-, 20-, 25-, and 35-days of age. Again, they found that after a 7- or 14-day delay, the three youngest age groups remembered much less than the older animals.

Stimulus-contingent tasks. Campbell and Campbell (1962) conditioned spatial avoidance in 5 groups of rats ranging in age from 18 to 100 days and then tested independent groups immediately after training or 7, 21, or 42 days later. Animals trained when over 30 days of age avoided the compartment in which they were shocked regardless of when tested, whereas animals trained at 18 to 23 days of age showed increasingly less avoidance the longer the retention interval. At the longest interval neither of the two youngest age groups showed any memory of original conditioning.

With a CER procedure, Campbell and Campbell (1962) also found that rats trained at 25 days of age showed less lick suppression after a 42-day delay than did rats trained as adults; however, the retention loss was considerably less than that observed with spatial avoidance. Following this up, Coulter, Collier and Campbell (1976) found that pups given tone–shock pairings as young as 17–19 days showed no loss of suppression 42 days after conditioning; however, rats conditioned at 14–16 days of age showed rapid forgetting of the CER. Even with suppression at asymptote 5 days after these young pups are conditioned, 28 days after the last tone–shock pairing CER is completely forgotten. Similarly, Alberts (1974) found excellent retention of a conditioned taste aversion after 28 and 56 days by rats conditioned at 18 days of age, but there was rapid forgetting of the aversion if conditioning took place at 10 days of age. Somewhat less rapid forgetting was observed in a group conditioned at 12 days of age, and there was virtually no forgetting by those conditioned at 15 days of age.

Thus, with stimulus-contingent tasks, an interesting pattern of results can be seen. Young animals are consistently shown to remember less well than older animals, but only when trained at much younger ages than that required to demonstrate retention losses of response–reinforcement contingencies. It would appear that as the task becomes simpler, susceptibility to forgetting can be observed only if animals are trained at increasingly younger ages.

Active avoidance and discrimination. In the first ontogenetic study of long-term retention of active avoidance, Kirby (1963) trained rats to make a runway response at 25, 50, or 100 days of age and then tested retention 1, 25, or 50 days later. Just as was described with escape learning, the youngest age group again remembered least well 25 or 50 days after training.

With the same age groups and retention intervals, Thompson, Koenigsberg, and Tennison (1965) tried to compensate for changes in the perceived size of the environment brought about by growth by increasing the size of the apparatus for the two youngest age groups when testing for retention. The outcome was inconclusive, however, since under these conditions the task was forgotten by all age groups. Feigley and Spear (1970) also increased the size of their apparatus when testing the retention of rats trained 25 days earlier at 23 or 100 days of age, and found that the younger rats still forgot more than the adults. But this result is clouded by the fact that with the same age groups and apparatus, but without changing apparatus size during the retention test, Parsons and Spear (1972) failed to obtain age differences in retention.

Studies involving retention of discrimination are also marked by complications. Doty (1968) found that with an avoidance task where rats were required to learn a brightness discrimination, pups trained at 23 days of age showed better retention than adults when relearning the task 60 days later. But this effect occurred only if rats had been exposed to extensive handling prior to training, a condition that could have improved the learning skills rather than the memory of the younger animals. Without such handling, retention by the younger animals was significantly poorer than that of adults. Fox (1971), also working with a brightness discrimination task, found that puppies ranging in age from 5 to 16 weeks when originally trained all relearned the task at the same rate; however, the puppies were explicitly extinguished during the retention interval, which could have eliminated any possible memory effects. When testing solely for the retention of a brightness discrimination task, Campbell, Jaynes and Misanin (1968) did observe marked forgetting by rats trained at 23−26 days of age whereas excellent retention was obtained in rats trained as adults.

In sum, then, with active avoidance, greater retention losses have been reported for animals trained when young than when trained as adults, although the results have not been as consistent as those reported for the tasks considered earlier. It should be noted, however, that the active avoidance studies described have all examined the retention of rats trained at well over 20 days of age. Since active avoidance is learned with relative ease, consistent forgetting would be expected only in animals trained at younger ages than so far studied. Interestingly, for the relatively difficult discrimination tasks, substantial retention losses have been observed even in rats trained at 30 days of age.

Passive avoidance. The research here has consistently found poorer retention of punished responses by young animals than by adults. Campbell *et al.* (1974) punished 16-, 20-, 25-, and 100-day-old rats when they stepped into the dark compartment of a two-compartment apparatus. Retention, as measured by latency to enter the black compartment, was tested either immediately, or 1, 7, or 21 days later. Adults consistently showed greater retention than the younger animals who showed virtually no memory of the task after 21 days. In similar step-through passive avoidance tasks employing three different shock intensities (Feigley & Spear, 1970) or different durations of shock (Schulenburg, Riccio, & Stikes, 1971) the long-term retention of younger rats was again found to be poorer than that of adults regardless of the strength or duration of punishment. Fox (1971) gave passive avoidance training to 3 groups of puppies ranging in age from 5 to 13 weeks by administering punishment for approach to a passive human observer. After 7 or 14 days, the youngest group showed virtually no memory of the original training while the older two groups showed no forgetting.

We earlier made the point that in order to convincingly establish that retention deficits in young organisms are independent of learning deficiencies, it is important that developmental studies of retention use tasks that are as easily learned by young animals as by adults. Since, as we discussed earlier, young animals have greater difficulty learning passive avoidance than adults, passive avoidance retention studies appear to violate this dictum. However, it should be pointed out that in the retention studies described, young animals were always trained to the same criterion as adults, that the size of the retention deficits reported is far out of proportion to the size of the original learning deficit, and that in at least one instance (Fox, 1971) the younger animals actually learned the task more rapidly than the older animals yet the same pattern of forgetting was observed. Thus, passive avoidance studies, if considered along with studies of tasks in which there are no apparent age differences in learning, provide additional evidence of memory deficits in immature organisms.

Ontogeny of memory: Recapitulation. There is clearly an urgent need to study the long-term retention of young animals over a wider range of species than represented in the literature. Nonetheless, the existing data, largely with juvenile rats, are strikingly consistent in demonstrating that young organisms remember less well than do adults. This relation has been observed in a variety of tasks including passive avoidance, active avoidance, escape, spatial avoidance, CER, and taste aversion. In general, the overall data strongly suggest that long-term memory for the events of infancy is either poor or nonexistent.

DETERMINANTS OF THE DEVELOPMENTAL
CHANGES IN LONG-TERM MEMORY

The data reviewed above have shown that young animals of a number of species are deficient in long-term memory and that this memory impairment appears to be independent of the animals' ability to learn. Apart from the inherent interest in this phenomenon as one with which we are all familiar, often described as infantile amnesia, it provides a scientific challenge, the solution of which may yield significant insights into the basic mechanisms of memory storage and retrieval.

We have arbitrarily categorized the processes known to influence memory storage and retrieval as "psychological" and "neurological." The two categories are clearly not mutually exclusive since both undoubtedly underlie each other and interact as they contribute to any behavioral phenomenon. At this stage of scientific evolution the relative contribution of these two kinds of processes to the poor memory of infancy is not understood. We shall describe below what little is known about the determinants of this phenomenon and speculate about the possible mechanisms that may underlie it.

Psychological Processes

These processes are dependent upon an organism's interaction with its external environment and can be viewed as resulting from "experience." They can be observed at any age but may be aggravated by the events which occur during development.

Retroactive and proactive interference. The retention of a response is known to be impaired by other responses which are acquired either before (proactive interference) or after (retroactive interference) the response in question is learned. The extent of interference depends upon many conditions including the similarity of the responses learned, the setting in which they were acquired, and the frequency with which they were experienced.

The question is a simple but unanswered one in the context of developmental psychology. How much do retroactive and proactive interference contribute to the basic phenomenon of poorer memory in infancy? The simplest model of proactive interference predicts that older animals will forget more rapidly because they have lived longer with a correspondingly higher probability of having previously learned responses which might interfere with retention of more recently learned responses. As the data reviewed above indicate, this prediction is contrary to fact.

Retroactive interference seems to be a somewhat more viable candidate than proactive interference as the basis for the rapid forgetting of infancy. The young of all species have to learn a great deal about the spatial–perceptual–social characteristics of their environment. The more they interact with stimuli in different ways and under varying conditions, the more they learn. In contrast, one could argue that older individuals, inactive and maintained in a familiar environment, learn less than their younger counterparts. It follows from this analysis that interference from learning occurring during the retention interval is likely to be higher in young than in adult animals.

In the only experimental test of this hypothesis, Parsons and Spear (1972) showed that housing infant and adult rats in enriched environments during a 60-day retention interval accelerated forgetting relative to animals housed in isolation. However, the younger rats were no more susceptible to retroactive interference than adults. This simple model is no more compelling at the human level. It is difficult to understand how it could predict either the quantitative or qualitative features of the poor memory of infancy. An enormous amount of learning occurs during all stages of development from infancy through adolescence. Memories for all of one's childhood should be interfered with and not just the first few years of life. One would also predict that as adult development progresses the continued learning would gradually erode all recollection of one's early life. On the basis of information currently available, it is impossible to single out any one stage of the complex human developmental sequence as responsible for more retroactive interference than another.

Some of the most compelling evidence that retroactive interference is a general degrader of memory comes from the literature on amnesic patients suffering from consolidation deficits. In reports of the classic case of H. M. (see Milner, Corkin & Teuber, 1968; Scoville & Milner, 1957), a patient who has shown little or no consolidation of new learning for over 14 postoperative years, it appears that he has a clearer recollection of the events of 20 years ago than do most normal adults of his age and intellectual capacity. Although it seems reasonable to assume that the continued acquisition of new knowledge would interfere with our memories of the past, there is no apparent reason why this new knowledge should interfere with memories of early childhood more than any other period.

Stimulus generalization and response differentiation. Stimulus events, by definition, are never reproduced exactly. Performance on each successive trial in a learning task is determined not only by the strength of the acquired response but also by the perceived similarity of the ongoing trial to previous trials. Presumably little stimulus generalization decrement occurs from trial to trial, even over long retention intervals in well-trained adult animals. However, in young animals growth-induced changes in body size and physiological makeup could substantially change the perception of the test environment resulting in significant performance decrements.

By far the most common assumption is that an age-induced stimulus generalization decrement occurs because of changes in the perceived size of the environment. For example, a young rat may perceive a maze as a great cavern from which escape requires a massive effort. On retest after a retention interval, the same maze may appear quite different. Both the visual angles from which the apparatus is viewed and the size of the apparatus, relative to the size of the animal, have changed. Similarly, the child's view of the world changes. At first it is populated by giants and distinguished by spots of gum underneath table tops.

Later it becomes the adult world we all know. This hypothesis is so intuitively appealing that some psychologists have considered it the major factor underlying the poor memory of infancy. Perkins (1965), for example, in references to Campbell and Campbell's (1962) report showing poor retention of fear in infant rats, states that, "The stimulus situation to which fear was learned may be altered so much by stimulus changes resulting from growth that there is a nearly complete generalization decrement resulting from maturation-induced stimulus changes [pp. 46–47]."

Just as perceptual changes may occur as a result of physical growth, so too may response patterns change. If the original response required precise movements, exact replication of these movements when the child or animal was older and physically larger would be inappropriate. A 10-year-old child might well find it impossible to ride a tricycle with the same response patterns that were necessary at age 3.

One cannot deny the importance of both stimulus generalization and response differentiation in those situations where original learning depended upon environmental parameters such as size, location, or distance. These factors must indeed be important in many studies, both in the original task and in the retention test. However, forgetting of tasks which have depended largely upon auditory, gustatory or visual stimuli such as brightness has been demonstrated consistently. It is difficult to see how these stimulus dimensions could be affected merely by physical growth. We also have noted instances where performance did not depend upon the memory of specific molecular responses. Avoidance, for example, can be performed in whatever manner is appropriate to the age. It in fact should occur automatically if the significance of the stimulus is retained. The forgetting is not selective. It does not occur only for spatially defined responses. The kind of memory failure we are interested in seems to occur for all kinds of responses over all kinds of stimulus parameters.

Even if physical growth is a critical source of forgetting, and under certain circumstances it might well be, it seems unlikely that its effects should be restricted to a single developmental period, infancy. Children continue to grow beyond age 7. Rats continue to grow beyond 30 days of age. Just as we noted the possible effects of retroactive interference, one can hardly completely explain a memory deficit confined to one period of development by such general processes as stimulus generalization and response differentiation.

Emerging unlearned responses. Many drastic changes take place in an animal's behavioral repertoire during the normal course of development. Some of these changes are learned, some are contingent upon changes in physical capability, some are preprogrammed in unknown ways such that they emerge at a particular stage when the proper stimulus appears, and still others are hormonally dependent. Male preweanling rats respond to the dam by rooting and suckling; at sexual maturity the same rat responds to the same female by copulating. Pain produces withdrawal and flight in the young animal and attack in the adult (Hutchinson, Ulrich, & Azrin, 1965), and unfamiliar environments may elicit more fear in older animals (Candland & Campbell, 1962; Sluckin, 1965). These age-related modifications of behavior could act to either permanently or temporarily interfere with the performance of a previously learned response.

There must be many situations in which an emerging unlearned response takes precedence over a previously learned response. The extent of this interference is undoubtedly proportional to the animal's repertoire of unlearned behaviors and is thus unlikely to be a major source of forgetting in man.

Changes in information-processing mechanisms. Just as emerging unlearned responses may interfere with previously learned responses, changes in mode or style of information processing may also interfere with the retrieval of previously learned material. In man, enormous changes take place in the way in which sensory information is processed. The most obvious changes occur in the use of language. To a preverbal child, a book is simply another object of his environment; later the object is verbally labeled as "book"; still later it is responded to by reading the title, either overtly or covertly; and finally the title evokes a variety of emotional or evaluative responses ranging from interest to aversion.

What effect do such changes have on memory? Are our early memories less accessible because the kind of information upon which they depend is processed differently now? This is a compelling possibility because the greatest changes in information processing and the transition between complete amnesia and the beginnings of recall for childhood events both occur in the immediate preschool and early school years. Language and the development of other cognitive skills must play a role in what is remembered about one's childhood. However, it is clear that animals which do not pass through such an obvious transition also show poor infantile memories.

Obviously, both the immaturity of the central nervous system and changes in information-processing mechanisms may play important roles in the ontogeny of memory. Early in development neurological factors may play the more significant role while later in development, particularly in man, altered modes of information processing may be the dominant factor.

Neurological Processes: General Considerations

Emergence of long-term memory. Before specifically considering neurological processes that may contribute to the poor memory of infancy, it may be useful to summarize the time course of memory development. In the rat, emergence of memory is not an all-or-none phenomenon. Although we did not emphasize the point earlier in this chapter, long-term memory for different tasks seems to develop at different times. Based on the experiments reviewed above, both from our laboratory and others, it seems that the development of long-term memory is complete for some tasks as early as 15 days (for example, learned aversions) and as late as 30 to 40 days for others (for example, passive avoidance). Development of long-term memory for other tasks appears to reach adult levels within these rather broad limits, and in no particular sequence.

The left panel of Figure 1 shows the rate of memory development for learned aversions and passive avoidance in the rat. The functions are hypothetical, but they do depict, within reasonable limits, the rate of the development of long-term memory for these two types of tasks. The origins, asymptotes and slopes of the curves are based upon the experiments reviewed above. Further research is needed to clarify the basis for the differential development of memory for these two tasks and to determine whether or not meaningful differences exist for other types of tests.

The absence of experimental data for man leaves the question of rate of memory development even more uncertain than in the rat. Child development psychologists have not yet studied memory over long time intervals. Our best estimates come from retrospective studies of early childhood memories. In the most quantitative of these studies Waldfogel (1948) determined the number of events recalled by college students at different childhood years. These data are shown in the right panel of Figure 1. What is clearly shown in these data is that college students are totally incapable of recalling anything from their infancy and early childhood. Even for age 8 only an average of 16 events are recalled,

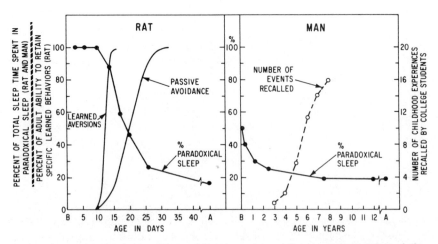

FIG. 1 Comparison of the emergence of long-term memory in rat and man with one index of central nervous maturity: percentage of total sleep time spent in paradoxical sleep. (The paradoxical sleep data are from Jouvet-Mounier et al. (1970) for rat and adopted from Roffwarg, et al. (1966) for man. The number of events recalled by college students of their early childhood is from Waldfogel (1948) and the theoretical functions describing development of memory in the rat are derived from research described in the text.)

suggesting that the clarity of recall continues to increase through the early school years. Asking any 50-year-old about his college days will demonstrate that this increased clarity of memory is a true developmental phenomenon and not a function of the decreasing retention interval.

We cannot overemphasize the differences between these indices of long-term memory in man and those used to study memory in the developing rat. The human is asked to recall events of early childhood in the absence of any stimuli associated with that era. The rat, on the other hand, is returned to a highly distinctive setting and asked to reproduce a specific response. If these same procedures were used with man it seems quite likely that evidence for long-term memory would appear much earlier. What we are certain of, however, is that long-term memory in man increases enormously during the course of onto-genesis.

General relationship of neural maturation to long-term memory. Both rat and man are born with immature central nervous systems, and both are deficient in long-term memory in infancy. As we have seen, psychological processes alone do not appear to be able to account for this memory deficit. That some degree of central nervous system maturity is necessary for the complex processes of memory storage and retrieval is self-evident. The embryonic neural tube is simply not capable of "learning," at least in the way in which we characterize that process in the adult. The issue is to determine the extent to which the memory deficit of infancy is due to neural immaturity. As we have seen, most young mammals pass through a stage in which their ability to learn approximates that of the adult, yet their long-term memory is markedly inferior.

In the rat, the ontogenetic period associated with poor long-term memory parallels a period of rapid central nervous system development (Campbell & Spear, 1972). However, this close correlation does not necessarily imply a causal relationship. This period is also marked by dramatic changes in the animals' behavior which could impair retention through psychological processes like those described earlier.

The strongest experimental support for the importance of general neural maturation as a critical substrate for the development of long-term memory comes from a recent study comparing neonatal rats and guinea pig (Campbell *et al.*, 1974). Both are rodents, and both have similar histories of breeding for laboratory use. They differ, however, in one critical dimension: maturity of the central nervous system at parturition. The guinea pig has a 65-day gestation period and is born with an almost fully developed central nervous system. Myelination is nearly complete, neural transmitters approximate adult levels, cellular differentiation is advanced, and cerebral electrical activity is similar to that of the adult. The rat, on the other hand, has a 21-day gestation period and its brain at birth is extremely underdeveloped. It is not until the rat is 20–30 days postpartum that the development of its central nervous system approxi-mates that of the newborn guinea pig.

Behaviorally, of course, both animals are naive at birth. Both will learn a great deal about its environment in the first few months of life. The psychological variables described above have the opportunity to impair the memory of infancy in both species. Yet when memory for tasks learned equally easily by young and adults of both species is determined, only the rat shows rapid forgetting. The guinea pig's capacity for long-term memory appears to be fully developed at birth while the rat's is not. Because of the similarity in the experiences both undergo during the course of development, it seems likely that the rapid forgetting shown by the neonatal rat is due primarily to immaturity of its central nervous system.

General mechanisms of neural maturation that may underlie long-term memory deficits. Neural growth not only leads to the development of an organism's full adult intellectual capabilities, but it may also obliterate or obscure many of the organism's prior memories. There are a variety of ways neural maturation might impair long-term memory and leave learning ability relatively unaffected. We briefly discuss some of the more compelling possibilities.

First, one might assume, in the tradition of Hughlings Jackson (Taylor, 1931, 1932), that learning in the young animal is mediated by earlier maturing brain centers that become subordinate to later maturing structures as development proceeds. Inferential support for this possibility comes from the well-documented fact that many reflexes disappear during the normal course of development but reappear following cortical injury or senile brain disease. The suckling and rooting reflexes of infancy, for example, are actively inhibited by the functional maturation of the cortex, but they reappear following cortical damage. It seems reasonable to postulate a similar developmental pattern for the disappearance of memories acquired in infancy.

Unfortunately the human clinical literature on this question is incomplete and ambiguous. There are many descriptions of behavioral regression in senile brain disease, but there is no compelling evidence for the reappearance of childhood memories. Cerebral injury in childhood often induces regression to a lower level of functioning (as from fifth grade to first grade), but again it is not apparent that there is a corresponding reappearance of memories previously associated with the earlier period of development (Blau, 1936).

The evidence from animal experimentation is no better. There are simply no reports showing that behaviors acquired early in development but subsequently forgotten reappear following cerebral insult. A study showing that a specific response acquired in infancy and forgotten during the normal course of development could be reinstated by one or more types of CNS dysfunction would be particularly valuable.

This line of reasoning can be applied to intrastructural development as well as to the sequential development of major cerebral structures. The neurons of the cerebral cortex, for example, begin as primitive undifferentiated cells without synaptic junctions. As development proceeds the dendritic and axonal structures become increasingly complex and the number of synaptic junctions increases astronomically. As Marcus Jacobson (1970) puts it, "Why are the memories of infancy beyond recall? Are they obliterated by the growth of dendrites and development of synapses that occur in the cerebral cortex during the first years after birth? [p. 344]" Intuitively this is probably the most intriguing neural explanation of the memory deficit of young animals. Unfortunately there is no evidence whatsoever to support this possibility.

A second possibility is that cerebral development may influence retrieval of childhood memories as a result of the striking change in the rate at which sensory—motor information can be processed. Conduction velocity in the immature, unmyelinated axon is markedly slower than in the adult (Purpura et al., 1964). In addition, the refractory period of immature cells is much longer (Scherrer, 1968). As a result, the central nervous system of the young animal potentially processes much less information per unit time than that of the adult.

If the immature central nervous system can process only limited amounts of information, then the amount of information encoded in a stimulus sequence preceding a criterion response is necessarily less in infancy than adulthood. Consequently, when an animal is tested for retention after a period during which neurological growth has occurred, the amount of information processed per unit time in the test environment would be greater than it was during original learning. Such changes could conceivably underlie generalization decrements leading to poorer performance. Changes in speed of transmission could also directly produce generalization decrements. For example, proprioceptive feedback would be more rapid in the adult than in the young rat.

A third possibility is that specific neural structures underlying the memory consolidation process are late in maturing. Considerable evidence suggests that some aspects of memory consolidation may span very long time periods. In man, retrograde amnesia resulting from cerebral insult can extend backwards in time for months or even years. Within the central nervous system, consolidation has been most often associated with the limbic system. In man surgical resection of the hippocampus and alcohol-induced damage of the mammillary bodies (Korsakoff's syndrome) both produce severe anterograde amnesia. Ontogenetically, limbic system structures may mature relatively slowly (Altman, 1967) giving some support to the possibility that long-term consolidation may be impaired in young mammals.

There are, of course, many other aspects of neural development that could underlie the long-term memory deficits of immature animals. Our purpose here has been to focus attention on the strong possibility that developmental changes in the central nervous system could underlie such deficits. In the next section we look more closely at the correlation between specific indices of neural maturation and the emergence of long-term memory.

Neurological Processes: Specific Indices of Neural Maturation
and the Emergence of Long-term Memory in Rat and Man

Since the potential exists for neural development to play a significant role in
memory development, it seems appropriate to look for correlations between
specific indices of neural maturation and the emergence of long-term memory in
rat and man. Aside from the usual hazards associated with a correlational
analysis, this analysis is complicated by the fact that little has been empirically
established about the locus or necessary substrates of memory storage. Thus, we
will not be able to examine the development of specific brain regions or
pathways. All we can do at the present time is to examine the overall maturation
of rat and human brain and look for some relationship between the emergence
of long-term memory and cerebral development in the two species. It is hoped
that such an analysis will be of heuristic value to the much needed additional
research.

Synaptic development. Whatever else the mechanisms of memory storage and
retrieval are finally shown to be, the synapse will certainly be an essential
component of the process. The synapse has already been shown to be the locus
of habituation in at least some preparations (see Castellucci & Kandel; Thompson & Glanzman in this volume). Thus, the appearance and functional maturation of synaptic junctions should be a significant index of the ability of any area
of the central nervous system to store and encode information.

Recently developed electron microscopic techniques allow the visualization
and counting of the number of synaptic junctions per unit volume of tissue
(Bloom & Aghajanian, 1966). Unfortunately there are very few comparative
studies using this direct method. In one study in rats, Aghajanian and Bloom
(1967) estimated the number of synaptic clefts in the molecular layer of the
parietal cortex as a function of age. The number of synaptic junctions increases
rapidly beginning at 10 days of age and reaches adult levels around 30 days of
age. It seems reasonable to assume that a similar pattern of development would
be found in other brain regions and other mammals, but at different rates
postnatally. Spinal cord and brainstem structures, for example, surely complete
synaptic development long before the cortex, although there is no direct data on
this point.

Although comparative studies using electron microscopic techniques are not
available, there are numerous studies using Golgi stains of development cortical
cells in both rat and man. The Golgi, light microscopic techniques provide an
estimate of synaptogenesis from the development of dendrites. Eayrs and Goodhead (1959) studied the development of pyramidal cells in the ganglionic layer
(layer V) of the rat cerebral cortex using a Golgi–Cox stain. They found that
dendritic arborization increased rapidly between 10 and 30 days of age. At birth
the pyramidal cells of the cortex are small and densely packed, the cortical
layers are not yet differentiated, and there are few visible dendrites either apical

or basal. Dendritic arborization becomes increasingly complex until it approximates the adult structure by around 30 days of age. In addition, Eayrs and Goodhead attempted to estimate the number of synaptic junctions present at different ages by counting the number of times dendrites of a given cell appeared to make axonal contact. Their findings are remarkably similar to those obtained by Aghajanian and Bloom in the molecular layer with the electron microscope. Even though these two layers probably mature at different rates in the rat as they do in man (Schadé & Van Groeningen, 1961), and the tissue samples were taken from somewhat different areas within the parietal cortex, the overall correspondence between electron microscopic and Golgi stain estimates of synaptogenesis suggest that dendritic arborization is a reasonable predictor of number of synaptic junctions present at different developmental ages.

The maturation of the human pryamidal cell, based on numerous Golgi–Cox studies, proceeds in a fashion not unlike that in the rat. It is, however, somewhat more developed at birth and its time course of development is much slower than in the rat (Schadé & Van Groeningen, 1961; Conel, 1939). Cells in cortical layer III are considerably less developed at birth than those in layer V, but 2 years of age cells from both layers approximate adult structure. Conel (1939) reports that dendritic growth in most cortical regions continues slowly for at least another 4 or 5 years. Undoubtedly, this continued dendritic growth is accompanied by continued synaptic formation, but the rate of synaptogenesis is unknown.

The relationship of dendritic arborization (and by implication synaptic development) to the emergence of long-term memory in rat and man is ambiguous. The available evidence suggests that the human brain at 2–4 years of age is at approximately the same level of neural development as the rat brain at 25–30 days of age. However, while long-term memory appears to reach adult levels by 30–40 days of age in the rat, it continues to develop at least through the early school years in man. It is possible, however, that the slow and subtle changes in dendritic structure occurring after age 4 (Conel, 1939) play a critical role in the complex forms of human memory.

Myelination. Flechsig (1896) was the first to observe that myelin was either absent or grossly deficient in neonatal mammals. In general, myelination proceeds developmentally in a caudocranial order, first appearing in the spinal cord, then in the medulla, pons, and midbrain, and finally in the telencephalon. The cerebral cortex also myelinates sequentially starting at the projection centers and ending at the association centers (Jacobson, 1963).

In the rat, the first evidence of myelination appears at about 2 days of age in the ventral spinal roots. It is not until about the tenth postnatal day that myelin begins to appear in the cerebrum. Thalamic fibers begin to myelinate between 10 and 12 days and are not fully myelinated until 40–50 days postnatally. Myelination does not begin in many regions of the cortex until 21 days and is not complete until the rat is approximately 60 days of age (Jacobson, 1963). The period of most rapid myelination occurs between 30 and 40 days following birth (Bass, Netsky & Young, 1969).

In man, myelination follows a similar course. However, as we noted for dendritic development, the human brain is more mature at birth than the rat brain, as indexed by the extent of myelination, and the time course of myelination is slower than in the rat. The ventral roots are fully myelinated at birth and there is evidence of myelin throughout the brainstem. By the end of the second year the infant brain is extensively myelinated except for the nonspecific thalamic radiations, cerebral commissures, and the cortex. Myelination in these regions continues slowly throughout the first decade and continues in the cortical association areas until the third or fourth decade of life (Yakovlev & Lecours, 1967).

Little correlation emerges between this index of central nervous system maturation and the development of memory in rat and man. Long-term memory in both species appears to be fully developed well before myelination is complete.

Development of spontaneous electrocortical activity.   Changes in spontaneous cortical electrical activity during development have been intensively studied for many years. Such changes undoubtedly reflect the general maturation of neural structure and function. In addition, changes in the electroencephalogram may be a general index of subtle changes in neural function that are difficult to detect with strictly morphological techniques.

In the rat, there is little or no spontaneous electrocortical activity for the first 6 to 7 postnatal days. Changes in both frequency and amplitude develop slowly from approximately the seventh to the twelfth postnatal day. Rapid development then begins and continues through 20–25 days of age (Deza & Eidelberg, 1967). The adult pattern of spontaneous electrocortical activity is attained by 30 days of age.

In man, this index again suggests a more mature central nervous system at birth than is found in the rat. The newborn shows continuous spontaneous electrocortical activity, with low frequency components predominating. There is a shift to higher frequency components as development proceeds, with the most dramatic changes occurring during the first three years of life. However, changes continue at a much reduced rate until early adolescence (Eichorn, 1970).

The development of spontaneous electrocortical activity as an index of general neural maturation shows a relatively close correlation with the development of long-term memory. In the rat, both memory and electrocortical activity reach adult levels between 30 and 40 days of age. The correlation for man is also good if we assume that long-term memory continues to improve up to early adolescence.

Development of sleep patterns.   All nonprecocial mammals show dramatic developmental changes in sleep patterns. Not only do newborn mammals sleep more than adults, but they also spend a greater percentage of their total sleep time in paradoxical sleep. As development proceeds, the percentage of paradoxical decreases while the percentage of slow wave sleep increases. By adulthood a much higher percentage of sleep time is spent in slow wave sleep than in paradoxical sleep. This developmental change in sleep patterns is thought to reflect the caudal to rostral sequence of brain development, with the appearance and dominance of slow wave sleep dependent upon functional maturation of the cerebral cortex (McGinty, 1971; Jouvet-Mounier, Astic, & Lacote, 1970). Thus, the percentage of total sleep time spent in paradoxical sleep is a potentially useful index of central nervous system maturity.

This index of neural maturation is shown in Figure 1 for rat and man. In the rat, as with the other measures of CNS maturation we have described, rapid changes occur between 10 and 25 days of age with relatively little change thereafter (Jouvet-Mounier, et al., 1970). Man shows a much lower percentage of paradoxical sleep at birth than the rat, suggesting once again a more mature neonatal central nervous system. Again the most dramatic changes in man occur during the first 3 years of life followed by a much slower rate of change for the next several years. Unfortunately, the human data upon which Figure 1 is based may have obscured any subtle changes in sleep patterns. The children are grouped over a fairly large age range. For example, the 7.5-year point includes children from 5 to 9 years of age (Roffwarg, Muzio, & Dement, 1966).

The development of sleep patterns as an index of neural maturation, not unlike the development of spontaneous electrocortical activity, shows a compellingly close correlation with the development of long-term memory. In the rat, long-term memory for all laboratory tasks investigated reaches maturity either before or at about the same time that the percentage of sleep time spent in paradoxical sleep declines to adult levels. In man, the ability to recall past events increases rapidly as sleep patterns assume their adult characteristics.

Conclusions

We have not discovered the determinants of the developmental changes in long-term memory from the data reviewed here. However, we do believe that the data force the conclusion that neural maturation, by whatever mechanism, is a major determinant of the poor memory of infancy. The primary support for this conclusion comes from the close correlations between a variety of measures of maturation of the central nervous system and the development of long-term memory in rat, man, and guinea pig. The guinea pig provides particularly compelling evidence since its central nervous system is almost completely mature at birth and it shows an adult capacity for long-term memory from birth. Thus, experiential factors must play a minimal role, at least in infraprimate mammals.

We simply do not know which dimensions of neural maturation are critical for the development of long-term memory in any species. It seems most probable that adult memory capacities derive from the development of an entire spectrum of interacting neural processes rather than from the development of any specific critical component.

OVERVIEW

We have had two major aims in this paper. First, we have tried to show that young animals are deficient in long-term memory and that this memory deficit cannot be accounted for by deficiencies in learning in the immature organism. Second, we have discussed possible mechanisms underlying the development of long-term memory and tried to show that maturation of the central nervous system plays a major role in that development.

Little if any of the data we have considered here dealt directly with habituation. However, if habituation is considered an elementary form of learning many of the same neurological and psychological mechanisms we have discussed may underlie the process. Although habituation often appears to be a relatively short-term process, retention of habituation under some conditions (Leaton, 1974) is prolonged enough to qualify as long-term memory. Those investigators who study habituation in infants or look for developmental changes in habituation may well find the material discussed here of heuristic value.

Very little experimental work has dealt with a developmental sequence for habituation but the possibility of developmental changes has been considered for children (Jeffrey & Cohen, 1971), and some recent data with the rat (Feigley *et al.*, 1972; Parsons, Fagan, & Spear, 1973) suggest a developmental sequence for habituation similar to that discussed here. Obviously, much more experimental work is needed in all species to establish a developmental sequence for habituation. Such research may well provide significant insights into the process of habituation, and the habituation paradigm may well be a particularly useful means of studying the development of memory.

REFERENCES

Aghajanian, G. K., & Bloom, F. E. The formation of synaptic junctions in developing rat brain: A quantitative electron microscopic study. *Brain Research*, 1967, *6*, 716–727.

Alberts, J. R. Ontogency of learned aversions in the rat. Paper presented at the Eastern Psychological Association meetings, Philadelphia, April, 1974.

Altman, J. Postnatal growth and differentiation of the mammalian brain, with implications for a morphological theory of memory. In G. C. Quarton, T. Melnechuk, & F. O. Schmitt (Eds.), *The neurosciences*. New York: Rockefeller University Press, 1967. Pp. 723–743.

Bacon, W. E. Stimulus control of discriminated behavior in neonatal dogs. *Journal of Comparative and Physiological Psychology*, 1971, *76*, 424–433.

Bacon, W. E. Aversive conditioning in neonatal kittens. *Journal of Comparative and Physiological Psychology*, 1973, *83*, 306–313.

Bacon, W. E., & Stanley, W. C. Avoidance learning in neonatal dogs. *Journal of Comparative and Physiological Psychology*, 1970, *70*, 448–452. (a)

Bacon, W. E., & Stanley, W. C. Reversal learning in neonatal dogs. *Journal of Comparative and Physiological Psychology*, 1970, *70*, 344–350. (b)

Bass, N. H., Netsky, M. G., & Young, E. Microchemical studies of postnatal development in rat cerebrum: I. Migration and differentiation of cells. *Neurology*, 1969, *19*, 258–268.

Blau, A. Mental changes following head trauma in children. *Archives of Neurology and Psychiatry*, 1936, *35*, 723–769.

Bloom, F. E., & Aghajanian, G. K. Cytochemistry of synapses: A selective staining method for electron microscopy. *Science*, 1966, *154*, 1575–1577.

Brennan, J. F., & Riccio, D. C. Stimulus control of shuttle avoidance in young and adult rats. *Canadian Journal of Psychology*, 1972, *26*, 361–373.

Brunner, R. L. Age differences in one-trial passive avoidance learning. *Psychonomic Science*, 1969, *14*, 134.

Brunner, R. L., Roth, T. G., & Rossi, R. R. Age differences in the development of the conditioned emotional response. *Psychonomic Science*, 1970, *21*, 135–136.

Caldwell, D. F., & Werboff, J. Classical conditioning in newborn rats. *Science*, 1962, *136*, 1118–1119.

Campbell, B. A., & Campbell, E. H. Retention and extinction of learned fear in infant and adult rats. *Journal of Comparative and Physiological Psychology*, 1962, *55*, 1–8.

Campbell, B. A., & Coulter, X. Ontogeny of learning and memory. In M. Rosenzweig & E. Bennett (Eds.), *Neural mechanisms of learning and memory*. Cambridge, Mass.: MIT Press, 1976.

Campbell, B. A., Jaynes, J., & Misanin, J. R. Retention of a light–dark discrimination in rats of different ages. *Journal of Comparative and Physiological Psychology*, 1968, *66*, 467–472.

Campbell, B. A., Misanin, J. R., White, B. C., & Lytle, L. D. Species differences in ontogeny of memory: Support for neural maturation as a determinant of forgetting. *Journal of Comparative and Physiological Psychology*, 1974, *87*, 193–202.

Campbell, B. A., & Spear, N. E. Ontogeny of memory. *Psychological Review*, 1972, *79*, 215–236.

Candland, D. K., & Campbell, B. A. Development of fear as measured by behavior in the open field. *Journal of Comparative and Physiological Psychology*, 1962, *55*, 593–596.

Conel, J. L. *The postnatal development of the human cerebral cortex* 8 vols. Cambridge, Mass.: Harvard University Press, 1939–1959.

Cornwall, A. C., & Fuller, J. L. Conditioned responses in young puppies. *Journal of Comparative and Physiological Psychology*, 1961, *54*, 13–15.

Coulter, X. Long-term retention of CER: Effects of number of CS–US pairings. Unpublished doctoral dissertation, Princeton University, 1974.

Coulter, X., Collier, A. C., & Campbell, B. A. Long-term retention of early Pavlovian fear conditioning in infant rats. *Journal of Experimental Psychology: Animal Behavior Processes*, 1976, *2*, 48–56.

Crockett, W. H., & Nobel, M. E. Age of learning, severity of negative reinforcement, and retention of learned responses. *Journal of Genetic Psychology*, 1963, *103*, 105–112.

D'Amato, M. R., & Jagoda, H. Age, sex, and rearing conditions as variables in simple brightness discrimination. *Journal of Comparative and Physiological Psychology*, 1960, *53*, 261–263.

Denenberg, V. H., & Kline, N. J. The relationship between age and avoidance learning in the hooded rat. *Journal of Comparative and Physiological Psychology*, 1958, *51*, 488–491.

Denenberg, V. H., & Smith, S. A. Effects of infantile stimulation and age upon behavior. *Journal of Comparative and Physiological Psychology*, 1963, *56*, 307–312.

Deza, L., & Eidleberg, E. Development of cortical electrical activity in the rat. *Experimental Neurology*, 1967, *17*, 425–438.

Doty, B. A. Age differences in avoidance conditioning as a function of distribution of trials and task difficulty. *Journal of Genetic Psychology*, 1966, *109*, 249–254.

Doty, B. A. Effects of handling on learning of rats. *Journal of Gerontology*, 1968, *23*, 142–144.

Doty, B. A., & Doty, L. Effects of age and chlopromazine on memory consolidation. *Journal of Comparative and Physiological Psychology*, 1964, *57*, 331–334.

Dye, C. J. Effects of interruption of initial learning upon retention in young, mature, and old rats. *Journal of Gerontology*, 1969, *24*, 12–17.

Eayrs, J. T., & Goodhead, B. Postnatal development of the cerebral cortex in the rat. *Journal of Anatomy*, 1959, *93*, 385–401.

Eichorn, D. H. Physiological development. In P. H. Mussen (Ed.), *Carmichael's manual of child psychology* (Vol. 1). New York: Wiley, 1970. Pp. 157–283.

Feigley, D. A., Parsons, P. J., Hamilton, L. W., & Spear, N. E. Development of habituation to novel environments in the rat. *Journal of Comparative and Physiological Psychology*, 1972, *79*, 443–452.

Feigley, D. A., & Spear, N. E. Effect of age and punishment condition on long-term retention by the rat of active- and passive-avoidance learning. *Journal of Comparative and Physiological Psychology*, 1970, *73*, 515–526.

Fields, P. E. The age factor in multiple discrimination learning by white rats. *Journal of Comparative and Physiological Psychology*, 1953, *46*, 387–389.

Flechsig, P. *Gehirn & Seele*. Leipzeig, 1896.

Fox, M. *Integrative development of brain and behavior in the dog*. Chicago: University of Chicago Press, 1971.

Frieman, J. P., Frieman, J., Wright, W., & Hegberg, W. Developmental trends in the acquisition and extinction of conditioned suppression in rats. *Developmental Psychology*, 1971, *4*, 425–428.

Frieman, J. P., Rohrbaugh, M., & Riccio, D. A. Age differences in the control of acquired fear by tone. *Canadian Journal of Psychology*, 1969, *23*, 237–244.

Frieman, J. P., Warner, L., & Riccio, D. C. Age differences in conditioning and generalization of fear in young and adult rats. *Developmental Psychology*, 1970, *3*, 119–123.

Fuller, J. L., Easler, C. A., & Banks, E. M. Formation of conditioned avoidance responses in young puppies. *American Journal of Physiology*, 1950, *160*, 462–466.

Goldman, P. S., & Tobach, E. Behavior modification in infant rats. *Animal Behavior*, 1967, *15*, 559–562.

Goodrich, C. L. Learning, retention, and extinction of a complex maze habit for mature, young and senescent Wistar albino rats. *Journal of Gerontology*, 1968, *23*, 298–304.

Green, P. C. Learning, extinction, and generalization of conditioned responses by young monkeys. *Psychological Reports*, 1962, *10*, 731–738.

Grote, Jr., F. W., & Brown, R. T. Rapid learning of passive avoidance by weanling rats: Conditioned taste aversion. *Psychonomic Science*, 1971, *25*, 163–164.

Harlow, H. F. The development of learning in the rhesus monkey. *American Scientist*, 1959, *47*, 458–479.

Harlow, H. F., Harlow, M. K., Rueping, R. R., & Mason, W. A. Performance of infant rhesus monkeys on discrimination learning, delayed response, and reversal learning. *Journal of Comparative and Physiological Psychology*, 1960, *53*, 113–121.

Hutchinson, R. R., Ulrich, R. E., & Azrin, N. H. Effects of age and related factors on the pain–aggression reaction. *Journal of Comparative and Physiological Psychology*, 1965, *59*, 365–369.

Jacobson, M. *Developmental neurology*. New York: Holt, Rhinehart & Winston, 1970.

Jacobson, S. Sequence of myelinization in the brain of the albino rat. A. Cerebral cortex, thalamus and related structures. *Journal of Comparative Neurology*, 1963, *121*, 5–29.

James, H., & Binks, C. Escape and avoidance learning in newly hatched domestic chicks. *Science*, 1963, *139*, 1293–1294.

James, W. T., & Cannon, D. J. Conditioned avoidance responses in puppies. *American Journal of Physiology*, 1952, *168*, 251–253.

Jeffrey, W. E., & Cohen, L. B. Habituation in the human infant. In H. W. Reese (Ed.), *Advances in child development and behavior* (Vol. 6). New York: Academic Press, 1971.

Jouvet-Mounier, D., Astic, L., & Lacote, D. Ontogenesis of the states of sleep in rat, cat, and guinea pig during the first post-natal month. *Developmental Psychobiology*, 1970, *2*, 216–239.

Kamin, L. J. The delay of punishment gradient. *Journal of Comparative and Physiological Psychology*, 1959, *52*, 434–437.

Kay, H., & Sime, M. E. Discrimination learning with old and young rats. *Journal of Gerontology*, 1962, *17*, 75–80.

Kirby, R. H. Acquisition, extinction, and retention of an avoidance response as a function of age. *Journal of Comparative and Physiological Psychology*, 1963, *56*, 158–162.

Klein, S. B., & Spear, N. E. Influence of age on short-term retention of active avoidance learning in rats. *Journal of Comparative and Physiological Psychology*, 1969, *69*, 583–589.

Leaton, R. N. Long-term retention of the habituation of lick suppression in rats. *Journal of Comparative and Physiological Psychology*, 1974, *87*, 1157–1164.

Lipsitt, L. P. Learning capacities of the human infant. In R. J. Robinson (Ed.), *Brain and early behavior: Development in the fetus and infant*. New York: Academic Press, 1969. Pp. 227–245.

Lipsitt, L. P. Infant learning: The blooming, buzzing confusion revisited. In M. E. Meyer (Ed.), *Second western symposium on learning: Early learning*. Western Washington State College, 1971. Pp. 5–19.

Mason, W. A., & Harlow, H. F. Formation of conditioned responses in infant monkeys. *Journal of Comparative and Physiological Psychology*, 1958, *51*, 68–70. (a)

Mason, W. A., & Harlow, H. F. Performance of infant rhesus monkeys on a spatial discrimination problem. *Journal of Comparative and Physiological Psychology*, 1958, *51*, 71–74. (b)

McGaugh, J., & Cole, J. Age and strain differences in the effect of distribution of practice on maze learning. *Psychonomic Science*, 1965, *2*, 253–254.

McGinty, D. J. Encephalization and the neural control of sleep. In M. B. Sterman, D. J. McGinty, & A. M. Adinolphi (Eds.), *Brain development and behavior*. New York: Academic Press, 1971. Pp. 335–357.

Meier, G. W. Differences in maze performance as a function of age and strain of house mice. *Journal of Comparative and Physiological Psychology*, 1964, *58*, 418–422.

Milner, B., Corkin, S., & Teuber, H. B. Further analysis of the hippocampal amnesic syndrome: 14-year follow-up study of H. M. *Neuropsychologia*, 1968, *6*, 215–234.

Moorcroft, W. H., Lytle, L. D., & Campbell, B. A. Ontogeny of starvation-induced behavioral arousal in the rat. *Journal of Comparative and Physiological Psychology*, 1971, *75*, 59–67.

Nagy, Z. M., & Murphy, J. M. Learning and retention of a discriminated escape response in infant mice. *Developmental Psychobiology*, 1974, *7*, 185–192.

Paré, W. P. Interaction of age and shock intensity on acquisition of a discriminated CER. *Journal of Comparative and Physiological Psychology*, 1969, *68*, 364–369.

Parsons, P. J., Fagan, T., & Spear, N. E. Short-term retention of habituation in the rat: A developmental study from infancy to old age. *Journal of Comparative and Physiological Psychology,* 1973, *84,* 545–553.

Parsons, P. J., & Spear, N. E. Long-term retention of avoidance learning by immature and adult rats as a function of environmental enrichment. *Journal of Comparative and Physiological Psychology,* 1972, *80,* 297–303.

Perkins, C. C., Jr. A conceptual scheme for studies of stimulus generalization. In D. I. Mostofsky (Ed.), *Stimulus generalization.* Stanford: Stanford University Press, 1965.

Peters, J., & Isaacson, R. Acquisition of active and passive responses in two breeds of chicken. *Journal of Comparative and Physiological Psychology,* 1963, *56,* 793–796.

Porter, K. L., & Thompson, R. W. The effects of age and CS complexity on the acquisition of an avoidance response in rats. *Psychonomic Science,* 1967, *9,* 447–448.

Purpura, D. P., Shofer, R. J., Housepian, E. M., & Noback, C. R. Comparative ontogenesis of structure–formation relationships in cerebral and cerebellar cortex. In D. P. Purpura & J. P. Schadé (Eds.), *Progress in brain research.* Vol. 4: *Growth and maturation of the brain.* Amsterdam: Elsevier, 1964.

Riccio, D. C., & Marrazo, M. J. Effects of punishing active avoidance in young and adult rats. *Journal of Comparative and Physiological Psychology,* 1972, *79,* 453–458.

Riccio, D. C., Rohrbaugh, M., & Hodges, L. A. Developmental aspects of passive and active avoidance in rats. *Developmental Psychobiology,* 1968, *1,* 108–111.

Riccio, D. C., & Schulenberg, C. J. Age-related deficits in acquisition of a passive avoidance response. *Canadian Journal of Psychology,* 1969, *23,* 429–437.

Roberts, W. A. Learning and motivation in the immature rat. *American Journal of Psychology,* 1966, *79,* 3–23.

Roffwarg, H. P., Muzio, J. N., & Dement, W. C. Ontogenetic development of the human sleep cycle. *Science,* 1966, *152,* 604–619.

Rohrbaugh, M., & Riccio, D. C. Stimulus generalization of learned fear in infant and adult rats. *Journal of Comparative and Physiological Psychology,* 1968, *66,* 530–532.

Rosenblatt, J. S. Learning in newborn kittens. *Scientific American,* 1972, *227,* 18–25.

Ruble, E. W., & Rosenthal, M. H. The ontogeny of auditory frequency generalization in the chicken. *Journal of Experimental Psychology: Animal Behavior Processes,* 1975, *2,* 287–297.

Schadé, J. P., & Van Groeningen, W. B. Structural organization of the human cerebral cortex. I. Maturation of the middle frontal gyrus. *Acta Anatomica* (Basel), 1961, *47,* 74–111.

Scherrer, J. Electrophysiological aspects of cortical development. In E. A. Asratyan (Ed.), *Progress in brain research.* Vol. 22: *Brain reflexes.* Amsterdam: Elsevier, 1968.

Schulenberg, C. J., Riccio, D. C., & Stikes, E. R. Acquisition and retention of a passive avoidance response as a function of age in rats. *Journal of Comparative and Physiological Psychology,* 1971, *74,* 75–83.

Scoville, W. B., & Milner, B. Loss of recent memory after bilateral hippocampal lesions. *Journal of Neurology, Neurosurgery and Psychiatry,* 1957, *20,* 11–21.

Sluckin, W. *Imprinting and early learning.* Chicago: Aldine, 1965.

Smith, N. Effects of interpolated learning on retention of an escape response in rats as a function of age. *Journal of Comparative and Physiological Psychology,* 1968, *65,* 422–426.

Snedden, D. S., Spevack, A. A., & Thompson, W. R. Conditioned and unconditioned suppression as a function of age in rats. *Canadian Journal of Psychology,* 1971, *25,* 313–322.

Stanley, W. C., Bacon, W. E., & Fehr, C. Discriminated instrumental learning in neonatal dogs. *Journal of Comparative and Physiological Psychology,* 1970, *70,* 335–343.

Stanley, W. C., Cornwall, A. C., Paggiani, C., & Trattner, A. Conditioning in the neonate puppy. *Journal of Comparative and Physiological Psychology,* 1963, *56,* 211–214.

Stone, C. P. The age factor in animal learning. I. Rats in the problem box and the maze. *Genetic Psychology Monographs,* 1929, *5,* 1–30. (a)

Stone, C. P. The age factor in animal learning. II. Rats on a multiple light discrimination box and a different maze. *Genetic Psychology Monographs,* 1929, *6,* 125–202. (b)

Taylor, J. *Selected writings of John Hughlings Jackson.* Vol. 1: *On epilepsy and epileptiform convulsions.* London: Hodder and Stoughton, 1931.

Taylor, J. *Selected writings of John Hughlings Jackson.* Vol. 2: *Evolution and dissolution of the nervous system.* London: Hodder and Stoughton, 1932.

Thoman, E., Wetzel, A., & Levine, S. Learning in the neonatal rat. *Animal Behavior,* 1968, *16,* 54–57.

Thompson, R. W. The effect of ECS on retention in young and adult rats. *Journal of Comparative and Physiological Psychology,* 1957, *50,* 644–646.

Thompson, R. W., Koenigsberg, L. A., & Tennison, J. C. Effects of age on learning and retention of an avoidance response in rats. *Journal of Comparative and Physiological Psychology,* 1965, *60,* 457–459.

Thorpe, W. H. *Learning and instinct in animals.* Cambridge, Mass.: Harvard University Press, 1956.

Waldfogel, S. The frequency and affective character of childhood memories. *Psychological Monographs,* 1948, *62*(4, Whole No. 291).

Wilson, L. M., & Riccio, D. C. CS familiarization and conditioned suppression in weanling and adult albino rats. *Bulletin of the Psychonomic Society,* 1973, *1,* 184–186.

Yakovlev, P. I., & Lecours, A. The myelogenetic cycles of regional maturation of the brain. In A. Minkowski (Ed.), *Regional development of the brain in early life.* Philadelphia: Davis, 1967. Pp. 3–65.

Zimmerman, R. R., & Torrey, C. C. Ontogeny of learning. In A. M. Schrier, H. F. Harlow, & F. Stollnitz (Eds.), *Behavior of nonhuman primates: Modern research trends* (Vol. 2). New York: Academic Press, 1965. Pp. 405–447.

Zimmerman, R. R. Analysis of discrimination learning capacities in the infant rhesus monkey. *Journal of Comparative and Physiological Psychology,* 1961, *54,* 1–10.

5

Developmental Study
of Habituation in Infants:
The Importance of Paradigm,
Response System, and State

Rachel Keen Clifton
Michael N. Nelson

University of Massachusetts

The phenomenon of habituation has received widespread attention among observers of infant behavior, who have regarded it as a means to study cognitive processes and their development over time. The impetus for this approach came from Soviet work (Bronshtein *et al.*, 1958; Sokolov, 1963) and animal experimentation (Sharpless & Jasper, 1956; Thompson & Spencer, 1966; Thorpe, 1963). Unlike the animal research which has been interested in the habituation phenomenon per se, research on infants has employed the habituation paradigm primarily for the study of other phenomena. The two primary purposes of the majority of infant habituation experiments have been: (1) to study the learning capacity of the infant by using a process that has been labeled by many as the simplest form of learning; and (2) to assess the infant's capacity to discriminate various stimuli by introducing novel stimuli following habituation. Recently, a third reason for studying habituation has been advocated by Lewis (1971), McCall (1971), and Kagan (1971). These authors contend that habituation may be used as a tool both to assess the infant's current cognitive processing and to predict future cognitive abilities. They suggest that habituation parameters reflect the efficiency with which the brain processes environmental events, allowing an infant's performance on a habituation task to be used as a predictor of mental functioning in other situations.

Thorpe (1963) described habituation as a simple type of learning, in which the animal learns to stop responding to insignificant or irrelevant stimuli. His description immediately interested developmental psychologists who were attempting to demonstrate learning in the newborn infant. If habituation could be demonstrated, the infant would be shown to be capable of rudimentary learning soon after birth. Classical conditioning had captured attention for precisely the same reason for a number of years. In the early 1960s, inconclusive results from studies of classical conditioning suggested that a simpler form of learning might be more easily demonstrated. The habituation paradigm had proved to be a simple and effective way of exploring modifications of animal behavior as a product of experience, although not everyone viewed such modifications as learning. For example, Razran (1971, p. 44) considers habituation a "rudimentary precursor" of learning, more prevalent among life forms lower on the phylogenetic scale. In animals higher on the scale, Razran maintains that other processes, such as inhibitory conditioning, supplant habituation as more efficient ways of learning what not to do (p. 56). Ratner (1970), commenting on the survival value of habituation, states that it is probably the oldest process for modifying an organism's behavior. Thorpe (1963) also emphasizes the adaptive nature of habituation, stressing the phenomenon's ubiquity across a wide range of animal species. All of these considerations suggest that habituation is an important phenomenon in the development of the immature human.

The translation of Sokolov's work (1963) on the orienting response (OR) made available to Western psychologists an attractive model for neural processes during habituation. According to Sokolov, when a novel stimulus is introduced into the organism's environment, an OR is elicited which consists of EEG activation and a complex of autonomic responses indicative of phasic, mild arousal. Upon repeated stimulus presentations the brain forms a neuronal model which incorporates the salient features of the stimulus, such as intensity, duration, and its temporal relationship to other stimuli. The OR rapidly habituates to repeated nonsignal stimuli, but returns when either a new stimulus is introduced, or some aspect of a previous stimulus is changed, including its omission after a regular time interval. A filter-feedback system was hypothesized to enable the organism to recognize the stimulus and discrepancies from it. Novelty, defined as the noncoincidence between a stimulus and the neuronal model, acts to increase the organism's discriminatory power for obtaining information about the new properties of the stimulus. Sokolov's theory of orienting posits negative afferent feedback arising from a match of the cortical model with a stimulus presented, while positive feedback arises from a mismatch. Negative feedback originating in the cortex reduces the effect of the stimulus by raising thresholds, and decreases cortical activation by inhibiting sensory inputs to the reticular activating system, resulting in habituation of the OR. On the other hand, positive feedback increases receptor sensitivity by lowering thresholds, and thus amplifies the effect of the stimulus.

Since the neuronal model was located in the cortex, developmental psychologists were immediately attracted to Sokolov's OR theory. Habituation of the OR should reflect the infant's cortical processing of stimulus information. Elicitation and habituation of the OR represented a new way of looking at activity controlled by higher nervous system functioning. Once again the interest was not in habituation per se, but in using it to identify and characterize the formation of cortical models during orienting.

BRIEF REVIEW OF EARLY
HABITUATION WORK WITH NEONATES

Except where indicated otherwise, this literature review has been limited to research conducted on newborn infants less than a week old. At this age the problems of experimental design, particularly those associated with specifying the subject's arousal level or state, are the greatest. Other chapters in this volume by Cohen, Jeffrey, and Olson cover the literature on older infants.

In the early 1960s, information concerning the newborn's sensory abilities was far from complete, with relatively little research conducted on this subject since the 1930s. Stimulated by reports of Soviet success with infants (Bronshtein *et al.*, 1958), the habituation paradigm was used to examine discrimination of tones, light patterns, odors, and other stimuli. The responses selected for measurement were usually indicated by the particular sensory system under study. For example, discrimination of odors was detected by a change in respiration, perception of visual images by ocular fixation or visual evoked responses, and loud sounds by body startle. To detect more subtle changes in auditory stimuli, such as duration of tone, pattern of tonal sequences, and small changes in decibel level, heart rate (HR) change has been measured. This autonomic response has proved particularly useful with auditory stimuli, as there is no reliable overt body movement to weak or moderately intense sounds in the very young infant.

This early work often carried the double purpose of first demonstrating that habituation could be obtained in the neonate, and second, showing that discrimination of some stimulus change could be made. In a typical experiment, several presentations of the same stimulus would result in a response decrement. The introduction of a novel stimulus was expected to reinstate or "dishabituate" the response back to its original strength.[1] Work by Bridger (1961, 1962), Bartoshuk (1962a, 1962b), and Keen (1964) typified this approach. Using HR and body startle, Bridger found that by reducing the interstimulus interval to 5 sec or less and increasing the stimulus duration to 40 sec, intense pure tones (decibel level not specified) would no longer produce startles. A frequency

---

[1] It should be noted that this usage of the term "dishabituation" does not correspond to the definition given by animal researchers (see Thompson & Spencer, 1966), and is not consistent with historical usage of the term based on the definition of the similar concept of "disinhibition" (Pavlov, 1927). Graham (1973) has indicated how inconsistent terminology and tests of dishabituation may have evolved. Nevertheless, increased responding to novelty following habituation trials is commonly referred to as "dishabituation" in the infant habituation literature, and we will frequently follow this usage of the term.

change of the tone produced a return of the full startle in some newborns. Attributing the response decrements to habituation is questionable, however, since auditory fatigue cannot be ruled out when intense auditory stimulation is presented for long periods (Thurlow, 1971). Using tones of lesser intensity and the sucking response, Keen (1964) found evidence of partial habituation but no increased responding to a frequency change of considerable magnitude (400 Hz versus 4000 Hz).

Several studies have found decrements in both amplitude and duration of HR acceleration to square wave stimuli under conditions that rule out auditory fatigue: brief duration, moderate intensity (70–80 dB) tones, with intertrial intervals of 60–90 sec (Bartoshuk, 1962a; Clifton, Graham, & Hatton, 1968; Graham, Clifton, & Hatton, 1968). Three characteristics of the neonatal habituated HR response should be noted: (1) the greatest decrement occurred quickly, within the first 6 trials; (2) the decrement was not linear, but showed spontaneous recovery on some trials; (3) responding was never completely absent, even after 40 trials (Bartoshuk, 1962b).

The most serious criticism that can be leveled at this pioneering work is that changes in the subjects' arousal level or state may have influenced the data. The newborns did not begin the session in a uniform state, and many changed state during the procedure. Graham *et al.* (1968) tabled state ratings obtained immediately before the first, sixth, and eleventh trials. Ratings changed significantly from a mean rating of "drowsy" at the beginning of the session, to a mean rating of "irregular sleep" before the eleventh trial. However, such changes in state ratings are not necessarily reflected by decreased responding—it depends on the response. This problem of state will be discussed at length below. Here, let it suffice to make the point that state was unreported or uncontrolled in this early work on habituation.

Investigations of olfactory discrimination (Engen, Lipsitt, & Kaye, 1963; Engen & Lipsitt, 1965) were performed with newborns in a constant sleep state. No stimuli were presented unless the infant had closed eyes, regular respiration, and little body movement. Additionally, mock trials and dishabituation to a different odor provided behavioral controls for state changes. As a further safeguard against a sensory adaptation explanation of response decrement, the dishabituation stimulus used in the 1965 study consisted of a component of a previous compound. These studies found habituation of respiratory responses within ten trials to odorants in combination, such as anise oil with asafoetida, and amyl acetate with heptanal. The response recovered when a single odorant of the same intensity as in the original combination was presented alone. These studies are unique in terms of control of state through subject selection and control of fatigue and sensory adaptation by the use of a proper paradigm.

Unlike the studies of olfactory and auditory habituation, studies using visual stimuli have built-in state control. That is, stimuli must be presented when the infant's eyes are open, virtually guaranteeing some degree of alertness. In newborn infants, Haith (1966) failed to obtain habituation to a moving light after 12 presentations, each 10 sec in duration. Wetherford and Cohen (1973) found a shift in habituation toward a preference for novelty between 6 and 12 weeks of age, with no habituation shown in infants 6–8 weeks old. Fantz (1964) showed a similar age change using different stimuli and a broader age range. In contrast, Friedman and Carpenter (1971) and Friedman (1972b) reported that newborn infants decreased their looking time to checkerboard stimuli after only 8 trials, each 60 sec long. The decrements, though statistically significant, were fairly small in absolute time, an average drop of about 6 sec from an initial mean fixation exceeding 55 sec. Friedman (1972b) used a design that controlled for state by producing differential rates of habituation in groups receiving redundant versus different stimuli on every trial. The "novel" group showed less response decrement than the redundant group. The presentation of novel stimuli might increase alertness, however, as Friedman reported significantly less fussing in the group which received novel stimuli. Still, this procedure offers new possibilities for equating ongoing state changes while manipulating important stimulus variables. New paradigms of this type need to be developed that will permit separation of the effects of stimulus repetition from other unrelated influences.

This brief review indicates that a wide variety of stimuli and responses have been used in habituation work with infants. In much of this work, only one response was recorded, yet results were extrapolated as though they represented a general process of habituation. The problem becomes critical if the experimenter classifies subjects as "rapid" or "slow" habituators, and uses this characterization to predict later cognitive development. In this case, one must ask what happens when multiple responses are recorded. Would rate of habituation and dishabituation differ, depending on the response system?

Six studies that measured habituation of HR and looking behavior to visual stimulation are presented in Table 1. In all of these studies visual stimuli were presented to groups of infants that included the four- to six-month age range, and attention and habituation were measured by recording the same responses. Thus, the studies seem truly comparable, yet the results do not agree as to which response is the better indicator of the infant's attention. Meyers and Cantor (1967) and McCall and Kagan (1967b) found increased HR deceleration to completely novel or discrepant stimuli following habituation trials, while visual fixation did not change. Kagan *et al.* (1966) also found HR to be the more sensitive response, as differential deceleration occurred to two types of facial stimuli while fixation did not differ. Kagan and Lewis (1965) found habituation in both response systems but did not test for response to novelty, perhaps omitting a more sensitive procedure for comparing the two responses than habituation alone. Of the last two experiments in the table, McCall and Kagan (1967a) found fixation to be sensitive to stimuli differing in amount of contour although HR decelerated equally to all stimuli; McCall and Kagan (1970) reported longer fixations to a change in the standard stimulus, while HR did not differ on change trials. As Table 1 shows, even when fairly comparable stimuli are repeatedly tested with

TABLE 1
Studies Which Have Measured Habituation of Both Heart Rate and Visual Fixation in Infants

Study	Stimulus description	Age (months)	Number of trials		Stimulus duration (& ISI) (sec)	Results
			Habituation	Dishabituation		
Meyers and Cantor (1967)	Colored pictures of ball and clown	6	16	8 familiar and 8 novel	7 (7+)	No habituation in either response measure during familiarization trials. During dishabituation or test trials, only males showed a larger HR deceleration to novel stimuli. Fixation did not differ.
McCall and Kagan (1967b)	Patterns of X's and Y's in different arrangements: 1 standard, 3 discrepant	3–4	Long-term exposure in the home	4 trials of each stimulus for 16 total	20 (15)	Habituation not assessed but assumed. Only females showed greater HR deceleration to increasingly discrepant stimuli. Fixation did not differ for the stimuli.

Study	Stimuli	Ages	Trials		Trial length	Results
Kagan, Henker, Hen-Tov, Levine, and Lewis (1966)	Pictures of regular, distorted, and blank faces	4, 8	16	none	30 (15)	Greater HR deceleration to regular than distorted faces at 4 mo. At 8 mo., distorted faces elicited more deceleration. No age or stimulus differences found for the fixation measure.
Kagan and Lewis (1965)	Blinking lights, face, geometric patterns	6, 13	12 trials of lights 30 trials of pictures	none	lights, 30 pictures, 12 (ISI-same)	Habituation found to both types of stimuli in both responses. Note: pictures were always presented first.
McCall and Kagan (1967a)	9 random shapes, varying in contour and complexity	4	9	none	30 (15)	Number of fixations increased with increasing contour. HR decelerated equally to all stimuli.
McCall and Kagan (1970)	3 complex toys mounted on a board	4	5 3 3 3	1 1 1	30 (15)	On change trials, the stimulus board differed by 1, 2, or all 3 components. There was longer looking to changed stimuli than to standard, but no discrepancy difference. HR was not different on change trials.

the same response systems, results of different studies conflict and fail to replicate, suggesting that conclusions about a general central process of habituation may be premature if they are based on data from a single response system. Until data from different response systems have been integrated and correlated with other relevant behaviors, the meaning of habituation in one response system but not another cannot be clearly interpreted in terms of general cognitive processes of the infant. Kagan (1971, p. 124) and Lewis and colleagues (Lewis & Goldberg, 1969; Lewis et al., 1966) have reported fairly high positive correlations in the range of .4–.7 between either total or first visual fixation and magnitude of cardiac deceleration. These correlations indicate that greater visual attention is associated with increased cardiac orienting on a particular trial. However, with respect to rate of habituation, the question of whether there is similar degree of concordance between these two response systems still needs to be tested.

Rather than seeking similarities in rate of habituation, we may find that differences in habituation across response systems reveal much about how behavior is organized. For example, HR acceleration in the newborn is difficult to habituate completely; after an early decrease in response amplitude, a small HR acceleration usually remains for many trials. If evoked HR acceleration is a component of a startle or defense response (Graham & Clifton, 1966), difficulty in habituation might be expected. Habituation of startle and defense reflexes is slower than habituation of OR's (Graham & Jackson, 1970; Sokolov, 1963), and experiments that examine habituation in infants are typically designed to be as short as possible, corresponding to the infant's brief periods of alertness. In addition, the newborn infant may have a lower threshold for elicitation of protective or startle reflexes (Graham, & Jackson, 1970), which may reduce the possibility of giving HR deceleration or other orienting behaviors. Thus, we cannot conclude that habituation is "slow" or impossible in the newborn because it does not appear in a particular response system. Under favorable experimental conditions cardiac deceleration and other orienting behaviors would be expected to habituate quickly (Adkinson & Berg, 1975). The challenge is to discover the linkage between habituation of certain responses and underlying central nervous system functioning.

DEVELOPMENTAL CHANGES IN RESPONSE SYSTEMS

The most common hypothesis concerning habituation as a function of age is that habituation rate should increase with increasing age, reflecting the older infant's more efficient information processing abilities. There are many difficulties in interpreting changes in response decrement across various ages. Maturational changes in the response system itself may affect the course of habituation, but have little influence on cognitive processes assumed to underlie habituation. Another age-related concern is whether certain responses may be inappropriate at some ages. Nonnutritive sucking appears to be such an age-dependent re-sponse, appropriate at younger ages (under six months) but difficult to use at older ages. Many reflexes that are prominent in the newborn infant gradually decrease in strength and drop out with age as new response patterns develop that inhibit and overlay some of the neonatal reflexes.

Visual fixation and HR change, the two most commonly used responses in infant habituation studies, have been used to measure response decrements from the premature infant to the adult. The assumption has usually been made that visual fixation is controlled by "attention," presumably a cortical process at all ages. However, functioning and control of visual fixation is affected by the rapid maturation of muscles controlling eye movements, and physiological develop-ments that increase acuity and accommodation during the first 6 months of life (Bronson, 1974). Less clear is the relationship of these maturational changes to habituation of the fixation response. Certainly there are striking age differences in the base rate or initial level of looking at visual stimuli. Younger infants, 3 months and under, appear to fixate longer than older babies. The lengthy fixations of Friedman's newborns (1972b; Friedman, Bruno, & Vietze, 1974) have already received comment. In a developmental study spanning 3–44 months of age, Lewis, Goldberg, and Campbell (1969) reported much longer fixations for the 3-month-olds than older infants. The 3-month-olds averaged greater than 20 sec out of a possible 30 on the first trial, while some groups of 13- and 18-month-olds looked about 5 seconds initially. Such striking dif-ferences in initial level were controlled for by expressing fixation times during habituation as percentages of responding on the first trial. However, the meaning of age differences in basal responding will remain unclear until we better understand what controls fixation at various ages. Cohen's distinction (1972) between "attention getting" and "attention holding" properties of stimuli repre-sents the type of information needed to answer this question (also see Cohen in this volume). If the same response is used to measure habituation over a wide age range, care must be exercised in assuming that the meaning of response decre-ment is equivalent across the entire range.

The question of developmental change in the HR response concerns the directionality of the response. Heart rate can either increase or decrease in response to a stimulus, and the meaning of an acceleration is apparently different from the meaning of a deceleration. Lacey's work (1959, 1967; Lacey et al., 1963) with adult humans led him to hypothesize that when subjects are "taking in" or anticipating stimulus input they show HR deceleration, whereas when they are rejecting or seeking to shut out stimulation, they show HR acceleration. Graham and Clifton (1966) related this directionality in responding to Sokolov's description (1963) of the orienting and defense responses. Until the early 1970's, studies of the newborn had found, practically without exception, that the HR response to various types of stimuli was acceleration. In contrast, again with almost no exception, older infants were found to show HR decelera-tion to many different types of stimuli. Graham and Jackson (1970) reviewed the literature on this subject, pointing out several factors that could produce this apparent developmental shift (such as arousal state, type of stimulus used, etc.), but they tentatively concluded that the newborn was incapable of the more mature decelerative response, considered to be a component of the OR. This suggestion launched investigations from a number of laboratories, each attempting to find the optimal state combined with an effective stimulus that would elicit an OR from the newborn (Adkinson & Berg, 1976; Gregg, Clifton, & Haith, 1976; Jackson, Kantowitz, & Graham, 1971; Kearsley, 1973; Pomerleau-Malcuit & Clifton, 1973; Sameroff, Cashmore, & Dykes, 1973). Although conflicting results emerged from these studies, the weight of evidence suggests that the OR can be elicited in the newborn if a slow rise time, moderately intense stimulus is presented to an alert newborn who is not manipulated into alertness through the use of pacifiers or other motor movements designed to "wake up" the baby.

The primary difficulty in obtaining an OR in the newborn probably lies in the transitory nature of spontaneously alert states and different thresholds for responding to various stimuli with an OR rather than a DR. For example, Pomerleau-Malcuit, Malcuit, and Clifton (1975) were able to evoke either direction of HR change in sleeping newborns by varying the tactile stimulus administered. A stroke on the cheek (a rooting stimulus) produced HR deceleration only if no motor response was evoked. A quick, gentle pinch of the ear lobe produced HR acceleration regardless of evoked motor movement.

In older infants, Berg (1974) attempted to find age differences between 6- and 16-week-old infants in various characteristics of orienting (developmental changes in HR responding for this age range have also been reported, that is, greater HR deceleration in older infants). He presented 1100-Hz sine waves (75 dB, 30 msec rise time) to these two age groups, comparing their magnitude of HR deceleration to stimulus onset and offset, habituation, and dishabituation to a different tone. In contrast to previous research (Graham et al., 1970; Rewey, 1973), no age differences in magnitude of HR deceleration to stimulus onset were found. Berg concluded that age differences in the decelerative HR–OR that had been reported earlier could be eliminated by controlling state within a narrow range of alertness, although Berg did report significantly greater HR deceleration to stimulus offset in older infants.

STATE CYCLE ONTOGENY DURING INFANCY[2]

A major concern of investigations of habituation in infants, especially newborn infants, must be the periodic cycling of sleeping and waking states (Ashton,

[2] To conserve space we have frequently cited reviews or summaries rather than primary experiments. Those interested in original reports are referred to the reference sections of the relevant recent reviews. The reader is also referred to Kleitman's classic work (1963,

1973b; Brown, 1964; Hutt, Lenard, & Prechtl, 1969; Korner, 1972). We will try to show that it is unwise to allow any change in state to occur during a habituation experiment, and that the potentially confounding influence of state change will vary as a function of the response system selected for study. Another factor is the basic rest–activity cycle (BRAC, see Kleitman, 1963), which in phylogeny has been observed in all of its basic stages (including the REM state of sleep) in virtually every mammal tested, as well as in birds and some other species (Tauber, 1974). The BRAC is influential during both sleep and waking, affecting transitions between the various stages of sleep (Sterman, 1972; Sterman & Hoppenbrouwers, 1971), and even producing reaction time rhythmicities in adult human subjects in vigilance experiments (Globus *et al.,* 1971). Over the course of human ontogeny the duration of the BRAC cycle lengthens from approximately 50 min in the newborn to 90–100 min in the adult (Kleitman, 1963). Our primary concern will be with the characteristics of various response systems as a function of state change, with the BRAC playing a role in terms of the duration of each state as it occurs within the cycle.

The concept of a basic cycle or rhythm underlying behavior suggests periodic quantitative changes in arousal level along a continuum. However, the evidence strongly supports the conclusion that responses do not wax and wane in a continuous fashion corresponding to underlying changes in arousal. Rather, qualitative changes in response organization occur as state changes (Korner, 1972; Prechtl, 1974; Wolff, 1966, 1973). The major state categories of interest are wakefulness, active sleep (commonly called REM or dreaming sleep), quiet sleep, and the transitional state of drowsiness (Parmelee & Stern, 1972; Petre-Quadens, 1974). These categories correspond to Wolff's (1973) alert activity and inactivity, irregular sleep, regular sleep, and drowsiness, respectively and to Prechtl's States 3 and 4, 2, and 1. Prechtl has not assigned a number to the transitional state of drowsiness (Prechtl, 1974). These gross categories do not take into account several important distinctions made in animals and adults, but represent a compromise based on the relatively greater difficulty of making more molecular classifications of the rather disorganized behavior of infants.

Three points can be emphasized concerning the major state categories defined in the newborn infant. First, these state categories become more distinct during ontogeny. Novel response organizations (or disorganizations) or states may be present in early infancy which gradually become less prominent as the central nervous system matures. For example, a portion of the sleeping activity observed during the newborn period has been characterized as either transitional (Parmelee, 1974), indeterminate (Korner, 1972), or periodic (Wolff, 1966) sleep. This additional sleep state, resembling active sleep in variability of activity, is

especially Chapter 15), and several recent books and reviews dealing with sleep (Akert, Bally, & Schadé, 1965; Chase, 1972; Clemente, Purpura, & Mayer, 1972; Freemon, 1972; Jouvet, 1967, 1969; Jovanović, 1971, 1973; Kety, Evarts, & Williams, 1967; Petre-Quadens & Schlag, 1974; Sterman, 1974; Weitzman, 1974).

mirrored by a complementary decrease in time classified as active sleep, especially in the premature infant (Parmelee *et al.,* 1967). The creation of the additional state category for the very young infant suggests that the organization of sleep states is not complete at birth, but also indicates genuine intermediate activity associated with prolonged or unstable state transitions.

Secondly, both the dominance and uninterrupted durations of various states change radically during early postnatal development, especially the first 3 months (Dittrichová, 1966). Those interested in the behavior of nonsleeping newborns for various theoretical or methodological reasons have available up to 7 hours of every 24 (Parmelee, Schultz, & Disbrow, 1961). During feedings a single period of alertness may last an hour or more, providing perhaps the best opportunity to test the newborn's capabilities for habituation and conditioning. In contrast, in the interval between feeding periods the newborn is alert and responsive to stimulation only briefly, with over 90% of alert periods lasting less than 10 min (Berg, Adkinson, & Strock, 1973; Prechtl, 1965; Wolff, 1965). Mean uninterrupted waking duration (excluding feeding periods) increases approximately linearly from 1 to 5 min in the newborn to about 30 min at 1 month, 40 at 2 months, and over 90 min in the 3-month-old (Wolff, 1973). The mean duration of quiet sleep increases very little and shows relatively low variability during the first 3 months, changing from approximately 20 min in the newborn (Prechtl, 1974; Wolff, 1966) to between 20 and 30 min in the 3-month-old (Paul & Dittrichová, 1974; Wolff, 1973). The mean duration of active sleep is also approximately 20 min in the newborn (Prechtl, 1974), but is misleading, as durations remain highly variable over the first 3 months, ranging from as low as 2–3 min in the newborn (Prechtl, 1965; Roffwarg, Muzio, & Dement, 1966), to as long as 50–60 min in both newborn and older infants (Roffwarg *et al.,* 1966; Wolff, 1973). The mean duration of active sleep episodes increases slightly over the first 3 months, although the percentage of total sleep time classified as active sleep decreases over this period from 50–60% to less than 40% at 3 months (Parmelee, 1974; Roffwarg *et al.,* 1966; Wolff, 1973). These data suggest that experiments requiring the presentation of many trials to an awake, alert infant are likely to be unsuccessful in infants less than a few weeks old, unless either repeated short sessions can be given on successive days, or testing can be conducted during the infant's normal feeding period. (It should be noted that the latter alternative is virtually impossible in most hospitals.) For early developmental comparisons, the optimal state in terms of mean uninterrupted duration would appear to be quiet sleep, a state of fairly long duration even at birth.

To further complicate the situation, state sequences show fairly rapid developmental change. For example, in the first two months approximately 60% of daytime quiet sleep is both preceded and followed by active sleep. By the third month, less than 50% of daytime quiet sleep can be categorized this way. In contrast, periods of daytime quiet sleep preceded or followed by drowsiness occur approximately 25% of the time over the first 2 months, but increase to over 40% in the 3-month-old (Wolff, 1973).

THE EFFECTS OF STATE CHANGE ON RESPONDING

Johnson (1970) has summarized a large body of data, much of it his own, which indicates that EEG and autonomic activity cannot be used alone to define states of consciousness in adults. He found that the same visceral and EEG changes can occur in different states, and concluded that the subject's state must be known prior to reaching any decisions concerning the patterns of autonomic activity observed. Since response characteristics change with state, developmental examination of response habituation cannot ignore state change, especially where state change produces response decrement resembling habituation. Depending on the response system selected, simply preparing a newborn infant for recording may be sufficient to produce a state change. Frequently the infant is swaddled to produce both motor quieting and less chance for disturbance of the electrode leads and other transducers. In addition, background white noise is often used to mask equipment and other extraneous sounds. Even without white noise, however, if the newborn infant is in the same room with the equipment (a not uncommon situation in crowded hospitals) the hum of the polygraph motor serves as a continuous background auditory stimulus. Both swaddling and continuous background noise are efficient procedures for rapidly producing sleep in newborns (Brackbill, 1973, 1975; Wolff, 1966). Wolff (1966) found that white noise presented to an alert newborn produced drowsiness within 90 sec 86.7% of the time, and presented to an infant in active sleep resulted in a transition to quiet sleep within 60 sec 98.5% of the time.

Several studies of habituation in newborns (Graham *et al.,* 1968; Eisenberg, Coursin, & Rupp, 1966; Keen *et al.,* 1965), all using auditory stimuli and the HR response, have reported changes of state toward sleep occurring during habituation trials. On the other hand, certain types of stimulation, especially strong, intermittent stimulation (Brackbill, 1970), may prolong a state, or produce a temporary state change in the direction of increased arousal. Apparently, state may change toward either greater alertness or toward sleep in a habituation experiment, depending on the specific stimulus parameters used.

In general, both organization across various response systems and direction and magnitude of responding within a response system alter as a function of state. The evidence supporting these conclusions for newborn infants is summarized in Table 2. The organization of state data is based primarily on the categories, supporting data, and considerations discussed previously in this and the preceding section. Across the top of the table are listed the major behavioral states of the newborn. Nomenclatures differ somewhat in different laboratories (see Ashton, 1973b; and Robinson, 1969, for listings of equivalent terms), but the

TABLE 2

Newborn Response System Changes as a Function of State

(Reference Numbers Correspond to Boldface Numbers Following Studies Listed in the Reference Section[a])

(+++, strong response; −, absent response; after Prechtl)

Response category	Response	Response measures	State (and mean uninterrupted state duration)				References
			Awake (4–6 min)	Drowsy (4–8 min)	Active sleep (15–25 min)	Quiet sleep (17–23 min)	
EEG[b]	EEG	Amplitude	15–50 µV	15–75 µV	15–50 µV Spikes to 100 µV	40–150 µV	23, 25, 27, 28, 35, 42, 58, 59, 60, 62, 63, 64, 65, 66, 72, 73, 75, 76, 78, 79, 94, 97
		Frequency	4–30 Hz	4–30 Hz	.5–15+ Hz	.5–8+ Hz	
		Characteristic waveform	Low voltage fast activity	Same as Awake, but with spikes	Much 4–8 Hz with spiking	Strong .5–3 Hz, trace alternant	
	Auditory evoked responses	Latency	Modal	~ Modal	~ Modal	Lengthened	2, 6, 39
		Peak to peak amplitude	Modal	~ Modal	~ Modal	Increased	55, 57, 95
		N_1 latency to peak	Modal	Modal	Modal	Lengthened	22, 39
		N_1 duration	Modal	Modal	Modal	Lengthened	
	Somato-sensory evoked responses	N_2 amplitude	Enhanced	Intermediate	Intermediate	Attenuated	
		P_2	Absent	Absent	Absent	Present	

Category	Measure					References
Autonomic						
Heart rate	Base level	125–155 bpm $\bar{X} \leqslant 140$ bpm	120–150 bpm $\bar{X} \leqslant 135$ bpm	115–145 bpm $\bar{X} \leqslant 130$ bpm	100–130 bpm $\bar{X} \leqslant 120$ bpm	1, 5, 10, 12, 15, 17, 19, 35, 37, 42, 43, 46, 49, 51, 52, 53, 63, 67, 72, 73, 75, 76, 80, 82, 83, 86, 88, 93
	Spontaneous activity or variability	Moderate–high	Moderate–high	High–moderate	Low	
	Evoked response[c]	Deceleration	Biphasic or acceleration	Acceleration	Acceleration	
Respiration	Base level	45–65/min $\bar{X} \leqslant 55$/min	40–60/min $\bar{X} \leqslant 50$/min	40–60/min $\bar{X} \leqslant 40$/min	35–45/min $\bar{X} \leqslant 40$/min	5, 12, 35, 42, 52, 63, 72, 73, 75, 76, 86, 87, 97
	Spontaneous activity or variability	Moderate	High for rate, low amplitude	High	Low	
	Evoked response[c]	Decreased rate	Increased rate	Increased rate	Increased rate	
Skin resistance[d]	Base level	Low	Low–moderate	Moderate–high	Highest	11, 18, 43, 44, 77, 86, 96
	Spontaneous activity or variability	Moderate	Moderate	Low ?	Lowest–highest (stages 1–4)?	
	Evoked response[c]	Highest	Lowest ?	Lowest ?	Moderate ?	
Skin potential	Base level	Most negative	Intermediate	Intermediate	Less negative	8, 13, 20, 21, 43, 86
	Spontaneous activity or variability	Low	Moderate–high	Moderate–high	Low–moderate	
	Evoked response[c]	Highest	Low–moderate	Moderate–low?	Moderate ?	
Behavioral (EMG = electromyogram)						
Arousal to shock	Magnitude[e]	++	+	+	±	30, 31, 38, 50, 81
EMG response to auditory stimuli	Magnitude[e]	+++	++	++	±	4, 24, 35, 42, 55, 69, 73, 85
Olfactory response	Magnitude[e]	+++	++	++	+	56, 69, 85

(continued)

TABLE 2 (*continued*)

Response category	Response	Response measures	State (and mean uninterrupted state duration)				References
			Awake (4–6 min)	Drowsy (4–8 min)	Active sleep (15–25 min)	Quiet sleep (17–23 min)	
	Gross body movements	Base level		≤ 80/hr	≤ 80–90/hr	≤ 20/hr	3, 14, 36, 42, 61, 63, 72, 76, 78, 79, 89, 97, 100
	Muscle twitches	Base level	++	++	+++	+	42, 63, 72, 73, 76, 79
	Muscle tone	Base level	++	+	±	+	42, 63, 72, 73, 76, 79, 89, 97
Reflexes[f]	Rooting and headturning	Spontaneous responses	+++	++	++	±	33, 34, 40, 70, 90, 92
		Evoked responses	+++	++	±	±	
	Nonnutritive Sucking	Base rate/min	60–120/min	60–100/min	< 60/min	Suppressed late in quiet sleep	9, 45, 48, 90, 97, 98, 99, 101
		Amplitude	+++	++	++	+	
	Mouthing	Base rate/min		~ 50–55/hr	~ 40–60/hr	~ 7–8/hr	47, 66, 97, 98
	Spontaneous startles[g]	Base rate	Absent	≤ 17/hr	≤ 12–13/hr	≤ 20/hr	66, 97, 100
	Moro	Evoked responding	+++	++	+	+++	7, 16, 40, 41, 42, 71,
		Amplitude	++		±	++	

174

Reflex	Measure				References
Ankle clonus	Amplitude	±	±	+++	73, 74, 75, 84, 90, 91, 97, 100
Patellar tendon	Amplitude	++	±	+++	
Lip jerk	Amplitude	++	±	+++	
Lip protrusion	Amplitude	+	++	−	
Babkin	Amplitude	++	+	−	
Palmar grasp	Amplitude	++	++	−	
Plantar grasp	Amplitude	++	+	−	
Nociceptive skin reflexes (including the Babinski reflex)	Amplitude	+++	+++	+++	

[a] Data from adults that appear to be consistent with newborn data are used occasionally. The specific values given in the table are often approximations based on conflicting data. Large variations between studies in stimuli used and recording conditions are probably responsible for much of the conflict and confusion, although most studies agree on the direction of response change as a function of state change. Cells in the table are left blank (especially in the "Drowsy" column) where information is not available or compelling.

[b] Visual-evoked potentials are not included for several reasons, the most important being the difficulty inherent in obtaining recordings during rapid eye movements occurring in active sleep. In addition, Ellingson (29) has reported great variability in the recordings obtained from neonates, and has failed to find any effect of state (see also the visual evoked potential data presented in Reference 39). The color of the light used to obtain evoked potentials may be important, however (54).

[c] Responding to low or moderate intensity stimuli. The use of very intense stimuli results in minimal state effects. For example, the cardiac response to intense stimulation is acceleration regardless of state. Cardiac decelerations can be obtained in sleep under some circumstances (68).

[d] Infant data may not be consistent with some of the entries based on adult data (marked as questionable). Infants differ from adults in skin potential activity in the direction of showing more spontaneous activity during active sleep than in quiet sleep (20, 21), the opposite of the adult pattern (43), and similar differences may exist for skin resistance.

[e] "Magnitude" represents the product of frequency and amplitude.

[f] Many of the reflexes listed are eventually suppressed, and cannot be evoked later in the first postnatal year (time of postnatal disappearance of many reflexes is tabulated in Reference 90). The time course of the postnatal disappearance of a reflex may be affected by the specific test of the reflex that is used, however (91).

[g] Not really mature startle reflexes, but superficially resemble Moro reflexes to startling (intense) stimuli, and are conveniently labeled as such (e.g., 97).

number of different state categories rarely exceeds four or five. Crying is omitted from consideration due to response measurement difficulties and paucity of interest and data concerning habituation in this state. The states of awake activity and inactivity are combined since virtually no research has systematically measured response differences between them. Drowsiness is included as an important state category due to the high probability of measuring responding in this state when awake newborns are selected for study. The previously discussed state that was labeled transitional, indeterminate, or periodic sleep by various newborn researchers is omitted due to measurement problems and available evidence frequently indicating little difference in responding between transitional and active sleep (Wolff, 1966).

Each state listed in Table 2 has its mean uninterrupted duration *in the absence of stimulation* given in minutes for neonates. The durations listed are typically observed in a period between feedings, when almost all neonatal research is conducted. It is unlikely that stimulation would prolong any state more than 4 or 5 min (Dittrichová, 1969; Wolff, 1966, 1969). The state labeled "Awake" includes all waking time save that labeled "Waking activity" (which apparently corresponds to fussiness) by Wolff (1966, 1973), and is distinguished primarily by the appearance of open, "shining eyes," visual pursuit with conjugate eye-movements, some motor activity for much of the time, and general responsiveness to stimulation. In this chapter the category "awake" is used to denote alert wakefulness.

Drowsiness, the state most likely to follow the awake state, involves alternately opening and closing eyes having a dull, glazed look, virtual absence of visual pursuit and conjugate eye movements, decreased motor activity, and increased variability in respiration and HR.

Active sleep, the state most likely to follow or precede drowsiness, is characterized by closed eyes, low-voltage-fast EEG, frequent bursts of REM's and occasional isolated REM's, some gross motor activity alternating with frequent muscle twitches (particularly of the facial musculature and extremities), smiling and other spontaneous facial expressions, frequent full or partial erections, and increased variability of ANS functions.

Quiet sleep in the newborn involves intermittent high amplitude, low frequency EEG (e.g., tracé alternant), slow and regular respiration and HR, little motor activity other than intermittent myoclonic jerks (spontaneous "startles") and occasional bursts of rhythmical mouthing. Due to limitations in the available data, the three to four stages of quiet sleep distinguished in adults have been treated in a unitary fashion in the table.

A large quantity of recent evidence indicates that a phasic—tonic rather than a REM—NREM distinction may be quite fruitful in understanding sleep (Grosser & Siegal, 1971). Unfortunately, this phasic—tonic distinction has been essentially ignored due to a paucity of relevant neonatal data. Where any relevant evidence exists (Petre-Quadens, 1974), however, we have noted distinctions concerning responding within the states as they are grossly divided. Sleep is a much more complex phenomenon than is indicated by Table 2, and the table should be considered as representing current knowledge rather than defining states for future reference.

To omit needless detail we will not discuss the effects of state for every response measure listed in the table. Rather, three major conclusions which follow from an overall examination of the Table will be stressed. First, information in adjacent columns indicates little empirical support for an underlying arousal continuum. If a continuum exists, the evidence indicates an extraordinarily complex relationship to various response measures. Moving from left to right, from the awake to the quiet sleep column, the rows labeled "evoked response" furnish examples of activity that do not uniformly decrease or increase, but rather change in complicated ways. The complex columnar organization of responding prohibits making a simple generalization concerning response change as a function of state.

A second conclusion based upon the data summarized in the table is that results obtained depend on the particular measure used within a response system. The distinction between spontaneous activity and evoked responding is especially important. The complexity involved in examining evoked versus spontaneous electrodermal responses during sleep in adults was clarified by Johnson's (1970) work, but an even finer grained analysis may be required, for example, in the case of respiration. Variability of respiratory frequency or rate is high during drowsiness in neonates, but the variability of amplitude is low (Wolff, 1966).

The third conclusion from the table is that changes in responding as a function of state change alone will mimic habituation for some response measures, but may suggest dishabituation or even sensitization for other response systems. Moving from left to right across the columns one can follow the state changes that are likely to occur in a newborn infant initially in an awake state. For example, the waking HR response to low to moderate intensity stimuli is HR deceleration. As the subject gets drowsy, this deceleration is replaced by acceleration, a result which is at least consistent with habituation of deceleration, especially for those researchers who score a HR response in the "wrong direction" as zero response. In contrast, HR variability, a measure which has enjoyed some recent popularity as an index of attention (Porges, 1974), gradually increases as the newborn infant progresses from the awake state, through drowsiness, to active sleep, resembling a sensitization effect, and then "habituates" to very low levels as the infant enters quiet sleep.

Under the heading of "Reflexes," Table 2 shows that spontaneous startles increase in frequency as the infant moves from the awake state to quiet sleep, an apparent "sensitization" effect. More complex results would obtain if spontaneous startles are not distinguished from other types of somatic activity. For example, gross body movements and muscle twitches change with state in a manner opposite to that observed for spontaneous startles, suggesting that state changes in motor activity would tend to cancel out if some composite motor response measure was used, such as total output from a stabilimeter. Interestingly, the nociceptive skin reflexes look uniquely promising, as they do not change as state changes. But failure of a response to alter as state changes does not necessarily imply optimal conditions for demonstrating habituation, as the process of habituation itself may be state dependent. While several monosynaptic reflexes weaken in active sleep and are strong in quiet sleep, polysynaptic reflexes change little as a result of transition from the awake state to active sleep, but weaken dramatically in quiet sleep. Clearly, the organization or patterning of reflexes and other responses changes dramatically from state to state, and so does the nature of potentially confounding influences of state change. Response decrement alone is grossly insufficient evidence of habituation.

The complexity of responding shown in Table 2 should not lead the reader to infer that neonatal responding as a function of state has been fully described. There are substantial individual differences between newborns in distinctiveness, consistency, range, and alterability of state as a function of stimulation (Korner, 1973). The variability of state characteristics and sequencing is especially high during the first postnatal week, with the first postpartum day being most different from subsequent days (Prechtl, 1974). Thereafter the neonate's state cycling becomes more stable. For example, by the end of the first postnatal week the state sequence, active sleep–quiet sleep–active sleep, is more common than all other daytime sleep sequences combined. During the first three postnatal months, 90% of all transitions from sleep to waking and vice versa involve either active sleep or drowsiness preceding or following daytime quiet sleep. Direct transitions from quiet sleep to wakefulness occur only about 1% of the time, and changes in the opposite direction may never occur (see Wolff, 1973, for more detail concerning daytime state transitions during the first three postnatal months).

Other research has indicated that the states surrounding active sleep are less stable than those proximate to regular sleep. Korner (1972) has shown that approximately one-fourth of active sleep periods are preceded by quiet sleep, while the remainder of active sleep periods are preceded most often by either drowsiness, crying, or waking activity, in that order. State transitions even vary with the direction of state change; it takes longer for the newborn to move from active to quiet sleep than vice versa (Prechtl, 1969). The sequence of states shown across the top of Table 2 is not immutable, then, but in general the infant does move through the intervening states when progressing from wakefulness to quiet sleep and vice versa.

Finally, it should be noted that state cycling and evoked responding are affected by feeding. The first episode of quiet sleep following a feed is longer than subsequent episodes (Dittrichová, 1969; Prechtl, 1969). In addition, Wolff

(1973) has indicated that breast-fed infants usually have their periods of alert wakefulness prior to feedings, while bottle-fed infants are alert after feedings. Auditory responsivity has been found to vary with prandial condition (Ashton, 1973a; Pomerleau-Malcuit & Clifton, 1973) but the distinction between breast-versus bottle-fed infants was not made.

RECENT DATA CONCERNING STATE
AND NEWBORN HR RESPONDING

Unpublished data from our own laboratory suggest subtle effects of state change on responding which go beyond the information given in Table 2. Figure 1 shows the HR response of 35 newborn infants to the first presentation of a 72-dB, 300-Hz, square-wave tone of 7 or 8 sec duration. Of the 21 infants stimulated in an awake state (behavioral ratings) who subsequently remained awake for more than 10 min, 19 showed HR deceleration to the novel tone. Of the 6 infants who were also rated behaviorally awake but who subsequently became drowsy or fell asleep within 5 min, half showed deceleration and half showed acceleration of HR. All 8 infants stimulated while drowsy or asleep gave HR accelerations to the novel tone. The three groups of infants were approximately equivalent in birth weight (7 lb) and age (2 days), had experienced a normal delivery, and did not differ substantially in the medication their mothers had received during labor and delivery. An assumption here is that the infants who stayed awake the longest were tested shortly after entering the alert state, while the infants who fell asleep within 5 min were tested near the end of their alert period. Possibly, the Awake < 5 min group simply had shorter alert periods, and therefore, fell asleep sooner. In any event, the most important point to be made is that HR responding may differ in two groups of awake infants depending on how soon the infants will be leaving the awake state, even when all infants are equivalently scored as awake and alert on the basis of behavioral ratings. Either habituation or a state change may cause an infant's HR response to shift from deceleration to acceleration. The 21 awake infants showing deceleration in Figure 1 habituated this response within 3 trials (requiring 1.5 min), giving accelerations rather than decelerations to the third stimulus presentation. In terms of the effect of state on the direction of HR responding, somewhat similar data have been reported for older infants. Lewis, Dodd, and Harwitz (1969) found that awake 2–6-week-old infants giving HR decelerations to initial tone presentations showed accelerations after falling asleep.

  The data presented in Figure 1 suggest the fruitfulness of measuring HR change concomitant with other measures of newborn orienting and attention. For example, in studies of habituation of visual fixation (Friedman et al., 1974) newborn infants have been rejected from a study for failure to habituate within a specified number of trials. Concomitant measurement of HR might have shown

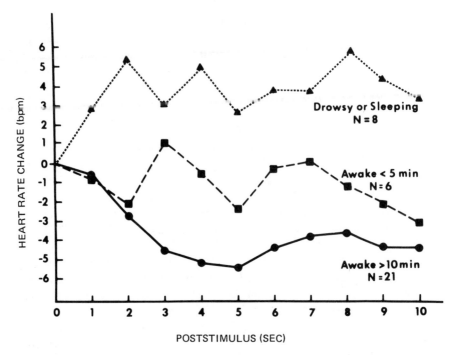

FIG. 1   Heart rate responses of newborn infants to the first presentation of a 72-dB, 300-Hz square wave tone. The infants rated behaviorally awake during stimulation subsequently remained awake for the numbers of minutes indicated. The abcissa shows second × second weighted average heart rate.

that "nonhabituators" gave HR accelerations or no consistent HR response. If such "nonhabituators" also fell asleep more rapidly following the termination of the experiment, the failure to habituate could probably be related to state, even though the infants may not have appeared to differ behaviorally. In this regard it should be noted that habituation of the eye-blink reflex in newborns occurs during both alert wakefulness and quiet sleep, but apparently does not occur in active sleep or transitional states (Martinius & Papoušek, 1970).

Many of the considerations discussed above in relation to the data presented in Figure 1 become less important as the newborn infant matures. Not only does wakefulness increase dramatically in duration over the early postnatal months (Dittrichová & Lapáčková, 1964; Wolff, 1973), but the behavioral indices of various states become less ambiguous as well. Most studies of newborn infants concentrate on the first few postnatal days not for theoretical reasons but because the infants are still in the hospital following delivery and thus are readily accessible for research. However, recent work indicates the wisdom of testing older infants. Even within the first three days of extrauterine life greater habituation has been found in older infants compared to younger infants in the sample (Adkinson & Berg, 1975; Friedman & Carpenter, 1971).

METHODOLOGICAL CONSIDERATIONS

Recent attempts have been made to circumvent some of the most obvious problems related to state. A study of HR responding to visual stimuli (Sameroff, Cashmore, & Dykes, 1973) introduced the methodological advance of completing all experimental preparations while the infants were asleep, and then waiting for them to awaken before presenting trials. This procedure eliminates the considerable amount of time lost in identifying infants as awake, transporting them to the laboratory, attaching electrodes, adjusting and calibrating equipment, etc. The full 5–10 min of available waking time can easily be consumed using the latter procedure.

Two other procedures have been used to shorten the recording period in an attempt to avoid state changes, but both have disadvantages. The first involves reducing the intertrial interval to the point where sufficient trials for habituation can be presented during the brief period of alertness that is available. Unfortunately, shortening the intertrial interval increases the risks of obtaining sensory adaptation, effector fatigue, or baseline changes due to incomplete recovery from previous responses. The last problem is especially important when long latency autonomic responses are recorded. Another approach is to reduce the number of trials while maintaining adequate intertrial intervals to allow responding from the previous trial to return to baseline and stabilize. But the reduction in trials may not allow enough stimulus experience to produce habituation.

In older infants where periods of alertness are not restrictively short, Koch's (1968) well designed study has shown how the effects of mutually interdependent rhythms associated with digestion and state cycles can be measured simultaneously by simply using an orthogonal design. Koch's procedure was to feed 4–6-month-old infants at 6 different times during successive long periods of alertness, but to measure conditioned head-turning reactions to auditory stimuli at the same 8 points in time within each alert period (10, 25, 40, 55, 70, 85, and 115 min after the onset of wakefulness). Head turning was reinforced by an opportunity to view various noise-making toys. In this manner, Koch examined changes in latency of the head-turning response separately in relation to the time of feeding, and in relation to the elapsed time within the waking period. He found that the latency of the conditioned head turning response first shortens and then lengthens as a function of duration of wakefulness alone, but changes in the opposite fashion with respect to time after feeding. This type of design could be used to measure more precisely the effects of state on habituation in infants, even allowing temporal effects within a single state category to be measured. Using an approach similar to Koch's, we presented data in Figure 1 that revealed differences in responding at different points within a period of wakefulness in newborns.

Another approach to the state problem has been to test the newborn in the longest and most unambiguous state, quiet sleep. Two of the best neonatal habituation experiments (Engen & Lipsitt, 1965; Engen et al., 1963) maintained neonates in the state of quiet sleep and reported both habituation and dishabitu-ation of respiratory responses to various olfactory stimuli. In older infants, Lewis et al. (1969a) reported habituation of HR change in quiet sleep, but not during wakefulness. (Unfortunately, Lewis et al., 1969a, were not able to present all 30 habituation trials without interruption to their awake 2–6-week-old infants, rendering the data collected in the awake state ambiguous.) On the other hand, Hutt et al. (1968) found no habituation in sleep but did find reliable response changes occurring as a function of state change. Research with adult subjects is also contradictory, some studies reporting both habituation and performance of conditioned responses during sleep (Firth, 1973; McDonald & Carpenter, 1975; Williams, Morlock, & Morlock, 1966), while other work has obtained habituation of biphasic HR responses in awake adults, but not in drowsy or sleeping adults (McDonald, Johnson, & Hord, 1964). Complex and contradictory results might be expected in view of recent complicated distinc-tions made between phasic and tonic phenomena of sleep (Grosser & Siegel, 1971; Rechtschaffen, 1973).

Relatively few neonatal experiments appear to have been designed with the state limitations of infants in mind. Tables 3A and 3B summarize the research designed to test either habituation over trials or average responding to neutral or nonsignal stimulation in both awake newborns (3A) and in sleeping newborns or those whose state was unrecorded or uncontrolled (3B). Studies of responding to nonsignal stimuli differ from habituation studies primarily in presenting an inadequate number of stimulus repetitions to assess habituation, or failing to examine changes in responding as a function of trials.

The critical feature of this table is the relation between the percentage of infants that could be expected to change state during the various studies listed, and the percentage of infants actually reported to have changed state. The expected percentages are based upon the state change and state duration criteria discussed earlier in this chapter. The percentages in columns 2–5 in Table 3A and column 4 in Table 3B are what would be expected for *unstimulated* infants who entered their specified initial state spontaneously. Depending on the type and intensity of stimulation the values given may be moved upward or down-ward. Although percentages are approximate they may be conservative, since initiation of an experiment coincident with the beginning of either the awake state (Table 3A), or the other states listed (Table 3B), is assumed.

Percentages in column 6 (3A) and column 5 (3B) were computed after omitting infants who were reported lost due to nonstate-related factors such as equipment failure, experimenter error, etc. The values given are based solely on the report of the experimenter, and do not take into consideration infants who might have been soothed by a pacifier or stimulated by the experimenter to increase wakefulness (see footnote h). That is, the percentages reported reflect loss rates incurred despite attempts to pacify or arouse the infants. Therefore, many of these percentages may also be conservative.

Note that although many of the experimental treatments listed in the tables were of sufficient length to reasonably expect state changes in over 90% of the infants, the state of the infants was either ignored, or reported state changes were considerably fewer than would be predicted. Either of two conclusions can be reached on the basis of the data reported in the table: (1) the stimuli presented in many of these studies were sufficiently arousing to maintain a greater than expected number of infants in an awake, alert state; or (2) the data of many infants may have been retained in the experiments despite state changes on the part of the subjects. The former conclusion is not as likely as it may seem, since repeated stimulation can have soporific effects (Roberts & Campbell, 1967). Even extensive wake-up procedures administered prior to an experiment are insufficient to maintain alertness for more than a few minutes (Clifton, Meyers, & Solomons, 1972). In summary, many of the studies listed in Table 3A and 3B show large discrepancies between the percentage of infants expected to change state on the basis of the extensive literature cited, such as in Table 2, and the actual subject loss reported in the study. The implication is that much of the infant habituation literature may have been contaminated to an unknown degree by response changes caused by alterations in state.

The points which follow from examination of Table 3A and 3B apply perhaps more strongly to conditioning experiments, as every neonatal conditioning experiment published over the last 45 years has been long enough to expect that over 90% of the infants may have changed state during the experiment. The least questionable studies have tested newborns just before feedings using food reinforcement, and thus may have capitalized on the point in the state cycle where the infants are maximally responsive to food and apt to have a relatively longer period of alertness.

THE HABITUATION PARADIGM:
A FEW BASIC RECOMMENDATIONS
FOR STUDIES OF INFANTS

In view of the difficulties referred to above, the design of habituation experiments using infant subjects becomes critically important. Most obviously, limitations imposed by behavioral state must determine the design, along with stimulus and response parameter considerations. In addition, behavioral state should be monitored using several indices, as no single behavioral or physiological measure is conclusive. An analogy to the infant researcher is the physiological

TABLE 3A
Newborn Studies of Habituation and Evoked Responding in Which Infants Were ≤ 7 Days Old and Initially Awake[a]

References	Number of trials[b]	Duration of study (min) and infants expected to change state (%)[c]				Infants reported to change state (%)	Disposition of data of infants who changed state[d]	Results[e]
		0–3 (0–30%)	4–6 (30–60%)	7–9 (60–90%)	10+ (>90%)			
Studies of habituation								
Adkinson and Berg (1976)	8			X		58	Discarded	H and DH
Barrett and Miller (1973)[f]	45				26+	10	Discarded	No H
Friedman (1972a)	>9				10–24+	44	Discarded	H and DH
Friedman (1972b)	8 or 10			X	11+	14	Discarded	H
Friedman, Bruno, and Vietze (1974)	>7			X	10+	41	Discarded	H and DH
Friedman and Carpenter (1971)	8			X		Unreported	?	H
Friedman, Nagy, and Carpenter (1970)	8			X		2[g]	Discarded	H
Haith (1966)[h]	24			X		34	Discarded	No H
Hutt, Bernuth, Lenard, Hutt, and Prechtl (1968)	≤180				≤120	100	Analyzed separately for different states	No H or DH
Jackson, Kantowitz, and Graham (1971, experiment 2)[h]	5–15		X		11	38	Discarded	H ?
Kaye (1966, experiment 2)	39				20	Unreported	?	H
Kaye and Levin (1963, experiment 1)	3				14	Unreported	?	No H
Keen (1964)[i]	50			X	16–22+	~4	Discarded	H, no DH
Moreau, Birch, and Turkewitz (1970)	40		X			Unreported	?	H
Sameroff (1970)	20/day				20+	>29	Discarded	H (inferred)
Semb and Lipsitt (1968)[i]	40				20	~17	Retained[j]	No H
Sigman, Kopp, Parmelee, and Jeffrey (1973)[h]	6			X		Unreported	?	H

Study			12	>0	?	No H
Stechler, Bradford, and Levy (1966)[h]	12					
Studies of responding to nonsignal stimuli						
Ashton (1973a, experiment 1)	≤6/state		≤12–13	>10	Discarded, and/or analyzed separately	State, etc, are important
(experiment 2)	≤6/state		≤12–13	Unreported	Discarded	Differential fixations
Fantz (1963)	12–48	X	10+	Low	Discarded	Differential fixations
Fantz and Miranda (1975)[h]	≤16	X		~20	Discarded	Differential fixations
Gregg, Clifton, and Haith (1976, tracking)[h]	4	X		50	Discarded	Visual attention
(stimulus dark)[h]	8			64	Discarded	
Hershenson (1964)[h]	6	X		~30	Discarded	Visual preferences
Hutt and Hutt (1970)	24+		18+	Unreported	?	LIV changes with state
Hutt, Hutt, Lenard, Bernuth, and Muntjewerff (1968)	4+	X		?	Analyzed separately for different states	Stimulus and state are important
Jackson, Kantowitz, and Graham (1971, experiment 3)[h]	4	X		59	Discarded	No HRR
Kearsley (1973)	4/day	X		Low	Discarded	Various HRRs
Kessen, Salapatek, and Haith (1972)[h]	5	X		47	Discarded	Visual attention
Miranda (1970)[h]	28		~15	Low	Discarded	Visual preferences
Pomerleau-Malcuit and Clifton (1973)	12	X		~19	Discarded	Various HRRs
Porges, Arnold, and Forbes (1973)[h]	4		11	<29	Discarded	Various HRRs
Porges, Stamps, and Walter (1974)[h]	4		10	57	Discarded	Various HRRs

(continued)

TABLE 3A (continued)

References	Number of trials[b]	Duration of study (min) and infants expected to change state (%)[c]				Infants reported to change state (%)	Disposition of data of infants who changed state[d]	Results[e]
		0–3 (0–30%)	4–6 (30–60%)	7–9 (60–90%)	10+ (>90%)			
Salapatek (1968)[h]	1		X			Low	Discarded	Visual scanning
Salapatek and Kessen (1966)[h]	2	X				<71	Discarded	Visual scanning
Salapatek and Kessen (1973)	2+/day	X	X			High	Discarded	Visual scanning
Sameroff (1967)	7/day				20	20	Discarded	Stimuli altered sucking
Sameroff, Cashmore, and Dykes (1973)	10	X				~50	Discarded	HR deceleration
Simner (1969)	1		X			19–26	Discarded	Various HRRs
Slater and Findlay (1972, experiment 2)	3	X				52	Discarded	Visual scanning
Stechler (1964)	9			X		13	Discarded	Drugs affect attention
Turkewitz, Moreau, Birch, and Davis (1970)	8–24		X		10–15+	57	Discarded	Nonequivalent responses
Wickelgren (1967, experiment 1)	8		X			≤55	Discarded	Poor convergence
Wickelgren (1967, experiment 2)	3	X				≤55	Discarded	

TABLE 3B

Newborn Studies of Habituation in Which Infants Were ≤7 Days Old and Initially Not Awake or in an Unspecified State

Study	Number of trials[b]	Duration of study (min)[b]	Infants' initial state	Infants expected to change state[c] (%)	Infants reported to change state (%)	Disposition of data of infants who changed state[d]	Results[e]
Aleksandrowicz and Aleksandrowicz (1974)	Unreported	Unreported	Sleep	?	Unreported	?	H
Bartoshuk (1962a, experiment 1)	24	24	Unreported	≥50	3	Discarded	H, no DH
(experiment 2)	71–81	70–80	Unreported	100	Unreported	?	H and DH
Bartoshuk (1962b)	40	15–40	Unreported	40–90+	Unreported	?	H
Brackbill, Kane, Manniello, and Abramson (1974, no drug)	37+	13	Sleep?	<50	Unreported	?	H
(drug)	74+	25	Sleep?	>50	Unreported	?	H
Bridger (1961)	30+	20–29	Unreported	≥50	High	Included	H and DH
Bronshtein, Antonova, Kamenetskaya, Luppova, and Sytova (1958)	1–10+	?	Unreported	Low ?	Unreported	?	H and DH
Bronshtein and Petrova (1967)	3–8+	3–11+	Unreported	Low to moderate	Unreported	?	H and DH
Campos and Brackbill (1973)	21–64	~15–60	Awake or active sleep	50–100	~100	Included, but analyzed separately	H
Clifton, Graham, and Hatton (1968)[h]	15	24–31	Unreported	≥50	<12	Discarded	H
Conway and Brackbill (1970)	42 & 75	7 & 12+	Sleep ?	Low	Unreported	?	H
Eisenberg, Coursin, and Rupp (1966)	21–73	3–12	Many states	Low to moderate	~100	Included, but analyzed separately	H and DH
Engen and Lipsitt (1965, experiment 1)	11	11	Quiet	≤10	<10	Discarded	H and DH
(experiment 2)	11	11	sleep	≤10	<10	Discarded	H and DH

(continued)

TABLE 3B (continued)

Study	Number of trials[b]	Duration of study (min)[b]	Infants' initial state	Infants expected to change state[c] (%)	Infants reported to change state (%)	Disposition of data of infants who changed state[d]	Results[e]
Engen, Lipsitt, and Kaye							
(experiment 1)	40	20	Quiet	~50	Unreported	?	No H
(experiment 2)	44	22	sleep	~50	Unreported	?	H and DH
Graham, Clifton, and Hatton (1968)[h]	15/day	27+	Awake or drowsy	>90	<19	Discarded	H
Gullickson & Crowell (1964)	15–21/day	~14	Unreported	Moderate ?	Unreported	?	H (inferred)
Keen, Chase, and Graham (1965)[h]	15/day	21+	Unreported	>50	<13	Discarded	H
Leventhal and Lipsitt							
(1964, experiment 1)	30	10	"Quiet"	Low to moderate	~19	Discarded	H, no DH
(experiment 2)	5–24	2–8	"Quiet"		20	Discarded	H and DH
Schachter, Williams, Khachaturian, Tobin, Kruger, and Kerr (1971)	110	197	Unreported	100	Unreported	Retained	No H
Stratton (1970)	46	38	Quiet sleep ?	90–100	Unreported	?	H and DH

Stratton and Connolly							
(1973, experiment 1)	30	21	Quiet	~50	Low	Retained	H and DH
(experiment 2)	19	16	sleep	<50	Low	Retained	H and DH

[a]In studies where the data for awake and sleeping infants were presented separately, only the data collected from awake infants are included.

[b]Variable, minimum, or mean values are given for studies in which a criterion of habituation rather than a fixed number of trials was used. For some studies blank or test trials are included in the total.

[c]In both Tables 3A and 3B percentages were arrived at without regard to arousing or pacifying procedures which may have been used. In 3A, where the duration of the experiment indicates greater than 90 percent subject loss, the actual duration of the study (in minutes) is given. For studies of variable length which used a habituation criterion, several intertrial intervals, etc., either variable or minimum durations have been given, or entries have been made in two or more columns.

[d]The entry "Discarded" applies only to the corresponding percentage of infants given in the previous column of the table, and does not cover pacified or aroused infants who might have been retained in a study.

[e]H = habituation, DH = dishabituation, LIV = "Law of Initial Values," HRR = heart rate response, HR = heart rate. The terms "habituation" and "dishabituation" are used uncritically, in correspondence with the conclusions of the studies listed. No endorsement of any study's conclusions should be assumed. An "H" has been listed for some studies which reported response decrement without definitely concluding that habituation had occurred. A "DH" has been listed for many studies which simply reported increased responding to a novel stimulus following habituation.

[f]Premature infants tested less than two weeks after birth at a mean conceptual age of 35.5 weeks.

[g]The study reported 5 of 320 trials were lost due to state changes.

[h]Some or all infants were stimulated by the experimenter or given a pacifier either before trials began, or between or during trials. Note: Studies of sucking in neonates are not footnoted as studies which used extraneous arousing or pacifying stimulation.

[i]State in these studies was not specified directly. Initial wakefulness was assumed from observed sucking rate.

[j]A session was interrupted if an infant stopped sucking, and sucking was allowed to recover during a period of no stimulation.

psychologist who must monitor several vital signs in order to maintain the proper level of anesthesia in an animal preparation. Specification of the infant's state throughout the experiment is of utmost importance for infants less than three months old, but even older infants can get drowsy or fussy during repetitive stimulation.

Several parameters of habituation should be manipulated so that internal consistency can be used to buttress conclusions concerning habituation. Using several stimulus intensities and intertrial intervals, for example, allows determination of whether the infant's habituation corresponds to the extensive parametric animal work (see Thompson & Glanzman, Chapter 2, this volume). If the same central process of habituation described by Thompson and his co-workers is controlling infant responding, then strong stimuli and long intertrial intervals should result in slower habituation rates, habituation beyond asymptote should result in slower spontaneous recovery, etc. Some response changes that occur as a function of state change resemble either habituation or sensitization, but a state change cannot easily produce alterations in responding that are consistent with several parameters of habituation. Greater confidence can be placed in the results of infant habituation studies that obtain internally consistent results after manipulating several parameters of habituation, as long as session length, an important state variable, does not vary significantly among parametric groups.

Another critical feature of the habituation paradigm is the use of discrimination trials following habituation. Certainly by now we know enough not to label any response decrement as "habituation." Discrimination trials (commonly referred to as "dishabituation trials" in the infant literature) may be used to test for sensory adaptation or effector fatigue, but can also be useful in assessing generalization of habituation. A novel stimulus might elicit no increase in responding on discrimination trials due to strong generalization of habituation to the new stimulus (see Geer, 1969, 1971). One method of reducing the confounding effects of generalization of habituation on discrimination trials might be to present several different stimuli from both the same and different stimulus dimensions or modalities (see Graham, 1973, for a review of the literature concerning generalization of autonomic responses to a test stimulus). Time permitting, several series of habituation and discrimination trials could be presented, just as series of conditioning, extinction, reconditioning, and re-extinction trials are used to demonstrate stimulus control in operant conditioning experiments. The former procedure has already been used with 5-month-old infants in the habituation research of McCall and Melson (1970; Melson & McCall, 1970), but may be prohibitively lengthy for awake newborns.

Because the use of discrimination trials introduces many problems, it deserves further discussion. The determination of the number of habituation trials to be given before the presentation of discrimination stimuli is a primary problem. Use of a fixed number of habituation trials does not appear advisable because many infants will not be habituated, while others will have been habituated beyond asymptote. In fact, when infants are dichotomized into groups of fast and slow habituators on the basis of a fixed number of habituation trials, the slow habituators may show no habituation whatsoever (Melson & McCall, 1970). One solution is to utilize these varying degrees of habituation by presenting different numbers of habituation trials to different groups of infants (McCall & Melson, 1970), including enough trials to virtually insure habituation in the group given the maximum.

Habituating all infants to some individualized performance criterion will also insure habituation prior to discrimination trials. Such criteria may consist of: (1) a response decrement to some percentage of the infant's initial level; (2) a specified number of nonresponse trials (usually consecutive); or (3) the same arbitrary amount of response decrement for all infants. In the first case the infants would be equated on relative amount of habituation, but could vary in absolute habituation. Using the second criterion, the infants would again be matched on relative decrement (100%), but would most likely show maximum variation in absolute amount of habituation. Finally, in the third example, the infants would vary in relative habituation while being equated for absolute decrement. These distinctions between criteria are not trivial, as Davis and Wagner (1968) have shown how stimulus intensity effects appear to be opposite depending on whether absolute or relative measures of habituation are used with one or more discrimination stimuli (Graham, 1973; Wagner, Chapter 3, this volume). The selection of habituation criteria should depend on the experimental design, the particular stimulus values used, and the parameters of habituation under investigation.

Statistical considerations may also be important in selecting a criterion of habituation. Any preselected criterion can be reached by chance if sufficient trials are presented. Bogartz (1965) formalized this problem and analyzed the risk of attaining various criteria by chance as a function of the probability of a response occurring on an individual trial. Bogartz constructed tables that specify both the maximum numbers of trials that should be presented for many different criteria, and attendant probabilities of Type 1 error. For example, if 5 consecutive trials of no response are adopted as the habituation criterion and the chance probability of no response on any single trial is .33; then no more than 21 trials can be presented if the investigator wishes to avoid reaching criterion by chance more than 5% of the time, that is, in more than 5% of the subjects. If the chance probability of no response is .25, then no more than 73 trials can be presented. Studies of habituation in newborn infants that have adopted the 5-trial criterion (Brackbill et al., 1974; Campos & Brackbill, 1973; Conway & Brackbill, 1970; Martinius & Papoušek, 1970) have uniformly reported that attainment of the habituation criterion requires 20 trials or more (range: 20–90+), but have failed to report the probability of a criterion trial occurring by chance. Specification of the probability of a criterion response should be based on the collection of adequate baseline or previous parametric data. In this way, empirically based estimates of response variation can be used to determine and evaluate various criteria of habituation.

HABITUATION AS AN INDEX
OF PSYCHOLOGICAL FUNCTIONING

Several researchers have used an individual infant's rate of habituation as an index of various complex cognitive processes (e.g., Lewis, 1971; McCall, 1971). The underlying hypothesis is that infants who show rapid response decrements are forming models or internal representations of stimuli faster than infants who habituate more slowly. Lewis (1971) stated that infants showing faster response decrement have "more efficient CNS function," implying superior abilities in general. Because older infants showed faster habituation than younger infants, Lewis et al. (1969b) argued that developmental increases in rate of habituation reflect developmental increases in the various cognitive abilities. The use of habituation data in this way is perhaps largely due to the nature of the habituation model adopted by the experimenter. Probably the two most widely held models are Thompson and Spencer's (1966; Thompson & Glanzman in this volume) and Sokolov's (1963). Lewis and McCall favor Sokolov's model, which posits the formation of a cortical model during repeated presentations of a stimulus, with discrepancies from the model eliciting OR's. In contrast, Thompson views response habituation as an intrinsic property of certain neurons in the CNS, possibly operating in similar ways in both the spinal cord and the brain (Groves & Thompson, 1973). To some extent the validity of a view of habituation rate as an index of higher cortical processing depends on which model of habituation receives the greatest empirical support. Since the question of the correct model has not been settled, however (Graham, 1973), it seems premature to test and classify infants as "fast" or "slow" learners, possessing efficient or inefficient CNS's, on the basis of their rate of response decrement.

The use of habituation rate as an index of developmental changes in cognitive abilities is encumbered by several confounding variables. First, many variables such as intertrial interval and stimulus intensity are known to affect the rate of habituation, but may change in importance developmentally. To avoid the inadvertent use of optimal habituation parameters for one group of infants and less optimal values for another group, several stimulus intensities, intertrial intervals, and various values of other habituation parameters should be used at each age level. Second, stimulus salience or attractiveness, inferred from visual fixation measures, also varies systematically with age (see the review by Bond, 1972). The solution seems to be the same—include a sufficiently wide range of stimulus values to insure that roughly equivalent stimuli get used at different ages.

Various social and emotional factors may also operate differently at different ages. Our tables don't touch on these factors, but they are of great importance in developmental research. Especially after 3–4 months of age, the novelty of the laboratory, new faces and voices of the experimenters, fear of strangers beginning as early as the sixth month, etc., all interfere with responding, probably to different extents depending on the response system selected (Lewis & Rosenblum, 1974; Parry, 1973). These characteristic problems of developmental research cannot be ignored if developmental parameters of response decrement are to bear any direct and meaningful relationships to the maturation of a central process of habituation.

Habituation, as a phylogenetically old and basic process of response modification, can be viewed as a learning process, albeit primitive (Harris, 1943; Humphrey, 1933; Thorpe, 1963). Faced with many of the problems of the comparative psychologist, the developmental researcher could spend fruitless hours attempting to equate learning situations for the different age subjects tested. In contrast, the methodological considerations specified by Gollin (1965) regarding the developmental study of learning could easily be applied to habituation as well (see Bitterman, 1965, for similar views regarding comparative research, especially "control by systematic variation"). That is, several major habituation parameters could be manipulated within each age range to see if they relate similarly to response decrement. Absolute comparisons of habituation processes and parameters at different ages should not be made. Rather, developmental changes involving interactions between major habituation parameters appear most fruitful. Virtually any organism can show response decrement to almost any selected stimulus for a variety of reasons. We must understand the process of habituation *within* age levels before accurate and meaningful developmental comparisons can be made.

ACKNOWLEDGMENTS

The preparation of this chapter was supported in part by NICHD grant HD-06753 to the first author. Both authors contributed equally to the preparation of the manuscript, so the ordering of the authors' names is arbitrary. The data collected by the authors that are reported in this chapter were collected at the Medical Center of Western Massachusetts. The invaluable assistance of the director of pediatrics, H. H. Shuman, M.D., and the nursing staff of the hospital is gratefully acknowledged. M. Nelson is now at the Illinois State Pediatric Institute.

REFERENCES

Note: Boldface numbers are references listed in Table 2.

Adkinson, C., & Berg, W. K. Cardiac deceleration in newborns: Habituation, dishabituation, and offset responses. *Journal of Experimental Child Psychology*, 1976, *21*, 46–60. **1**

Akert, K., Bally, C., & Schadé, J. P. (Eds.). *Progress in brain research.* Vol. 18. *Sleep mechanisms.* New York: Elsevier, 1965.

Akiyama, Y., Schulte, F. J., Schultz, M. A., & Parmelee, A. H., Jr. Acoustically evoked responses in premature and full term newborn infants. *Electroencephalography and Clinical Neurophysiology*, 1969, *26*, 371–380. 2

Aleksandrowicz, M. K., & Aleksandrowicz, D. R. Obstetrical pain-relieving drugs as predictors of infant behavior variability. *Child Development*, 1974, *45*, 935–945.

Anders, T. F., & Hoffman, E. The sleep polygram: A potentially useful tool for clinical assessment in human infants. *American Journal of Mental Deficiency*, 1973, *77*, 506–514.

Aserinsky, E., & Kleitman, N. A motility cycle in sleeping infants as manifested by ocular and gross bodily activity. *Journal of Applied Physiology*, 1955, *8*, 11–18. 3

Ashton, R. The influence of state and prandial condition upon the reactivity of the newborn to auditory stimulation. *Journal of Experimental Child Psychology*, 1973, *15*, 315–327. (a) 4

Ashton, R. The state variable in neonatal research: A review. *Merrill–Palmer Quarterly*, 1973, *19*, 3–20. (b)

Ashton, R., & Connolly, K. The relation of respiration rate and heart rate to sleep states in the human newborn. *Developmental Medicine and Child Neurology*, 1971, *13*, 180–187. 5

Barnet, A. B., & Goodwin, A. M. Averaged evoked electroencephalographic responses to clicks in the human newborn. *Electroencephalography and Clinical Neurophysiology*, 1965, *18*, 441–450. 6

Barrett, T. E., & Miller, L. K. The organization of non-nutritive sucking in the premature infant. *Journal of Experimental Child Psychology*, 1973, *16*, 472–483.

Bartoshuk, A. K. Human neonatal cardiac acceleration to sound: Habituation and dishabituation. *Perceptual and Motor Skills*, 1962, *15*, 15–27. (a)

Bartoshuk, A. K. Response decrement with repeated elicitation of human neonatal cardiac acceleration to sound. *Journal of Comparative and Physiological Psychology*, 1962, *55*, 9–13. (b)

Beintema, D. J. *A Neurological study of newborn infants*. Clinics in Developmental Medicine No. 28. Lavenham, Suffolk, England: Lavenham Press, 1968. 7

Bell, R. Q. Sleep cycles and skin potential in newborn studies with a simplified observation and recording system. *Psychophysiology*, 1970, *6*, 778–786. 8

Bell, R. Q., & Haaf, R. A. Irrelevance of newborn waking states to some motor and appetitive responses. *Child Development*, 1971, *42*, 69–77. 9

Berg, W. K. Cardiac orienting response of 6- and 16-week-old infants. *Journal of Experimental Child Psychology*, 1974, *17*, 303–312.

Berg, W. K., Adkinson, C. D., & Strock, B. D. Duration and frequency of periods of alertness in neonates. *Developmental Psychology*, 1973, *9*, 434.

Berg, K. M., Berg, W. K., & Graham, F. K. Infant heart rate response as a function of stimulus and state. *Psychophysiology*, 1971, *8*, 30–44. 10

Berkson, G., & Mooney, D. J. Basal skin resistance of premature infants. *Perceptual and Motor Skills*, 1971, *33*, 1138. 11

Bitterman, M. E. Phyletic differences in learning. *American Psychologist*, 1965, *20*, 396–410.

Bogartz, R. S. The criterion method: Some analyses and remarks. *Psychological Bulletin*, 1965, *64*, 1–14.

Bond, E. K. Perception of form by the human infant. *Psychological Bulletin*, 1972, *77*, 225–245.

Brackbill, Y. Acoustic variation and arousal level in infants. *Psychophysiology*, 1970, *6*, 517–526.

Brackbill, Y. Continuous stimulation reduces arousal level: Stability of the effect over time. *Child Development*, 1973, *44*, 43–46.

Brackbill, Y. Continuous stimulation and arousal level in infancy: Effects of stimulus intensity and stress. *Child Development,* 1975, *46,* 364–369.

Brackbill, Y., Kane, J., Manniello, R. L., & Abramson, D. Obstetric premedication and infant outcome. *American Journal of Obstetrics and Gynecology,* 1974, *118,* 377–384.

Brady, J. P., & Tooley, W. H. Cardiovascular and respiratory reflexes in the newborn. In L. S. James (Ed.), *The pediatric clinics of North America* (Vol. 13). Philadelphia: Saunders, 1966. **12**

Brazelton, T. B. Observations of the neonate. *Journal of the American Academy of Child Psychiatry,* 1962, *1,* 38–58.

Bridger, W. H. Sensory habituation and discrimination in the human neonate. *American Journal of Psychiatry,* 1961, *117,* 991–996.

Bridger, W. H. Sensory discrimination and autonomic function in the newborn. *Journal of the American Academy of Child Psychiatry,* 1962, *1,* 67–82.

Bronshtein, A. I., Antonova, T. G., Kamenetskaya, A. G., Luppova, N. N., & Sytova, V. A. On the development of the functions of analyzers in infants and some animals at the early stage of ontogenesis. In *Problems of evolution of physiological functions.* Moscow: USSR Academy of Sciences, 1958 (translation available from the Office of Technical Services, U. S. Department of Commerce, Washington, D. C.).

Bronshtein, A. I., & Petrova, E. P. The auditory analyzer in young infants. In Y. Brackbill & G. G. Thompson (Eds.), *Behavior in infancy and early childhood.* New York: The Free Press, 1967.

Bronson, G. The postnatal growth of visual capacity. *Child Development,* 1974, *45,* 873–890.

Broughton, R. J., Poiré, R., & Tassinari, C. A. The electrodermogram (Tarchanoff effect) during sleep. *Electroencephalography and Clinical Neurophysiology,* 1965, *18,* 691–708. **13**

Brown, J. L. States in newborn infants. *Merrill–Palmer Quarterly,* 1964, *10,* 313–327.

Bryan, E. S. Variations in the responses of infants during first ten days of post-natal life. *Child Development,* 1930, *1,* 56–77.

Campbell, D. Motor activity in a group of newborn babies. *Biologia Neonatorum,* 1968, *13,* 257–270. **14**

Campos, J. J., & Brackbill, Y. Infant state: Relationship to heart rate, behavioral response and response decrement. *Developmental Psychobiology,* 1973, *6,* 9–19. **15**

Chase, M. H. Patterns of reflex excitability during the ontogenesis of sleep and wakefulness. In C. D. Clemente, D. P. Purpura, & F. E. Mayer (Eds.), *Sleep and the maturing nervous system.* New York: Academic Press, 1972. **16**

Chase, M. H. (Ed.), *The sleeping brain. Perspectives in the brain sciences* (Vol. 1). Los Angeles: Brain Information Service/Brain Research Institute, UCLA, 1972.

Clemente, D. C., Purpura, D. P., & Mayer, F. E. (Eds.). *Sleep and the maturing nervous system.* New York: Academic Press, 1972.

Clifton, R. K. Cardiac conditioning and orienting in the infant. In P. A. Obrist, A. H. Black, J. Brener, & L. V. DiCara (Eds.), *Cardiovascular psychophysiology: Current issues in response mechanisms, biofeedback and methodology.* Chicago: Aldine, 1974. **17**

Clifton, R. K., Graham, F. K., & Hatton, H. M. Newborn heart-rate response and response habituation as a function of stimulus duration. *Journal of Experimental Child Psychology,* 1968, *6,* 265–278.

Clifton, R. K., Meyers, W. J., & Solomons, G. Methodological problems in conditioning the headturning response of newborn infants. *Journal of Experimental Child Psychology,* 1972, *13,* 29–42.

Cohen, L. B. Attention-getting and attention-holding processes of infant visual preferences. *Child Development,* 1972, *43,* 869–879.

Conway, E., & Brackbill, Y. Delivery medication and infant outcom: An empirical study. *Monographs of the Society for Research in Child Development,* 1970, *35*(No. 4), 24–34.

Crowell, D. H., Davis, C. M., Chun, B. J., & Spellacy, F. J. Galvanic skin reflex in newborn humans. *Science,* 1965, *148,* 1108–1111. 18

Crowell, D. H., Jones, R. H., Nakagawa, J. K., & Kapuniai, L. E. Information processing and human newborn heart rate response. In F. J. Mönks, W W Hartup, & J. De Wit (Eds.), *Determinants of behavioral development.* New York: Academic Press, 1972. 19

Curzi-Dascalova, L., Pajot, N., & Dreyfus-Brisac, C. Relationships between some phasic and autonomic events and the spontaneous skin potential responses (SPR) during sleep of premature and full-term babies. In W. P. Koella & P. Levin (Eds.), *Sleep: Physiology, biochemistry, psychology, pharmacology, clinical implications.* Basel, Switzerland: Karger, 1973. 20

Curzi-Dascalova, L., Pajot, N., & Dreyfus-Brisac, C. Spontaneous skin potential responses in sleeping infants between 24 and 41 weeks of conceptional age. *Psychophysiology,* 1973, *10,* 478–487. 21

Davis, M., & Wagner, A. R. Startle responsiveness after habituation to different intensities of tone. *Psychonomic Science,* 1968, *12,* 337–338.

Desmedt, J. E., & Manil, J. Somatosensory and evoked potentials of the normal human neonate in REM sleep, in slow wave sleep and in waking. *Electroencephalography and Clinical Neurophysiology,* 1970, *29,* 113–126. 22

Dittrichová, J. Development of sleep in infancy. *Journal of Applied Physiology,* 1966, *21,* 1243–1246.

Dittrichová, J. Development of sleep in infancy. In R. J. Robinson (Ed.), *Brain and early behaviour.* New York: Academic Press, 1969. 23

Dittrichová, J., & Lapáčková, V. Development of the waking state in young infants. *Child Development,* 1964, *35,* 365–370.

Dittrichová, J., & Paul, K. Responsivity in newborns during sleep. *Activitas Nervosa Superior (Praha),* 1974, *16,* 112–113. 24

Dreyfus-Brisac, C. The bioelectrical development of the central nervous system during early life. In F. Falkner (Ed.), *Human development.* London: Saunders, 1966. 25

Dreyfus-Brisac, C. Organization of sleep in prematures: Implications for caregiving. In M. Lewis & L. A. Rosenblum (Eds.), *The effect of the infant on its caregiver.* New York: Wiley, 1974. 26

Dustman, R. E., & Beck, E. C. The effects of maturation and aging on the wave form of visually evoked potentials. *Electroencephalography and Clinical Neurophysiology,* 1969, *26,* 2–11.

Eisenberg, R. B., Coursin, D. B., & Rupp, N. R. Habituation to an acoustic pattern as an index of differences among human neonates. *Journal of Auditory Research,* 1966, *6,* 239–248.

Ellingson, R. Methods of recording cortical evoked responses in the human infant. In A. Minkowski (Ed.), *Regional development of the brain in early life.* Oxford: Blackwell Scientific Publications, 1967. 27

Ellingson, R. J. The study of brain electrical activity in infants. In L. P. Lipsitt & C. C. Spiker (Eds.), *Advances in child development and behavior* (Vol. 3). New York: Academic Press, 1967. 28

Ellingson, R. J. Variability of visual evoked responses in the human newborn. *Electroencephalography and Clinical Neurophysiology,* 1970, *29,* 10–19. 29

Ellingson, R. J., & Ellis, R. R. Motor response thresholds to electrical stimulation at the wrist in human newborns. *Developmental Psychobiology,* 1969, *2,* 202–206. 30

Ellis, R. R., & Ellingson, R. J. Responses to electrical stimulation of the median nerve in the human newborn. *Developmental Psychobiology,* 1973, *6,* 235–244. 31

Emde, R. N., & Metcalf, D. R. An electroencephalographic study of behavioral rapid eye movement states in the human newborn. *Journal of Nervous and Mental Disease,* 1970, *150,* 376–386. **32**

Engen, T., & Lipsitt, L. P. Decrement and recovery of responses to olfactory stimuli in the human neonate. *Journal of Comparative and Physiological Psychology,* 1965, *59,* 312–316.

Engen, T., Lipsitt, L. P., & Kaye, H. Olfactory responses and adaptation in the human neonate. *Journal of Comparative and Physiological Psychology,* 1963, *56,* 73–77.

Fantz, R. L. Pattern vision in newborn infants. *Science,* 1963, *140,* 296–297.

Fantz, R. L. Visual experience in infants: Decreased attention to familiar patterns relative to novel ones. *Science,* 1964, *146,* 668–670.

Fantz, R. L., & Miranda, S. B. Newborn infant attention to form to contour. *Child Development,* 1975, *46,* 224–228.

Firth, H. Habituation during sleep. *Psychophysiology,* 1973, *10,* 43–51.

Freemon, F. R. *Sleep research. A critical review.* Springfield, Illnois: Charles C Thomas, 1972.

Friedman, S. Habituation and recovery of visual response in the alert human newborn. *Journal of Experimental Child Psychology,* 1972, *13,* 339–349. (a)

Friedman, S. Newborn visual attention to repeated exposure of redundant vs. "novel" targets. *Perception and Psychophysics,* 1972, *12,* 291–294. (b)

Friedman, S., Bruno, L. A., & Vietze, P. Newborn habituation to visual stimuli: A sex difference in novelty detection. *Journal of Experimental Child Psychology,* 1974, *18,* 242–251.

Friedman, S., & Carpenter, G. C. Visual response decrement as a function of the age of human newborn. *Child Development,* 1971, *42,* 1967–1973.

Friedman, S., Nagy, A. N., & Carpenter, G. C. Newborn attention: Differential response decrement to visual stimuli. *Journal of Experimental Child Psychology,* 1970, *10,* 44–51.

Geer, J. H. Generalization of inhibition in the orienting response. *Psychophysiology,* 1969, *6,* 197–201.

Geer, J. H. Effect of presenting matching stimuli on the orienting response. *Perceptual and Motor Skills,* 1971, *33,* 187–191.

Gentry, E. F., & Aldrich, C. A. Rooting reflex in the newborn infant: Incidence and effect of it on sleep. *American Journal of Diseases of Children.* 1948, *75,* 528–539. **33**

Globus, G. G., Drury, R. L., Phoebus, E. C., & Boyd, R. Ultradian rhythms in human performance. *Perceptual and Motor Skills,* 1971, *33,* 1171–1174.

Goldie, L., & Hopkins, I. J. Head turning towards diffuse light in the neurological examination of newborn infants. *Brain,* 1964, *87,* 665–672. **34**

Goldie, L., & Velzer, C. V. Innate sleep rhythms. *Brain,* 1965, *88,* 1043–1056. **35**

Gollin, E. S. A developmental approach to learning and cognition. In L. P. Lipsitt & C. C. Spiker (Eds.), *Advances in child development and behavior* (Vol. 2). New York: Academic, 1965.

Gordon, N. S., & Bell, R. Q. Activity in the human newborn. *Psychological Reports,* 1961, *9,* 103–116. **36**

Graham, F. K. Habituation and dishabituation of responses innervated by the autonomic nervous system. In H. V. S. Peeke & M. J. Herz (Eds.), *Habituation.* Vol. 1. *Behavioral studies.* New York: Academic Press, 1973.

Graham, F. K., Berg, K. M., Berg, W. K., Jackson, J. C., Hatton, H. M., & Kantowitz, S. R. Cardiac orienting responses as a function of age. *Psychonomic Science,* 1970, *19,* 363–365.

Graham, F. K., & Clifton, R. K. Heart-rate change as a component of the orienting response. *Psychological Bulletin,* 1966, *65,* 305–320.

Graham, F. K., Clifton, R. K., & Hatton, H. M. Habituation of heart rate response to repeated auditory stimulation during the first five days of life. *Child Development*, 1968, *39*, 35–52.

Graham, F. K., & Jackson, J. C. Arousal systems and infant heart rate responses. In H. W. Reese & L. P. Lipsitt (Eds.), *Advances in child development and behavior* (Vol. 5). New York: Academic Press, 1970. 37

Grogg, C., Clifton, R., & Haith, M. A possible explanation for the frequent failure to find cardiac orienting in the newborn infant. *Developmental Psychology*, 1976, *12*, 75–76.

Grosser, G. S., & Siegal, A. W. Emergence of a tonic-phasic model for sleep and dreaming: Behavioral and physiological observations. *Psychological Bulletin*, 1971, *75*, 60–72.

Groves, P. M., & Thompson, R. F. A dual-process theory of habituation: Neural mechanisms. In H. V. S. Peeke & M. J. Herz (Eds.), *Habituation*. Vol. 2: *Physiological substrates*. New York: Academic Press, 1973.

Gullickson, G. R., & Crowell, D. H. Neonatal habituation to electrotactual stimulation. *Journal of Experimental Child Psychology*, 1964, *1*, 388–396. 38

Haith, M. M. The response of the human newborn to visual movement. *Journal of Experimental Child Psychology*, 1966, *3*, 235–243.

Harris, J. D. Habituatory response decrement in the intact organism. *Psychological Bulletin*, 1943, *40*, 385–422.

Hershenson, M. Visual discrimination in the human newborn. *Journal of Comparative and Physiological Psychology*, 1964, *58*, 270–276.

Hrbek, A., Hrbková, M., & Lenard, H. Somato-sensory, auditory and visual evoked responses in newborn infants during sleep and wakefulness. *Electroencephalography and Clinical Neurophysiology*, 1969, *26*, 597–603. 39

Humphrey, G. *The nature of learning in its relation to the living system*. New York: Harcourt, Brace and Company, 1933.

Humphrey, T. Postnatal repetition of human prenatal activity sequences with some suggestions of their neuroanatomical basis. In R. J. Robinson (Ed.), *Brain and early behavior*. New York: Academic Press, 1969. 40

Hunt, W. A., Clarke, F. M., & Hunt, E. B. Studies of the startle pattern: IV. Infants. *Journal of Psychology*, 1936, *2*, 339–352. 41

Hutt, C., Bernuth, H. V., Lenard, H. G., Hutt, S. J., & Prechtl, H. F. R. Habituation in relation to state in the human neonate. *Nature (London)*, 1968, *220*, 618–620.

Hutt, C., & Hutt, S. J. The neonatal evoked heart rate response and the law of initial value. *Psychophysiology*, 1970, *6*, 661–668.

Hutt, S. J., Hutt, C., Lenard, H. G., Bernuth, H. V., & Muntjewerff, W. J. Auditory responsivity in the human neonate. *Nature (London)*, 1968, *218*, 888–890.

Hutt, S. J., Lenard, H. G., & Prechtl, H. F. R. Psychophysiological studies in newborn infants. In L. P. Lipsitt & H. W. Reese (Eds.), *Advances in child development and behavior* (Vol. 4). New York: Academic Press, 1969. 42

Jackson, J. C., Kantowitz, S. R., & Graham, F. K. Can newborns show cardiac orienting? *Child Development*, 1971, *42*, 107–121.

Johnson, L. C. A psychophysiology for all states. *Psychophysiology*, 1970, *6*, 501–516. 43

Jouvet, M. Neurophysiology of the states of sleep. *Physiological Reviews*, 1967, *47*, 117–177.

Jouvet, M. Biogenic amines and the states of sleep. *Science*, 1969, *163*, 32–40.

Jovanović, U. J. *Normal sleep in man*. Stuttgart: Hippokrates Verlag Stuttgart, 1971.

Jovanović, U. J. (Ed.). *The nature of sleep*. Stuttgart: Gustav Fischer Verlag, 1973.

Kagan, J. *Change and continuity in infancy*. New York: Wiley, 1971.

Kagan, J., Henker, B. A., Hen-Tov, A., Levine, J., & Lewis, M. Infants' differential reactions to familiar and distorted faces. *Child Development*, 1966, *37*, 519–532.

Kagan, J., & Lewis, M. Studies of attention in the human infant. *Merrill-Palmer Quarterly,* 1965, *11,* 95–127.

Kaye, H. Skin conductance in the human neonate. *Child Development,* 1964, *35,* 1297–1305. 44

Kaye, H. The effects of feeding and tonal stimulation on non-nutritive sucking in the human newborn. *Journal of Experimental Child Psychology,* 1966, *3,* 131–145.

Kaye, H. Infant sucking behavior and its modification. In L. P. Lipsitt & C. C. Spiker (Eds.), *Advances in child development and behavior* (Vol. 3). New York: Academic Press, 1967. 45

Kaye, H., & Levin, G. R. Two attempts to demonstrate tonal suppression of non-nutritive sucking in neonates. *Perceptual and Motor Skills,* 1963, *17,* 521–522.

Kearsley, R. B. The newborn's response to auditory stimulation: A demonstration of orienting and defensive behavior. *Child Development,* 1973, *44,* 582–590. 46

Keen, R. Effects of auditory stimuli on sucking behavior in the human neonate. *Journal of Experimental Child Psychology,* 1964, *1,* 348–354.

Keen, R., Chase, H., & Graham, F. K. Twenty-four hour retention by neonates of habituated heart rate response. *Psychonomic Science,* 1965, *2,* 265–266.

Kety, S. S., Evarts, E. V., & Williams, H. L. (Eds.). *Sleep and altered states of consciousness.* Baltimore: Williams & Wilkins, 1967.

Kessen, W., Salapatek, P., & Haith, M. The visual response of the human newborn to linear contour. *Journal of Experimental Child Psychology,* 1972, *13,* 9–20.

Kleitman, N. *Sleep and wakefulness* (2nd ed.). Chicago: University of Chicago Press, 1963.

Koch, J. The change of conditioned orienting reactions in 5-month-old infants through phase shift of partial biorhythms. *Human Development,* 1968, *11,* 124–137.

Korner, A. F. REM organization in neonates. *Archives of General Psychiatry,* 1968, *19,* 330–340. 47

Korner, A. F. State as variable, as obstacle, and as mediator of stimulation in infant research. *Merrill-Palmer Quarterly,* 1972, *18,* 77–94.

Korner, A. F. Early stimulation and maternal care as related to infant capabilities and individual differences. *Early Child Development and Care,* 1973, *2,* 307–327.

Lacey, J. I. Psychophysiological approaches to the evaluation of psychotherapeutic process and outcome. In E. A. Rubinstein & M. B. Parloff (Eds.), *Research in psychotherapy* (Vol. 1). Washington, D.C.: American Psychological Association, 1959.

Lacey, J. I. Somatic response patterning and stress: Some revisions of activation theory. In M. H. Appley & R. Trumbull (Eds.), *Psychological stress: Issues in research.* New York: Appleton–Century–Crofts, 1967.

Lacey, J. I., Kagan, J., Lacey, B. C., & Moss, H. A. The visceral level: Situational determinants and behavioral correlates of autonomic response patterns. In P. H. Knapp (Ed.), *Expression of the emotions in man.* New York: International Universities Press, 1963.

Leventhal, A. S., & Lipsitt, L. P. Adaptation, pitch discrimination, and sound localization in the neonate. *Child Development,* 1964, *35,* 759–767.

Levin, G. R., & Kaye, H. Nonnutritive sucking by human neonates. *Child Development,* 1964, *35,* 749–758. 48

Lewis, M. Individual differences in the measurement of early cognitive growth. In J. Hellmuth (Ed.), *Exceptional infant. Vol. 2. Studies in abnormalities.* New York: Brunner/Mazel, 1971.

Lewis, M. The cardiac response during infancy. In R. F. Thompson & M. M. Patterson (Eds.), *Bioelectric recording techniques.* Part C. *Receptor and effector processes.* New York: Academic Press, 1974. 49

Lewis, M., Dodd, C., & Harwitz, M. Cardiac responsivity to tactile stimulation in waking and sleeping infants. *Perceptual and Motor Skills,* 1969, *29,* 259–269. (a)

Lewis, M., & Goldberg, S. The acquisition and violation of expectancy: An experimental paradigm. *Journal of Experimental Child Psychology,* 1969, *7,* 70–80.

Lewis, M., Goldberg, S., & Campbell, H. A developmental study of information processing within the first three years of life: Response decrement to a redundant signal. *Monographs of the Society for Research in Child Development,* 1969, *34*(No. 9). (b)

Lewis, M., Kagan, J., Campbell, H., & Kalafat, J. The cardiac response as a correlate of attention in infants. *Child Development,* 1966, *37,* 63–71.

Lewis, M., & Rosenblum, L. A. (Eds.), *Origins of fear.* New York: Wiley, 1974.

Lewis, M., & Spaulding, S. J. Differential cardiac response to visual and auditory stimulation in the young child. *Psychophysiology,* 1967, *3,* 229–237.

Lipsitt, L. P., & Levy, N. Electrotactual threshold in the neonate. *Child Development,* 1959, *30,* 547–554. 50

Lipton, E. L., & Steinschneider, A. Studies on the psychophysiology of infancy. *Merrill–Palmer Quarterly,* 1964, *10,* 102–117. 51

Lipton, E. L., Steinschneider, A., & Richmond, J. B. The autonomic nervous system in early life. *New England Journal of Medicine,* 1965, *273,* 147–153, 201–208. 52

Lipton, E. L., Steinschneider, A., & Richmond, J. B. Autonomic function in the neonate: VII. Maturational changes in cardiac control. *Child Development,* 1966, *37,* 1–16. 53

Lodge, A., Armington, J. C., Barnet, A. B., Shanks, B. L., & Newcomb, C. N. Newborn infants' electroretinograms and evoked electroencephalographic responses to orange and white light. *Child Development,* 1969, *40,* 267–293. 54

Martinius, J. W., & Papoušek, H. Responses to optic and exteroceptive stimuli in relation to state in the human newborn: Habituation of the blink reflex. *Neuropädiatrie,* 1970, *1,* 452–460.

McCall, R. B. Attention in the infant: Avenue to the study of cognitive development. In D. N. Walcher & D. L. Peters (Eds.), *Early Childhood. The development of self-regulatory mechanisms.* New York: Academic Press, 1971.

McCall, R. B., & Kagan, J. Attention in the infant: Effects of complexity, contour, perimeter, and familiarity. *Child Development,* 1967, *38,* 939–952. (a)

McCall, R. B., & Kagan, J. Stimulus-schema discrepancy and attention in the infant. *Journal of Experimental Child Psychology,* 1967, *5,* 381–390. (b)

McCall, R. B., & Kagan, J. Individual differences in the infant's distribution of attention to stimulus discrepancy. *Developmental Psychology,* 1970, *2,* 90–98.

McCall, R. B., & Melson, W. H. Amount of short-term familiarization and the response to auditory discrepancies. *Child Development,* 1970, *41,* 861–869.

McDonald, D. G., & Carpenter, F. A. Habituation of the orienting response in sleep. *Psychophysiology,* 1975, *12,* 618–623.

McDonald, D. G., Johnson, L. C., & Hord, D. J. Habituation of the orienting response in alert and drowsy subjects. *Psychophysiology,* 1964, *1,* 163–173.

Melson, W. H., & McCall, R. B. Attentional responses of five-month girls to discrepant auditory stimuli. *Child Development,* 1970, *41,* 1159–1171.

Meyers, W. J., & Cantor, G. Observing and cardiac responses of human infants to visual stimuli. *Journal of Experimental Child Psychology,* 1967, *5,* 16–25.

Miranda, S. B. Visual abilities and pattern preferences of premature infants and full-term neonates. *Journal of Experimental Child Psychology,* 1970, *10,* 189–205.

Monod, N., & Garma, L. Auditory responsivity in the human premature. *Biologia Neonatorum,* 1971, *17,* 292–316. 55

Moreau, T., Birch, H. G., & Turkewitz, G. Ease of habituation to repeated auditory and somesthetic stimulation in the human newborn. *Journal of Experimental Child Psychology*, 1970, *9*, 193–207.

Murray, B. W. Habituation and the state variable in the human newborn. Unpublished doctoral dissertation, Queen's University, Kingston, Ontario, Canada, 1971. **56**

Ornitz, E. M., Ritvo, E. R., Lee, Y. H., Panman, L. M., Walter, R. D., & Mason, A. The auditory evoked response in babies during REM sleep. *Electroencephalography and Clinical Neurophysiology*, 1969, *27*, 195–198. **57**

Ornitz, E. M., Wechter, V., Hartmen, D., Tenguay, P. E., Lee, J. C. M., Ritvo, E. R., & Walter, R. D. The EEG and rapid eye movements during REM sleep in babies *Electroencephalography and Clinical Neurophysiology*, 1971, *30*, 350–353. **58**

Parmelee, A. H., Jr. Ontogeny of sleep patterns and associated periodicities in infants. In F. Falkner, N. Kretchmer, & E. Rossi (Eds.), *Modern problems in pediatrics* (Vol. 13). Basel, Switzerland: Karger, 1974.

Parmelee, A. H., Jr., Akiyama, Y., Schultz, M. A., Wenner, W. H., Schulte, F. J., & Stern, E. The electroencephalogram in active and quiet sleep in infants. In P. Kellaway & I. Petersen (Eds.), *Clinical electroencephalography of children.* New York: Grune & Stratton, 1968. **59**

Parmelee, A. H., Jr., Akiyama, Y., Stern, E., & Harris, M. A. A periodic cerebral rhythm in newborn infants. *Experimental Neurology*, 1969, *25*, 575–584. **60**

Parmelee, A. H., Jr., Brück, K., & Brück, M. Activity and inactivity cycles during the sleep of premature infants exposed to neutral temperatures. *Biologia Neonatorum*, 1962, *4*, 317–339. **61**

Parmelee, A. H., Jr., Schulte, F. J., Akiyama, Y., Wenner, W. H., Schultz, M. A., & Stern, E. Maturation of EEG activity during sleep in premature infants. *Electroencephalography and Clinical Neurophysiology*, 1968, *24*, 319–329. **62**

Parmelee, A. H., Jr., Schultz, H. R., & Disbrow, M. A. Sleep patterns of the newborn. *Journal of Pediatrics*, 1961, *58*, 241–250.

Parmelee, A. H., Jr., & Stern, E. Development of states in infants. In C. D. Clemente, D. P. Purpura, & F. E. Mayer (Eds.), *Sleep and the maturing nervous system.* New York: Academic Press, 1972. **63**

Parmelee, A. H., Jr., Wenner, W. H., Akiyama, Y., Schultz, M., & Stern, E. Sleep states in premature infants. *Developmental Medicine and Child Neurology*, 1967, *9*, 70–77.

Parmelee, A. H., Jr., Wenner, W. H., Akiyama, Y., Stern, E., & Flescher, J. Electroencephalography and brain maturation. In A. Minkowski (Ed.), *Regional development of the brain in early life.* Oxford: Blackwell Scientific Publications, 1967. **64**

Parry, M. H. Infant wariness and stimulus discrepancy. *Journal of Experimental Child Psychology*, 1973, *16*, 377–387.

Paul, K., & Dittrichová, J. Development of quiet sleep in infancy. *Physiologia Bohenoslovaca*, 1974, *23*, 11–18. **65**

Pavlov, I. P. *Conditioned reflexes. An investigation of the physiological activity of the cerebral cortex.* London: Oxford University Press, 1927.

Petre-Quadens, O. Sleep in the human newborn. In O. Petre-Quadens & J. D. Schlag (Eds.), *Basic sleep mechanisms.* New York: Academic Press, 1974. **66**

Petre-Quadens, O., Hardy, J. L., & De Lee, C. Comparative study of sleep in pregnancy and in the newborn. In R. J. Robinson (Ed.), *Brain and early behavior.* New York: Academic Press, 1969.

Petre-Quadens, O., & Schlag, J. D. (Eds.), *Basic sleep mechanisms.* New York: Academic Press, 1974.

Pomerleau-Malcuit, A., & Clifton, R. K. Neonatal heart-rate response to tactile, auditory, and vestibular stimulation in different states. *Child Development*, 1973, *44*, 485–496. **67**

Pomerleau-Malcuit, A., Malcuit, G., & Clifton, R. K. An attempt to elicit cardiac orienting and defense responses in the newborn to two types of facial stimulation. *Psychophysiology*, 1975, *12*, 527–535. 68

Porges, S. W. Heart rate indices of newborn attentional responsivity. *Merrill–Palmer Quarterly*, 1974, *20*, 231–254.

Porges, S. W., Arnold, W. R., & Forbes, E. J. Heart rate variability: An index of attentional responsivity in human newborns. *Developmental Psychology*, 1973, *8*, 85–92.

Porges, S. W., Stamps, L. E., & Walter, G. F. Heart rate variability and newborn heart rate responses to illumination changes. *Developmental Psychology*, 1974, *10*, 507–513.

Pratt, K. C. The neonate. In L. Carmichael (Ed.), *Manual of child psychology* (2nd ed.). New York: Wiley, 1954. 69

Prechtl, H. F. R. The directed head turning response and allied movements of the human baby. *Behavior*, 1958, *13*, 212–242. 70

Prechtl, H. F. R. Problems of behavioral studies in the newborn infant. In D. S. Lehrman, R. A. Hinde, & E. Shaw (Eds.), *Advances in the study of behavior* (Vol. 1). New York: Academic Press, 1965. 71

Prechtl, H. F. R. Polygraphic studies of the full-term newborn: II. Computer analysis of recorded data. In R. MacKeith & M. Bax (Eds.), *Studies in infancy*. Clinics in developmental medicine No. 27. Lavenham, Suffolk, England: Lavenham Press, 1968. 72

Prechtl, H. F. R. Brain and behavioural mechanisms in the human newborn infant. In R. J. Robinson (Ed.), *Brain and early behaviour*. New York: Academic Press, 1969. 73

Prechtl, H. F. R. Patterns of reflex behavior related to sleep in the human infant. In C. D. Clemente, D. P. Purpura, & F. E. Mayer (Eds.), *Sleep and the maturing nervous system*. New York: Academic Press, 1972. 74

Prechtl, H. F. R. The behavioural states of the newborn infant (a review). *Brain Research*, 1974, *76*, 185–212. 75

Prechtl, H. F. R., Akiyama, Y., Zinkin, P., & Grant, D. K. Polygraphic studies of the full-term newborn: I. Technical aspects and qualitative analysis. In R. MacKeith and M. Bax (Eds.), *Studies in infancy*. Clinics in developmental medicine No. 27. Lavenham, Suffolk, England: Lavenham Press, 1968. 76

Ratner, S. C. Habituation: Research and theory. In J. H. Reynierse (Ed.), *Current issues in animal learning*. Lincoln: University of Nebraska Press, 1970.

Razran, G. *Mind in evolution*. Boston: Houghton Mifflin, 1971.

Rechtschaffen, A. The psychophysiology of mental activity during sleep. In F. J. McGuigan & R. A. Schoonover (Eds.), *The psychophysiology of thinking. Studies of covert processes*. New York: Academic Press, 1973.

Rewey, H. H. Developmental change in infant heart rate response during sleeping and waking states. *Developmental Psychology*, 1973, *8*, 35–41.

Richter, C. P. High electrical resistance of the skin of new-born infants and its significance. *American Journal of Diseases of Children*, 1930, *40*, 18–26. 77

Roberts, B., & Campbell, D. Activity in newborns and the sound of a human heart. *Psychonomic Science*, 1967, *9*, 339–340.

Robinson, R. J. Nomenclature of the stages of sleep. In R. J. Robinson (Ed.), *Brain and early behavior*. New York: Academic Press, 1969.

Roffwarg, H. P., Dement, W. C., & Fisher, C. Preliminary observations of the sleep–dream pattern in neonates, infants, children and adults. In E. Harms (Ed.), *Problems of sleep and dreams in children*. Monographs on child psychiatry, No. II. New York: Pergamon, 1964. 78

Roffwarg, H. P., Muzio, J. N., & Dement, W. C. Ontogenetic development of the human sleep-dream cycle. *Science*, 1966, *152*, 604–619. 79

Salapatek, P. Visual scanning of geometric figures by the human newborn. *Journal of Comparative and Physiological Psychology,* 1968, *66,* 247–258.

Salapatek, P., & Kessen, W. Visual scanning of triangles by the human newborn. *Journal of Experimental Child Psychology,* 1966, *3,* 155–167.

Salapatek, P., & Kessen, W. Prolonged investigation of a plane geometric triangle by the human newborn. *Journal of Experimental Child Psychology,* 1973, *15,* 22–29.

Sameroff, A. J. Non-nutritive sucking in newborns under visual and auditory stimulation. *Child Development,* 1967, *38,* 443–452.

Sameroff, A. J. Respiration and sucking as components of the orienting reaction in newborns. *Psychophysiology,* 1970, *7,* 213–222.

Sameroff, A. J., Cashmore, T. F., & Dykes, A. C. Heart rate deceleration during visual fixation in human newborns. *Developmental Psychology,* 1973, *8,* 117–119.   80

Schachter, J., Williams, T. A., Khachaturian, Z., Tobin, M., Kruger, R., & Kerr, J. Heart rate responses to auditory clicks in neonates. *Psychophysiology,* 1971, *8,* 163–179.

Schmidt, K., & Birns, B. The behavioral arousal threshold in infant sleep as a function of time and sleep state. *Child Development,* 1971, *42,* 269–277.   81

Schmidt, K., Rose, S. A., & Bridger, W. H. The law of initial value and neonatal sleep states. *Psychophysiology,* 1974, *11,* 44–52.   82

Schulman, C. A. Effects of auditory stimulation on heart rate in premature infants as a function of level of arousal, probability of CNS damage, and conceptional age. *Developmental Psychobiology,* 1969, *2,* 172–183.   83

Schulte, F. J., Linke, I., Michaelis, R., & Nolte, R. Excitation, inhibition, and impulse conduction in spinal motoneurones of preterm, and small-for-dates newborn infants. In R. J. Robinson (Ed.), *Brain and early behaviour.* New York: Academic Press, 1969.   84

Semb, G., & Lipsitt, L. P. The effects of acoustic stimulation on cessation and initiation of non-nutritive sucking in neonates. *Journal of Experimental Child Psychology,* 1968, *6,* 585–597.

Sharpless, S., & Jasper, H. Habituation of the arousal reaction. *Brain,* 1956, *79,* 655–681.

Sigman, M., Kopp, C. B., Parmelee, A. H., Jr., & Jeffrey, W. E. Visual attention and neurological organization in neonates. *Child Development,* 1973, *44,* 461–466.

Simner, M. L. The cardiac self-stimulation hypothesis and nonnutritive sucking in human infants. *Developmental Psychology,* 1969, *1,* 569–575.

Slater, A. M., & Findlay, J. M. The measurement of fixation position in the newborn baby. *Journal of Experimental Child Psychology,* 1972, *14,* 349–364.

Sokolov, E. N. *Perception and the conditioned reflex.* New York: Pergamon, 1963.

Spears, W. C., & Hohle, R. H. Sensory and perceptual processes in infants. In Y. Brackbill (Ed.), *Infancy and early childhood.* New York: Basic Books, 1967.   85

Stechler, G. Newborn attention as affected by medication during labor. *Science,* 1964, *144,* 315–317.

Stechler, G., Bradford, S., & Levy, H. Attention in the newborn: Effect on motility and skin potential. *Science,* 1966, *151,* 1246–1248.

Steinschneider, A. Developmental psychophysiology. In Y. Brackbill (Ed.), *Infancy and early childhood.* New York: Basic Books, 1967.   86

Steinschneider, A. Sound intensity and respiratory responses in the neonate. *Psychosomatic Medicine,* 1968, *30,* 534–541.   87

Steinschneider, A. Determinants of an infant's cardiac response to stimulation. In D. N. Walcher & D. L. Peters (Eds.), *Early childhood. The development of self-regulatory mechanisms.* New York: Academic Press, 1971.   88

Sterman, M. B. The basic rest–activity cycle and sleep: Development considerations in man and cats. In C. D. Clemente, D. P. Purpura, & F. E. Mayer (Eds.), *Sleep and the maturing nervous system.* New York: Academic Press, 1972.

Sterman, M. B. Sleep. In L. V. DiCara (Ed.), *Limbic and autonomic nervous systems research.* New York: Plenum Press, 1974.

Sterman, M. G., & Hoppenbrouwers, T. The development of sleep–waking and rest–activity patterns from fetus to adult in man. In M. B. Sterman, D. J. McGinty, & A. M. Adinolfi (Eds.), *Brain development and behavior.* New York: Academic Press, 1971.   89

Stern, E., Parmelee, A. H., Jr., & Harris, M. A. Sleep state periodicity in prematures and young infants. *Developmental Psychobiology,* 1973, *6,* 357–365.

Stratton, P. M. The use of heart rate for the study of habituation in the neonate. *Psychophysiology,* 1970, *7,* 44–56.

Stratton, P. M., & Connolly, K. Discrimination by newborns of the intensity, frequency and temporal characteristics of auditory stimuli. *British Journal of Psychology,* 1973, *64,* 219–232.

Taft, L. T., & Cohen, H. J. Neonatal and infant reflexology. In J. Hellmuth (Ed.), *Exceptional infant. Vol. 1. The normal infant.* New York: Brunner/Mazel, 1967.   90

Tauber, E. S. Phylogeny of sleep. In E. D. Weitzman (Ed.), *Advances in sleep research* (Vol. 1). New York: Spectrum Publ., 1974.

Thompson, R. F., & Spencer, W. A. Habituation: A model phenomenon for the study of neuronal substrates of behavior. *Psychological Review,* 1966, *73,* 16–43.

Thorpe, W. H. *Learning and instinct in animals* (2nd ed.). Cambridge, Massachusetts: Harvard University Press, 1963.

Thurlow, W. R. Audition. In J. W. Kling & L. A. Riggs (Eds.), *Woodworth & Schlosberg's experimental psychology* (3rd ed.). New York: Holt, 1971.

Touwen, B. C. L. A study on the development of some motor phenomena in infancy. *Developmental Medicine and Child Neurology,* 1971, *13,* 435–446.   91

Turkewitz, G., & Birch, H. G. Neurobehavioral organization of the human newborn. In J. Hellmuth (Ed.), *Exceptional infant.* Vol. 2: *Studies in abnormalities.* New York: Brunner/Mazel, 1971.   92

Turkewitz, G., Moreau, T., Birch, H. G., & Davis, L. Relationships among responses in the human newborn: The non-association and non-equivalence among different indicators of responsiveness. *Psychophysiology,* 1970, *7,* 233–247.

Vallbona, C., Desmond, M. M., Rudolph, A. J., Pap, L. F., Hill, R. M., Franklin, R. P., & Rush, J. B. Cardiodynamic studies in the newborn. II: Regulation of the heart rate. *Biologia Neonatorum,* 1963, *5,* 159–199.   93

Vitová, Z., & Hrbek, A. Ontogeny of cerebral responses to flickering light in human infants during wakefulness and sleep. *Electroencephalography and Clinical Neurophysiology,* 1970, *28,* 391–398.

Watanabe, K., & Iwase, K. Spindle-like fast rhythms in the EEGs of low-birth-weight infants. *Developmental Medicine and Child Neurology,* 1972, *14,* 373–381.   94

Watanabe, K., Iwase, K., & Hara, K. Visual evoked responses during different phases of quiet sleep in pre-term infants. *Neuropädiatrie,* 1973, *4,* 427–433.

Weitzman, E. D. (Ed.) *Advances in sleep research* (Vols. 1–2). New York: Spectrum Publ., 1974.

Weitzman, E. D., & Graziani, L. J. Maturation and topography of the auditory evoked response of the prematurely born infant. *Developmental Psychobiology,* 1968, *1,* 79–89.   95

Weller, G. M., & Bell, R. Q. Basal skin conductance and neonatal state. *Child Development,* 1965, *36,* 647–657.   96

Wetherford, M. J., & Cohen, L. B. Developmental changes in infant visual preferences for novelty and familiarity. *Child Development,* 1973, *44,* 416–424.

Wickelgren, L. W. Convergence in the human newborn. *Journal of Experimental Child Psychology,* 1967, *5,* 74–85.

Williams, H. L., Morlock, H. C., & Morlock, J. V. Instrumental behavior during sleep. *Psychophysiology,* 1966, *2,* 208–216.
Wolff, P. H. The development of attention in young infants. *Annals of the New York Academy of Sciences,* 1965, *118,* 815–830.
Wolff, P. H. The causes, controls, and organization of behavior in the neonate. *Psychological Issues,* 1966, *5*(17, Whole No. 1), 1–105. 97
Wolff, P. H. The serial organization of sucking in the young infant. *Pediatrics,* 1968, *42,* 943–956. 98
Wolff, P. H. Discussion following Dittrichová paper. In R. J. Robinson (Ed.), *Brain and early behaviour.* New York: Academic, 1969.
Wolff, P. H. The interaction of state and non-nutritive sucking. In J. F. Bosma (Ed.), *Third symposium on oral sensation and perception: The mouth of the infant.* Springfield, Illinois: Charles C Thomas, 1972. 99
Wolff, P. H. Organization of behavior in the first three months of life. In J. I. Nurnberger (Ed.), *Biological and environmental determinants of early development.* Vol. 51 of the Research Publications of the Association for Research in Nervous and Mental Disease. Baltimore: Williams & Wilkins, 1973. **100**
Wolff, P. H., & Simmons, M. A. Nonnutritive sucking and response thresholds in young infants. *Child Development,* 1967, *38,* 631–638. **101**

6
Habituation of
Infant Visual Attention

Leslie B. Cohen

University of Illinois, Champaign–Urbana

Research on infant habituation is of relatively recent origin. Although comprehensive investigations of infant learning, perception, cognition, and social development date back at least to the 1930's, the first studies of habituation in the human infant began to appear in the literature less than 15 years ago. Even as late as 1971 one could conclude only that by 2 or 3 months of age infants could habituate to stimuli from a variety of modalities, and that the habituation procedure might prove useful in assessing the beginnings of other psychological processes (Jeffrey & Cohen, 1971).

A great deal has changed since 1971. Abundant evidence now exists on infant habituation, and new experiments continue to be published at an ever increasing rate. These recent experiments are investigating more than just whether or not an infant is capable of habituating. Habituation is now a common tool for answering basic questions about how the infant perceives, processes, and remembers information in his environment. The results of these experiments are slowly producing a fundamental change in our conception of the infant. Once thought of as a passive recipient of stimulation, the infant is proving to be an active participant in his interaction with the environment who is able to control the onset, duration, and termination of external information.

The proliferation of research on infant habituation has been most pronounced for studies of early visual attention. In these experiments habituation is usually defined as a reduction in fixation time to a repeated visual stimulus. The definition has two components: first, it must be demonstrated that an infant's fixation time decreases over time or trials; and second, that the decrease is specific to the stimulus which was repeated. The latter portion of this definition is particularly crucial in infant research. One recurring problem in investigations of infant behavior is determing whether alterations in an infant's responsiveness over time reflect changes in his reaction to a particular stimulus or more general changes in state. For example, most newborn infants can maintain an alert state for only a few minutes and then tend to fall asleep (Berg, Adkinson, Strock, 1973; Clifton & Nelson, Chapter 5, this volume) while many older infants become increasingly fussy or irritable over time (Cohen, DeLoache, & Rissman, 1975). Either change can cause a reduction in attention, but most investigators would not consider the reduction habituation. More detailed accounts of the procedures required to assess the role of state changes in an infant habituation paradigm have been presented elsewhere (Cohen & Gelber, 1975; Jeffrey & Cohen, 1971). It is sufficient to note here that most recent studies of infant habituation have adequately controlled for state changes by introducing one or more novel stimuli at the end of a series of habituation trials. If the infant's attention decreases during the habituation trials and then increases again to a novel stimulus of equal intensity, the decrease will have been specific to the originally repeated stimulus, general changes in state can usually be ruled out, and the infant is said to have habituated.

The first impression one gets from reviewing the literature on infant habituation is that a number of programmatic attempts have been made to answer the same general question: What are the optimal conditions for producing habituation in the human infant? While many might agree with this characterization of the field, others recently have begun to believe it may be incomplete. A more meaningful description might be that over the past ten years infant habituation research has tended to progress more in a stepwise fashion along a series of levels or plateaus. At each level certain specific questions were asked about infants' abilities, and procedures were developed to test these questions. Sooner or later dissatisfaction with existing techniques, contradictory data, or both, produced a modified conceptualization of the infant, and a new plateau was reached with different questions and techniques becoming relevant. To be sure, not all that was learned at one level was discarded at the next level. In fact many investigators have been conducting research at several levels concurrently. Nevertheless, it does seem that over the last few years research questions have changed somewhat as have assumptions about the infant's role in the habituation process.

This characterization of the field will be made more explicit in the remainder of the chapter which is organized in terms of these plateaus. At least four distinct levels can be identified, and in research from our laboratory, we may have, by accident, stumbled upon a fifth.

LEVEL 1: DEMONSTRATION
OF INFANT HABITUATION

Interest in infant habituation originated primarily from two sources. In the 1950s investigators of animal behavior were becoming increasingly disenchanted with traditional drive reduction theories such as those of Hull (1943) and Spence

(1956), and were discovering that a wide variety of organisms would approach or explore a stimulus for no reason other than that it was novel (Welker, 1961). Spontaneous alternation behavior was observed in animals as diverse as paramecia (Lepley & Rice, 1952), rats (Dember, 1961), and man (Iwahara, 1959), and attempts to explain alternation usually included either an avoidance of familiarity (Glanzer, 1953) or an approach to novelty (Dember, 1956). New motivational theories were proposed which put the reinforcing effects of novelty or stimulus change on a par with other more primary reinforcers such as food, water, and sex. Some of these theories also assumed the notion of an "optimal level of stimulation," according to which a moderate degree of novelty was presumed to be more reinforcing than either greater or lesser novelty (e.g., Berlyne, 1960; Hebb, 1955; Leuba, 1955). Ontogenetic changes in the effects of novelty or stimulus change were also reported. (See Welker, 1961, for a summary.) As animals became older, their optimal level tended to increase.

Given this background, it was natural for developmental psychologists to wonder at what age young children or even infants would be more attracted to novel than familiar stimuli. Would infants also exhibit an optimal level, and, as with the animal literature, would that level increase with age?

The second source of interest in infant habituation stemmed from the work of Sokolov (1963, 1969) on the orienting reflex (OR). The OR is actually a constellation of physiologic and behavior responses (heart rate change, EEG activation, head turning, eye movements, etc.) which occurs to the first presentation of a novel stimulus. According to Sokolov (1969), "The peculiar feature of the orienting reflex is that after several applications of the same stimulus (generally 5–15) the response disappears (or as the general expression goes 'is extinguished'). However, the slightest possible change in the stimulus is sufficient to reawaken the response [p. 673]."

Thus Sokolov, working from a totally different perspective than the psychologists investigating animal exploratory motivation, also found that both animals and man would respond differentially to novel and familiar stimuli. Sokolov, however, went further in two respects. First, he made explicit the habituation paradigm (repeatedly presenting one stimulus followed by a novel one) which was to become the standard procedure for studying infant habituation. And second, he proposed a neuronal model which linked habituation to memory.

According to Sokolov, the orienting reflex is not simply a reaction to current stimulation. Rather, it is a product of the discrepancy between current inputs and the neuronal trace or memory of prior ones. He assumed that within certain limits, the magnitude of the OR was proportional to the difference between the trace and the stimulus operating at a given moment. Since this discrepancy should be greatest when a novel stimulus is first presented, the largest OR should also occur. Repeated presentations of the same stimulus should lead to a buildup of the trace of that stimulus, reducing the discrepancy and thereby producing habituation of the OR. At this point, introduction of a new stimulus should reactivate the OR since the discrepancy between current and prior stimulation would once again be large. In fact it was the recovery of the OR to novel stimulation which indicated that habituation of the orienting reflex reflected more than just adaptation. It also indicated the acquisition and storage of some aspect of prior stimulation.

To developmental psychologists interested in assessing infant perceptual and cognitive development, the habituation paradigm seemed a promising technique. Even in the youngest infant one can measure behavioral and physiological responses to the initial presentation of a stimulus. The obvious question was what was the earliest age an infant's response would habituate and recover to a novel stimulus? If the infant responded differentially to a novel and familiar stimulus, it would indicate both that he could discriminate between them and that he remembered something about the familiar one. Using infants' reactions to novel versus familiar stimuli as an indicant of early cognitive development was especially attractive because the data fit into existing theoretical formulations. Optimal level theories developed to explain animal exploratory behavior were remarkably similar to Piaget's notion that inputs moderately different from those an infant had assimilated should be the most highly motivating (Hunt, 1961).

Thus several independent lines of investigation seemed to be converging on the same common theme: differential reactions to novelty and familiarity indicated some kind of memory; that this memory, however primitive, was available to a wide variety of organisms, perhaps even to human infants; that simple techniques (applicable to infants), had been developed to assess this memory; and that examination of infant memory might shed some light on more advanced forms of cognitive abilities in older children and adults.

The first developmental study of infant attention to novel versus familiar visual stimuli was reported by Fantz (1964). Earlier, Fantz (1958) had devised a technique for measuring visual preferences in infants by recording the percentage of time that patterns were reflected off an infant's cornea. Now he used the same corneal reflection technique to investigate infant recognition memory. Twenty-eight infants between the ages of 1 and 6 months were shown 2 complex pictures cut from magazines. The pictures were presented simultaneously. Ten 1-min-trials were given and 1 of the stimuli remained constant from trial to trial while the other was varied (Figure 1). Infants under 2 months of age tended to fixate the 2 pictures equally, but those over 2 months looked relatively less at the constant than at the changing picture as the session progressed. One cannot tell from these results whether actual habituation (a decrease in fixation time to the constant stimulus) occurred, or whether the "relative" decrease was produced by an increase in fixation time to the changing stimulus. However, infants did look at the novel and familiar stimuli differentially, which implies both discrimination and memory as early as 2 months of age.

Several other experiments more specifically on habituation of infant attention began appearing in the literature at about the same time or shortly

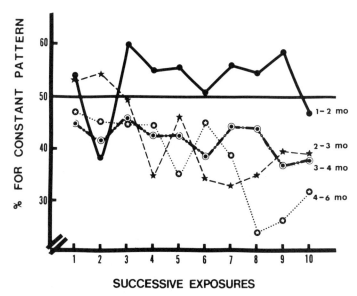

FIG. 1 Change in relative duration of fixation of a repeatedly exposed (constant) pattern relative to a novel (variable) pattern (the position of each being controlled) during a series of exposure periods. Each curve is the mean for six to eight infants. (Adapted from Fantz, 1964. Copyright 1964 by the American Association for the Advancement of Science.)

thereafter (Caron & Caron, 1969; Cohen, 1969a; Kagan & Lewis, 1965; Lewis *et al.,* 1966; Saayman, Ames, & Moffett, 1964). In all of them a single visual stimulus was presented repeatedly for a number of trials and fixation time recorded. By current standards most of the studies had some shortcoming: stimuli were not counterbalanced; following habituation no test was given with a novel stimulus; or if it was given, infant attention did not increase. Nevertheless, the majority of the experiments were consistent in showing that beginning at 2 or 3 months of age, repetition of the same visual stimulus produced a decrease in fixation time, and the older the subject the more rapid the decrease.

One of the more appropriately designed studies was reported by Wetherford and Cohen (1973). Infants between the ages of 6 and 12 weeks were repeatedly shown the same simple geometric pattern, and the Fantz procedure was used to record fixation times. Of the 17 15-sec trials given, 14 were with the familiar stimulus and Trials 2, 9, and 16 with novel ones. The experiment actually involved a combined cross sectional—longitudinal design, but since the cross sectional data produced the clearest results, only those will be reported here. Changes in fixation time over trials to the familiar pattern are shown in Figure 2. Consistent with the findings of earlier research, both 10- and 12-week-old infants decreased their fixation time over trials, while 6- and 8-week-old infants did not. By the end of the experiment the 10- and 12-week-olds also looked longer at the novel

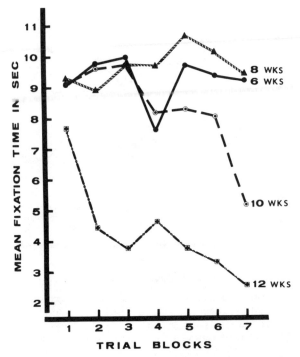

FIG. 2 The age × trial blocks interaction in the 14-trial familiarization period. (From Wetherford & Cohen, 1973.)

than at the familiar patterns (Figure 3). Somewhat surprisingly, even though fixation times of the 6- and 8-week-olds did not change, the infants responded more to the familiar than to the novel pattern.

Performance of the older subjects met the assumptions for both habituation and memory. Ten- and 12-week-olds both decreased their fixation time to the familiar stimulus and increased it again to a novel one. Performance of the younger subjects, however, required a more complex explanation. Even though they did not reduce their fixation time, they did respond differentially to novel and familiar stimuli. That result, by itself, indicated 6- and 8-week-old infants remembered something. Apparently, a decrement in looking is a sufficient, but not a necessary condition for storing information about the visual environment.

This preference for familiarity at about 6 weeks of age has been reported by other investigators as well (Greenberg, Uzgiris, & Hunt, 1970; Uzgiris & Hunt, 1970; Weizmann, Cohen, & Pratt, 1971). These investigators considered the evidence supportive of theories proposing a developmental change in the "optimal level" of novelty. According to the theories, younger infants should have a lower optimal level (that is they should prefer lower levels of novelty) than older infants. That would cause the younger ones to look longer at a moderately novel than at a highly novel stimulus.

Although "optimal level" explanations had considerable appeal at the time, recent evidence suggests that given the proper conditions, infants under two months of age are indeed capable of habituating. In a series of studies Friedman (1975) has repeatedly demonstrated that newborn infants can reduce their attention to a repeated checkerboard pattern and increase it again when the checkerboard is changed. Similarly, Hunter and Ames (1975), also using checkerboard stimuli, obtained habituation of attention and preference for novelty in five-week-old infants. Two procedural changes may have been responsible for these recent successes at obtaining habituation in infants under two months. The first is the use of simple black and white checkboard patterns. Recent evidence indicates that even though newborn infants have a relatively immature visual system, they will shift their gaze and attend to high contrast, vertically oriented black and white edges (Haith, 1968).

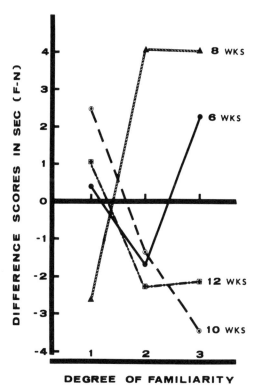

FIG. 3 The age X degree of familiarity interaction in the novelty preference data. (From Wetherford & Cohen, 1973.)

Possibly the multicolored or intricate patterns used in earlier studies were beyond the newborn's primitive visual capabilities. The second significant change was the use of a criterion for habituation rather than running all infants the same fixed number of trials. This provided infants with considerably more exposure time to the habituation stimulus. Perhaps if the earlier studies had provided additional trials, younger as well as older infants would have habituated.

For whatever the reason, the demonstration of habituation in newborn infants forced a change in the type of research question posed by investigators of infant attention, a change which we are considering characteristic of a new plateau or level. Instead of asking what is the earliest age an infant can habituate or remember, the question for level 2 research became: To what type of visual information is the infant's attention habituating? Rather than the demonstration of habituation being an end in itself, habituation became a means for investigating early information processing and memory ability.

LEVEL 2: THE TYPE OF INFORMATION PROCESSED BY THE INFANT

No great methodological advance marked the onset of Level 2. Appropriate controls were beginning to be used, and a test for novelty at the end of habituation was becoming routine. The major change was in emphasis from being primarily concerned about the infant's behavior during habituation, to being concerned about his behavior in the test. In Level 1 little regard was given to the type of stimulus presented to the infant. In Level 2 the stimuli were carefully selected to assess the type of information the infant processed and stored.

A typical example of Level 2 research is the experiment reported by Cohen, Gelber, and Lazar (1971). Sixty-four, 4-month-old infants were given 12, 15-second trials with a simple, colored geometric pattern followed by 8 test trials with the same or novel patterns. The experimental design is presented in Figure 4. The test included 2 trials with the original habituation stimulus, 2 with a novel color but familiar form, 2 with a familiar color but novel form, and 2 with novel color and form. A change in either form or color produced some increase in fixation time, and a change in both produced the greatest increase. Any increase in fixation time would signify that the infant had attended to that dimension. The results indicated, therefore, that by 4 months of age infants were capable of attending to and storing information about a visual pattern's color and form.

A recent study by Welch (1974) supported and extended the Cohen *et al.* (1971) findings. Welch's procedure differed somewhat from a true habituation paradigm. Although her infants were familiarized to a visual stimulus, she did not examine any reduction in attention, or habituation which might have resulted. However, she was interested in a subsequent preference for novelty

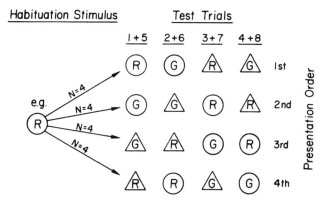

FIG. 4   Latin square design used for the test trials. Shown above is the case in which infants were habituated to the red circle. The same Latin square was used when one of the other three patterns was the habituation stimulus.

over familiarity. Her 4-month-old infants received the same complex pattern (multiple colored squares arranged in a bullseye) on both left and right sides of a screen for a 60-sec trial. This familiarization trial was followed by 3 10-sec test trials during which a novel stimulus replaced one of the familiar ones. The novel stimulus could vary in any of 3 dimensions, color, form, or arrangement of elements. A linear relationship was found between number of novel dimensions and percent fixation of the novel pattern, with the greater the novelty, the higher the percentage. Element arrangement, then, can be added to the list of dimensions which infants can process, discriminate and store.

Habituation and preference for novelty techniques are now among the most common methods for investigating a wide range of perceptual abilities in the infant. They have been successfully used to show that infants under six months of age can remember and discriminate between a variety of patterns (Fantz, Fagan, & Miranda, 1975), hues (Oster, 1975), orientation (McGurk, 1970), and even faces (Fagan, 1975). The techniques have also been employed with older infants and young children to demonstrate recognition of meaningful events (Golinkoff, 1975) and conceptual categories (Faulkender, Wright, & Waldron, 1974).

In one of the most imaginitive uses of the habituation paradigm, Golinkoff (1975) examined 14–18-month-old infants' ability to distinguish between the concepts of agent and recipient. Each infant was first shown 6 repetitions of a short movie in which a man pushed a table from left to right, and fixation times were recorded. One of 3 transformations of the movie was then presented. In the "position-direction" transformation the man pushed the table from right to left. The initial positions or locations of the man and table were reversed as was the direction of movement. But, the agent–recipient relationship remained unchanged. It was still the man pushing the table. In the "action role–position" transformation, the table pushed the man from left to right. In this case the direction of movement remained unchanged, but the agent and recipient were reversed as was the position of the table and man. Finally the "action role–direction" transformation, the table pushed the man from right to left. In this case the initial positions remained the same, but the agent and recipient, and direction of movement were reversed. The question of interest, of course, was which types of transformation would be most significant for the infant. Would infants' fixation times increase more when the perceptual characteristics of the movie (the position and direction) were maximally changed? Or would they increase more when the meaning of the event changed (agent–recipient reversal) even though there were fewer perceptual alterations? Unfortunately, Golinkoff's results must be considered somewhat tentative. The greatest increase seemed to occur when the role of agent and recipient were reversed. However, the difference was only marginally significant. Also it was unclear whether the increase in fixation time could be considered recovery of a previously habituated response or was simply a function of viewing the anomalous event of a table pushing a man. In any case, use of the habituation procedure to investigate preverbal infants' processing of higher-order meaningful events has considerable merit, and several investigators are following up Golinkoff's initial explorations in this area.

Level 2 research has already provided valuable information regarding an infant's ability to process visual stimulation. In all probability it will continue to do so in the future. However, there are some drawbacks to considering habituation simply as a tool for investigating perceptual discrimination and recognition. It directs attention away from the question of what the infant is actually doing in the testing situation. To what extent is he being controlled by the pictures presented in front of him? Is his turning to look at a pattern or subsequent fixation of a pattern merely automatic reflexive response, and is he gradually and inevitably reducing his fixation time to the same pattern because a match is slowly developing between what is stored and what is being seen at the moment? Or is he more actively controlling the stimulation he is receiving, determining for himself when, how long, and under what conditions he will look? The active versus passive role an infant plays may never be disentangled completely. But research from Levels 3, 4, and 5 suggests he is playing a more active role than had previously been assumed.

LEVEL 3: ATTENTION GETTING
AND ATTENTION HOLDING

It should be obvious that when a visual stimulus is presented in the periphery at least three discrete responses are involved in the act of attending: orienting to the stimulus; fixating it; and finally, turning away. Yet in Levels 1 and 2 no distinction was made among these three. All were presumably linked to the one common response measure, "total fixation time per trial." Research conducted at Level 3 produced the first break in that linkage. Procedures were developed to distinguish between orientation to a visual pattern or an "attention getting process" and maintenance of a fixation or an "attention holding process." Some research at this level indicated that attention getting involved more than an automatic orienting reflex. It also included an operant component. That is, orientation to a peripheral pattern was at least partially an active response under the control of the infant.

As we have noted repeatedly (Cohen, 1969b, 1972; Cohen et al., 1975), total fixation time per trial can be a misleading measure. One infant may look once for 10 sec during a trial, while another may look five times, with each look being 2 sec; yet both infants would be recorded as having identical 10-sec fixation times. Furthermore, as trials with the same stimulus continued, total fixation time would decrease, but it would be unclear whether the decrease resulted from a reduced tendency to turn to the stimulus or a reduction in the duration of each fixation. One might expect the former to occur from a Sokolovian viewpoint since turning toward a stimulus is one component of the orienting reflex. However, one might also expect the latter from an information processing point of view, since an infant must fixate a stimulus in order to process, store, and compare currently presented information with previously stored information.

In order to assess the relative importance of turning versus looking, Cohen (1969b) reported 3 experiments in which total fixation time per trial was separated into number of fixations and mean duration of a fixation. Infants in all 3 studies were between 3 and 6 months of age. Two of the experiments were on visual preferences rather than on habituation per se. In one study the preference stimuli consisted of a single blinking light which varied in its probability of a movement. The light appeared in a 6 X 6 matrix and either remained stationary or moved randomly among 3, 9, or 27 positions. If one considered only the total fixation time data, the results would seem straightforward. Infants looked longer if the light moved at all than if it never moved. However, both number of fixations and mean fixation duration data provide different pictures. The number of fixations increased linearly as the probability of movement increased. On the other hand the duration of a look remained constant to the 1, 3, and 9 position stimuli but dropped off markedly to the 27 position one. The conclusion of the study was that degree of movement in the periphery might get an infant to turn toward the stimulus initially, but other factors such as the redundancy of the movement or ability to follow the light determined how long the infant would continue fixating.

In the second experiment reported by Cohen (1969b) infants were shown checkerboard patterns that varied both in overall size and number of squares. Again, number of fixations and mean fixation duration produced different results. Turning to a pattern was more a function of size than number of squares while just the opposite was true of fixation duration.

In the final experiment Cohen reanalyzed data from a previously reported habituation study (Pancratz & Cohen, 1970). Four-month-old infants were shown a simple geometric form pattern for 10 15-sec trials, followed by a six-trial test containing alternating trials of the familiar and a novel pattern.

Changes in total fixation time during the habituation phase of the experiment are presented in Figure 5. As is apparent from these curves, male infants displayed habituation over trials while female infants did not. A significant difference between the linear trend scores for the two groups indicated that their curves differed from one another in slope.

The important question which must be examined next is whether this habituation of total fixation time is reflected in number of fixations, mean duration of a fixation or both measures. Figure 6 gives changes in number of fixations over trials in the habituation phase. There is no evidence either of habituation or of a difference between male and female infants. On the other hand, Figure 7 which gives the fixation duration data presents a different picture. Although these data are more variable than those from total fixation time, the general downward trend of the curve for boys and the difference in performance between boys and girls can be seen. Evidently in the habituation portion of the experiment, the total fixation time data are more a reflection of mean duration of a fixation than of number of fixations.

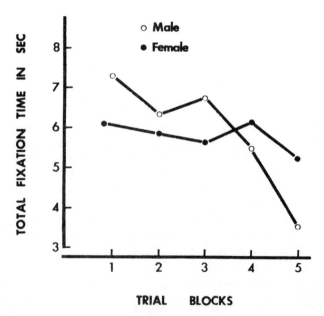

FIG. 5   Total fixation times during the habituation phase of the Pancratz and Cohen study. (From Cohen, 1973.)

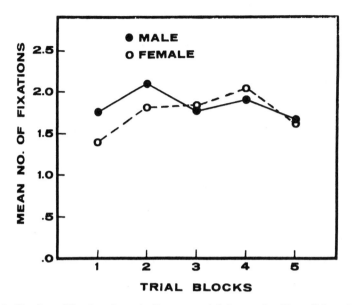

FIG. 6   Number of fixations from the Pancratz and Cohen study. (From Cohen, 1973.)

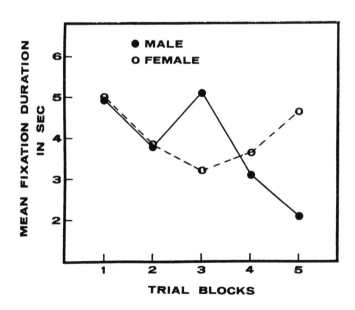

FIG. 7   Mean fixation durations from the Pancratz and Cohen study. (From Cohen, 1973.)

The same conclusion can be drawn from infants' performance during the test. As might be expected, total fixation time indicated that boys, but not girls, looked significantly longer at the novel than the familiar stimulus. No differences were found in number of fixations, but recovery to the novel stimulus in males did occur in the mean duration measure.

Thus, findings from all three studies point to the necessity of separating an infant's turning from his looking. Apparently two distinct processes are at work; an attention-getting process which results in the infant's orienting to a stimulus in the periphery when it moves or is sufficiently large, and an attention-holding process which results in the infant's maintaining his fixation when the stimulus is intricate, unpredictable, or novel, (Cohen, 1972).

One difficulty with using number of fixations and mean fixation duration as independent measures of attention getting and holding is that in a fixed trial procedure the two can be negatively correlated. An infant who begins a trial with one long look cannot possibly turn to look several times on the same trial, whereas one who has nothing but short fixations has ample opportunity to turn and look again. The fixed trial procedure has other limitations as well (Cohen, 1972, 1973; Horowitz, 1975; Horowitz et al., 1972). How does one score an infant who never looks during a trial? Would a fixation time of zero accurately reflect his interest in the stimulus? Perhaps he was just engaged in looking at something else when the stimulus came on. What about an infant who is fixating when the trial ends and the stimulus goes off? Would his fixation really have ended at that instant if the slide had remained on? A new procedure was needed which would eliminate these difficulties and at the same time allow for independent assessment of attention getting and attention holding.

One such procedure has been reported by Cohen (1972). It was first used in an experiment attempting to replicate and extend the study reported earlier on infant visual preferences for checkerboard patterns (Cohen, 1969b). Four-month-old infants were placed in an infant seat facing a display screen. Each trial began with a light blinking on and off on one side of the screen. The light was used to attract the infant's attention at the start of each trial and to control where the infant was looking when a checkerboard pattern was presented. As soon as the infant fixated the light, it went off and a checkerboard appeared on the opposite side of the screen. The infant's latency in turning from the light to the pattern constituted the measure of attention getting. Nine different checkerboard patterns were presented in all. They varied from trial to trial in total size of the pattern and in number of squares. The infant was allowed one unlimited fixation of the pattern per trial, and the duration of this fixation was the measure of attention holding. As soon as the infant turned away from the pattern, it went off and the blinking light came on once again to mark the start of the next trial.

The results with this new procedure replicated those found earlier. Latency of turning toward the pattern was determined more by the size of the checkerboard than by the number of squares, while the duration of a fixation was more a function of the number of squares than the size. These results, then, lend further support to the contention that infant attention should be divided into separate attention getting and attention holding processes.

Finally, Cohen *et al.* (1975) used the new procedure to examine the roles of attention getting and holding in an habituation paradigm. Eighteen male and 18 female, 4-month-old infants were given a total of 20 trials. They were all shown a red circle on trials 1 and 2, followed by 16 trials with either a 2 X 2, 8 X 8, or 24 X 24 checkerboard pattern. On the last 2 trials all infants were again shown the red circle.

Once more the data replicated those obtained earlier using a fixed trial procedure (Pancratz & Cohen, 1970). Fixation duration decreased over trials to the repeated checkerboard pattern in males but not females. Furthermore neither males nor females showed any significant change in latency over those same checkerboard trials. Thus, further evidence was provided that habituation, at least in male infants, occurs in the attention-holding but not the attention-getting process.

Although latencies did not decrease or habituate during the checkerboard trials, some interesting effects involving latency did occur. The infants did turn more rapidly to a 24 X 24 checkerboard than to an 8 X 8 or a 2 X 2. (The difference appeared to be more true for females than males, although the sex X stimulus interaction did not reach significance). This finding of shorter latencies to the 24 X 24 checkerboard contrasts with those obtained in the Cohen (1972) experiment where the type of checkerboard pattern had little effect on speed of turning for either sex. One clue to the different results obtained in the 2 studies could be that in Cohen (1972) infants saw a different checkerboard on each trial, while in Cohen *et al.* (1975) infants saw the same checkerboard repeated 16 times. If turning were elicited solely by the pattern currently in the periphery, the two studies should have obtained similar results. The fact that they did not suggests that latency of turning on one trial is also affected by what the infant has seen on previous trials. Apparently, attention getting is not the simple reflexive orientation to a peripheral stimulus it was once assumed to be.

The hypothesis that attention getting involves more than just an automatic turning of the head or eyes was further supported by the latency data from the first two and last two red circle trials. Both male and female infants responded differently at the end of the experiment than they had at the beginning. Males turned more rapidly to the final red circles than to the initial ones regardless of what they had seen in between. Females, on the other hand, turned more rapidly if they had previously seen the 24 X 24 pattern, did not change their latency if they had seen the 8 X 8, and slowed down their turning if they had seen the 2 X 2. Since, at the end of the experiment, the same red circle was presented to *all* infants, any differential rate of turning must have been produced by what was seen on the preceding checkerboard trials. Thus both in the checkerboard and red circle phases of the experiment, attention getting in females seemed to be a function of the type of pattern viewed in the past, while this relation was not as strong in males. The reasons for this sex difference are unknown. Cohen *et al.* (1975) hypothesized that whereas males were storing information about the pattern and showing it through habituation, females were storing information either about the contingency between turning to one side and seeing a pattern or about how long they had looked on previous trials. Actually this statement may be worded a bit too strongly. The males' latencies did decrease from the beginning to the end of the experiment, and their attention getting may also have been influenced somewhat by seeing a checkerboard in the past.

From this one experiment it is difficult to estimate the generality of these sex differences. At this point it seems worthwhile to assume that attention getting in some infants is sensitive to the type of pattern seen on earlier trials and to try to explain why that might be the case. At least two hypotheses are tenable regarding differential latencies to the red circles found in the preceding experiment.

The first is that repeatedly looking at the 24 X 24 checkerboard pattern results in a higher state of activation or arousal than looking at the 8 X 8 or 2 X 2. If that were true, some infants in the 24 X 24 condition would become more active or alert and consequently would turn more rapidly to any stimulus subsequently presented. A second possible hypothesis is that some infants were being operantly conditioned to turn their heads to the pattern. Since infants looked longest at the 24 X 24 checkerboard, one could reasonably assume the 24 X 24 pattern was also the most interesting or reinforcing. It could be argued that a clear look at the pattern was contingent upon turning toward it, and those infants who saw an interesting pattern would learn to turn more rapidly than those who saw a dull one.

Two experiments were conducted in order to assess the validity of the arousal versus conditioning explanations and to see if the sex differences would continue to occur when the procedure was slightly modified (DeLoache, Wetherford, & Cohen, 1972). In both, 4-month-old infants were repeatedly shown the same checkerboard patterns. The first experiment used a modified-paired-comparison procedure. Each trial began with a central blinking light. As soon as an infant fixated the light, it went off and 2 checkerboard patterns appeared, one on the left and one on the right. There were four experimental groups. For group 1, the pattern on both sides was a 2 X 2 checkerboard. For group 2, a 24 X 24 was on the left and a 2 X 2 was on the right. For group 3, a 2 X 2 was on the left and a 24 X 24 was on the right; and for group 4, a 24 X 24 was on both sides. The infants could look at either pattern but were allowed only 1 fixation per trial. As soon as they turned away, both checkerboards went off and the blinking light reappeared to start the next trial. Sixteen trials with the checkerboard patterns were presented in all.

If attention getting were a function of nonspecific arousal, one would predict that while an infant might turn more rapidly on later trials, the direction and speed of turning should not be influenced by whether the attractive pattern was on the right or left. On the other hand, if the patterns served as differential reinforcers and the infant's turning was operantly conditioned, one would predict more head turns and shorter latencies to the side with the more attractive pattern.

The results supported the conditioning interpretation, and no reliable sex differences were found in the attention-getting measures. As can be seen from Figure 8, the infants had a strong right turn bias. When the same pattern was shown on both sides (Conditions 1 and 4), they turned to the right over 70% of the time, and when the more attractive pattern was on the right (Condition 3) they turned right more than 90% of the time. That bias was overcome, however, when the 24 X 24 pattern was on the left and the 2 X 2 was on the right, (Condition 2). In this condition more than 80% of the turns were to the left. The difference in responding found between conditions 2 and 3 cannot be attributed to arousal. Both groups looked primarily at the 24 X 24 checker-

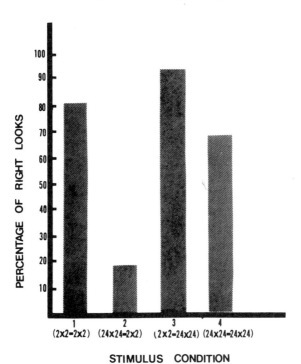

FIG. 8 Percentage of right looks in 16 checkerboard trials from experiment 1 of DeLoache, Wetherford and Cohen (1972).

board, yet one group turned left and the other turned right. There is no reason why increased arousal should make infants who are receiving approximately the same stimulation more likely to turn in one direction under one condition and in the opposite direction under another.

The latency data also suggested conditioning rather than arousal. As shown in Figure 9, latencies were significantly slower for the infants receiving only 2 X 2 checkerboards (Condition 1) than for those receiving only 24 X 24 ones (Condition 4). One could argue that the difference between these groups was due to arousal. However, that interpretation is discounted by the fact that there was no difference between Conditions 1 and 4 in latency of turning back to the light. If the arousal level of Condition 4 were higher, one would have expected them to turn more rapidly to the light as well.

Although evidence from this study tends to negate the importance of generalized arousal as an explanation of changes in latency over trials, it does not provide any direct evidence for conditioning. In all the experiments presented thus far, visual stimuli were presented at the discretion of the experimenter rather than the infant. In the early fixed trial studies, the stimulus came on at some predetermined time. In the later blinking light studies it came on when the infant was looking at the light. In neither type of experiment was the onset of

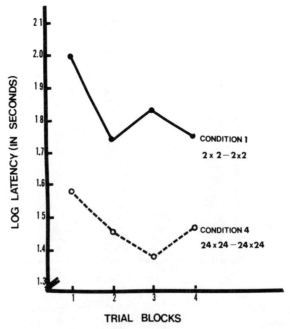

FIG. 9   Log latency of turning to either 2 X 2 or 24 X 24 checkboards from Experiment 1 of DeLoache, Wetherford, and Cohen (1972).

stimulation actually made contingent on the infant's turning to it. Of course one can argue that when an infant turns toward a visual pattern, the type of stimulation he is receiving is necessarily changing and thus is, to some extent, contingent on his turning. Nevertheless, it would be instructive to set up a situation in which the infant must turn before he receives any pattern stimulation, a situation in which the onset of the pattern is truly contingent on the infant's prior orienting response. If four-month-old infants can be easily conditioned in this type of situation, it would strengthen the case for conditioning in the more typical visual preference or habituation paradigms, and for the necessity of an operant component in the attention-getting process. That was the goal of the second experiment in De Loache et al. (1972).

DeLoache et al. again used four-month-old infants and the same stimuli and apparatus as in the previous experiment. Each trial began with the central blinking light. When the infant looked at the light it went off, but this time no checkerboard pattern automatically appeared in the periphery. The checkerboard was not presented until 1 sec after the infant either turned his head approximately 45° in the proper direction or fixated on the place the pattern would later appear. Infants were divided into two groups. For one group a head turn produced a 2 X 2 checkerboard, and for the other it produced a 24 X 24 checkerboard.

Changes in latency over the 16 checkerboard trials are shown in Figure 10. As in the preceding experiment there were no sex differences. Two significant effects did occur, both of which would have been predicted from earlier research. First, latencies decreased from the first to the second block of trials. This was essentially the conditioning effect DeLoache et al. were attempting to demonstrate; second, latencies were longer to the 2 X 2 checkerboard than to the 24 X 24. This result would follow from the prediction that the 2 X 2 checkerboard was less interesting or reinforcing than the 24 X 24. Thus, evidence from this experiment further supports the hypothesis that 4-month-old infants can rapidly learn to turn their head in order to obtain an interesting visual stimulus and that a complete account of the attention-getting process should include the learning or operant conditioning component. The lack of sex differences in both DeLoache et al. studies also indicates that this conditioning is more general than the Cohen et al. (1975) results would suggest. Apparently, by 4 months of age both males and females can learn to turn more rapidly to an interesting than to an uninteresting visual stimulus. The evidence is also consistent with other experiments (Caron, 1967; Siqueland & DeLucia, 1969) which have established the reinforcing power of interesting visual stimuli for young infants.

To summarize, Level 3 research has produced considerable new information about the mechanisms underlying infant attention and memory. The need to separate attention getting from attention holding has been clearly demonstrated. The fact that attention getting includes more than a simple reflexive turning

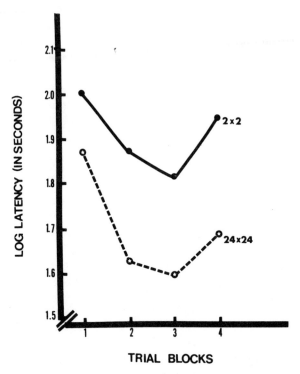

FIG. 10 Log latency in turning to 2 × 2 or 24 × 24 checkerboards in the conditioning experiment (experiment 2) of DeLoache, Wetherford, and Cohen (1972).

toward a peripheral stimulus, that turning can also be a response emitted by the infant in order to obtain something interesting to look at, suggests the infant is more actively involved in the experimental situation than had previously been supposed. By turning more rapidly to some stimuli than to others and by modulating his turning on the basis of what he has seen previously, the infant is actively attempting to control his visual inputs.

    In the next section on Level 4 research we shall attempt to show that after the infant turns he is actively involved in processing information as well. That argument will be developed more fully in the next section along with the contention that habituation of infant visual attention does not really proceed in a gradually decreasing manner so characteristic of group habituation curves. A slight change in the blinking light procedure and a new way of looking at fixation duration data over trials suggest that infant attention habituates much more rapidly than had previously been supposed.

LEVEL 4: ATTENTION HOLDING
AND INFANT MEMORY

Investigators of infant habituation now generally agree that an infant's reduction in attention to a repeated visual stimulus followed by his increased response to a novel stimulus implies some type of recognition memory. The theory most often invoked is a variant of Sokolov's. When the infant fixates a pattern, he encodes some information about that pattern. This current information is then compared to whatever has been stored about prior patterns. If a match occurs between what is being encoded at the moment and what has been stored in the past, the infant will stop looking. If no match occurs, the infant will maintain his fixation.

While this rather superficial analysis of infant memory allows one to predict both the occurrence of habituation and the preference for novelty over familiarity, it ignores one basic aspect of the infant's attending behavior. It does not explain why an infant will turn away from a stimulus on those early trials before he has habituated completely and before a model has been formed.

Even more difficult for Sokolovian type models to explain are those infants who do not show any evidence of habituation during the course of an entire experiment. They repeatedly turn away from the stimulus, but are they storing information about the stimulus or not? If they are, why don't they habituate? Several studies have already been mentioned in which 6–8-week-old infants (Wetherford & Cohen, 1973) or 4-month-old females (Cohen *et al.,* 1971) do not seem to habituate. One would have to assume from the Sokolovian model that they are not remembering the stimulus and therefore should never turn away. The evidence obviously indicates the contrary. In fact, the duration of nonhabituators' fixations on the early trials is usually no longer than the fixations of those who later habituate. Clearly, some mechanism over and above a Sokolovian type of match between prior stored information and currently available information is needed to explain termination of an infant's fixation. Both Levels 4 and 5 research examine that point.

One could really consider Level 4 research as beginning with the question of whether those infants who did not habituate in earlier experiments would be able to do so if given more optimal conditions. The obvious way to investigate this is to give habituation trials to a criterion of habituation rather than for a fixed number of trials. It will be recalled that early attempts to discover the age at which an infant first habituates used a fixed-trials procedure. Subsequently, two studies, one by Friedman (1972) and one by Hunter and Ames (1975) did obtain habituation in infants under two months of age. Both experiments used a criterion.

We have also incorporated a criterion in our blinking light procedure. Any of several possible criteria could have been selected, an absolute decrease, a proportional decrease, a decrease to some common level (Cohen & Gelber, 1975); but a reexamination of prior data indicated that most infants reached asymptote when their attention dropped to about half of what it was originally. We therefore assumed infants to have habituated when their fixation time on 3 consecutive trials averaged 50% or less of what it had been on the first 3 trials. We also included posthabituation trials with the same stimulus to insure that infants had in fact habituated and had not reached the criterion by chance.

Several experiments with four-month-old infants have now been conducted in our laboratory using this criterion. In one (DeLoache, 1976) infants were shown a simple colored geometric pattern, and in two others still in progress they were shown a photograph of a face. Females as well as males habituated in all three experiments. While it is unclear just why four-month-old females had not habituated in earlier experiments, these recent studies demonstrate females are certainly capable of habituating when a criterion is used. Thus, data from infants under two months and from four-month-old females are comparable in that both groups will habituate if the procedure includes a criterion.

Use of a criterion permitted us to ask more detailed questions about the course of habituation. It has been known for some time that the typical gradually increasing group learning curve may be misleading. For example, Zeaman and House (1963) have shown that even though retardate discrimination learning appears to be incremental, when the performance of individual subjects is plotted backwards from criterion, retardates learn in an all-or-none manner on a single trial. The slope of the typical learning curve is actually an artifact produced by averaging across subjects who reach criterion on different trials.

The same artifact may be present in group habituation curves, except in this case the curves would be gradually decreasing rather than increasing. In order to test this notion, data from several infant habituation studies have now been plotted backward as well as forward. Figure 11 is a composite of the results of these experiments. In all the studies 4-month-old infants were tested with the blinking light procedure. Habituation trials were given until the subject's fixation time declined to 50% of initial looking time. Fixation times were plotted backwards from that criterion. Two posthabituation trials with the same stimulus were also included to test for an accidental decrease rather than habituation. The only major difference between studies was the type of stimulus presented to the infant. An examination of Figure 11 reveals several interesting facts. First, it is clear that 4-month-old infants did not habituate in a gradual fashion. They had one or more long fixations and then dropped down suddenly on a single trial. Second, prior to habituating, the duration of a fixation was determined by the type of stimulus they had been viewing. They looked longest at a photograph of a face, next longest at a 24 × 24 checkerboard, next at an 8 × 8 checkerboard, and at a pattern containing four colored geometric forms; and least at a 2 × 2 checkerboard. In general the duration of a fixation prior to habituation was a function of the complexity or intricacy of the stimulus. Third, regardless of how long the infants looked initially, once they did habituate, their looking dropped

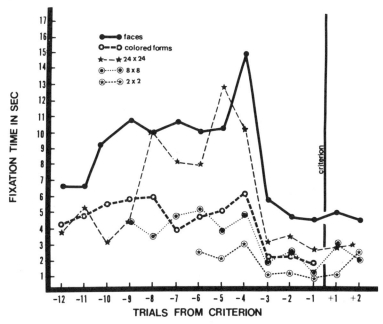

FIG. 11   Backward habituation curves to faces, colored forms and checkerboard patterns. (Checkerboard data adapted from Cohen & Gelber, 1975.)

substantially, and remained low on the posthabituation trials with the same stimulus. Finally, there is some evidence with the more complex stimuli that fixation times actually increased or reached a peak just prior to habituation.

Let's consider the significance of each of these facts in turn. The abruptness of the habituation tends to refute the commonly held belief that infant attention habituates in a gradual fashion. On prehabituation trials the infants may be gradually accumulating a more accurate representation of the stimulus, but habituation appears to be more of a threshold phenomenon than an incremental one. When the representation is sufficiently similar to current input, the infant will look only briefly; but before the representation reaches this level of similarity, infants respond as if there had been nothing stored at all. Also, on prehabituation trials infants do terminate their fixations. They do not continue to look indefinitely. If an accurate representation of the stimulus (in the Sokolovian sense) has not yet been formed, what causes them to stop looking?

At least two possibilities may be considered. One, suggested by Cohen and Gelber (1975) is that two types of memory, long-term and short-term, are involved in infant attention. On each trial, as the infant fixates a pattern, a short-term representation of the pattern is stored. Once there is a match between this short-term memory and current input, the infant looks away. However, that short-term representation dissipates between trials, so that on the next trial the infant will look approximately as long as he did on the preceding one. At the same time a long-term representation of the stimulus is also gradually forming. This representation persists across trials and is what Sokolov was referring to as the "neuronal model" of a stimulus. It is this long-term model which eventually produces habituation, albeit not in the gradual fashion supposed by Sokolov.

A second hypothesis concerning the prehabituation trials is than no information at all is being stored even in short-term memory. The infant turns away simply because he is becoming tired of looking in the same direction. This interpretation is negated by the fact that on the prehabituation trials infants look more at complex than at simple stimuli. If they were simply becoming fatigued, they should have turned away after the same length of time, regardless of what they were looking at. That their fixation time was related to the type of stimulus being viewed supports the short-term, long-term memory hypothesis.

One possible criticism of plotting habituation curves backward from criterion is that the precipitous drop in responding would be present even if the data were essentially random, and infants had not habituated at all. If a sufficient number of trials were run, one would expect fixation times to drop 50% simply by chance. By placing all those low chance trials together on Trials −1, −2, −3, one would expect precisely what was obtained, little or no change in attention until Trial −4 and then an abrupt decrease. The problem with this interpretation of data is that if only chance factors were operating, one would expect an equally abrupt increase in attention on the post-habituation trials. Since fixation times remained low during posthabituation, the evidence supports an habituation interpretation. The occurrence of habituation is further supported by the finding (not shown in Figure 11) that in all the experiments, presentation of a novel stimulus following posthabituation produced an increase in attention.

Inspection of Figure 11 also reveals a peak in responding just prior to habituation for groups shown either a face or a 24 × 24 checkerboard. This peak is difficult to interpret. Cohen and Gelber (1975) have suggested that it might reflect the onset of concerted attention and processing information in long-term memory. On the other hand, two factors argue against this view. First, some of the peak is undoubtedly artifactual since if an infant happens to have a low score just prior to habituation, that score will in all probability be placed at Trial −3 rather than at −4. Exclusion of low scores from −4 will tend to inflate the mean and produce a higher fixation time than Trials −5, −6, etc. which do include low as well as high scores. Attempts are currently underway to estimate the size of the artifactual increase so that it can be removed statistically, but until that is done one can only guess the actual magnitude of the peak. The second factor is that a few infants take one long look and then habituate immediately. Their long first fixation tends to inflate the group mean on Trial −4 and gives the false impression that all infants increase their fixation time prior to habituation.

However, even when these subjects' data are removed, backward habituation curves still show an increase in fixation time just prior to the decrease.

One recent study from our laboratory (Walter, unpublished paper) may have some bearing on the nature of the peak. Three-month-old infants were habituated to a 24 X 24 checkerboard pattern using the blinking light procedure, and heart rate changes were recorded along with fixation time. On trials prior to the peak infants tended to exhibit cardiac acceleration; on Trials −4 and −3 they tended to show cardiac deceleration. On posthabituation trials, however, little or no change in heart rate occurred. This effect was more marked for slow habituators then for fast ones. The changes in heart rate suggest different processes at work on the early trials and on the trials just before and following habituation.

Increased attention to a familiar stimulus just prior to habituation may also help explain the confusing developmental change in preferences for novelty or familiarity. It will be recalled that some Level 1 research reported a preference for familiarity in 6–8-week-old infants followed by a preference for novelty in older infants. Since the infants were not run to a criterion, one possible explanation could be that the younger ones had not yet habituated and were being tested at the point where they would normally show a peak. Hunter and Ames (1975) tested this explanation directly. One group of five-week-old infants was habituated (to a 50% criterion) with an 8 X 8 checkerboard and then tested with the 8 X 8 and 2 X 2. This group clearly preferred the novel pattern. A second group was given only half the number of familiarization trials as the first group, so that they did not habituate. When tested, the second group clearly preferred the familiar checkerboard. Hunter and Ames (1975) concluded:

1. that five-week-old infants *do* habituate to visual stimuli;
2. that previous failures to demonstrate habituation have been due to stimulus and procedural limitations rather than to any inherent inability of young infants; and
3. that preference for novelty is found following the attainment of a stringent individual habituation criterion, while preference for familiarity is found following a period of familiarization too short to permit the attainment of such a criterion [p. 7].

The peak also makes sense in terms of optimal level of stimulation theories. If a moderate level of novelty is more reinforcing or attractive to infants than either a greater or lesser degree of novelty, one would expect first an increase in fixation time as a stimulus becomes more familiar and then a decrease. The abruptness of the decrease would not be predicted, but the general curvilinear function would.

Several explanations of the peak are possible. Does it result mainly from a motivational change as proposed by optimal level theories? Or does it signal a different way of processing visual information? A somewhat novel approach was used in a study from our laboratory by Rissman (1976), to test whether or not the peak is a necessary condition for storing information in long-term memory.

Four-month-old infants were again habituated to a 24 X 24 checkerboard using the blinking light procedure. In the free looking group, infants were allowed to fixate as long as they wished on each trial. The restricted group received anywhere from 1 to 12 trials in which the stimulus was turned off after the infants had looked for 4 sec even though they were still fixating. The restricted trials were then followed by free looking trials identical to those in the other group. The main question was whether the restricted group would store information about the stimulus in long-term memory during the restricted trials, even though the 4-sec cutoff prevented them from showing a peak. If they did, the restricted group's total fixation time prior to habituation (including both 4-sec and free trials) should be the same as the free looking group's total fixation time. If they did not, the restricted group's fixation time on free trials alone should be the same as the free looking group's. The results clearly indicated the former. Total fixation times across all prehabituation trials were the same for both groups. Apparently even on the restricted trials, infants were encoding information used later to produce habituation.

Thus, Level 4 research has provided interesting new information about infant visual memory. Sokolov's model was shown to be incomplete at least in terms of infant visual attention. The course of habituation can best be explained in terms of separate short- and long-term memory processes, each involving a match between incoming and stored information. The match in long-term memory, and perhaps in short-term as well, seems to fit an all—or—none model better than a gradual probabilistic one, but that does not necessarily mean information is stored in memory on a single trial. The occurrence of a peak in fixation time prior to attainment of criterion, the pre- to postcriterion changes in heart rate, and preferences for familiarity prior to habituation all suggest that something special is happening just before the infant habituates, perhaps something that involves encoding information in long-term memory. On the other hand, the restricted trials experiment suggests that information is being stored in long-term memory from the very first trial even when a peak is prevented from occurring.

Whatever the eventual outcome regarding the reality and/or significance of the peak, it is clear that Level 4 research represents an advance over previous levels. Questions are now directed toward specific processes underlying infant habituation and memory, rather than just asking whether habituation and memory will or will not occur. New and more refined theories (Cohen, 1973; Olson, Chapter 7, this volume) are beginning to appear to explain these phenomena which were once thought so simple and are now seen to be highly complex. These theories assume the infant plays a much more active role in the attention-holding process than previously believed. He is looking, abstracting certain properties of a stimulus, encoding the information in both short- and long-term memory, comparing new and old information, and terminating his fixation when the two match. Still undecided is whether the match produces an automatic releasing of attention or whether the act of turning away from a stimulus is also under active, voluntary control. That is the topic covered below.

LEVEL 5: THE ATTENTION RELEASING PROCESS

Very little is known about the processes involved when an infant turns away from a visual stimulus. Memory models of infant habituation seem to assume that the release from attention occurs automatically whenever a match exists between current and prior stimulation, but recent research from our laboratory suggests that it is not quite as automatic as these models seem to imply. Our investigation of the attention releasing process began somewhat serendipitiously with a reexamination of the merits of the blinking light procedure.

Although the procedure has several advantages, it also has a drawback. Infants are essentially on line with the equipment. When they look at the light, it goes off and a pattern comes on. When they turn away from the pattern, it goes off and the blinking light reappears. All these changes in stimulation are manually controlled by an observer. The difficulty arises when the infant makes a response that leads the observer to erroneously conclude that fixation has been terminated. Occasionally an infant will blink, move his head but not his eyes away from the pattern, or momentarily cover his eyes with his hands. This behavior does not really constitute termination of a fixation, but may induce the observer to release the switch controlling the pattern presentation, and once the observer releases this switch, it is too late to correct the mistake.

In order to eliminate these errors, we modified our equipment by including a .5-sec delay interval before terminating the pattern. If the infant fixated the pattern again within the half second, the pattern remained on and the fixation was scored as if the infant had never turned away. Use of the delay interval turned out to be more of a handicap than a help. We soon found that many more infants would not complete our experiment. Whereas with the original procedure we would lose 30–40% due to crying or fussing, we were now losing nearly 80%. A close look at videotaped recordings under the two procedures revealed a surprising phenomenon. With the old procedure many infants were not just turning away from the pattern, they were turning away in a highly stereotyped manner. Some infants would consistently look down to the left. Others would move their heads quickly to the right and then back to the center. One infant, on trial after trial, would arch his back and look over his left shoulder. While individual infants might vary from one another in the technique they used to turn off the pattern, a given infant would often be highly consistent, doing the same thing for a number of trials. The consistency was disrupted, however, when the half second-delay was included. Infants would turn away, the pattern would remain on, and they would turn back to look at it.

Sometimes their reorientation was rapid enough to maintain the pattern. Other times they would be a bit too slow, and just as they turned back, the pattern would go off. Our preliminary evaluation was that the half second-delay had introduced an element of uncertainty or unpredictability into the situation. Without the delay the infants were in control of the stimulation. When they were through looking at it, they were learning (albeit superstitiously) to turn it off by making a specific type of response. With the delay this control was reduced or eliminated, and infants became upset and started to cry.

Since these initial observations we have begun to investigate consistency in the attention-releasing process more thoroughly. We eliminated the half second-delay, developed an objective measure of consistency, and are in the process of comparing consistent and inconsistent infants both across age and over a number of experimental conditions.

A consistency score was developed by going back to the videotaped records and recording the direction the infant turned away from the pattern on each trial. A template was made consisting of a central point with 16 numbered lines emanating from the point at 22.5° intervals. The template was placed on the television screen with the point superimposed on the infant's pupil. As the infant turned away, the direction his eyes moved was compared to the closest line and his turn was given the number corresponding to that line. Consecutive turns that were two lines or less (45°) apart were rated as consistent, all others as inconsistent. Since infants differed in the number of trials needed to habituate, an overall consistency score during habituation was computed for each infant by dividing the number of consistent responses during habituation by the total number of consistent and inconsistent ones. Thus far we have been able to evaluate only a limited amount of data using this proportional measure of consistency, but the results look promising.

The data came from two of our most recent experiments on infant habituation to face photographs. In the first, 32, 4-month-old infants were habituated to either a front or side view of an adult male face. They were then tested with the same and a similar face in the original and novel orientation. In general the results showed that by 4 months of age infants can discriminate between different faces and between the same face in a different orientation. More to the point of the present discussion, some of our measures of infant attention were also related to consistency scores. Infants varied greatly in how consistent they were in turning away from the photographs. The mean score was .67, and scores ranged from 1.00 (perfect consistency) to .30 (little consistency). Moreover, when infants were split at the median into consistent and inconsistent, some highly significant differences appeared. Although both groups habituated and responded more to novel than familiar faces, the inconsistent infants had much longer latencies in turning to the photographs (30.4 sec versus 12.2 sec) and after they turned, looked much longer before turning away (15.3 sec versus 9.2 sec). In fact, the correlation between fixation time on the first three trials and consistency was a remarkable −.73.

The meaning of these results is still unclear, but it may have something to do with the infant's maturational level. The second face experiment, which is still in progress, is essentially a replication of the first but with infants being tested at 14, 18, and 22 weeks. Although the number of subjects is still quite small, preliminary indications are that the 14-week-olds have longer latencies and fixation times and are less consistent than the 18-week-olds. If these results are reliable, we may have stumbled upon a way of determining degree of maturation both between ages and within the same age. One obvious next step is to compare consistent and inconsistent infants on the way they process and store visual information. For example, one goal of experiment 2 is to see if younger and/or less consistent infants respond differently to a change in faces or in orientation than do older and/or more consistent infants.

One other point should be mentioned regarding the behavior of our 14-week-old infants. It may well be that the reason they have longer fixation times is that they have difficulty releasing their attention from the visual stimulus. We get the subjective impression when observing some of these infants that they look intently for a while, then become increasingly agitated with their eyes still glued to the pattern, and finally avert their gaze in an inconsistent manner. It is almost as if they wanted to turn away earlier, but couldn't. Several investigators (Ames & Silfen, 1965; Stechler & Latz, 1966; Friedman, 1975) have commented on the distinction between an infant being captured by a stimulus and his capturing that stimulus. The long fixation times followed by inconsistent turns in our 14-week-old subjects may be a reflection of the same phenomenon. If it is, the consistency score may turn out to be the first objective way of measuring the degree of control an infant has over his own visual attention.

Whether one considers consistency to be a measure of learning to turn off a stimulus or a measure of voluntary rather than obligatory attention, it appears that the attention releasing-process, like attention getting and holding, involves more active control by the infant than had previously been assumed. Understanding the nature of this control and how it develops requires much more information than is presently available. It may still be too early to give research on the attention releasing-process the status of a new level. However, it is clear that the consistency of turning away from a visual stimulus does reflect an aspect of infant attending which has not been thoroughly investigated in the past. We are just beginning such an investigation and hope in the near future to have a much better indication of the role played by the attention releasing-process in infant visual attention and habituation.

SUMMARY AND CONCLUSIONS

This chapter has tried to emphasize the changing nature of research on infant visual attention and habituation. The field, as an active area of investigation, is quite young, less than 15 years old. Yet considerable progress has been made in that short time. Evolving out of a literature on animal learning and motivation, the field has taken on a character of its own. As researchers have become more immersed in the study of infant habituation they have become more attuned to the subjects they have been observing. Early attempts to demonstrate the youngest age an infant could habituate have been replaced by attempts to discover the types of visual information infants attend to and remember. Early models of infant habituation stressed that infant memory requires a match between what is old and what is new. These models have now been replaced by more refined ones which posit separate short- and long-term memory mechanisms. Research on infant memory has led to a more analytic view of the attending response itself. It is now evident that infant attention is not a simple phenomenon. Each time an infant attends to a visual stimulus he must turn to it, look at it, and turn away from it. The view of the infant that has gradually emerged is that by 3 or 4 months of age he is actively in control of all three of these processes. The age at which an infant changes from being a passive recipient of stimulation to an active participant in his interaction with the environment is still unknown; but it is undoubtedly much earlier than we had previously believed.

ACKNOWLEDGMENTS

Preparation of this chapter and much of the research conducted by the authors was supported in part by research grant HD 03858 to L. B. Cohen from the National Institute of Child Health and Human Development. I wish to thank A. Broga, J. DeLoache, L. Lundgren and M. Strauss for their assistance on this manuscript.

REFERENCES

Ames, E. W., & Silfen, C. K. Methodological issues in the study of age differences in infants' attention to stimuli varying in movement, complexity, and novelty. Paper presented at the Society for Research in Child Development meeting, Minneapolis, 1965.

Berg, W. K., Adkinson, C. D., & Strock, B. D. Duration and frequency of periods of alertness in neonates. *Developmental Psychology.* 1973, *9,* 434.

Berlyne, D. E. *Conflict, arousal, and curiosity.* New York: McGraw-Hill, 1960.

Caron, R. F. Visual reinforcement of head-turning in young infants. *Journal of Experimental Child Psychology,* 1967, *5,* 489–511.

Caron, R. F., & Caron, A. J. Degree of stimulus complexity and habituation of visual fixation in infants. *Psychonomic Science,* 1969, *14,* 78–79.

Cohen, L. B. Observing responses, visual preferences, and habituation to visual stimuli in infants. *Journal of Experimental Child Psychology,* 1969, *7,* 419–433.   (a)

Cohen, L. B. Alternative measures of infant attention. Paper presented at the meeting of the Society for Research in Child Development, Santa Monica, March, 1969.   (b)

Cohen, L. B. Attention-getting and attention-holding processes of infant visual preferences. *Child Development,* 1972, *43,* 869–879.

Cohen, L. B. A two-process model of infant visual attention. *Merrill-Palmer Quarterly,* 1973, *19,* 157–180.

Cohen, L. B., DeLoache, J. S., & Rissman, M. The effect of stimulus complexity on infant visual attention and habituation. *Child Development,* 1975, *46,* 611–617.

Cohen, L. B., & Gelber, E. R. Infant visual memory. In L. Cohen & P. Salapatek (Eds.), *Infant perception.* New York: Academic Press, 1975. Pp. 347–403.

Cohen, L. B., Gelber, E. R., & Lazar, M. A. Infant habituation and generalization to differing degrees of stimulus novelty. *Journal of Experimental Child Psychology,* 1971, *11,* 379–389.

DeLoache, J. Rate of habituation and visual memory in infants. *Child Development,* 1976, *47,* 145–154.

DeLoache, J., Wetherford, M., & Cohen, L. B. The effects of motivation and conditioned head turning on infant attention to patterns of varying complexity. Paper presented at the meeting of the Midwestern Psychological Association, Cleveland, Ohio, 1972.

Dember, W. N. Response by the rat to environmental change. *Journal of Comparative Physiology and Psychology,* 1956, *49,* 93–95.

Dember, W. Alternation behavior. In D. Fiske & Maddi, S. (Eds.), *Functions of varied experience.* Homewood. Dorsey Press, 1961. Pp. 227–252.

Fagan, J. F. Infant recognition of faces. Paper presented at the Midwestern Psychological Association, Chicago, 1975.

Fantz, R. L. Pattern vision in young infants. *Psychological Record,* 1958, *8,* 43–49.

Fantz, R. L. Visual experience in infants: Decreased attention to familiar patterns relative to novel ones. *Science,* 1964, *146,* 668–670.

Fantz, R., Fagan, J., & Miranda, S. Early visual selectivity. In L. B. Cohen & P. Salapatek (Eds.), *Infant perception: From sensation to cognition.* New York: Academic Press, 1975. Pp. 249–341.

Faulkender, P., Wright, J., & Waldron, A. Generalized habituation of concept stimuli in toddlers. *Child Development,* 1974, *45,* 1002–1010.

Friedman, S. Habituation and recovery of visual response in the alert human newborn. *Journal of Experimental Child Psychology,* 1972, *13,* 339–349.

Friedman, S. Infant habituation: Process, problems and possibilities. In N. R. Ellis (Ed.), *Aberrant development in infancy.* Hillsdale, New Jersey: Lawrence Erlbaum Assoc., 1975. Pp. 217–237.

Glanzer, M. Stimulus satiation: An explanation of spontaneous alternation and related phenomena. *Psychology Review,* 1953, *60,* 257–268.

Golinkoff, R. Semantic development in infants: The concepts of agent and recipient. *Merrill-Palmer Quarterly,* 1975, *21,* 181–193.

Greenberg, A., Uzgiris, I. C., & Hunt, J. McV. Attentional preference and experience: III. Visual familiarity and looking time. *Journal of Genetic Psychology,* 1970, *117,* 123–135.

Haith, M. Visual scanning in infants. Paper presented at the Society for Research in Child Development meeting, Clark University, 1968.

Hebb, D. O. Drives and the central nervous system (conceptual nervous system). *Psychological Review,* 1955, *62,* 243–254.

Horowitz, F. D. Infant attention and discrimination. Methodological and substantive issues. In F. D. Horowitz (Ed.), *Monographs of the Society for Research in Child Development,* 1975, *39,* 105–115.

Horowitz, F., Paden, L., Bhana, K., & Self, P. An infant-control procedure for studying infant visual fixations. *Developmental Psychology,* 1972, *7,* 90.

Hull, C. L. *Principles of behavior.* New York: Appleton-Century-Crofts, 1943.

Hunt, J. McV. *Intelligence and experience.* New York: Ronald Press, 1961.

Hunter, M. A., & Ames, E. W. Visual habituation and preference for novelty in five-week-old infants. Paper presented at meeting of the Society for Research in Child Development, Denver, 1975.

Iwahara, S. Studies in spontaneous alternation in human subjects: III. A developmental study. *Japanese Psychological Research*, 1959, *8*, 1–8.

Jeffrey, W. E., & Cohen, L. B. Habituation in the human infant. In H. Reese (Ed.), *Advances in child development and behavior*, New York: Academic Press, 1971, Pp. 63–97

Kagan, J., & Lewis, M. Studies of attention in the human infant. *Merrill-Palmer Quarterly*, 1965, *11*, 95–127.

Leply, W. M., & Rice, G. E., Jr. Behavior variability in paramecia as a function of guided act sequences. *Journal of Comparative Psysiology and Psychology*, 1952, *5*, 283–286.

Leuba, C. Toward some intergration of learning theories: The concept of optimal stimulation. *Psychological Review*, 1955, *1*, 27–33.

Lewis, M., Fadel, D., Bartels, B., & Campbell, H. Infant attention: The effect of familiar and novel visual stimuli as a function of age. Paper presented at Eastern Psychological Association, New York, 1966.

McGurk, H. The role of object orientation in infant perception. *Journal of Experimental Child Psychology*, 1970, *9*, 363–373.

Oster, H. S. Color perception in ten-week-old infants. Paper presented at the Society for Research in Child Development, Denver, 1975.

Pancratz, C. N., & Cohen, L. B. Recovery of habituation in infants. *Journal of Experimental Child Psychology*, 1970, *9*, 208–216.

Rissman, N. W. Effects of interrupted attention on visual memory. Unpublished doctoral dissertation. University of Illinois, 1976.

Saayman, G., Ames, E. W., & Moffett, A. Response to novelty as an indicator of visual discrimination in the human infant. *Journal of Experimental Child Psychology*, 1964, *1*, 189–198.

Siqueland, E., & DeLucia, C. A. Visual reinforcement of nonnutritive sucking in human infants. *Science*, 1969, 1144–1146.

Sokolov, E. N. The modeling properties of the nervous system. In M. Coles & I. Maltzman (Eds.), *A handbook of contemporary Soviet psychology*. New York: Basic Books, 1969. Pp. 671–704.

Sokolov, E. N. *Perception and the conditioned reflex.* New York: Macmillan, 1963.

Spence, K. *Behavior theory and conditioning.* New Haven: Yale University Press, 1956.

Stechler, G., & Latz, E. Some observations on attention and arousal in the human infant. *Journal of the American Academy of Child Psychiatry*, 1966, *5*, 517–525.

Uzgiris, I. C., & Hunt, J. McV. Attentional preference and experience: II. An exploratory longitudinal study of the effect of visual familiarity and responsiveness. *Journal of Genetic Psychology*, 1970, *117*, 109–121.

Walter, G. The relationship between visual attention and heart rate changes in infant habituation. Unpublished paper.

Weizmann, F., Cohen, L. B., & Pratt, R. J. Novelty, familiarity, and the development of infant attention. *Developmental Psychology*, 1971, *4*, 149–154.

Welch, M. M. Infants' visual attention to varying degrees of novelty. *Child Development*, 1974, *45*, 344–350.

Welker, W. I. An analysis of exploratory and play behavior in animals. In D. Fiske & S. Maddi, *Functions of varied experience.* Homewood: Dorsey Press, 1961. Pp. 175–226.

Wetherford, M. J., & Cohen, L. B. Developmental changes in infant visual preferences for novelty and familiarity. *Child Development*, 1973, *44*, 416–424.

Zeaman, D., & House, B. J. The Role of attention in retardate discrimination learning. In H. R. Ellis (Ed.), *Handbook of mental deficiency*, New York: McGraw-Hill, 1963. Pp. 159–223.

7

An Information-Processing Analysis of Visual Memory and Habituation in Infants

Gary M. Olson

University of Michigan

One of the major developments in contemporary experimental psychology has been the attempt to sketch the general nature of the adult's cognitive system. Research on perception, memory, attention, language, and problem solving has been integrated into a reasonably coherent picture of mature cognitive processing. But despite the fact that standard summaries of this new approach have surveyed a wide range of phenomena (e.g., Broadbent, 1971; Lindsay & Norman, 1972; Neisser, 1967; Posner, 1973), and though there have been some preliminary attempts at formulating comprehensive theories (e.g., Anderson & Bower, 1973), there is no readily identifiable *theory* of human information processing. Rather, there is a consistent point of view from which research questions are viewed, and there is consensus about the kinds of empirical phenomena that ought to be central to a theory of information processing. Further, there is an enthusiastic faith that out of this point of view a coherent, formal theory of cognition will soon emerge.

Given the eclectic, quasitheoretical status of the human information-processing approach to cognition, it is not surprising that there is no information-processing theory of cognitive development. There have been increasing numbers of attempts to apply information-processing terminology to developmental questions (Farnham-Diggory, 1972). Since developmental psychology has always had a strong cognitive tradition, an information processing "revolution" would be little more than an updating of terminology. But there is much to be gained by treating comparable phenomena in children and adults from the same point of view, since this can serve to clarify both the changeable and the invariant features of cognitive development. Further, it could serve to point out aspects of development ignored by earlier viewpoints.

This chapter will focus on the prelinguistic child's ability to remember visual stimuli, and will present a preliminary sketch of the infant's visual information processing system. Change and invariance will be central themes. Though the nature and the developmental course of infant information processing skills are largely unknown, it is already clear that the infant possesses a wide range of interesting abilities. There is much about the infant's performance in habituation and in visual memory tasks that suggests that the infant's information-processing abilities are similar to those of older children and adults. It will be argued that visual recognition memory abilities represent an ontogenetically primitive characteristic of information processing in humans, and that these abilities do not undergo radical developmental changes.

The first section of this chapter reviews the hypothesized structure of the mature information processor, and provides a few details concerning the adult's visual memory skills. The next section provides an overview of the development of memory abilities, and again focuses on visual memory. The third and major section reviews some recent research on the nature of the infant's memory abilities, focusing in particular on theoretical issues of general interest to information processing models. The fourth section provides a preliminary sketch of the infant's visual information processing system and will examine some of its tested and untested predictions. The final section briefly considers the early development of visual recognition memory in light of some broader issues of cognition and development.

THE MATURE INFORMATION PROCESSOR

Information processing theories of cognition attempt to show how the environmental–behavioral or behavioral–behavioral correlations that we observe are related to internal mental activities. Among the major objectives of such theories are descriptions of: (a) the overall structure or organization of the information processing system; (b) the kinds of internal codes available for representing information; (c) the dynamtic laws governing the fate of internal representations as a function of processing activities; (d) the control processes which provide organization to the information processing; (e) the interfacing of internal processes and structures with external events (stimuli and responses); and (f) the unique demands of particular tasks and how these govern the form of information processing in interaction with organismic factors. By and large these questions are questions of memory, since one of the hallmarks of the information processing approach is to tie questions about specific cognitive processes to general questions about memory.

Within the past decade or so several factors have led to attempts to characterize the adult memory system in a comprehensive fashion. First, the explosion of research on short-term memory during the 1960s, following the pivotal contributions of Miller (1956), Broadbent (1958), and Peterson and Peterson (1959), led to the suggestion that short-term memory might be functionally distinct from long-term memory. Wickelgren (1973) has recently reviewed the kinds of arguments used to support this inference. Second, a set of plausible theoretical concepts about memory processes and structures was introduced into psychological theory from computer science. For instance, one way of describing the organization of information processing in a computer is to describe the properties of its memory stores, registers, and buffers. Given the evidence that long-term and short-term memory may be distinct in humans, aspects of the multistore architecture of typical computer systems provided a rich source of hypotheses about human information processing. Finally, a third influence, closely related to the second, has been the effort to view a variety of complex cognitive phenomena as influenced or constrained by the nature of the memory system. For instance, certain linguistic structures may be perceptually complex because of demands made upon limited memory capacities, or certain problem-solving heuristics could result from the melding of demands of real time-, rate-pressured information processing with capacity limitations.

The end product of these kinds of theoretical pressures has been what Murdock (1967, 1974) has called the "modal model" of human memory. Figure 1 shows a representative flow chart for such models. This scheme emphasizes the logical distinctness of various memory stores and input–output buffers, treating information processing as a set of sequentially ordered activities whose primary forms are the result of system architecture and individual component properties.

The receptors are the loci for perceptual processing and feature extraction, and some kind of input buffering is assumed to occur in what are called sensory stores (Atkinson & Shiffrin, 1968; Norman & Rumelhart, 1970). These are special purpose memories having very brief residence times. The properties of these stores can be studied only under special experimental conditions, and in general will not be important in the discussions in this chapter. However, the

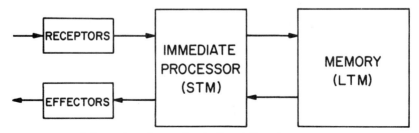

FIG. 1   Flow diagram for the "modal" model of memory.

general feature extraction process which occurs at this stage will be a central source of developmental change within the period of three to six months.

The immediate processor has a significant role in cognition because it serves as a major capacity limitation on the flow of information. Miller (1956) first called attention to this property, and over the ensuing years it has generally been agreed that the capacity of the immediate processor (or short-term memory, STM) is on the order of five to seven units of information. Though it was thought for a time that the immediate processor held information in only a limited number of formats, now it is generally believed that virtually any kind of information can be held there (Wickelgren, 1973). Further, the capacity restriction can be somewhat alleviated by efficient coding of information. For instance, the symbols in short-term memory might be codes for search or computation routines that are stored in long-term memory. Short-term memory is often equated with a computational or working memory, though recently Baddeley and Hitch (1974) have cautioned against simpleminded extrapolations from data in different paradigms. Short-term memory has usually been thought of as a store that is distinct from the rest of the memory system (Wickelgren, 1973), although it has also been proposed that what we think of as short-term memory is merely the currently active portion of a continuous, single-store system (Craik & Lockhart, 1972; Herriot, 1974). Regardless of which view is taken concerning the number of stores, there is little doubt about the existence of a state of information characterized by rapid forgetting, fixed symbol capacity, and rapid, flexible throughput. In this sense, Posner's (1973) label of "active memory" seems more neutral and appropriate, and will be used in the remainder of the chapter to refer to the immediate processor.

In contrast, long-term memory appears to be, for all practical purposes, of indefinite capacity, with very slow rates of information loss and a much more complex organization. It is, of course, the store of all knowledge, experience, and skills. Though information in long-term memory is relatively permanent and usually can be retrieved very quickly, it takes considerable time and effort to store new information. Newell and Simon (1972) have reviewed evidence which suggests storage time is several orders of magnitude longer than searchless retrieval time. In problem solving (Newell & Simon, 1972), language processing (Olson, 1972), or mental arithmetic (Hunter, 1968), where there are pressures due to the limited capacity of active memory and forced serial processing in real time, limitations on the rate of entry of new information into long-term memory can serve as another constraint on the overall complexity of processing. This property will be important in the model of infant visual memory to be proposed later.

Not surprisingly, the modal model has attracted criticism, not so much because it is in principle wrong or inconsistent with data but because it offers an incomplete account of the nature of memory processes. Critics have felt that its emphasis on architectural characteristics of memory has led to an oversimplification of the relation between coding processes and retention. Alternative models like the "levels of processing" approach (Craik & Lockhart, 1972; Herriot, 1974) have focused instead on the memorial consequences of various kinds of stimulus processing. The experiments of Hyde and Jenkins (1969, 1973) are a typical case, where in an incidental learning paradigm subjects who processed words semantically were found to remember them much better than subjects who processed a superficial characteristic like phonetic or graphemic properties. As stated by Craik and Lockhart (1972), "the memory trace can be understood as a byproduct of perceptual analysis and . . . trace persistence is a positive function of the depth to which the stimulus has been analyzed [p. 671] ."

The modal model and the levels of processing approach do not seem to be contradictory. Though Craik and Lockhart (1972) correctly point out that some of the arguments for assuming separate stores are not viable, Wickelgren (1973) has reviewed other arguments which are consistent with a multistore inter- pretation. But there is an important sense in which the claim concerning separate, distinct stores is not the central claim of the modal model. Rather, the functional distinctions between active memory and long-term memory appear to be more critical. These functional differences have been captured quite nicely within the production system formalism of the Carnegie–Mellon project on complex information processing (Newell, 1972, 1973; Newell & Simon, 1972). Long-term memory is viewed as a set of production rules specifying which actions or processes take place given specified inputs, while active memory holds the current arguments or conditions that will trigger the operation of particular rules. This conceptualization places less emphasis on storage systems, coding differences, and other classic hallmarks of the modal model, and focuses on the functional distinctions between inputs that control processing and representa- tions of the processing rules themselves.

At present, the modal model and the levels of processing approach may be viewed primarily for their heuristic value in generating theoretical issues or research paradigms. Under conditions where memory representations are con- structed as a by-product of other behaviors, the levels of processing approach provides a useful way of conceptualizing the memorial consequences of such acts. On the other hand, in tasks where memory dynamics operate as limiting factors in information processing, especially in tasks with temporal rate or information overload constraints (Carpenter & Just, 1975; Newell & Simon, 1972), the modal model provides a framework for relating memory considera- tions to a range of mental operations. Within the broad range of retention tasks per se, which lie between these extremes, both approaches offer useful concep- tualizations.

Visual Memory

Most research on human memory has used verbal stimuli, but recently there has been a resurgence of interest in memory for pictures and other visual stimuli. There seems little doubt now that one form of internal representation is processed in a manner suggestive of isomorphisms with perceptual processing (see Bower, 1972; Paivio, 1969, 1971; Shepard, 1975), though many important conceptual issues plague discussions of mental imagery and memory (Pylyshyn, 1973). Recent information processing conceptualizations of mental imagery and internal picture processing have suggested that there are in principle theoretical solutions to such difficulties (Baylor, 1971; Winston, 1973, 1975). While it is naive to suppose that we literally store mental pictures in long-term memory, there is no objection to the supposition that whatever *is* stored can be processed in ways which are analogous to processing pictorial information.

Given that visual information can be remembered in a manner distinct from verbal information, does such retention fit into the general scheme for information processing just outlined? Since virtually the entire empirical foundation for models of memory comes from research on verbal retention, this is an important question both for evaluating the generality of these models and for assessing their applicability to the concerns of this chapter. The evidence on visual memory is sketchy, and it will not be possible to assess this question in detail, but some general similarities and dissimilarities between verbal and visual retention can be outlined.

What about some of the basic functional distinctions? Is there a contrast between active memory and long-term memory for visual stimuli? Are processes like rehearsal in the absence of external stimulation found for visual stimuli as they are for verbal stimuli? It is important in asking questions like these to be sure we are studying visual memories and not the verbal memories that often accompany them. Subjects examining a picture activate a number of purely verbal associations, all of which could serve to mediate retention of the picture. To control this, special procedures are used which selectively focus on the visual memories themselves. Pictures having very low codability are presented, or the pictures are presented very rapidly or in very large numbers so that verbal coding is difficult, or selective interference procedures are used which affect only that portion of the encoding of a stimulus that is visual.

There have been several studies of the kind employing rapid presentations (Loftus, 1974; Hintzman & Rogers, 1973; Potter, 1975; Potter & Levy, 1969; Shaffer & Shiffrin, 1972). Stimulus exposures range from less than 100 msec up to several seconds. Recognition memory performance is poor at the faster presentation rates, but is above chance values for all except the very briefest presentation. Potter and Levy (1969) and Loftus (1974) have reported recency effects in such experiments, and such effects in recognition memory have been used as circumstantial evidence for the existence of active memory, (Waugh & Norman, 1965). But the tests of recency effects in the studies using rapid presentations have not been obtained under conditions which would lend clear support for the notion that they were mediated by a short-term, active trace.

However, there is evidence from short-term memory experiments that a short-lived visual trace can be established. Pellegrino, Siegel, and Dhawan (1975) found, using a Peterson and Peterson (1959) short-term retention paradigm, that when subjects had to remember a visual item, working on an embedded figures task during the retention interval impaired the recall of the name of the visual item, whereas the embedded figures task did not interfere with auditory presentations of the name (though the standard counting backwards did). The retention functions they obtained are difficult to compare, since the initial levels are quite different for verbal and visual items, but over the course of a 15-sec retention interval performance declined by the same amount for both types of items under conditions of selective interference. Other studies have also shown that visual interference can produce rapid loss of visual information under conditions approximating standard short-term memory tasks (Murray & Newman, 1973). Baddeley and Hitch (1974) have reviewed other data suggesting there exists an active visual memory. As with the serial position data, these findings are only circumstantial evidence for an active memory for visual information. But the existence of qualitative similarities between verbal and visual memory performance lends some credence to the generality of the principles of information processing outlined earlier.

The question of rehearsal is somewhat different, however. Atkinson and Shiffrin's (1968) influential version of the modal model emphasized the importance of rehearsal processes in verbal active memory. Rehearsal serves to maintain a verbal item in active memory after it has been presented and also plays a role in the establishment of a more permanent memory trace in long-term memory. But visual memory seems to be quite different. Shaffer and Shiffrin (1972) and Potter and Levy (1969) reported that the level of recognition of a rapidly presented picture was entirely a function of the exposure duration of the picture and was unrelated to the duration of the intertrial intervals where supposedly rehearsal would take place. Though others have argued that rehearsal does seem to play a role in visual memory (Pellegrino et al., 1975), the direct evidence is certainly weak. Results like those of Loftus' (1972), which show that visual recognition memory performance can be predicted by the number of eye fixations made during the scanning of a picture, suggest that the analogue to rehearsal for visual memory may be the fixation. But this is a different sense of rehearsal, since the fixation serves to aid in establishing a permanent memory representation but an external memory (the picture itself) must maintain the memory trace in active memory.

Another striking characteristic of visual memory is that once a representation is formed, it seems remarkably resistant to forgetting. In a number of studies, it has been found that recognition memory for pictures following exposure to hundreds or even thousands of examples is very good, and continues to be reliably above chance levels for up to a year (Shepard, 1967; Nickerson, 1968; Standing, Conezio, & Haber, 1970). These facts have often been pointed to as distinguishing visual memory from verbal, where such remarkable levels of performance are not usually found (one well-known but unpublished exception, a study by Wallace, Turner, and Perkins (1957), used words that were highly imagable). But it must be remembered that many theoretically relevant variables are not equated in studies of picture and word recognition memory. Further, these remarkable levels of performance are limited to codable or meaningful stimuli (Freedman & Haber, 1974; Goldstein & Chance, 1971). Nonetheless, by a rough metric, visual recognition memory for meaningful items is very good, and as we will see later, is essentially as good throughout development, in marked contrast to verbal memory.

Whatever the exact form of visual coding, subjects can process a visual stimulus to varying degrees as in the levels of processing studies with verbal stimuli. This is of course a truism with respect to sensory and perceptual analysis. But under conditions where coding is more leisurely, namely, under incidental learning conditions typically used for testing the levels of processing view, similar findings emerge. Bower and Karlin (1974) had subjects judge pictures of faces for sex (superficial coding) or likableness (deep coding) and found that depth of processing predicted later recognition memory for the faces. Freedman and Haber (1974) reported better recognition memory for ambiguous forms "seen" as faces than those not seen as faces, and Loftus and Bell (1975) found that recognition memory for pictures was based on two levels of coding that they called "specific details" and "general visual information." Such flexibility in coding or processing will also be an important feature of infant visual recognition memory.

In general, then, though there are many parallels between visual memory and verbal memory in adults, the correspondence is certainly inexact. In the present chapter it will be assumed that comparable principles of representation and memory dynamics will hold for the processing of visual experiences as well as verbal ones, though the evidence to support this assumption is at best circumstantial and detailed analogies would clearly be inappropriate. But then it is the nature of preliminary, working hypotheses to be inexact.

MEMORY DEVELOPMENT

General Picture

It scarcely takes systematic empirical verification to support the general claim that memory abilities improve throughout early development. But it is less clear what underlies such broad change. The current state of knowledge about memory development at least allows some descriptive claims to be made. In a nutshell, it looks like the most salient characteristics of memory development are: (a) an increasingly fine-grained repertoire of mental features or categories with which experience can be represented; (b) an increasingly sophisticated repertoire of encoding and retrieval strategies, largely involving language, to aid in recovering memories; and (c) increasingly accurate knowledge about the nature of one's own memory system, which in turn yields a more realistic selection of strategies and tasks. Thus, memory development is a species of general cognitive development: as the child learns more about the world and about the cognitive capacities available to itself, it both more realistically and effectively stores and retrieves experiences. Let us look at a few illustrations of these aspects of development.

It is a truism that the more organized knowledge one has about a subject, the easier it is to remember material pertaining to it. Retention in general is organized and meaningful, and is aided by having some preexisting context to embed an experience in. This thought has been at the heart of the developmental theories of Gibson (1969) and Piaget and Inhelder (1972). As an illustration, experienced chess players can remember meaningful board positions better than naive players, though both do poorly on randomly arranged boards (Simon & Gilmartin, 1973). Knowledge organizes our experience, making it easier to sort out the details of the events we witness. Piaget and Inhelder (1972) reported that even in the absence of active rehearsal or practice, a child's memory of an event can improve if in the meantime it has acquired knowledge which gives it an effective epistemological classification for the previous experience. Hagen, Jongeward, and Kail (1975) have other evidence which supports the mnemonic importance of knowledge acquisition.

Children also acquire various strategies to aid their retention. For instance, the use of verbal labels is an obvious and well-studied example. If you want to be able to remember a series of pictures shown to you, it helps to think of the names of the objects in the pictures. This verbal mediation effect has been demonstrated repeatedly with children (Flavell, 1970; Hagen et al., 1975). So, to become more efficient at remembering events children must learn that planful encoding strategies like verbal labeling, clustering, and elaborative imagery facilitate retention.

However, acquiring such strategies and actually using them are quite different matters. Even at a point in development when they are capable of doing so, young children do not spontaneously use memory aids like verbal labeling (Flavell, 1970; Hagen et al., 1975). Young children have inaccurate or incomplete knowledge about the nature of remembering and the nature of their own retentive abilities, and thus do not appreciate the usefulness of various memory strategies. Younger children will overestimate the amount of information they can remember, will inaccurately assess the relative difficulty of two lists of information, will give poor suggestions for planning their retention, and will in general show that they do not take the properties of their own memory system into account to the extent that older children and adults do (Flavell, Friedrichs & Hoyt, 1970; Kreutzer, Leonard & Flavell, 1975). For instance, Kreutzer et al. (1975) report that young children do not think that performing a distracting activity between looking up a telephone number and dialing it would affect retention, whereas older children realize they had better dial it before it slips away. This somewhat neglected aspect of memory, which Kreutzer and co-workers term "metamemory," is clearly important, for the selection of appropriate strategies and plans for remembering depends in large part upon knowing one's limitations and knowing when the extra effort required by elaborate encoding will be required.

Little systematic work has been done on the general organization of information processing in children, though there is interest in the kinds of models of memory proposed for adult performance (Hagen *et al.*, 1975). There certainly is ample evidence for qualitative features of performance that parallel those found with adults, but there is little research directed toward the question of what aspects of information processing change. Do basic structural characteristics like storage capacity, transfer rates, rehearsal rates, and the like change with development? There is not much evidence, but a recent review of developmental research on temporal rates of information processing (Wickens, 1974) concluded that most of the observed changes in performance in reaction time tasks, tachistoscopic recognition tasks, and other tasks requiring rapid information processing could be attributed to nonstructural variables like level of practice, motivation, or attention. Wickens felt there was some evidence for developmental changes in the rate parameters of very early perceptual processing and pattern recognition, and that young children seem to be slightly more "single channel" than older children, but the evidential basis for even these claims was slight. What is more impressive about his review is how little change there seems to be in basic temporal parameters when the nonstructural variables mentioned before are controlled. The issue of possible invariances in development is important enough so that we will return to it again. But first let us review the data on children's visual memory abilities, since it will enter into our consideration of developmental invariances.

Visual Memory

The dramatic improvements in retention of verbal information are obvious, but in tasks where verbal coding is only minimally involved, there appears to be little or no change with development. A variety of studies have shown either no developmental changes at all or very small ones very early in development on tasks using recognition of pictorial material (Brown & Scott, 1971; Nelson, 1971; Corsini, 1969; Hoffman, 1971). At all levels of development, from preschool through adulthood, picture recognition memory is very good and very long lasting. Even when possible ceiling effects are controlled by using a recency judgment task with pictorial materials, essentially no developmental differences are found (Brown, 1973). Such experiments argue for viewing picture recognition performance as a basal, developmentally invariant aspect of the memory system, and might offer a paradigm within which one could study the subtle issue of change versus constancy in development.

Invariance and Change

Change is always the most salient characteristic of development, but in attempting to specify the functional changes that underly observed performance it is important to separate out factors which might be invariant. This is a difficult task, since it usually takes converging evidence to support a claim of invariance of function when the data are observed changes. An important example from the memory development literature will illustrate this. It is an overwhelmingly well-documented fact that digit span recall improves systematically with age. The improvement is so regular that such performance is used in assessing intelligence. Does this improved ability to remember a random string of digits indicate that the capacity of active memory is changing? This interpretation is not illogical, but neither is it necessary. Both Olson (1973) and Simon (1974) have argued, independently, that given current conceptions of chunking and active memory (Miller, 1956), the improvement in digit span could either be a change in the capacity of active memory, a change in the ability to code numbers, or possibly both. Simon (1974) pointed to correlational evidence which suggests that capacity remains invariant. Given that we already know that improvement in coding is a fundamental source of developmental change (Hagen *et al.,* 1975), it is not at all unreasonable to take the strong view that active memory capacity does not change. This conclusion could in turn be used to support the argument that basic structural characteristics of the information processing system do not change with development. The data on picture recognition memory and Wickens' (1974) review of information processing parameters are further support. Though the evidential basis for this claim is sketchy, it offers an interesting heuristic, especially given that the well-documented changes that do occur fit very nicely with this conception.

Of course, during the first months of life the infant is not a neurologically stable organism. The rapid development of primary sensorimotor cortex and the somewhat slower development of association cortex must certainly affect even the most primitive memory abilities during the early postnatal months. Thus, one would not want to insist on invariant characteristics of information processing during the early months; and even after three or four months, when the rate of neurological change within sensory systems has slowed down, basic information processing capabilities could plausibly be affected by such factors. But it is also reasonable, given the data on neurological development, to suspect that after the first three or four months such changes should play a decreasingly important role in cognitive development, especially within the realm of visual information processing.

INFANT VISUAL MEMORY

This section will focus on the ages from three to six months, largely because most of the data on infant visual recognition memory has been collected from subjects in this age range. It is harder to study visual memory in infants younger than three months (Cohen & Gelber, 1975; Fantz, 1964; Jeffrey & Cohen, 1971), though exactly why is difficult to determine. The visual system, which is immature at birth, changes quite rapidly during the first three or four months (Haynes, White, & Held, 1965), and Bronson (1974) has recently suggested some ways in which this neurological immaturity could affect early cognitive development. The novelty preference that is at the heart of the most common techniques for assessing infant memory is not strongly established during this early period (Fisher, Sperber & Zeaman, 1973; Wetherford & Cohen, 1973). Further, complications of state of alertness make the measurement of cognitive functions in the early weeks of life very difficult (Clifton & Nelson, Chapter 5, this volume). But beyond three months the data are quite clear and plentiful, and the kinds of factors which complicate the study of memory in the first few months are much less of a problem.

Sufficient data are available to attempt to sketch the infant's visual memory capacities during this period. Further, the developmental changes that occur during this period can also be given a principled explanation. The model to be presented in the next section is based both on general principles of information processing derived from research on mature cognition and from important features of the data reviewed below. Though in general the striking similarities between infant memory performance and that of older subjects are emphasized, there are important differences that cannot be ignored. Since many of these differences result from characteristics of the memory paradigms typically employed, we must turn our attention to matters of methodology prior to examining pertinent data.

Methodology

Though there are other ways to study visual memory in infants, most of the data have been collected in habituation experiments or in studies employing methods based on habituation. The underlying logic is simple, and derives from Sokolov (1963), who first emphasized that habituation to a stimulus is due to the formation of a memory trace. An infant is familiarized with a stimulus, perhaps for a fixed number of trials or for a fixed period of time, or perhaps to a prespecified level of decline in looking. Then a new stimulus is presented to demonstrate that the infant can discriminate the new stimulus from the old one, and to show that the decline in looking to the old one is not due to sensory adaptation, receptor fatigue, and other nonmemory causes (Thompson & Spencer, 1966). Thus, in the habituation paradigm, it is the recovery from the decline in level of looking that is the critical feature that allows the inference of a memory trace. Standard reviews of infant habituation experiments are readily available (Cohen, Chapter 6, this volume; Cohen & Gelber, 1975; Jeffrey & Cohen, 1971; Kessen, Haith, & Salapatek, 1970).

Fantz (1964) and Fagan (1970) developed a special adaptation of the habituation procedure which has proved to be quite useful in studying infant visual memory. The infant is exposed to a visual stimulus and then is tested for retention by being presented two stimuli simultaneously, the old one and a new one. Relatively greater looking toward the new stimulus implies retention. Data from experiments using this paired-comparison procedure will be the primary focus of the present review, in part because data from pure habituation tasks have been adequately reviewed elsewhere and in part because most of the evidence pertinent to the model to be presented later has come from such tasks. But in discussing the dynamics of information storage, habituation data will play a central role.

A brief methodological note on the paired-comparison procedure is in order here so the review can focus on substantive issues. As just mentioned, memory is tested in this paradigm by presenting an old and a new stimulus simultaneously and observing the extent to which the new stimulus elicits more looking (there is no reason why reliably more looking toward the old stimulus could not be used to argue for retention, but in the period from three to six months there is generally no evidence for such behavior). Though it is tempting to view this procedure as an analogue of the forced-choice recognition test, this is inappropriate, since there is no notion of "correct choice" for the infant that guides its selection of stimuli. Rather, the paired-comparison test is a species of choice or preference task, in which the experimenter monitors the subject's choice between two stimuli. That such behavior has multiple determinants is obvious. Figure 2 summarizes the kinds of factors which might govern an infant's choice between Pictures A and B. The relative novelty—familiarity of the stimuli is of primary importance for the memory experiment. In order to measure memory effects independent of the other determinants of choice, investigators typically do two things: (a) they try to choose stimuli which infants look at about equally often prior to familiarization with one of them; and (b) they counterbalance stimulus assignments over subjects, so that equal numbers see A and B as old stimuli in each condition of an experiment. The counterbalancing insures that experimental effects averaged over stimulus assignments are memory effects, and by choosing stimuli that elicit comparable levels of looking prior to familiarization the experimenter attempts to control the variance due to stimulus assignments interacting with nonmemory factors.

But many interesting questions about memory performance cannot be easily asked when the above are the only kinds of controls used. For instance, important memory effects might emerge under conditions where there are strong a priori biases with a given pair of stimuli. Further, any scheme which partitions

Determinants of paired-comparison looking

DISCRIMINABILITY

Interstimulus contrast
Codability

PREFERENCE

Perceptual features
Interpretation
Novelty-familiarity

RESPONSE BIASES

Position habits
Criteria for shifting gaze
State

FIG. 2   Determinants of looking on paired-comparison tests.

subjects on the basis of some characteristic of performance (e.g., features of familiarization looking) would not preserve the exact counterbalancing and thus would make it difficult to infer the memorial consequences of these performance characteristics. So, an alternative procedure is to determine the a priori choice levels empirically, either by testing subjects both before and after familiarization in a memory experiment or by collecting choice data from a comparable group of subjects. The first of these is best, since it takes into account individual variation in a priori choice factors. But in cases where retention is being studied in relation to relatively brief experience with the stimuli, pretests of choice might interfere with the experimental manipulations. In this case, group choice data might be the only recourse. Data reported from the author's laboratory have made use of such group choice data to compute an empirical "chance" value for each subject. However, to preserve comparability with reports from other laboratories, all scores reported here have been arithmetically rescaled so that discrepancies from these empirical chance values are measured with respect to the conventional 50% chance value for the two-choice situation. The computation procedure is to first obtain the algebraic difference between the percentage of time a memory subject looked at the novel stimulus and the percentage of time a nonmemory subject looked at the same stimulus when given the same test pair without any prior familiarization. Then this difference score is added algebraically to the 50% scale value to yield the final memory score.

Incidentally, the multiple determinants of paired-comparison looking summarized in Figure 2 have another important effect on recognition memory experiments with infants. The observed percent-to-novel scores in such studies rarely exceed 60% to 70%. Novelty preferences as high as 80% to 90% are simply not observed, and this should be kept in mind when interpreting data from such experiments.

Memory Codes

The sealing wax metaphor of Plato suggested that we store copies of experience in memory, but the more accurate view is that we store encodings or interpretations of experience. Such encodings are purchased at the cost of veridical memories, but the benefits are enormous. Through coding we can abstract invariances from the flux of experience. Luria's mnemonist is dramatic testimony to the usefulness of abstraction, for his veridical memories repeatedly interfered with his intellectual functioning (Luria, 1968).

To show retention on a paired-comparison test, an infant must be able to represent one or more of the features that differentiate the old and the new items. At any particular stage of development, the infant's retentive skills are going to depend upon perceptual coding abilities. Some perceptual categories are going to develop primarily through maturation (Blakemore & Cooper, 1970; Freeman, Mitchell & Millodot, 1972; Hirsch & Spinelli, 1970), while others will be acquired through experience (Gibson, 1969), and it is clear that infancy is a period of rapid change. It will be important to know about infants' coding abilities in examining their visual information processing skills. To this end, we will review data from recognition memory experiments for the period from three to six months. Though some theorists (Bruner, 1964; Piaget, 1952) have suggested that motoric codes may play a role in the infant's internal representations, the present chapter will focus exclusively on the purely visual features of internal codes.

The data to be considered are admittedly imperfect from a logical point of view. The underlying assumption employed in this review is that if infants can differentially orient to two stimuli on the basis of prior experience with one of them, then some aspect of their difference was encoded in memory. However, the failure to find such differentiation does not imply the failure of the infant to encode some particular feature. Thus, technically, no conclusion can be drawn from negative evidence. But failures to differentiate can be used as circumstantial evidence regarding coding abilities, especially in a developmental context. If infants at one developmental level do not discriminate two stimuli on a recognition memory test while those at a later developmental level do, then it is plausible to assume that, at the very least, the encoding of the differences has become more automatic at the later stage. These developmental contrasts are the kind we are most interested in here.

Table 1 summarizes the available data on three to six month old infants' abilities to encode visual experiences. These data are for the comparisons that have actually been tested, so are understandably piecemeal when examined across developmental levels. Nonetheless, some important generalizations emerge. The most striking developmental change is that as the infant gets older it is able to make finer and finer discriminations from memory, given approximately equivalent nominal levels of familiarization. While it could be argued that the overall rate of visual information processing is slower in the younger infants, it is more sensible, given the data, to assume that the differences are due to the automaticity with which particular features can be coded. For example, a right-side-up face and an upside-down one are of equivalent nominal complexity, yet the five-month-old infant can easily remember the former but not the latter.

The positive evidence for three-month infants all comes from contrasts where, to speak loosely, the stimuli vary multidimensionally.[1] If only the form or the color or the arrangement of a set of objects varies, the three-month-old has difficulty. But just a month later there is positive evidence for mnemonic discrimination of more subtle contrasts like arrangement or form. Though Cohen, Gelber, and Lazar (1971) found positive evidence in four-month-old males for memory discriminations based on color alone using a habituation task, comparable positive evidence with paired-comparison tasks has not been found until after six months (Miranda & Fantz, 1974).

It has already been noted by others, most notably Gibson (1969), that there is a regular progression during the first year in the ability to encode features of the human face. Gibson reviewed earlier data that supported her model of the acquisition of the distinctive features of the human face, and a recent habituation

---

[1] Though the term "multidimensional" is perhaps not the best term for describing the stimulus contrasts referred to here, it was chosen because it has been used frequently in the literature to refer to "sharply contrasting, black and white patterns [Fagan, 1970, p. 220]," in contrast, say, to sets of patterns varying in just outline shape, number or size of elements, arrangement of elements, or color. The study by Miranda and Fantz (1974), referred to several times in Table 1, used such highly contrasting stimuli in color on white versions as well as black on white. Thus, multidimensional stimuli varying in pattern or color alone refer, respectively, to variations in the sharply contrasting patterns or in the color of the patterns.

TABLE 1

Paired-Comparison Data on Developmental Changes in Recognition Memory for Specific Stimulus Contrasts

Nature of stimulus contrast	Amount of familiarization (exposures, sec)	Source
3 Months—Positive evidence		
Highly contrasting photographs and magazine ads	repeated 60-sec exposures	Fantz (1964)
Simple figures differing in both form and color	270	Saayman, Ames, and Moffett (1964)
Black and white stimuli varying multidimensionally	120	Fagan (1970)
Multidimensional stimuli varying in pattern alone[a]	30 and 60	Miranda and Fantz (1974)
3 Months—Negative evidence		
Photographs of faces	60	Miranda and Fantz (1974)
Simple figures varying only in form or color	270	Saayman et al. (1964)
Small elements in differing arrangements	60	Miranda and Fantz (1974)
Multidimensional stimuli varying in color only[a]	30 and 60	Miranda and Fantz (1974)
4 Months—Positive evidence		
Photographs of faces when paired with upside down face	60	Fagan (1972)
Highly contrasting photographs and magazine ads	repeated 60-sec exposures	Fantz (1964)
Small elements differing in arrangement	120	Fagan (1970)
	60	Cornell (1975)
Black and white stimuli varying multidimensionally	120	Fagan (1970)
Multidimensional stimuli varying in at least 2 of the following dimensions: color, arrangement of elements, shape of elements	60	Welch (1974)
Two-dimensional funnel-shaped objects	80	McGurk (1970)
Fabric swatches varying in color and pattern	60	Olson (unpublished data)
Red and yellow figures varying in shape only	60	Olson (unpublished data)
Black and white patterns of circular forms	60	Olson (unpublished data)
Simple rotating forms	30, 60, and 120	Adams (1973)

(continued)

TABLE 1 (continued)

Nature of stimulus contrast	Amount of familiarization (exposures, sec)	Source
4 Months—Negative evidence		
Photographs of faces when paired with other upright faces	60	Fagan (1972)
	6 10-sec exposures	Cornell (1974)
Three-dimensional face masks	60	Fagan (1972)
Three-dimensional face masks paired with upside-down face mask	80	McGurk (1970)
Schematic faces	60	Olson (unpublished data)
5 Months—Positive evidence		
Highly contrasting photographs and magazine ads	repeated 60-sec exposures	Fantz (1964)
Black and white patterns varying multidimensionally	120	Fagan (1970, 1971)
Photographs of faces presented in normal orientation	60 and 120	Fagan (1972)
	6 10-sec exposures	Cornell (1974)
Three-dimensional face masks in normal orientation	60	Fagan (1972)
Photograph of familiar face in new pose versus unfamiliar face	6 10-sec exposures	Cornell (1974)
Photograph of unfamiliar face in same sex versus unfamiliar face in opposite sex	6 10-sec exposures	Cornell (1974)
5 Months—Negative evidence		
Photographs of faces presented upside down	60 and 120	Fagan (1972)
Three-dimensional face masks presented upside down	60	Fagan (1972)
Line drawings of faces	60	Fagan (1972)
6 Months—Positive evidence		
Black and white patterns varying multidimensionally	120	Fagan (1973)
Small elements in differing arrangements	120	Fagan (1973)

Photographs of faces	60	Miranda and Fantz (1974)
	120	Fagan (1973)
Three-dimensional face masks versus upright face masks	60	Miranda and Fantz (1974)
	120	Fagan (1973)
Three-dimensional face masks versus upside-down face masks	80	McGurk (1970)
Multidimensional stimuli varying in pattern only[a]	30 and 60	Miranda and Fantz (1974)
Three-dimensional nonsense object	120	Schaffer and Parry (1970)
Two-dimensional funnel-shaped object	80	McGurk (1970)
6 Months—Negative evidence		
Multidimensional stimuli varying in color only[a]	30 and 60	Miranda and Fantz (1974)

[a]See footnote 1.

study by Caron, Caron, Caldwell and Weiss (1973) provided detailed experimental confirmation of Gibson's proposals. These data show that infants are able to encode the eyes earlier than they are able to encode the mouth, and that the inner face configuration is codable later than the overall outer face shape. This fits with data on perceptual scanning of simple figures (Salapatek, 1975). Though the data shown in Table 1 do not permit such detailed inferences about mnemonic codes as the Caron et al. (1973) data allow, they certainly support the distinctive feature analysis of Gibson. The contrast already noted at five months between the recognition of right-side-up faces but not upside-down ones is the clearest case.

Current theories of adult recognition memory (e.g., Anderson & Bower, 1972, 1974; Tulving & Thomson, 1973; Watkins & Tulving, 1975) represent the mnemonic code of an experience in association with a representation of the context within which it was experienced. Thus, a subject who learns to recognize a word in a typical recognition memory experiment suffers when forced to recognize it within an altered context. Of course most of these studies involved the subjects' ability to remember items (words) that were already well known, so that the subject's task was in essence to learn an association between the item and the experimental context. Such context effects are probably not as strong when the material is unfamiliar, and may account in part for the very high retention shown for unfamiliar pictures.

The role of context variables in infant visual recognition has not been systematically studied, and those results that do exist are not straightforward. Weizman, Cohen, and Pratt (1971) tested babies in either the same bassinet as used during the familiarization phase or in a different one, but found that the effect of familiar versus novel context on recognition performance was different for males and females. Males fixated a novel stabile more frequently in a familiar bassinet, while females fixated a novel stimulus more frequently in a novel bassinet. It is difficult to determine on the basis of Weisman et al.'s (1971) data whether or not the contextual cues contributed to the level of recognition performance, but there does not seem to be any indication of inferior performance in a novel context unless one were to generalize to males only. Weisman and co-workers reviewed other studies which showed differential effects of novel and familiar contexts for males and females, but none of these studies specifically contrasted memory performance in altered versus constant contexts vis-à-vis acquisition. Thus, though their data are quite suggestive, the general hypothesis that recognition memory is mediated by learned associations between representations of specific items and of the context of acquisition has not been adequately tested with infants.

Short-Term versus Long-Term Processes

Earlier we reviewed some of the circumstantial evidence for a distinction between short-term and long-term processes in adult visual recognition memory.

Similar circumstantial evidence is available for infants. Cohen (1973; Cohen & Gelber, 1975) has proposed that performance details observed by plotting habituation data backward from the trial of habituation suggest a two-process interpretation of infant memory. The short-term looking away from the stimulus prior to habituation is accounted for by a rapidly forgotten short-term visual trace, while the longer-term loss of interest defined as habituation is evidence of the presence of a long-term trace. Cohen does not find a gradual decline in interest prior to attaining a criterion of habituation, so that the short-term process seems to have the steady-state properties characteristic of the STM state of earlier Markov models of multistore memory processes (Atkinson & Crothers, 1964; Kintsch, 1966, 1967; Olson, 1969). Just as with the earlier all-or-none controversies surrounding the development of these kinds of models, the all-or-noneness of habituation data will probably depend upon the complexity of the stimuli (Bower, 1967). Thus, until a wider range of stimulus materials and presentation schedules are examined, Cohen's interpretation of his backward curves must be viewed with caution. But his general argument for the existence of short-term and long-term processes in habituation is plausible, and certainly fits well with physiological and behavioral data on habituation in simple organisms (Carew & Kandel, 1974).

A series of experiments in the author's laboratory have examined infant recognition memory for a list of briefly presented visual stimuli. An infant is shown a series of 4 stimuli drawn from a class of related items, with familiarization periods of 10 or 15 sec duration, depending upon the experiment. The familiarization periods are timed from the infant's first look toward the stimuli. After the list is presented one of the items from the list is chosen and paired with a new item from the same stimulus class.[2] These two items constitute a paired–comparison test for the serial position of the old item. Over the course of the experiment each infant is tested on each serial position once, with each list constructed from a different class of stimuli (examples of classes are geometric shapes, nonsense shapes, fabric swatches, schematic faces).

The infant is seated in front of a partition in a semidarkened room. Stimuli are projected onto a rear-projection screen, and an observer monitors the corneal reflections of the stimuli in the infant's eyes through a small peephole just below the rear-projection screen. An image of the stimulus the infant is looking at is reflected from the center of the pupil. The observer records the durations of the infant's fixations of the stimuli via microswitches mounted on a console below the peephole. All experimental events and data recording are handled by an online minicomputer system interfaced with the slide projector and the observer's console.

---

[2] The paired-comparison tests are always presented in two parts with the position of old and new stimuli counterbalanced, since it is well known that infants have very strong position preferences when looking at a pair of stimuli (Cohen, 1972; Olson, unpublished data).

Data for two such experiments are shown in Figures 3 and 4. These experiments differed only in the length of the familiarization interval, with the 48 infants in Figure 3 presented each item for 10 sec and the 32 infants in Figure 4 presented each item for 15 sec. All of the infants were 17–20 weeks old, and were equally divided between the two sexes. A remarkable pattern of results emerged from these studies. The most striking serial position effect was the primacy effect, not the recency one. The males' recognition memory for serial position one in both experiments was statistically significant, while male recognition memory for serial position two in the second experiment approached significance. No significant recency was found in these overall data, which are averaged over the various stimulus classes used in the 2 experiments. Further, the females showed no significant retention for any serial position in these overall results. Cohen and Gelber (1975) stated that "no topic is more confusing, no evidence more contradictory than that on sex differences in infant attention and memory [p. 47]." The superior performance shown by males in Figures 3 and 4 is in the same direction as the sex differences Cohen has found in a number of studies on visual habituation. But data from other laboratories sometimes show different effects, and until someone researches these sex differences in a more systematic fashion their precise meaning will remain unexplicated.

Upon closer examination of the data in these experiments, reliable recency effects were found within one of the classes of items presented. This class consisted of swatches of brightly colored and patterned fabrics, which had been

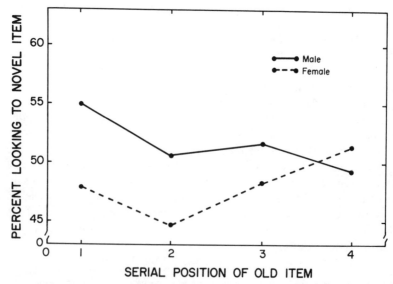

FIG. 3   Mean percentage of looking to novel items for females and males (familiarization time = 10 sec).

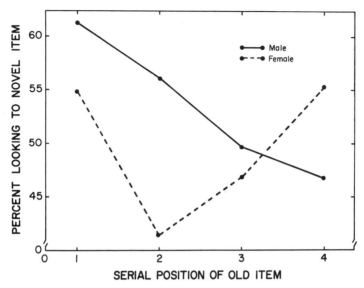

FIG. 4   Mean percentage of looking to novel items for females and males (familiarization time = 15 sec).

stretched over a standard size frame and photographed for presentation. These stimuli elicited a great deal of interest from the 17–20-week infants, and as shown in Figure 5, elicited a significant recency effect for both males and females. This is a theoretically important result. The fabric swatches constituted a class of items that were relatively heterogeneous, since the members of this category differed extensively in color and pattern. By contrast, the other stimulus classes used were much more homogeneous. For instance, two of the categories had items which were always the same color but differed only in outline, while another differed in internal detail but not in color or shape.

How should one interpret such data, which are in marked contrast to the patterns of serial position effects found with adults for either verbal or visual items? The typical adult findings for recognition show recency but seldom if ever primacy, and recency effects are in general minimally influenced by stimulus similarity (Wickelgren, 1973). The explanation seems to lie in the nature of the task used to assess infant memory. Recall that the task is basically a choice task, and there is of course no instructionally induced intent to learn or remember the stimuli. Infants habituate to repeated presentation of the same stimulus, and such habituation generalizes to similar stimuli. Thus, for classes of items that are homogeneous, the infants look actively at the first member of the series but as the items are presented, the infant habituates to the class and attends less to the later items. For a heterogeneous class, the level of attention remains high, and each stimulus is processed more completely. This explains why

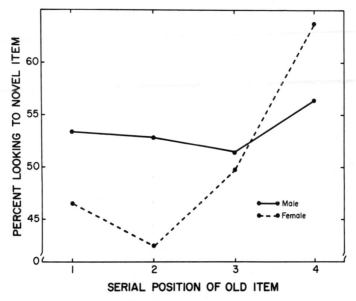

FIG. 5   Mean percentage of looking to novel items with fabric swatch stimuli.

primacy effects are more widespread in the data and why the heterogeneous classes alone show recency and also accounts for the general effect of increased familiarization time on the earlier serial positions (Figures 3 and 4). But it also suggests that the level of retention for all serial positions in the heterogeneous list ought to be high, and the data in Figure 5 do not seem to support this (though there are only 10 observations for each point). Thus, several new experiments are in progress to explore further the interactions of stimulus series heterogeneity and primacy–recency effects, and until these are completed the interpretation above must be viewed as tentative. All that can be said for it is that it is consistent with habituation phenomena (Cohen & Gelber, 1975) and is supported by certain qualitative details of the data. For instance, parameters of the infants' familiarization data are consistent with the habituation interpretation, in that for the homogeneous classes average looking time and average fixation length decline over the series of items, while these same statistics rise over the series for the heterogeneous items. But these effects are small and are in need of replication before they can be used as serious evidence for this interpretation.

The elevated performance on the last serial position for the heterogeneous class of items (Figure 5) is consistent with the idea that there is an active memory for visual stimuli in infants. By itself such an effect is not persuasive, but in the next section further evidence from a different kind of experiment will be presented which is consistent with this interpretation.

Storage

Under the conditions of typical infant memory experiments, it is difficult to infer the nature of the infant's storage processes. Unlike typical incidental learning procedures used with older children or adults, infant memory experiments do not permit precise experimental control of the infant's level of processing. As shown in the discussion of serial position effects, infants' looking and subsequent memory performance are influenced by the kinds of pictures seen before and after they view a target picture. Thus, some marginal control over the level of the infant's processing can be obtained by various manipulations of stimuli and presentation schedules. Further, under the assumption that an infant habituates because of the formation of a memory trace (Cohen & Gelber, 1975; Sokolov, 1963), some measure of the loss of interest in a picture could be interpreted as the attainment of an adequate memory trace.

Numerous attempts have been made to predict the infant's recognition performance from looking behavior during familiarization. Such parameters as the total looking time, number of looks toward a picture, and average length per look have been examined, with generally negligible results when individual looking was correlated with subsequent retention (Cornell, 1972; Fagan, 1972, 1973; Olson & Strauss, 1974). When group looking parameters are controlled experimentally, it is clear that the more time that is available the better a group of infants does in remembering the picture (Adams, 1973; Fagan, 1974) (Figures 3 and 4). Attempts to control experimentally individual parameters of looking have not been made.

Cohen's (1973; Cohen & Gelber, 1975) discussion of short-term versus long-term processes in infant habituation suggested a different approach to the issue of predicting an infant's recognition memory performance from looking behavior during familiarization. If habituation is due to the formation of a long-term memory trace, then looking for evidence of habituation during the familiarization interval ought to be a good predictor of long-term retention. However, if there is also a short-term trace that persists for seconds, then evidence of habituation during the familiarization interval ought to be a poorer predictor of immediate retention. As a check on this, some retention data collected in the author's laboratory were examined. In this experiment, the infants observed a picture during a 60-sec familiarization period and then were given an immediate paired-comparison test. A series of four familiarization test presentations were used, with stimuli from four different categories. Following completion of this series of study intervals and immediate recognition tests, a 5–7-min delay was introduced, during which time the infant was removed from the test apparatus. Then the infant was returned to the apparatus and a series of delayed retention tests were administered. Details of the stimuli and the general testing procedure were similar to the studies of serial position effects described above.

The primary results from this study appear in Table 2. Since there were in general no sex differences in these data, they are shown for both sexes com-

TABLE 2

Percentage of Looking to Novel Item on Immediate and Delayed Tests
for Each Stimulus Class[a]

Stimulus class	Immediate test		Delayed test	
	$\overline{X}(s)$	t	$\overline{X}(s)$	t
Fabric swatches	59.2 (17.4)	3.67***	57.6 (17.1)	3.09**
Geometric shapes	55.7 (18.1)	2.18*	55.7 (17.1)	2.29*
Circular forms	56.2 (15.1)	2.85**	54.8 (15.4)	2.17*
Schematic faces	50.5 (18.0)	0.17	56.1 (15.9)	2.65*

[a]$n = 48$.
*$p < .05$.   **$p < .005$.   ***$p < .0005$.

bined. The only exception was for the schematic faces, where the superior delayed retention was due entirely to the girls, as shown in Table 3. For the other three stimulus classes, there was reliable retention on both the immediate and the delayed test, and there was no difference between performance on immediate and delayed tests. This relative lack of forgetting will be discussed in the next section.

In an effort to assess whether habituation during the familiarization interval is a predictor of delayed retention, each infant's familiarization looking behavior was examined for evidence of habituation. The first 20 sec of the interval were compared with the last 20 sec, and an infant was classified as an habituator if the level of looking declined by at least 40%.[3] The retention data for those babies classified as habituators and nonhabituators by this criterion are shown in Table 4. These data show mixed results. For males, having habituated during the familiarization interval led to relatively higher delayed retention for all stimulus classes. But the girls only showed a comparable effect for the fabric swatches. Habituation performance often differs for males and females (Cohen & Gelber, 1975; Maccoby & Jacklin, 1974), and the most frequent pattern is that when sex differences are found it is the males that show better habituation or recognition memory. Thus, observed consistency of the male data with the hypothesis is quite encouraging. But while evidence of habituation is a possible predictor of long-term retention, it is not the only one. There is a suggestion in the data, though the numbers are too small for one to be certain, that holding level of habituation constant, longer total looking times lead to better long-term retention. This would imply, contrary to Cohen and Gelber (1975), that even though there was no behavioral indication of memory storage (habituation), considerable information was being stored. Given the lack of conclusiveness and the

[3] Though a criterion of 50% loss of interest is what Cohen and Gelber (1975) report using, the lower criterion was chosen for these data in order to get a reasonable number of habituators.

TABLE 3

Percentage of Looking to Novel Item on Immediate and Delayed Tests
for Each Sex for Schematic Faces

Sex of subject	Immediate test			Delayed test		
	$\bar{X}$	(s)	t	$\bar{X}$	(s)	t
Females[a]	48.4	(22.9)	−0.56	59.3	(16.9)	2.71*
Males[a]	53.5	(10.9)	1.58	52.8	(14.5)	0.96

[a] n = 24 per group.
*$p < .01$.

small samples in these post hoc analyses of one set of retention data, a new series
of experiments is in progress in the author's laboratory which experimentally
manipulate the level of habituation and the total looking time by making the
duration of the familiarization interval contingent upon the infant's looking
behavior. This will provide better control of the parameters involved in testing
the hypothesis, and will in turn lead to a clearer picture of the nature of storage
processes in infant memory.

Forgetting and Interference

Given that an infant can remember some particular stimulus, how long will the
infant be able to discriminate the to-be-remembered stimulus from a new one?

TABLE 4

Percentage of Looking to Novel Item on Immediate and Delayed Tests for
Habituators and Nonhabituators[a]

Group	Habituators			Nonhabituators		
	N	$\bar{X}$ (immediate)	$\bar{X}$ (delayed)	N	$\bar{X}$ (immediate)	$\bar{X}$ (delayed)
Males						
Fabric swatches	4	54.1	62.4	20	63.7	57.2
Geometric shapes	7	50.5	60.5	17	57.0	54.0
Circular forms	7	58.9	62.2	17	52.9	55.7
Schematic faces	7	53.4	57.0	17	53.5	51.1
Females						
Fabric swatches	5	44.8	61.9	19	59.5	55.9
Geometric shapes	12	61.1	52.9	12	51.6	57.9
Circular forms	13	57.4	47.9	11	58.2	57.0
Schematic faces	5	51.6	53.3	19	46.3	60.9

[a] Each subject's score has been adjusted to reflect the a priori preference for the novel
stimulus, using the formula (% novel on memory − % novel on choice + 50) (see discussion
on pages 251–253).

Though tests of delayed retention have been used in habituation paradigms, we will focus on paired–comparison data since a wider range of retention intervals and stimulus classes have been examined. Further, it is likely that the paired–comparison procedure is more sensitive for picking up memory effects at long delays.

The simplest generalization is that infants in the range of 3 to 6 months do not forget visual stimuli very rapidly if they have had a sufficiently long initial exposure and if there is relatively little specific interference. Representative data are shown in Figure 7. The data from Fagan's laboratory are for 21–25-week-old infants, while those from the author's lab are for 17–20-week-old infants. Also most of the older babies had stimulus exposures twice the duration of those for the younger ones. So the differences in overall level of retention are not surprising. Though the general trend of these curves is downward, their rate of decline is strikingly low. As long as 2 weeks later the older infants can recognize a photograph of a face seen originally for a couple of minutes. The rate of forgetting seems comparable over a wide range of stimulus classes and for both the older and younger babies. This slow rate of forgetting for picture recognition memory is just what we found earlier for adults and older children. On the basis of data like these, it seems plausible to assume that visual recognition memory

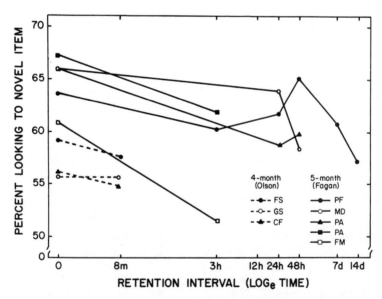

FIG. 6 Long-term recognition memory performance in paired-comparison tasks. FS = fabric swatches; GS = geometric shapes; CF = circular forms; PF = photographs of faces; MD = black and white stimuli varying multidimensionally; PA = small elements varying in pattern or arrangement; FM = three-dimensional face masks. Time scale is in log (minutes), but for ease of reading is shown in minutes (m); hours (h); and days (d). (Data for four-month-old infants from Olson unpublished, and for five-month-olds from Fagan, 1973.)

abilities might remain invariant with development, once the performance has been scaled for level of initial familiarity and for the kinds of perceptual features available for encoding at a particular stage. This conclusion is merely suggested by the currently available data, and there are profound conceptual difficulties involved in comparing infant data with recognition memory data for older children and adults. But it is a hypothesis deserving of further empirical examination.

Of course infants do forget, especially when stimuli are presented briefly or are presented among interfering stimuli. Fagan (1970, 1973) reported general interference effects, and has studied some of the stimulus characteristics and temporal relations responsible for such effects. The data shown in Figures 3 and 4 also show forgetting (see also Olson and Strauss, 1974). But as we noted earlier in reviewing visual memory with older subjects, the striking findings are the high levels of delayed recognition as shown in Figure 6.

A MODEL OF INFANT VISUAL MEMORY

An overview of the infant's visual information processing system is shown in Figure 7. The data summarized in Table 1 make an attribute or multicomponent model of memory representations a natural beginning place (Bower, 1967). Such models assume that the perceptual and memory encodings of events consist of a vector of features that characterize the distinctive attributes of the event. Clearly, even for simple two-dimensional figures of the kind most often used in infant visual recognition research, this conceptualization is simple minded. More

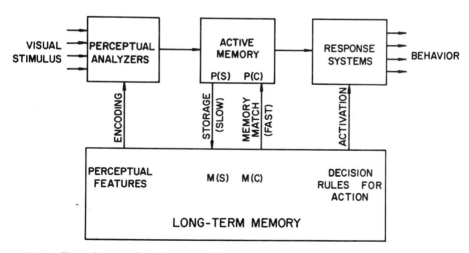

FIG. 7 Flow diagram for infant visual information processing. P( ) and M( ) refer, respectively, to perceptual and memory vectors; S refers to the target stimulus and C to the context.

sophisticated representational schemes of the kinds discussed in artificial intelligence work on picture processing are more appropriate (Hunt, 1975; Minsky, 1975; Winston, 1973). But for present purposes the simplification to a vector of features will suffice. These features are one of the major determinants of developmental change. Following Gibson (1969), it is assumed that the available set of encodings will change as the system learns to differentiate aspects of the stimuli it encounters.

Once the stimulus is encoded, a vector of perceptual features is held in active memory, where two processes occur simultaneously. A memory matching process searches long-term memory for a memory vector that is similar to the perceptual vector. Though the details of memory search for visual stimuli are unclear, it is reasonable to assume that this process is quite fast. The net result of the match process is a single valued match score that will ultimately be used in decision routines that control behavior, in this case eye movements. The second process is memory storage, and consists of the transfer of information to long-term memory, that is, in the transformation of a perceptual vector into a memory vector. For the moment the issue of whether storage involves the establishment of multiple copies or the adjustment of the relative strengths of features of an established copy will be ignored, since so far nothing in the infant data even begins to suggest an answer to this. Two characteristics of the storage process are important. First, we assume that what is stored is an associative representation of the perceptual vector for the specific stimulus with a representation of the context in which it was experienced. This seems uncontroversial, but the exact nature of such associations and their involvement in the decision routines that direct behavior will have to be worked out in light of new evidence. The second property of importance is that the storage process is relatively slow. As noted in the first section of this chapter, quantitative research on learning and memory in adults suggests a marked asymmetry between retrieval time for searchless retrieval and storage time for new information. This asymmetry is assumed here as well, and helps to explain certain details of infant performance in visual recognition memory tasks.

Decision rules stored in long-term memory are responsible for producing the behavioral consequences of memory events. Figure 8 is an example of what such decision processes might be like. No attempt has been made to capture all known memory effects, nor have the other determinants of performance in paired–comparison paradigms been treated (Figure 2). The first phase is a global check for match between the current representation of the stimulus in active memory and any pertinent representations in long-term memory. If an insufficient match is found, a more sequential, detailed feature-by-feature examination of the current stimulus follows until a short-term criterion of habituation is reached. Thus, this system has affinities with current multistage matching models for adult recognition memory or semantic memory tasks (Atkinson, Herrmann & Wescourt, 1974; Smith, Shoben & Rips, 1974), and with Cohen's multistage model of habituation (1973; Cohen & Gelber, 1975).

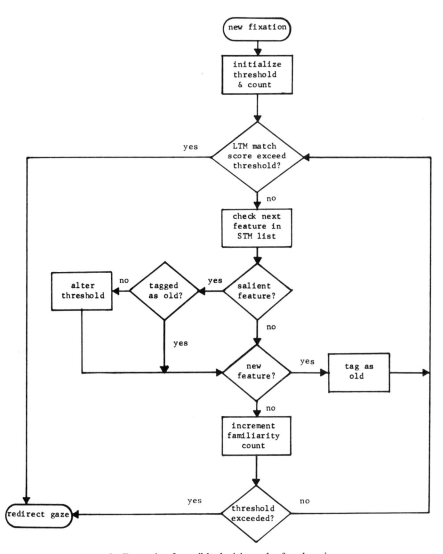

FIG. 8   Example of possible decision rules for changing gaze.

Let us look at a few of the predictions of this model. The fast memory match from a long-term memory and the slower short-term examination of the stimulus are needed to account for several features of infant habituation. Once an infant has habituated, it will rapidly look *away* from the familiar stimulus once it has fixated it. Thus, habituation should be marked by briefer fixations but not necessarily fewer fixations. The data used in constructing Table 4 support this, as do Cohen's findings. But infants also look away from the stimulus prior to reaching a criterion of habituation. Thus, the long-term process, whose critical component is the fast memory match, accounts for the rapid looking away found after habituation, while the short-term process accounts for the slower looking away found prior to habituation. The threshold mechanism is used to account for: (a) the flat precriterion phase of backward habituation curves noted by Cohen; (b) the differential interest (and differential rates of habituation) infants show for different kinds of stimuli. The temporal asymmetry between the matching and storage processes accounts for the suddenness of habituation revealed by Cohen's backward curves. However, unlike Cohen's model (1973; Cohen & Gelber, 1975), the current scheme states that memory information is being stored throughout the prehabituation phase. What is needed are habituation data where tests—preferably paired—comparison ones—are interspersed throughout the prehabituation phase. The clear prediction is that there ought to be a steady growth of the strength of the long-term memory representation prior to attainment of habituation.

The model in Figure 7 contains two loci of developmental change. The first is the set of perceptual features available for encoding the stimuli, and the second is the set of decision rules available for directing fixation behavior. We have already considered the first of these, and noted that it is consistent with a variety of data. The second source of change also has support. It has been noted by several investigators (Wetherford & Cohen, 1973; Fisher, Sperber & Zeaman, 1973; Zeaman, Chapter 9, this volume) that the strength and even the direction of the preference for novelty undergoes developmental change. This change could be incorporated within the decision rules component of the model schematized in Figure 7. Further, it has also been noted that global characteristics of an infant's scan of visual figures undergoes developmental change (Harris, 1973; Salapatek, 1975). In part such changes would be determined by the set of perceptual features, but it is also plausible to assume they would be due to changes in the behavioral consequences of memory-based decision rules. In contrast, it is assumed that the rate and organization of information processing would not change with development. As noted, Wickens (1974) could not marshall evidence from older children to suggest much change in these factors. So up to the limits of the currently available evidence, the scheme proposed in Figures 7 and 8 seems to capture the essential features of infant visual memory performance.

CONCLUSIONS

The study of visual memory in infants has implications for a wide range of important psychological issues, the most obvious being those pertaining to the development of memory and the nature of mature memory abilities. Though the assumption that visual memory abilities represent a primitive, essentially un-changing foundational component of the memory system is exceedingly tentative at this point, it does seem to be a useful working hypothesis for further research. The data on early infant memory may also be useful in studies of general memory dynamics across a broad range of developmental levels and stimuli. For instance, the lack of developmental change in forgetting rate observed in Figure 6 has been noted by other investigators studying both picture and word memory in children and adults over a wide span of ages (Fajnsztejn-Pollack, 1973; Wickelgren, 1975). Though much difficult empirical and theoretical work remains to be done, findings like these suggest that the contrast between invariance and change in memory development may have some interesting theoretical outcomes.

The information processing point of view maintains that memory is a critical component of virtually all forms of cognition. Thus, a theory of memory development will be intimately related to a general theory of cognitive development. Studies of early cognitive development are increasingly examining the role of memory in various cognitive skills (Bower, 1974; Gratch, 1975; Olson, 1973; Piaget & Inhelder, 1972). An especially interesting illustration of this is the development of wariness toward novel persons and objects during infancy (e.g., Bronson, 1972). To become wary of a novel object or person requires that the infant be able to discriminate familiar and unfamiliar events. There is substantial evidence that between three and six months the infant learns to discriminate familiar and unfamiliar faces (Caron *et al.*, 1973; Fagan, 1972; Fitzgerald, 1968). Thus, the onset of wariness toward unfamiliar persons during the second half-year follows nicely from the memory data. Despite considerable interest in the subject, the exploration of general cognitive development from the perspective of memory development has scarcely begun. Hopefully, the kinds of structures and processes sketched in this chapter can be refined and elaborated to allow useful insights into cognitive development during the preverbal and eventually the verbal periods of early childhood.

Until recently habituation was often dismissed as a rudimentary form of behavioral adaptation of little interest to the psychological theorist. The chapters in this volume provide ample evidence of the more favorable contemporary attitude. In addition to attracting much interest as a phenomenon in and of itself, habituation is coming to play an important methodological role in the study of other psychological processes. As this and other chapters on infancy in this volume have demonstrated, habituation paradigms and their derivatives provide useful tools for the study of more complex forms of information processing in human infants. This makes possible the developmental study of information processing across a very wide range of ages, and an approach to resolving classic empiricist—nativist controversies about the mind.

ACKNOWLEDGMENTS

The author's research is supported by a grant from the Grant Foundation of New York. Hi Fitzgerald, Joan Olson, and Gordy Wood provided useful critiques of an earlier draft of this chapter.

REFERENCES

Adams, W. V. *Infant memory: Effect of familiarization time.* Paper presented at the meetings of the American Psychological Association, Montreal, August 1973.

Anderson, J. R., & Bower, G. H. Recognition and retrieval processes in free recall *Psychological Review,* 1972, 79, 97 123.

Anderson, J. R., & Bower, G. H. *Human associative memory.* Washington, D.C.: Winston, 1973.

Anderson, J. R., & Bower, G. H. A propositional theory of recognition memory. *Memory and Cognition,* 1974, 2, 406–412.

Atkinson, R. C., & Crothers, E. J. A comparison of paired-associate learning models having different acquisition and retention axioms. *Journal of Mathematical Psychology,* 1964, 1, 285–315.

Atkinson, R. C., Herrmann, D. J., & Wescourt, K. T. Search processes in recognition memory. In R. L. Solso (Ed.), *Theories in cognitive psychology: The Loyola symposium.* Hillsdale, N. J.: Lawrence Erlbaum Assoc., 1974.

Atkinson, R. C., & Shiffrin, R. M. Human memory: A proposed system and its control processes. In K. W. Spence & J. T. Spence (Eds.), *The psychology of learning and motivation* (Vol. 2). New York: Academic Press, 1968.

Baddeley, A. D., & Hitch, G. Working memory. In G. H. Bower (Ed.), *The psychology of learning and motivation* (Vol. 8). New York: Academic Press, 1974.

Baylor, G. W. *A treatise on the mind's eye.* Institute de Psychologie, Universite de Montreal, July 1971.

Blakemore, C., & Cooper, G. F. Development of the brain depends on the visual environment. *Nature (London),* 1970, 228, 477–478.

Bower, G. H. A multicomponent theory of the memory trace. In K. W. Spence & J. T. Spence (Eds.), *The psychology of learning and motivation* (Vol. 1). New York: Academic Press, 1967.

Bower, G. H. Mental imagery and associative learning. In L. Gregg (Ed.), *Cognition in learning and memory.* New York: Wiley, 1972.

Bower, G. H., & Karlin, M. B. Depth of processing pictures of faces and recognition memory. *Journal of Experimental Psychology,* 1974, 103, 751–757.

Bower, T. G. R. *Development in infancy.* San Francisco: Freeman, 1974.

Broadbent, D. E. *Perception and communication.* New York: Pergamon Press, 1958.

Broadbent, D. E. *Decision and stress.* New York: Academic Press, 1971.

Bronson, G. W. Infants' reactions to unfamiliar persons and novel objects. *Monographs of the Society for Research in Child Development,* 1972, 37(Whole No. 148).

Bronson, G. The postnatal growth of visual capacity. *Child Development,* 1974, 45, 873–890.

Brown, A. L. Judgments of recency for long sequences of pictures: The absence of a developmental trend. *Journal of Experimental Child Psychology,* 1973, 15, 473–480.

Brown, A. L., & Scott, M. S. Recognition memory for pictures in preschool children. *Journal of Experimental Child Psychology,* 1971, 11, 401–412.

Bruner, J. S. The course of cognitive growth. *American Psychologist,* 1964, 19, 1–15.

Carew, T. J., & Kandel, E. R. Synaptic analysis of the interrelationships between behavioral modifications in *aplysia.* In M. V. Bennett (Ed.), *Synaptic transmission and neuronal interaction.* New York: Raven Press, 1974.

Caron, A. J., Caron, R. F., Caldwell, R. C., & Weiss, S. J. Infant perception of the structural properties of the face. *Developmental Psychology,* 1973, 9, 385–399.

Carpenter, P. A., & Just, M. A. Sentence comprehension: A psycholinguistic processing model of verification. *Psychological Review,* 1975, 82, 45–73.

Cohen, L. B. Attention-getting and attention-holding processes of infant visual preferences. *Child Development,* 1972, *43,* 869–879.

Cohen, L. B. A two process model of infant visual attention. *Merrill–Palmer Quarterly,* 1973, *19,* 157–180.

Cohen, L. B., & Gelber, E. R. Infant visual memory. In L. Cohen & P. Salapatek (Eds.), *Infant perception: From sensation to cognition* (Vol. 1). New York: Academic Press, 1975.

Cohen, L. B., Gelber, E. R., & Lazar, M. A. Infant habituation and generalization to differing degrees of stimulus novelty. *Journal of Experimental Child Psychology,* 1971, *11,* 379–389.

Cornell, E. H. *The effects of activity during familiarization on infants' subsequent preferences for novel stimuli.* Paper presented at the meetings of the Eastern Psychological Association, Boston, April 1972.

Cornell, E. H. Infants' discrimination of photographs of faces following redundant presentations. *Journal of Experimental Child Psychology,* 1974, *18,* 98–106.

Cornell, E. H. Infants' visual attention to pattern arrangement and orientation. *Child Development,* 1975, *46,* 229–232.

Corsini, D. A. Developmental changes in the effect of non-verbal cues on retention. *Developmental Psychology,* 1969, *1,* 425–435.

Craik, F. I. M., & Lockhart, R. S. Levels of processing: A framework for memory research. *Journal of Verbal Learning and Verbal Behavior,* 1972, *11,* 671–684.

Fagan, J. F., III. Memory in the infant. *Journal of Experimental Child Psychology,* 1970, *9,* 217–226.

Fagan, J. F., III. Infants' recognition memory for a series of visual stimuli. *Journal of Experimental Child Psychology,* 1971, *11,* 244–250.

Fagan, J. F., III. Infants' recognition memory for faces. *Journal of Experimental Child Psychology,* 1972, *14,* 453–476.

Fagan, J. F., III. Infants' delayed recognition memory and forgetting. *Journal of Experimental Child Psychology,* 1973, *16,* 424–450.

Fagan, J. F., III. Infant recognition memory: The effects of length of familiarization and type of discrimination task. *Child Development,* 1974, *45,* 351–356.

Fajnsztejn-Pollack, G. A developmental study of decay rate in long-term memory. *Journal of Experimental Child Psychology,* 1973, *16,* 225–235.

Fantz, R. L. Visual experience in infants: Decreased attention to familiar patterns relative to novel ones. *Science,* 1964, *146,* 668–670.

Farnham-Diggory, S. (Ed.). *Information processing in children.* New York: Academic Press, 1972.

Fisher, M. A., Sperber, R., & Zeaman, D. Theory and data on developmental changes in novelty preference. *Journal of Experimental Child Psychology,* 1973, *15,* 509–520.

Fitzgerald, H. D. Autonomic pupilary reflex activity during early infancy and its relation to social and nonsocial visual stimuli. *Journal of Experimental Child Psychology,* 1968, *6,* 470–482.

Flavell, J. H. Developmental studies of mediated memory. In H. W. Reese & L. P. Lipsitt (Eds.), *Advances in child development and behavior* (Vol. 5). New York: Academic Press, 1970.

Flavell, J. H., Friedrichs, A. G., & Hoyt, J. D. Developmental changes in memorization processes. *Cognitive Psychology,* 1970, *1,* 324–340.

Freedman, J., & Haber, R. N. One reason why we rarely forget a face. *Bulletin of the Psychonomic Society,* 1974, *3,* 107–109.

Freeman, R. D., Mitchell, D. E., & Millodot, M. A neural effect of partial visual deprivation in humans. *Science,* 1972, *175,* 1384–1386.

Gibson, E. J. *Principles of perceptual learning and development.* New York: Appleton-Century-Crofts, 1969.

Goldstein, A. G., & Chance, J. E. Visual recognition memory for complex configurations. *Perception and Psychophysics,* 1971, *9,* 237–241.

Gratch, G. Recent studiès based on Piaget's view of object concept development. In L. Cohen & P. Salapatek (Eds.), *Infant perception: From sensation to cognition* (Vol. 2). New York: Academic Press, 1975.

Hagen, J. W., Jongeward, R. H., Jr., & Kail, R. V., Jr. Cognitive perspectives on the development of memory. In H. Reese (Ed.), *Advances in child development and behavior* (Vol. 10). New York: Academic Press, 1975.

Harris, P. L. Eye movements between adjacent stimuli: An age change in infancy. *British Journal of Psychology,* 1973, *64,* 215–218.

Haynes, H., White, B., & Held, R. Visual accommodation in infants. *Science,* 1965, *148,* 528–530.

Herriot, P. *Attributes of memory.* London: Methuen, 1974.

Hintzman, D. L., & Rogers, M. K. Spacing effects in picture memory. *Memory and Cognition,* 1973, *1,* 430–434.

Hirsch, H. V. B., & Spinelli, D. N. Visual experience modifies distribution of horizontally and vertically oriented receptive fields in cats. *Science,* 1970, *168,* 869–871.

Hoffman, C. D. *Recognition memory for pictures: A developmental study.* Paper presented at the meetings of the Eastern Psychological Association, New York, April 1971.

Hunt, E. B. *Artificial intelligence.* New York: Academic Press, 1975.

Hunter, I. M. L. Mental calculation. In P. C. Wason & P. N. Johnson-Laird (Eds.), *Thinking and reasoning.* Baltimore: Penguin, 1968.

Hyde, T. S., & Jenkins, J. J. Differential effects of incidental tasks on the organization of recall of a list of highly associated words. *Journal of Experimental Psychology,* 1969, *82,* 472–491.

Hyde, T. S., & Jenkins, J. J. Recall for words as a function of semantic, graphic, and syntactic orienting tasks. *Journal of Verbal Learning and Verbal Behavior,* 1973, *12,* 471–480.

Jeffrey, W. E., & Cohen, L. B. Habituation in the human infant. In W. H. Reese (Ed.), *Advances in child development and behavior* (Vol. 6). New York: Academic Press, 1971.

Kessen, W., Haith, M. M., & Salapatek, P. H. Human infancy: A bibliography and guide. In P. H. Mussen (Ed.), *Carmichael's manual of child psychology* (3rd ed., Vol. 1). New York: Wiley, 1970.

Kintsch, W. Recognition learning as a function of the length of retention interval and changes in the retention interval. *Journal of Mathematical Psychology,* 1966, *3,* 412–433.

Kintsch, W. Memory and decision aspects of recognition learning. *Psychological Review,* 1967, *74,* 496–504.

Kreutzer, M. A., Leonard, C., & Flavell, J. H. An interview study of children's knowledge about memory. *Monographs of the Society for Research in Child Development,* 1975, *40*(Whole No. 159).

Lindsay, P. H., & Norman, D. A. *Human information processing.* New York: Academic Press, 1972.

Loftus, G. R. Eye fixations and recognition memory for pictures. *Cognitive Psychology,* 1972, *3,* 525–551.

Loftus, G. R. Acquisition of information from rapidly presented verbal and nonverbal stimuli. *Memory and Cognition,* 1974, *2,* 545–548.

Loftus, G. R., & Bell, S. M. Two types of information in picture memory. *Journal of Experimental Psychology: Human Learning and Memory*, 1975, *104*, 103–113.

Luria, A. R. *The mind of a mnemonist.* New York: Avon, 1968.

Maccoby, E. E., & Jacklin, C. N. *The psychology of sex differences.* Stanford, Calif.: Stanford University Press, 1974.

McGurk, H. The role of object orientation in infant perception. *Journal of Experimental Child Psychology*, 1970, *9*, 363–373.

Miller, G. A. The magical number seven, plus or minus two: Some limits on our capacity for processing information. *Psychological Review*, 1956, *63*, 81–97.

Minsky, M. A framework for representing knowledge. In P. Winston (Ed.), *The psychology of computer vision.* New York: McGraw-Hill, 1975.

Miranda, S. B., & Fantz, R. L. Recognition memory in Down's syndrome and normal infants. *Child Development*, 1974, *45*, 651–660.

Murdock, B. B., Jr. Recent developments in short-term memory. *British Journal of Psychology*, 1967, *58*, 421–433.

Murdock, B. B., Jr. *Human memory: Theory and data.* Hillsdale, N.J.: Lawrence Erlbaum Associates, 1974.

Murray, D. J., & Newman, F. M. Visual and verbal coding in short-term memory. *Journal of Experimental Psychology*, 1973, *100*, 58–62.

Neisser, U. *Cognitive psychology.* New York: Appleton-Century-Crofts, 1967.

Nelson, K. E. Memory development in children: Evidence from nonverbal tasks. *Psychonomic Science*, 1971, *25*, 346–348.

Newell, A. A theoretical exploration of mechanisms for coding the stimulus. In A. W. Melton & E. Martin (Eds.), *Coding processes in human memory.* Washington, D.C.: Winston, 1972.

Newell, A. Production systems: Models of control structures. In W. G. Chase (Ed.), *Visual information processing.* New York: Academic Press, 1973.

Newell, A., & Simon, H. A. *Human problem solving.* Englewood Cliffs, N.J.: Prentice-Hall, 1972.

Nickerson, R. S. A note on long-term recognition memory for pictorial material. *Psychonomic Science*, 1968, *11*, 58.

Norman, D. A., & Rumelhart, D. E. A system for perception and memory. In D. A. Norman (Ed.), *Models of human memory.* New York: Academic Press, 1970.

Olson, G. M. Learning and retention in a continuous recognition task. *Journal of Experimental Psychology*, 1969, *81*, 381–384.

Olson, G. M. *Sentence comprehension: The emerging psycholinguistic model and an alternative.* Paper presented at the Third Annual Meeting on Structural Learning, Graduate School of Education, University of Pennsylvania, April 1972.

Olson, G. M. Developmental changes in memory and the acquisition of language. In T. E. Moore (Ed.), *Cognitive development and the acquisition of language.* New York: Academic Press, 1973.

Olson, G. M., & Strauss, M. S. *Short-term visual memory in infants.* Paper presented at the meetings of the Midwestern Psychological Association, Chicago, May 1974.

Paivio, A. Mental imagery in associative learning and memory. *Psychological Review*, 1969, *76*, 241–263.

Paivio, A. *Imagery and verbal processes.* New York: Holt, Rinehart & Winston, 1971.

Pellegrino, J. W., Siegel, A. W., & Dhawan, M. Short-term retention of pictures and words: Evidence for dual coding systems. *Journal of Experimental Psychology: Human Learning and Memory*, 1975, *104*, 95–102.

Peterson, L. R., & Peterson, M. J. Short-term retention of individual verbal items. *Journal of Experimental Psychology*, 1959, *58*, 193–198.

Piaget, J. *The origins of intelligence in children.* New York: International Universities Press, 1952.

Piaget, J., & Inhelder, B. *Memory and intelligence.* New York: Basic Books, 1972.

Posner, M. I. *Cognition: An introduction.* Glenview, Ill.: Scott, Foresman, 1973.

Potter, M. C. Meaning in visual search. *Science,* 1975, *187,* 965–966.

Potter, M. C., & Levy, E. I. Recognition memory for a rapid sequence of pictures. *Journal of Experimental Psychology,* 1969, *81,* 10–15.

Pylyshyn, Z. W. What the mind's eye tells the mind's brain: A critique of mental imagery. *Psychological Bulletin,* 1973, *80,* 1–24.

Saayman, G., Ames, E. W., & Moffett, A. Response to novelty as an indicator of visual discrimination in the human infant. *Journal of Experimental Child Psychology,* 1964, *1,* 189–198.

Salapatek, P. Pattern perception in early infancy. In L. B. Cohen & P. Salapatek (Eds.), *Infant perception: From sensation to cognition* (Vol. 1). New York: Academic Press, 1975.

Schaffer, H. R., & Parry, M. H. The effects of short-term familiarization on infants' perceptual-motor coordination in a simultaneous discrimination situation. *British Journal of Psychology,* 1970, *61,* 559–569.

Shaffer, W. O., & Shiffrin, R. M. Rehearsal and storage of visual information. *Journal of Experimental Psychology,* 1972, *92,* 292–296.

Shepard, R. N. Recognition memory for words, sentences, and pictures. *Journal of Verbal Learning and Verbal Behavior,* 1967, *6,* 156–163.

Shepard, R. N. Form, formation, and transformation of internal representations. In R. Solso (Ed.), *Information processing and cognition: The Loyola symposium.* Hillsdale, N.J.: Lawrence Erlbaum Associates, 1975.

Simon, H. A. How big is a chunk? *Science,* 1974, *183,* 482–488.

Simon, H. A., & Gilmartin, K. A simulation of memory for chess positions. *Cognitive Psychology,* 1973, *5,* 29–46.

Smith, E. E., Shoben, E. J., & Rips, L. J. Structure and process in semantic memory: A featural model for semantic decisions. *Psychological Review,* 1974, *81,* 214–241.

Sokolov, E. N. *Perception and the conditioned reflex.* New York: Macmillan, 1963.

Standing, L. G., Conezio, G., & Haber, R. N. Perception and memory for pictures: Single trial learning of 2,500 visual stimuli. *Psychonomic Science,* 1970, *19,* 73–74.

Thompson, R. F., & Spencer, W. A. Habituation: A model phenomenon for the study of neuronal substrates of behavior. *Psychological Review,* 1966, *73,* 16–43.

Tulving, E., & Thomson, D. M. Encoding specificity and retrieval processes in episodic memory. *Psychological Review,* 1973, *80,* 352–373.

Wallace, W. H., Turner, S. H., & Perkins, C. C. *Preliminary studies of human information storage.* Signal Corps Project 132C, Institute for Cooperative Research, University of Pennsylvania, Philadelphia, 1957.

Watkins, M. J., & Tulving, E. Episodic memory: When recognition fails. *Journal of Experimental Psychology: General,* 1975, *104,* 5–29.

Waugh, N., & Norman, D. Primary memory. *Psychological Review,* 1965, *72,* 89–104.

Weizmann, F., Cohen, L. B., & Pratt, J. Novelty, familiarity, and the development of infant attention. *Developmental Psychology,* 1971, *4,* 149–154.

Welch, M. J. Infants' visual attention to varying degrees of novelty. *Child Development,* 1974, *45,* 344–350.

Wetherford, M. J., & Cohen, L. B. Developmental changes in infant visual preferences for novelty and familiarity. *Child Development,* 1973, *44,* 416–424.

Wickelgren, W. A. The long and short of memory. *Psychological Bulletin,* 1973, *80,* 425–438.

Wickelgren, W. A. Age and storage dynamics in continuous recognition memory. *Developmental Psychology*, 1975, *11*, 165–169.

Wickens, C. D. Temporal limits of human information processing: A developmental study. *Psychological Bulletin*, 1974, *81*, 739–755.

Winston, P. Learning to identify toy block structures. In R. L. Solso (Ed.), *Contemporary issues in cognitive psychology: The Loyola symposium.* Washington, D.C.: Winston, 1973.

Winston, P. (Ed.), *The psychology of computer vision.* New York: McGraw-Hill, 1975.

8

Habituation as a Mechanism for Perceptual Development

W. E. Jeffrey

University of California, Los Angeles

As I pondered the focus of this book, I realized that I have been less interested in what I could do for habituation than in what habituation could do for me. My abiding concern over the years has been in perceptual development. That may not appear obvious from my research but that is because I, and many of my peers, are living examples of the rather hoary story of the drunk who, because of the better visibility, looked for his watch in the gutter under the street light rather than in the dark alley where he had dropped it.

For the empiricist it was a matter of faith that perception was very primitive at birth. To the learning theorist, who was also an empiricist, it was obvious that perceptual development was the result of conditioning. Therefore, early attempts to evaluate perceptual development in the human infant primarily used the classical conditioning paradigm. Failure to obtain stable simple conditioning, however, discouraged anyone from attempting more complicated stimulus differentiation procedures. There were a few visual tracking studies, and a study or two that used activity level as a dependent variable with either hue or illumination level being manipulated, but for the most part the investigation of perceptual development was dropped in the late 1930s.

After a hiatus of some ten years, and as the result of the increased sophistication of the discrimination learning procedures developed with rats and chimpanzees, child psychologists found it simplest in the 1950s to focus on discrimination learning with children of four to five years of age, and older. We knew how to manage children of this age, and with collossal naivete, assumed that a child's failure to respond differentially indicated inability to perceive critical differences. Correspondingly, differential responses were taken to indicate that the child was now able to perceive differences between the two stimuli. Of course, one could not quarrel with the latter assertion. When one attempted to use discrimination learning techniques with children of increasingly younger ages, however, he was confronted with an absurdity. Two- and three-year-old children did not respond differentially to stimuli that better sense, and some data on infants, told us could be differentiated.

It took a pediatrician (Bridger, 1961) to retrieve from the past the long neglected habituation–recovery paradigm, and to show us that it could be used to evaluate the perceptual capacity of infants. We did not take to it quickly, however. Learning theorists were never very comfortable with habituation. In spite of its ubiquitousness, habituation was generally considered a rather low level, insignificant activity of the nervous system. Moreover, it was not assumed to be an important mode of behavior acquisition and no one was interested in it as a test of sensory capacity. Psychologists of the early 1960s remained burdened with the legacy of the 1930s and 1940s that perception was not something to be evaluated but to be learned. Thus, one did not test infant perception, but rather one established what the infant could learn to discriminate, or under what conditions he might learn to discriminate.

Changing attitudes, attributable for the most part to the rise of ethology, the work of Hebb (1949), Harlow (1961), and finally Fantz's (1965) pioneering visual fixation studies, forced a number of us to reconsider some of our philosophical and methodological biases. It was clearly time to look at infant perception again. Given Fantz's success with visual fixation one might reasonably question why the habituation paradigm became the method of choice for so many. I suspect that even if many have reservations about habituation as a true example of learning, there is some appeal that accrues from basic similarity between the habituation and learning paradigms. For example, the habituation paradigm permits the evaluation of behavior change over trials, and moreover, the change in response appears to be relatively permanent. Inasmuch as our focus was now on perception, however, few developmental psychologists attempted very seriously to establish the characteristics of habituation beyond assuring ourselves it was a useful indicator response. That position has changed somewhat in the last few years but only in a limited way (Jeffrey & Cohen, 1971).

HABITUATION: SOME PROBLEMS OF TERMINOLOGY

For the most part, those of us who have been looking specifically at the habituation of behavioral responses to relatively complex stimuli have been content to use Sokolov's (1963) model for habituation of the orienting reflex. We have done so rather uncritically and sometimes inappropriately. But this usage was gratuitous anyway. We depended on few of the subtleties or intricacies of Sokolov's model, and the language of that model, as well as the language of habituation in general, has been used rather poorly.

We frequently use the term dishabituation to refer to the elicitation of an habituated response by a generalized or different stimulus whereas it classically refers to the recovery of an habituated response, that is, the response reoccurs to the original adequate stimulus following an extraneous, and usually strong stimulus. I know of only one study that has looked for or seen such behavior with infants (Ruff, 1975). More recently it has become popular to use the term recovery in place of dishabituation, but recovery like dishabituation implies the occurrence of the habituated response to the originally adequate stimulus. What we are interested in most typically is the condition where a novel or generalized stimulus elicits a response that is no longer elicited by a previously repeated stimulus. Whatever neural modification accounts for the failure of the response to be elicited by the habituated stimulus still exists. Indeed, to assure ourselves that we are dealing with habituation rather than effector fatigue, we typically make certain the response in question can be elicited by an alternate stimulus of equal or lesser intensity. What is being demonstrated then is that the neural modification that occurs with repeated exposure does not generalize to, or involve the same pathways as, the novel stimulus. Which is, of course, precisely what we wanted to show. Therefore, our terminology should emphasize not the recovery of a response, but the discriminative nature of the process.

From my reading of the physiological literature, similar terminological problems exist there. For one thing, researchers in that area typically are quite unconcerned as to whether the phenomena they are studying meet the Thompson and Spencer (1966) criteria. Buchwald and Humphrey (1973) even suggest such concerns are irrelevant. Also a distinction is made between sensory and response habituation that appears to rest primarily on whether the responses being measured are electrical (evoked potentials or unit activity) or behavioral. This distinction may be useful in some way to the neurophysiologist but I believe that to speak of response habituation is very misleading. The change that occurs with habituation is a change in the capacity of a stimulus to elicit a response, not in the capacity of the response to occur. As already indicated, our control groups are typically directed toward showing that the response is still elicitable by other stimuli.

I propose that it would be very useful for us to develop a more precise language. As long as we speak so loosely not only do we communicate poorly among ourselves, but also it is quite likely that our conceptualizations are equally poor, and thus, we may overlook subtleties in our results that implicate or suggest other mechanisms.

HABITUATION AND PERCEPTUAL DEVELOPMENT

As I indicated above, the classical and operant conditioning models had proved inadequate for assessing perceptual development except among those who were content to accept that if behavior had changed, learning had undobtedly taken place. For some of us, the accumulating evidence indicated that the neonate was considerably more proficient perceptually than we had previously surmised. Furthermore, it became clear that additional perceptual development occured very rapidly over the first few months. Although habituation had been used by developmental psychologists primarily as an indicator response, from my observations of infants I proposed that habituation of the orienting reaction might provide a mechanism with which to explain perceptual development (Jeffrey, 1968, 1969).

At the time I wrote the aforementioned articles Eleanor Gibson's book (1969) was not yet available, but James Gibson's (1966) was, and I was much impressed with his dynamic exorcism of some hoary models of perception. I was not ready to go quite as far as he goes in placing perception outside the organism, but I did subscribe to the notion that the detection and abstraction of features of the environment was a very critical operation in perceptual development. The crucial question, however, was how to account for this process, and how to study it, particularly without reducing the infant to 80% of normal body weight and providing him a squirt of milk only when appropriate discriminative operants occurred. I did try the latter, actually, giving the squirt of milk for discriminative operants, but I did not reduce the child to 80% of normal body weight, and this is probably why I failed to obtain a stable response.

As with any early model, because there were so few specific empirical data for it to handle, my serial habituation model could be quite elegant in its simplicity. The propositions were broad and minimal. First, it was asserted that stimuli in the environment differ in their salience, where salience is defined in terms of either the likelihood of a stimulus eliciting an observing response, or of the magnitude of the orienting reflex. Second, with attention to the most salient cue, its salience will wane and attention will shift to an initially less salient cue. With attention to the second cue, however, the salience of the first cue will show partial recovery and the infant's attention will return to the first cue. Third, with repeated habituation the salience of all cues observed will be reduced and the rate at which a number of cues might be scanned, as well as the number of cues scanned, will increase. Obviously, cue salience differences are attributable to both natural stimulus differences as well as to experience with a stimulus. Also it should be noted that the likelihood of a stimulus eliciting an observing response differs in some absolute sense as well as with competition from other stimuli.

The process described in the above three propositions could certainly account for the systematic scanning of cues in the environment. However, whether a veridical percept developed as the result of such scanning would depend upon whether the cues that are scanned were systematically organized in a single stimulus complex. For example, given a stimulus such as a mother's face, an infant might first look at the eyes, then upon habituating to the eyes, would look at the mouth. While attending to the mouth, however, the salience of the eyes should recover so that the infant would look back at the eyes, only to return again to the mouth as the salience of the eyes habituated and that of the mouth recovered. One can see that these two stimuli could become finally a unitary percept to which additional facial attributes, such as nose, ears, and hair could be attached. In the end, this response to the configuration of cues in the face would be isolated from the background because there would be no constant relationship between background and facial cues. Indeed, insofar as mother's hair contour, or hair color changed markedly, those cues would not become a critical perceptual feature of mother's face.

For the sake of example I have probably presented one aspect of the infant's perceptual development out of order. It is quite likely that before the facial features became an organized percept the infant would already have been attracted by the differential movement of brightness contours in his environment and would have developed some perception of depth through the observation of motion parallax. Therefore, the isolation of mother's head from the background probably occurs first and the delineation of facial detail would occur subsequently.

In my description of this model I have already altered the language to be consonant with the viewpoint I expressed earlier in this chapter. In place of responses habituating, I have referred to the habituation of the salience of the stimulus. Having done that, I feel only slightly more virtuous. Although it may be appropriate to say that the salience of the stimulus wanes or habituates, I wish we had a way to make it clearer where the locus of the action is, that it is a change in the processing of the stimulus, rather than in the stimulus itself. The appeal of Sokolov's orienting reflex model was, of course, that it proposed a neurological model of habituation. However, as the orienting reflex is operationally defined, I have a feeling we are missing something. That is, cue processing at this level must go on considerably beyond the disappearance of most signs of the orienting reflex. Possibly Sokolov would agree that his measures are rather gross. Certainly the cessation of heart rate deceleration does not signal the cessation of all stimulus processing.

I must also make note of the grossness of my model, or at least of the example I presented. The description of the process of perceiving mother's face could be equally well applied to the eye alone, given a different focal range. But maybe this fact only indicates that percepts can be and are formed at a variety of levels. This assertion, however, brings us to a consideration of what is formed in the habituation process, or more precisely, what are the changes that mediate the alterations in behavior associated with habituation.

I had generally accepted the notion that the result of serial habituation would be some internal representation. Sokolov used the term "neurological model." I substituted "schema" in one paper (Jeffrey, 1968) and "percept" in a second (Jeffrey, 1969). After reading Eleanor Gibson's book (1969) and more recently Garner's book (1974) I am increasingly convinced that they are right in eschewing notions that internalize perceptions. There is diverse, complex, and structured information available in the environment. One need not necessarily encode this information nor construct a model, but rather, I would suggest that one must develop a processing program. The serial habituation hypothesis suggests a way in which a processing program might develop.

RELEVANT RESEARCH

Before attempting to refine the model it would be useful to see what support it currently has, and what data suggest a need for change. Although several attempts have been made to test the serial habituation hypothesis it has proved rather difficult to select stimuli of appropriate salience levels for the various age groups one might use. A stimulus complex must be salient enough to capture the subject's attention, simple enough that habituation will occur relatively rapidly, but not so simple that the subject will have scanned and habituated to all of the features of the stimulus within a short time. The most successful study was conducted by Miller (1972). She used 36 male infants, 4 months of age. Their visual fixations were viewed on a television monitor and were also video taped. The stimuli she presented are seen in Figure 1.

In addition to these stimuli there were 5 colorful Kodachrome slides. The presentation sequence was as follows: 2 color slides, the 3 parts of the standard stimulus presented separately, 2 color clides, then the standard presented 8 times, each of the 3 parts again, followed by the standard, and finally another color slide. That sequence can be represented symbolically as $N N P P P N N S S S S S S S S P P P S N$, where N refers to a colored slide, P to a presentation of only part of the stimulus, and S to the standard intact stimulus. The 20 slides were presented for 20 sec each without interruption. In order to vary the order in which the parts were presented and tested, 3 different stimulus sequences were used with each of the 2 stimulus sets.

All response information was taken from the video tape by an observer who was informed of the presentation of a slide only by a signal light on the video monitor. Three different fixation measures were taken on three

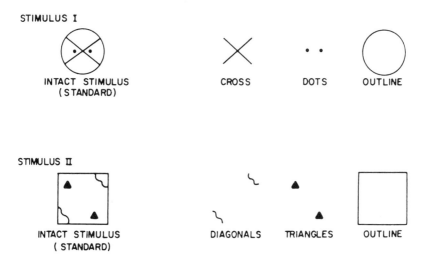

FIG. 1 Intact stimuli (used as standards) and respective parts used in a study by Miller (1972). (From Miller, 1972. Copyright 1972 by the American Psychological Association. Reproduced by permission.)

independent viewings of the tape. For my purposes it is sufficient to consider only the total fixation time for each slide. These data are presented in Figure 2. Note that there were differences in looking time to the part stimuli, thus indicating they differ in salience. The salience order for the parts differed among individuals, however, and therefore P_1, P_2, and P_3 do not refer to specific parts but to the salience order found during the first exposure. The prehabituation measures are presented at the right hand side of the figure for easy comparison with the posthabituation scores. Note also that there is habituation over trials to the standard yet the presentation of a test stimulus and a colored stimulus at the end of the sequence elicited a substantial response, thus indicating the response decrement is attributable to habituation rather than to a fatigue. The most interesting data, however, are the changes in exposure times to each of the parts when magnitude of preexposure responding was used to index the relative salience of parts. It can be seen that the fixation time for the most salient cue is reduced whereas the time to the least salient cue increased. This decline is of interest whether attributable to the repeated exposure of the standard or only to the preexposure of the parts. Unfortunately, although the decline in responding to the most salient part is very significant, the increase in responding to the least salient cue is significant only between the 5 and 10% level. These are not overpowering data but they are encouraging given the difficulties of doing research with infants.

Other evidence of attention to specific cues of a stimulus complex is provided in a study by Caron *et al.* (1973). In an habituation–discrimination

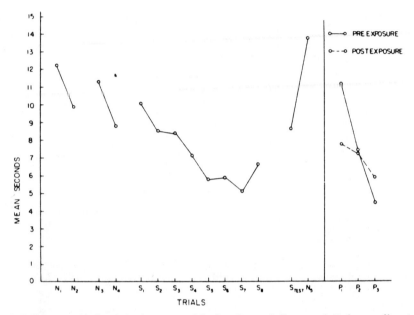

FIG. 2 Mean total fixation time per trial. P_1, P_2, and P_3 are plotted according to each individual's stimulus preference. (From Miller, 1972. Copyright 1972 by The American Psychological Association. Reprinted by permission.)

paradigm with schematic faces as stimuli, their data on a four-month-old group of infants suggest greater attention to eyes, than to nose and mouth. Although Caron *et al.* did not attempt to see how attention could be manipulated, they did test an older group (five months) who proved to be equally as responsive to nose and mouth cues as to eyes. Thus, a cue salience hierarchy that changes with age is indicated, but one cannot infer the mechanism behind the change from this study.

Because a study by Fantz and Miranda (1975) confirmed my assumption that infants would be more responsive to the perimeter of a form than to cues within the perimeter, we were encouraged to devise an experiment to evaluate the change in responsiveness to various parts of a stimulus over repeated exposures. In this experiment we followed Fagan's (1970) procedure, which involves first the presentation of a stimulus, usually in duplicate on the left and right, for a short period of time. These stimuli are removed and then reexposed with one of the two stimuli altered in some way. To counteract position preferences the altered stimulus is inserted for a brief period first on one side and then the other. This procedure has the advantage of not requiring complete habituation in order to find response to novelty. Rather, preference may be shown for a novel cue after relatively brief exposures.

Our stimuli were projected through a window into a sound shielded room, and onto a screen set at such an angle as to be roughly perpendicular to the infant's line of sight and 46 cm in front of him as he rested in an infant seat. A video camera lens inserted in the center of the screen permitted video taping of the infant's visual fixations.

The stimuli and sequence in which they were presented can be seen in Figure 3. The first stimulus pair was presented for 20 sec and the four test pairs for 10 sec each.

Thirty-two 19-week-old infants served as subjects. It was expected that if these infants were actually attending first to the perimeter of the stimulus as would be predicted from the Fantz and Miranda study then they should

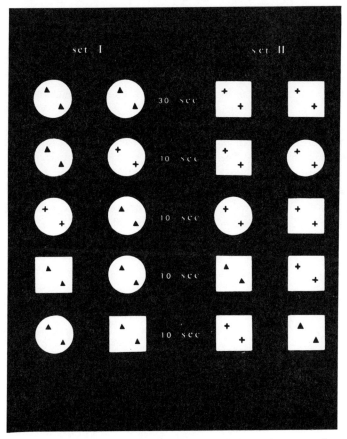

FIG. 3 Stimuli shown to infants. The first stimulus pair in each set are the standard sets. The order of changes in either center detail or perimeter was counterbalanced across sets.

respond in the early tests to changes in the form of the perimeters, but only with repeated exposures should we see a response to substitutions within the stimuli. Table 1 shows the mean percentage of preference for 32 infants, with 16 receiving the round and 16 the square stimuli as the standard set. The left—right position of the novel stimulus and the order of outside versus inside features changes were counterbalanced.

These data, like those of the Miller study, suggest that to obtain the appropriate effect will require a very careful balance between stimulus complexity, exposure time, and age of subject. One can only presume that with additional exposures one might obtain more substantial evidence for attention developing to inside features.

Another implication of the serial habituation hypothesis is that stimuli that are similar in cue salience level yet discriminably different will produce more shifts in visual fixation than will the presentation of two stimuli that are markedly different. A study by Ruff provides evidence for this. Ten stimuli were first ranked in terms of fixation duration for a sample of 18 3-month-old infants (Ruff & Birch, 1974). Subsequently, Stimuli 1, 5, and 9 from that series were presented paired together in all possible combinations, including each paired with itself, to 36 infants equally divided in 9-, 14-, and 19-week age groups (Ruff, 1975). The primary results are presented in Table 2. An analysis of variance confirmed that there was significantly more shifting for similar than for different pairs ($p < .01$). There was also a significant age by degree of similarity interaction ($p < .01$) indicating that the effect was seen primarily for the 14-week-old infants.

Ruff also found that over trials there was first an increase and then a decrease in number of shifts per second as one would predict from the serial habituation hypothesis.

TABLE 1
Percentage of Visual Fixation on the
Novel Stimulus on Test Trials
Following Each of Three Exposures
of the Standard Stimulus

	Novel feature	
Test trial	Inside	Outside
1	59.28	51.81
2	47.91	56.41
3	59.34*	63.75**

*$p<.05$.   **$p<.001$.

TABLE 2
Mean Number Shifts per Second in an Age X Similarity Design

| Age (weeks) | Degree of similarity | | | |
	Different	Medium	Same	Age mean
9	.086	.111	.106	.101
14	.287	.500	.509	.432
19	.555	.580	.564	.566
Mean for each condition:	.309	.397	.393	

DATA REQUIRING SPECIAL CONSIDERATION

Cohen's backward plots of his habituation data (Chapter 6, this volume) show an increase in visual fixation time as the criterion of habituation is approached, and that attainment of criterion is associated with a sudden sharp decline in fixation time. This implies something like "one-trial" habituation. These curves are, of course, quite startling in comparison with what is typically reported. I would like to credit Cohen with genius, but all I can think about is how stupid so many of the rest of us are to keep fooling ourselves with group data plotted in the traditional forward manner. Particularly in the face of Zeaman's data of almost 15 years (Zeaman & House, 1963).

The notion of "one-trial" habituation should not have been all that unsettling to anyone who has observed a large number of infants. It is also important to note that Cohen's data are collected in a novel way. The person who is interested primarily in habituation typically chooses a simple stimulus and presents it repeatedly with fixed intensity, duration, and interstimulus interval. Cohen, however, presents a stimulus more naturally in that the infant is permitted to look as long as he likes, but the stimulus is terminated as soon as he looks away. In looking away, however, the infant's attention is caught by another stimulus specifically chosen for its attention getting rather than attention-holding power (Cohen, 1973). As soon as the infant attends to the latter stimulus, the habituation stimulus is represented and the infant returns to that stimulus unless habituation has occurred.

In my presentation of the serial habituation model I described the situation simpler than it actually is. I am referring particularly to the fact that scanning behavior is more erratic than the model would suggest. Except for the very young infant, no single fixation lasts very long, and even given an interesting stimulus complex, there will be numerous glances away from it. It is these glances away that provide Cohen his trial. With his procedure he finds that these glances away are less likely to occur just before "complete" habituation. Thus, his data suggest something more complex than what we have traditionally presumed to be involved in the simple habituation model.

To explain Cohen's data I would present two alternatives to the memory model he proposoo. If I were to retain the original serial habituation model then I would take recourse to a theoretical curve, presented in an earlier paper (Jeffrey, 1968), to explain the inverted U-shaped curve that is typically found to relate fixation time, or visual preference, to stimulus complexity.

Unfortunately, in the original article that curve lacked an adequate label. I present it to you here in a form that is more understandable.

What this figure says is that although simple cues may be highly salient, little time will be spent with them, that is, habituation will occur quite quickly because of this simplicity. I would think that cues such as corners, edges, hues, etc. could be categorized as simple. Given greater complexity, however, such as more corners combined with more edges, and more complex brightness or hue transitions, the bits and pieces may be of lesser salience, but once one attends to them there is more to assimilate, and thus habituation would occur more slowly. Further, it is not unreasonable to assume that the very young infant and other simple organisms tend not to engage their information processing systems with anything very complex.

Once any particular simple yet salient features of a stimulus complex are attended to, evaluated, processed, and found to contain little information, the organism may well turn away. Given nothing else in his environment more engaging, a situation we contrive in an experiment, he may then return to the stimulus now quite possibly to attend to the more complex but less salient features. As indicated in Figure 4, with these less salient and more complex cues, habituation proceeds more slowly. Thus, Cohen's finding (in this volume) of longer fixation times on later trials with a 24 × 24 checkerboard stimulus than with an 8 × 8, or 2 × 2 checkerboard is consistent with this model (cf. Figure 11, page 229).

I believe I would now opt, however, for a second, less parsimonious approach, that provides a more detailed explanation. Cohen's data with complex stimuli suggests to me that the habituation curve may be separated into two phases. I would propose that two different types of habituation are associated with these two phases.

The first phase of the curve might be presumed to reflect a targeting reflex. This is Konorski's (1967) term and it accentuates the arousal and receptor orienting aspect of what is typically called the orienting reflex. I propose that the targeting reflex is elicited by rather simple but salient stimulus properties such as sharp brightness or hue difference contours and movement. It is reasonable to assume that such a reflex would be related motivationally to basic alimentary and defensive systems.

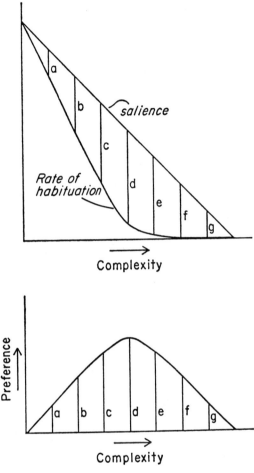

FIG. 4 The differences between the two theoretical curves in the top figure produce the inverted U curve below. (From Jeffrey, 1968. Copyright 1968 by the American Psychological Association. Reproduced by permission.)

The targeting reflex clearly has an arousal component which is, I suspect, what we see habituating rather quickly when using heart rate deceleration as a measure of the orienting reflex. This reflex probably includes a high sensitization component. Thus, whether the targeting reflex occurs or not is to a considerable extent a function of arousal or motivational factors rather than sensory factors. I presume that the targeting reflex system would be involved in what Cohen has called the attention getting aspect of a stimulus. Furthermore, when a simple stimulus is presented there is nothing but the targeting reflex to habituate, and therefore the individual habituation curve would approximate the classic group curve for habituation.

With a complex stimulus, however, I propose that a second system takes over before the targeting reflex habituates. It is this second system that accounts for the second phase of an infant's fixation behavior. I would call this second system an information processing system and now suggest that the serial habituation process operates primarily in this second phase. I also believe that in this second phase the arousal system and the degree of arousal may be different from that involved in the targeting reflex in that the information processing arousal system is not related to alimentary or defensive needs but to the extraction of information from the environment (Hunt, 1963).

Fixation times would be expected to increase during the information-processing phase of the habituation curve because as the serial habituation hypothesis dictates, the subject begins responding to more than one cue. In doing so time is permitted for spontaneous recovery of cue salience, and the more cues observed, the more recovery time there is. Thus, it seems quite likely that there would be an increase in fixation time. Furthermore, given serial attention to multiple cues, wherever habituation is taking place, it must be spread out over a wider range of pathways and points. Although I am not eager to generalize to perceptual development in human infants from the wiping response in the frog, Kimble and Ray (1965) found that when the stimulus site was varied there was an increase in responsiveness over trials prior to habituation.

Given the extent to which we are now willing to recognize the motivational and reinforcing aspects of information processing it also seems reasonable to suggest that as the organism discovers the richness of the stimulus complex some arousal would occur. Our observations certainly suggest that there is some excitement that occurs in active processing but I am not certain that it is the kind of arousal that would show up in the gross measures used for the orienting reflex.

Although the stipulation of two intervening processes in attending behavior does increase the complexity of the model, it also increases its testability. A single-process theory is always isomorphic to empirical relationships whereas, as Underwood (1975, p. 131) indicates, to have a testable theory it is necessary to have at least two intervening processes that interact in some way to relate independent variables to the dependent variable. In this instance, by assuming two different processes involved with two different phases of the habituation curve, it should be possible to manipulate the shape of the curve by varying the salience of the components of the habituating stimulus as well as the salience of the alternate (attention-getting) stimulus. The less salient the attention getting stimulus, and the border or surround of the attention holding stimulus, the more quickly an infant should become engaged with the less salient internal cues, thus producing an earlier peak response component. On the other hand, high salience of those cues controlling targeting, and less salient internal cues would prolong the first phase, possibly even to the exclusion of the second phase. It should be remembered that shifts in attention occur as the result of competition from other cues. Thus, if the discrepancy between the salience of external and internal cues is large, other stimuli in the environment are more likely to engage the organism's attention than the less salient internal features of a stimulus complex. We seldom exhaust all the stimulus information available from an object.

Having accounted for the initial decrement and subsequent increment in visual fixation the next problem is to account for the rapid final decrement. The serial habituation hypothesis would predict that during the process of forming a percept, cues of lesser salience are scanned only after stronger cues have been reduced in salience several times. Thus, the previously most dominant cues would be recovering less and less, if at all, and the last cues to be picked up are, of course, the weakest by definition. Thus, the whole scanning process would essentially collapse into a single extended glance once the least salient cues were finally included.

Given a longer lapse of time, and repeated habituation, it might be expected that only a few of the more salient cues would recover. Thus, upon meeting a familiar stimulus one would expect to see a targeting response of some magnitude, but only a very brief reaction to the most salient features of the stimulus.

It is quite likely that as with most aspects of human performance, uneconomical responses in a sequence are squeezed out. I would expect this to be equally true of perception. Thus, when one becomes very familiar with an object, attending responses to the less salient or less critical features do not occur even when those features are altered. More than one of us have been chagrined to find that the absence of a previously much maligned beard or mustache is not necessarily immediately noted by its severest critic. Thus, novelty does not automatically elicit an orienting reflex.

THE QUESTION OF MEMORY

Finally I would like to consider the question of just what is stored in the process of habituation. In this instance, in dedication to parsimony, and for the sake of argument, I would propose that the critical aspect of what is stored is some neurological change that affects the responsiveness of the organism. Thus, to say that one remembers an object need not mean more than that minimal but orderly processing occurs. That does not say that one has encoded the stimulus or has an image of the stimulus. Although the subject may later attach a label to the object and may associate stimulus features with that label, or with the scanning procedure, these activities are not necessarily basic to perception, and hence not to memory at this level of analysis.

Thus, rather than suggesting a neurological model of the stimulus as does Sokolov, or memory storage as does Cohen, I would propose, in line with Buchwald's suggestions (1973), that in the sensory habituation that takes place with repeated exposures some more general inhibitory process must be developed, probably in the limbic system, that blocks arousal. But given the arousal of a targeting response, which occurs relatively easily, an observation sequence would follow automatically. For simple perception or recognition to occur we need not propose anything so involved as a memory store or a neurological model. If the organism has had sufficient experience with the stimulus complex in the past he will spend little time with it, if he has not, or if there is a salient novel element, additional processing will automatically occur.

In closing I would like to comment on Cohen's explanation for his own data. He identifies the two phases in his backward habituation curve with short-term and long-term memory processing. Although he is clearly aware of the complexity of the memory concept, and puts forth his ideas with appropriate reservations, I do not feel that his approach will prove fruitful. The memory literature is a very sophisticated body of knowledge and there is no doubt but that the flow diagrams memory theoreticians generate are impressive. The great majority of this work, however, is with adult human subjects. It typically uses stimuli that have well overlearned labels, or else the subject is presented with written labels or letters that are highly meaningful and readily decoded. But then because of the past experience involved these stimuli are presented in situations that are contrived either to make it difficult to perceive the critical aspects of the stimuli, or else if sufficient time is provided to perceive and encode the stimuli, something is introduced to interfere with the opportunity to rehearse the codes. Thus, one is playing quite a different game than the one played with perceptual development.

If one is to insist on saying there is memory anytime information is retained, or the nervous system is modified, then I would argue only against trends toward wholesale adoption of the concepts of current information-processing and memory models to handle this level of information storage. For example, one would presume from most memory models that rehearsal is prerequisite to placing something in long-term memory. It appears very tenuous to me to assume that the infant is capable of such rehearsal strategies. Although the serial habituation hypothesis provides a mechanism that might be considered similar to rehearsal, to confuse serial habituation with the rehearsal strategies of the older child is not likely to be productive.

It is unfortunate that our memory research and theories grew primarily out of the verbal learning paradigm rather than from the more recent research on recognition memory. The latter provides an example of memory at a much more basic level and I believe would have led us to consider memory more as Meacham (1972) proposes; not as a faculty but as an epiphenomenon of perceptual and cognitive activities.

REFERENCES

Bridger, W. H. Sensory habituation and discrimination in the human infant. *American Journal of Psychiatry*, 1961, *117*, 991–996.

Buchwald, J. S., & Humphrey, G. L. In E. Stellar & J. M. Sprague (Eds.), *Progress in physiological psychology* (Vol. 5). New York: Academic Press, 1973.

Caron, A. J., Caron, R. F., Caldwell, R. C., & Weiss, S. J. Infant perception of the structural properties of the face. *Developmental Psychology*, 1973, *9*, 385–399.

Cohen, L. B. A two process model of infant visual attention. *Merrill–Palmer Quarterly*, 1973, *19*, 157–180.

Fagan, J. F. Memory in the infant. *Journal of Experimental Child Psychology*, 1970, *9*, 217–226.

Fantz, R. L. Visual perception from birth as shown by pattern selectivity. *Annals of the New York Academy of Sciences*, 1965, *118*, 793–814.

Fantz, R. L., & Miranda, S. B. Newborn infant attention to form of contour. *Child Development*, 1975, *46*, 224–228.

Garner, W. R. *The processing of information and structure*. Hillsdale, N. J.: Lawrence Erlbaum Assoc., 1974.

Gibson, E. J. *Principles of perceptual learning and development*. New York: Appleton-Century-Crofts, 1969.

Gibson, J. J. *The senses considered as perceptual systems*. Boston: Houghton Mifflin, 1966.

Harlow, H. The development of affectional patterns in monkeys. In B. M. Foss (Ed.), *Determinants of infant behavior* (Vol. I). New York: Wiley, 1961.

Hebb, D. O. *The organization of behavior*. New York, Wiley, 1949.

Hunt, J. McV. Motivation inherent in information processing and action. In O. J. Harvey (Ed.), *Motivation and social interaction*. New York: Ronald Press, 1963.

Jeffrey, W. E. The orienting reflex in cognitive development. *Psychological Review*, 1968, *75*, 323–334.

Jeffrey, W. E. Early stimulation and cognitive development. In J. P. Hill (Ed.), *Minnesota symposium on child psychology* (Vol. 1). Minneapolis: The University of Minnesota Press, 1969.

Jeffrey, W. E., & Cohen, L. B. Habituation in the human infant. In H. W. Reese (Ed.), *Advances in child development and behavior* (Vol. 6). New York: Academic Press, 1971.

Kimble, D. P., & Ray, R. S. Reflex habituation and potentiation in *Rana pipicus*. *Animal Behavior*, 1965, *13*, 530–533.

Konorski, J. *Integrative activity of the brain: An interdisciplinary approach*. Chicago: University of Chicago Press, 1967.

Meacham, J. A. The development of memory abilities in the individual and society. *Human Development*, 1972, *15*, 205–228.

Miller, D. J. Visual habituation in the human infant. *Child Development*, 1972, *43*, 483–493.

Ruff, H. A. The function of shifting fixations in the visual perception of infants. *Child Development*, 1975, *46*, 857–865.

Ruff, H. A., & Birch, H. G. Infant visual fixation: The effect of concentricity, curvilinearity and number of directions. *Journal of Experimental Child Psychology,* 1974, *17,* 460–473.

Sokolov, E. N. *Perception and the conditioned reflex.* New York: Macmillan, 1963.

Thompson, R. F., & Spencer, W. A. Habituation: A model phenomenon for the study of neuronal substrates of behavior. *Psychological Review,* 1966, *73,* 16–43.

Underwood, B. J. Individual differences as a crucible in theory construction. *American Psychologist,* 1975, *30,* 128–139.

Zeaman, D., & House, B. J. The role of attention in retardate discrimination learning. In N. R. Ellis (Ed.), *Handbook of mental deficiency.* New York: McGraw-Hill, 1963. Pp. 159–223.

9
The Ubiquity of Novelty— Familiarity (Habituation?) Effects

David Zeaman

University of Connecticut

Mythology has it that the reason psychologists studied rats so much is that they could not keep them out of the laboratory. Studying other animals required food to be kept around. Rats came in uninvited, to help themselves, so psychologists decided (it shouldn't be a total loss) to study them.

I am also told that a physicist (Compton, I believe) had a sign over his laboratory which said "Cosmic Ray Lab." Since cosmic rays were not his object of study the sign raised questions about the appropriateness of the sign. The answer was: "Well, we can't keep them out."

Habituation is like rats and cosmic rays. If you are a psychologist, it is hard to keep it out of your laboratory.

As an experimentalist and developmental psychologist, I never planned to study habituation, but I have been continually plagued throughout my research career by a problem closely related to, if not identified with, habituation: differential responsiveness to new and old stimuli.

My troubles began in the late 1940s. Dr. House and I were interested in studying the discrimination learning of rats at a single choice point. We had a little T maze in the basement of one of the old houses that constituted the Psychology Laboratory at Brown in those days. The usual procedure in studying discrimination was to give the rat a series of trials in which it had a free choice of the rewarded and unrewarded arms of the T maze. Our guiding theory was the Hull–Spence formulation in which discrimination was derived from interaction of excitation and inhibition resulting from reward and nonreward, and generalization between the discriminative stimuli. Habituation certainly played no role in this scheme.

House and I decided that theoretical interpretations might be simplified if the experimenter rather than the rat determined the pattern of rewarded and nonrewarded responses. This meant blocking off one or another arm of the T maze and forcing the rat to make either a rewarded or unrewarded response. In one of our extreme conditions we forced the rats to go to the rewarded arm 10 times in quick succession, then opened up the blocked arm to allow a free choice; we were not prepared for what happened.

The Law of Effect dictated strong preferences for the rewarded side, and this was our theoretical expectation. As most readers will know, the theory was exactly 180° out of phase with the results. Every last rat—100% of them—preferred the side that had previously been blocked; not a one chose the side that had been rewarded 10 times (Zeaman & House, 1951). The Law of Effect, that day, gave way to some more powerful law.

Being good Hullians at the time, we appealed to a law of fatigue using Hull's concept of reactive inhibition.

A flood of subsequent research showed us the error in our thinking. The rats alternated their response not because they were tired of the old response but because they preferred the new stimuli over the old (habituated?) stimuli (Fowler, 1965). It occurred to us then as it has many times since that the Law of Effect must always be at war with some Law of Habituation as long as subjects have some preference for novelty.

We discovered quite accidentally that novelty preference is by no means universal, even in so curious an animal as the rat. If you inadvertently drop a rat, pinch its tail, or upset it in any way, it temporarily loses its curiosity or novelty preference. Rats that had been shocked recently were not good alternators. In short, worried rats like familiar, not novel, stimuli. In an early review of the literature on spontaneous alternation, Dember and Fowler (1958) describe studies showing the reduction in alternation (and response variability in general) produced by noxious stimuli.

It can be seen from all this that habituation obtruded itself on our research through the *motivational* properties of new or old stimuli. At the mammalian level, at least, a familiar or habituated stimulus does not always lead to a response decrement. It depends on the motivational state of the subject.

If habituation can be identified with differential response to novel and familiar stimuli, the next obtrusion of habituation in my research manifested itself not through preferences for novel over familiar stimuli but through the unexpectedly strong cue values of novel stimuli. Again the discovery was serendipitous. Dr. House and I were running retarded children, in the early 1950s, on two-choice visual discrimination problems, and many of our subjects were doing very badly solving such problems, despite endless training sessions. On one occasion a child who for 20 daily sessions had been at chance performance level walked, unasked, to a laboratory rack before the beginning of the twenty-first session and picked out from an array of several hundred stimulus objects the very two that were *his,* the ones on which he had been failing for so long. We were surprised. He may not have been discriminating the difference between the two stimuli, but he could certainly tell the difference between both these old stimuli and many other new stimuli quite similar in appearance.

We reasoned then that if this subject were so good at seeing the difference between old and new, why not try to use this capacity to help him learn the difference between the right and wrong stimulus in the standard discriminative learning problem. So what we did was to get a bunch of subjects who had been failing the discriminative problem for hundreds of trials, and then suddenly introduce either a new positive stimulus together with the old negative, or a new negative stimulus together with the old positive stimulus. The results were gratifying, and consequently published (Zeaman, House, & Orlando, 1958). Most of these long-term failing subjects solved the problem and maintained solution after novelty had worn off. The results are not interpretable in terms of novelty preference since a new negative stimulus also had a facilitating effect. The only interpretation that fits is that the novelty–familiarity dimension has strong attention, or cue, value. If the right and wrong stimuli in a discriminative problem also differ in novelty then a highly salient redundant dimension has been added which will markedly facilitate solution.

We have over the course of many years continued to rediscover the remarkable effects of stimulus novelty in a variety of experimental contexts, some of which I will describe. The effects are to be seen not only in the behavior of rats and retardates; they work on you and me as well.

The application of novelty–familiarity dynamics to learning in normal adult subjects was brought home to me, again quite accidentally, in 1960. Teaching machines were hot topics in those days, and a colleague of mine, Walter Kaess, and I did a study using college students, testing a then current idea that contingent learning was better than noncontingent (Kaess & Zeaman, 1960). That is, letting a student *discover* a right answer was presumed better than telling him what it was straightaway. What we wanted our college students to learn was some technical definitions of psychological terms. To allow them to learn contingently we presented a term together with five alternative definitions from which they could choose, and we had a device which told them immediately whether a choice was correct or incorrect. On each item our subjects continued to choose until they made the correct response. One of our comparison groups had no contingencies at all—the psychological term was presented followed by only one definition, the correct one. A large number of items was trained in those two ways, contingently and noncontingently, followed by identical test trials of the information learned using the standard multiple-choice (five alternatives) test format.

What were our expectations? Well, the contingent condition had a lot going for it. For one, there was the joy of discovery. That was supposed to have some additional reinforcing properties. Secondly, in the contingent condition the training and test stimuli were identical (one term and five alternative definitions) which was not true in the noncontingent condition (one term and one definition) so there would be no generalization decrement between training and test trials in the contingent condition. Thirdly, the contingent group was given more information in the sense that they learned not only what definitions were correct but also which were incorrect. And finally, the contingent group took much longer to complete their training trials so their total study time on the learning materials are longer.

Despite all these advantages, the noncontingent group outdid the contingent group by far. There was virtually no overlap in the distributions. And why was this? Because the noncontingent group on every test item needed only to go through the alternative answers and pick the familiar one. All novel choices were wrong. I suspect that the subjects could have done equally as well if we hadn't presented the psychological terms at all. They had a basis for solution of each test trial merely on the basis of novelty or familiarity of the choices, and no associative learning of the kind we were trying to measure may have occurred in this condition.

In short, the experiment was magnificently confounded, and although the study was published in the *Journal of Experimental Psychology,* neither the authors nor the editors of this journal were at that time sufficiently aware of the confounding effects of novelty and familiarity in learning experiments to catch the error.

This ignorance has been rectified, largely through the efforts of Underwood and his associates, who rediscovered quite independently the effects I have described in what is now a sizable literature generally confirmatory of Underwood's *Frequency Theory* of discrimination learning (Ekstrand, Wallace, & Underwood, 1966). The major postulates of the theory are that the correct or positive cue of a discriminative problem becomes more familiar than the negative cue, and that simple discriminative learning is largely a matter of approaching the more familiar rather than novel cue. He has shown that the frequency of prefamiliarization trials can strongly determine the rate of solution of discriminative problems in adult subjects. Note here that adult humans are assumed to prefer familiar, habituated stimuli in this theory.

Roughly at about this time in my personal history of struggle with novelty–familiarity effects, Dr. House and I were embarked on a small program of research to assess the relative use of positive and negative cues in the discriminative learning of retardates. Two competing theories of retardate learning deficit implicate either excitatory or inhibitory processes. To get an experimental handle on this issue, we were trying to measure the relative uses of positive and negative cues in discriminative learning under the assumption that positive cue usage tapped excitatory processes while the negative cue tapped inhibitory processes. Several methods were available to us, all having a common strategic property: interference in some way with either the positive or negative cue followed by a measure of the resulting performance decrements.

A method we devised ourselves deprived the subjects of the use of a positive cue not by removing it but by making it variable from trial to trial. Thus on each successive trial of the two-choice problem, the same negative stimulus would appear accompanied by a different positive stimulus. Any excitatory tendencies attached to a particular positive stimulus would be unable to contribute to problem solution. The same operations were applied to the negative stimulus by making it variable from trial to trial, thus presumably eliminating inhibitory processes from problem solution (House, Orlando, & Zeaman, 1957). The trial-by-trial changes in stimulus displays under the variable negative condition and variable positive condition are illustrated in Figure 1.

By now the reader should be able to guess the nature of the difficulties that emerged. Instead of eliminating the positive or negative stimulus by these strategies, we had merely given the subjects a different kind of stimulus dimension that could be used as either a positive or negative cue. That dimension was, of course, novelty–familiarity. All the subject need learn is that the novel stimulus is correct in the variable positive condition, or that the novel stimulus is always incorrect in the variable negative condition.

We were led to this interpretation by the appearance of interproblem improvement or learning set which did not appear with these subjects in standard problems having nonvariable positive and negative cues. Internal analysis of the data suggested strongly that the source of the learning set was a learned tendency to use variability or novelty as a cue. It all seemed so obvious after the fact, but not before. Needless to say, our published report of this work was unable to come to any very definite conclusions about our target problem—the relative use of positive and negative cues—because of the complicating intrusion of novelty dynamics.

TRIALS	CONDITIONS			
	VARIABLE NEGATIVE		VARIABLE POSITIVE	
	POSITIVE CUE	NEGATIVE CUE	POSITIVE CUE	NEGATIVE CUE
1	A	B	B	A
2	A	C	C	A
3	A	D	D	A
⋮	⋮	⋮	⋮	⋮
N	A	Z	Z	A

FIG. 1 Stimulus displays used by House, Orlando, and Zeaman to assess relative usages of positive and negative cues in two-choice discriminative learning. The letters A, B, C, . . . designate different stimuli used as positive or negative cues.

Another method that we were using at about this time to study the control of discriminative learning by positive and negative cues was the Moss–Harlow design, named after its originators (Moss & Harlow, 1947). In one condition of this experimental design, just the positive stimulus is presented to the subject and response to it is rewarded. A series of test trials immediately follows with both positive and negative stimulus presented simultaneously on each trial with differential reinforcement. The other condition of the design presents just the negative stimulus which is nonrewarded, followed again by the series of test trials with both positive and negative cues presented simultaneously as before. Differences in performance under the two conditions were attributable to the relative importance of acquisition and extinction (or excitation and inhibition) in discriminative learning. Using monkeys as subjects, Moss and Harlow found that performance on test trials was relatively better after a single nonreinforced presentation of the negative stimulus than after the reinforced positive stimulus. This result leads naturally enough to the conclusion that inhibitory contributions to discriminative learning are greater than excitatory, and this conclusion is entirely consonant with Harlow's error factor theory of discriminative learning which describes the learning process in terms of the extinction or inhibition of a large number of error tendencies.

We used the Moss–Harlow design with some moderately retarded children and got similar results, but came to rather different conclusions (House & Zeaman, 1958). Observe that the stimulus arrangements in Figure 2 are precisely the experimental operations for a single-trial habituation experiment. The performance outcomes for the test trial are widely divergent. One might be tempted to conclude on the basis of the 45 versus 84% comparison that inhibition is greater

MOSS-HARLOW EFFECT

	REWARD	NONREWARD
TRAIN:	S_1 △	S_2 ○
TEST:	S_1 △ S_2 ○	S_1 △ S_2 ○
% CORRECT	45%	84%

FIG. 2 Arrangement of stimuli in the two conditions of the Moss–Harlow design used by House and Zeaman with retarded children. Under each condition a single training trial displays only one stimulus (rewarded or nonrewarded) followed by a second (test) trial providing a choice of a new and old stimulus. Performances are shown in the bottom row.

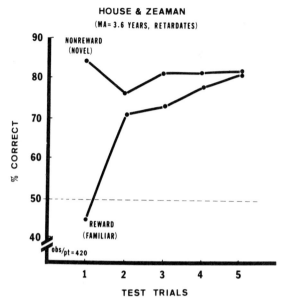

FIG. 3 Performance on four subsequent test trials identical to those shown in Figure 2. (From House & Zeaman, 1958. Copyright 1958 by the American Psychological Association. Reproduced by permission.)

than excitation, but there are some suspicious aspects of the data that make this interpretation questionable. There is, for example, that puzzling figure of 45% correct in the reward or positive condition. This percentage is based on 420 observations and is reliably below chance. Unless the odd assumption were made that reward had some inhibitory properties, some other factor than reward must be pushing this percentage below chance level. By this time in our mental development we were sufficiently aware of the nature of the "other" factor. These young children were approaching the novel stimulus. The 45% is artifactually reduced by novelty preference, the 84% is artifactually raised.

Some confirmation of this is seen in Figure 3 which shows performance on four subsequent test trials. On these test trials the positive and negative stimuli are not quite so different in novelty and familiarity, since they both have been seen on previous trials. The loss in differential novelty is accompanied by a drawing together of the two functions; the nonreward curve drops, the reward condition rises. It is hard to think of a model of excitation—inhibition dynamics that would produce this curious funneling of the two functions. The inference of novelty confounding fits it nicely.

It should be emphasized here that the subjects showing novelty preference were developmentally quite young, with mental ages (MAs) of about $3\frac{1}{2}$ years. In 1966 an important study appeared by Cross and Vaughter which demonstrated that the Moss–Harlow effect had a strong developmental parameter. They used the Moss–Harlow design with 2 groups of normal children, one with a mean age of 3½ years, the other 5½ years. Their results are shown in Figure 4. At the 3½ year level the percentages of correct responses under the two conditions of the experiment were very close to those of our retardates with MAs of 3½ years. Especially significant is the subchance performance when the children were required to approach a familiar rewarded stimulus.

Contrast these results with those of the 5½-year-old children. For them the approach to the familiar (rewarded) stimulus is far stronger than avoidance of the unrewarded stimulus. There are, as I have pointed out, two ways of interpreting those developmental differences. One is in terms of the Moss–Harlow explanation which would say that for older children approach is stronger than avoidance (or excitation is stronger than inhibition, or acquisition is stronger than extinction), while in younger children the reverse is true. The other interpretation is that younger children prefer novelty; older children prefer familiarity. Cross and Vaughter chose the approach–avoidance explanation but did not consider the confounding by novelty and familiarity preferences. Unlike us, these investigators apparently did not have such a long history of having been faked out by novelty.

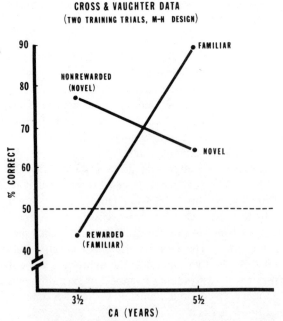

CROSS & VAUGHTER DATA
(TWO TRAINING TRIALS, M–H DESIGN)

FIG. 4 Test trial performances with a Moss–Harlow design for normal children at two age levels. The younger children show novelty preference; the older children prefer familiar stimuli. (Data from Cross & Vaughter, 1966.)

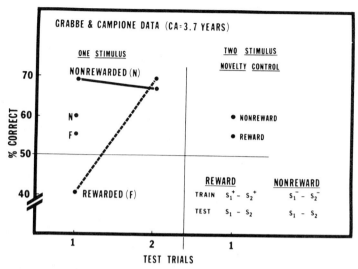

FIG. 5 The Moss–Harlow design was used by Grabbe and Campione to obtain the data shown in the panel at left. In the panel at right are the data from a control condition paradigmed at bottom right and described in the text. The data points of the control condition are replotted at left (labeled N and F) for comparison. (From Grabbe & Campione, 1969.)

Three years later, Grabbe and Campione (1969) came out with a study which attempted to show experimentally that the Moss–Harlow effect in younger children was not attributable to approach–avoidance differences but to novelty preferences. They mounted a control for novelty and found the differential effects of a single reward or nonreward to be negligible. Figure 5 presents their design and data. At the bottom right of the figure are shown the two stimulus arrangements of their control condition. Under the reward condition two stimuli are presented simultaneously and whichever is chosen is rewarded. The test trial following is a standard discriminative trial with the same two stimuli re-presented. Under the nonreward condition 2 stimuli are presented simultaneously and whichever is chosen is nonrewarded. A standard test trial follows. Test-trial performances are plotted for these two conditions, showing a small difference, about 60 and 55% for the effects of nonreward and reward respectively. Novelty was presumed under control in this comparison since all stimuli had been seen exactly once before the test trial.

At the left of the figure are the data from a Moss–Harlow design. Only one stimulus was presented on the training trial and the results were as expected from previous experiments, including the subchance performance after reward, and the funneling of the reward–nonreward curves on the second test trial. The points labeled N and F are simply replots of the control data.

The conclusion drawn by Grabbe and Campione was that the Moss–Harlow effect is entirely due to novelty preferences in young children, since the effect disappears when novelty is eliminated.

There are some difficulties with the Grabbe and Campione control data in that the experimental conditions are confounded with possible stimulus preferences that would artificially raise the reward point (since the correct test stimulus is initially preferred), and lower the nonreward point (the correct test stimulus is initially nonpreferred). But even if the experimental control of novelty failed in this study because of the introduction of this confounding variable, the replication of the two critical features of the data in the Moss–Harlow conditions (the below-chance point, and the sharp funneling of the curves) so clearly implicate the operation of novelty preference that not much confidence can be put in the excitation–inhibition argument.

Being developmental psychologists, we were intrigued by the age trends in the Moss–Harlow effects. We interpreted them as age changes in novelty preference, but we did not know whether the age changes were those of MA or chronological age (CA). To answer the question with the population of retarded children available to us we used the Moss–Harlow design with a group of children varying in MA, CA, and IQ. All three of these developmental variables showed some control of the performances in the two conditions of the Moss–Harlow design, with subjects who were lower in MA, CA, and IQ showing greater novelty preference (or excitation or approach tendency), and those higher in those three developmental variables showing greater familiarity preference (or inhibition, or avoidance tendency).

The group of us who did this experiment (Fisher, Sperber, & Zeaman, 1973) were well aware that we needed some way of teasing out of the Moss–Harlow data separate indices of learning and novelty–familiarity preferences. So we constructed a little model of what we thought was going on in the Moss–Harlow experiment.

Figure 6 presents the model. It is assumed that there are just three theoretical variables: a novelty preference N, a familiarity preference F, and learning state L. On training trials (with just one stimulus presented) the subject becomes familiar with the demonstrated object and learns something about its reward or nonreward value. On the test trial, it is assumed that the subject observes the novelty–familiarity difference between the two stimuli and has relative preferences, expressed as probabilities, N and F, in favor of the novel and familiar stimuli, respectively. These preferences may be overridden or enhanced by the learning which has taken place on the training trial. If the subject, because of novelty or familiarity preference, tends *covertly* to choose the wrong stimulus, then he has a conditional probability, L, of overcoming this tendency and making the correct response.

On any test trial, then, the probability of a correct response is completely determined by three theoretical probabilities: N, F, and L. In the positive condi-

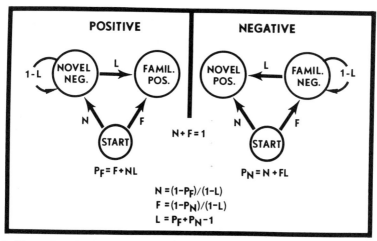

FIG. 6 Theoretical flow diagrams for the positive (reward) and negative (nonreward) conditions of the Moss–Harlow paradigm. N, F, and L are probabilities of transition to the novel, familiar, and learned stimuli, respectively. Once these probabilities bring the subject to the positive stimulus, he remains there with a probability of 1. Equations relating theoretical and empirical variables are shown at bottom. P_F and P_N are the empirical percentages of correct response under the positive and negative conditions, respectively. (From Fisher, Sperber, & Zeaman, 1973.)

tion of the Moss–Harlow design, where to be correct the subject must approach the familiar positive stimulus on the test trial, the probability of a correct response is shown by the equation at left. Under the negative condition, where to be correct the subject must approach the novel positive stimulus, the probability of a correct test choice is shown by the equation at right. It is assumed that the subject prefers either the novel or familiar stimulus but not both, so we can also write the equation $N + F = 1$. This gives us three equations and three theoretical unknowns. The equations can be solved for N, F, and L, if we have empirical measures of P_F and P_N from the percentages of correct responses in the two conditions of the Moss–Harlow design. Furthermore, we can get estimates of N, F, and L for a single subject by running the subject many times under each condition on a set of homogeneous problems. This is what we did in our experiment and the results are shown in Figure 7.

We plotted the values of novelty preference (N) against mental age. The complementary values of familiarity preference (F) are scaled by the ordinate at right. The solid line is the regression line for object stimuli, which were easier for these subjects to discriminate than picture stimuli. The plotted points are the averages of objects and pictures. Observe that for these average points the transition from novelty to familiarity preference occurs between four and five years of mental age. The data points from the three other studies described earlier (Cross &

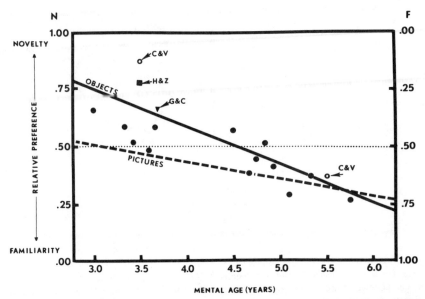

FIG. 7 Changes in novelty–familiarity preferences with mental age using pictures or objects as stimuli. Regression lines are graphed separately for the pictures and objects. Solid circles are the average for each subject over both experiments. Other points (designated by initials) were recomputed from studies of Cross and Vaughter (1966), Grabbe and Campione (1969), and House and Zeaman (1958). (From Fisher, Sperber, & Zeaman, 1973.)

Vaughter, 1966; Grabbe & Campione, 1969; House & Zeaman, 1958) confirm the general trend.

A CA function could also be plotted here, but regression on CA was not statistically reliable. IQ and MA were partially confounded in this experiment. The correlation of IQ and novelty preference was $-.71$. MA and N correlated $-.85$. Partial correlations showed that it was MA rather than IQ that accounted for the larger portion of the regression.

I have not mentioned the fate of the learning variable L. It did *not* covary significantly with any of the developmental parameters. Over the mental age range of 3–6 years, learning rates were constant but novelty preferences changed drastically over this period. Let me emphasize that the model we have used to derive our measures of learning and novelty–familiarity preferences in no way constrains the developmental changes that may occur in these measures. As far as the theory is concerned, the values of N and L can go in any direction they want as mental age increases. The constancy of learning rates did not surprise us at all, since all our other quantitative analyses of discriminative learning have led us to the same conclusion.

We were gratified, however, to have arrived at a quantitative evaluation of maturational changes in novelty preferences with theoretical controls offered for possible learning rate changes. The model we have offered, simple as it may be, is the only one I know of relating discriminative performance to both novelty–familiarity preference and learning measures.

We wondered next whether novelty preferences might also play some role in ordinary simultaneous two-choice visual discrimination learning. It might seem that the presentation of the same two stimuli on each trial of a standard discriminative problem would control adequately for novelty–familiarity preferences since both positive and negative stimuli are presented equally often. We recalled however that Underwood's frequency theory postulated that positive stimuli gain more familiarity than negative stimuli, and this possibility guided an unpublished experiment by Dr. Mary Ann Fisher, in our laboratory. She presented a series of 10 2-choice concurrent problems each for just one trial. That is, there were 20 stimuli, 10 positive and 10 negative, presented pairwise for 10 standard discriminative learning trials. On each training trial the subject chose one stimulus; if it was correct the choice was rewarded and the next problem presented. If incorrect, no candy was given and the child allowed to correct by picking up the positive stimulus. After 10 such trials, one each on the different problems, a test was performed to find out if the child could recognize which he had seen before. To do this Dr. Fisher paired each of the 10 positive and 10 negative stimuli with novel stimuli not presented before, and asked the subject to "point to the one you have seen before." That is, of course, a recognition test of novelty–familiarity.

The question of interest was whether the positive stimuli would be recognized as familiar to a greater extent than the negative stimuli. Separate counts were made for problems on which the correct response was made on the training trial and those on which incorrect responses were made.

When the subjects picked up the positive stimulus (by guessing of course), they were able to recognize the positive stimuli as familiar with 82% accuracy. The negative stimuli were recognized as familiar with only a 57% accuracy. For the problems on which the subjects chose the negative stimulus on the training trial (again by guessing) the recognition scores for positive and negative stimuli were about the same (82 and 80% respectively). Remember that correction technique was used here so that a choice of the negative stimulus meant that both positive and negative stimuli were handled. In summary, there was differential familiarity for positive and negative stimuli on roughly half of the problems of this experiment. Couple this with the fact that during the ordinary simultaneous discriminative experiment, with many training trials, the subjects pick up the positive stimulus more and more frequently, and it can be seen that differential familiarity of positive and negative cues is the normal state of affairs even though the experimenter has presented all stimuli equally often. Furthermore, a similar mechanism could obtain in discrimination learning experiments featuring a noncorrection technique. If there is posited some learning in early trials independent of novelty–familiarity influences, as preference for the positive stimulus grows it will become more and more familiar with a consequent snowballing effect as learning and familiarity preference summate.

Let us assume now that we have demonstrated two facts: (1) in discriminative learning the positive cue becomes more familiar than the negative; and (2) as subjects get older they change from novelty preference to familiarity preference.

What are the implications of these two facts? As a developmental psychologist, I think they are profound. They mean that younger children, preferring novelty, will consequently tend to do badly on discriminative learning tasks, whereas older children, preferring familiarity, will tend to do better—not because the older learn faster but because they prefer familiarity (and positive stimuli are more familiar). The developmental psychologist interested in the relation of maturation and learning must know that the Law of Effect is continually at war with novelty preferences. We had to learn this the hard way, but I do not believe that even today it is common knowledge.

No trait or process has been more closely identified, historically, with the maturation of intelligence than learning rate. But now we see that raw empirical measures of discriminative learning may be seriously confounded with mere preference differences for novelty and familiarity, which change developmentally. Why do I say *mere* preference differences? The answer is that novelty–familiarity preferences are so easily changed. Not only will affective states change the preference (worried subjects become wary and avoid novel stimuli), but also novelty and familiarity preferences can be changed in the laboratory with a nickle's worth of training.

This has been shown by Daryl Greenfield in a master's thesis study run recently in our laboratory. He had 2 groups of retarded children, one with MAs averaging about $3\frac{1}{2}$ years, the other about $5\frac{1}{2}$ years. The design was Moss–Harlow, in which either the positive stimulus was demonstrated on Trial 1 or the negative stimulus. The difference between this experiment and our previous Moss–Harlow studies was that each subject stayed in one condition of the design for many problems instead of alternating between them, so that the subjects could learn to use novelty or familiarity as a cue; that is, a correct solution to all the problems was either "choose the novel cue" or "choose the familiar stimulus," depending upon the condition.

The results are displayed in Figure 8. Trial 2 performances are plotted over 10 days of training with 6 problems per day. The panel at left, for the low MA subjects, showed the usual, strong novelty preference effect at the outset of training. Over the course of 60 problems there was a huge improvement in the performance of subjects who had the positive stimulus demonstrated on each problem. This interproblem improvement is attributable to a learned use of familiarity as a cue. It is not attributable to any generalized learning set formation since these same subjects given an equal number of standard two-stimulus problems in another condition showed no interproblem improvement, as would be expected if they were simply learning to learn. The subjects in the

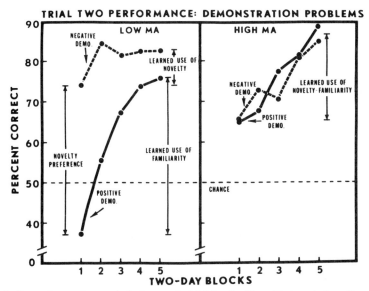

FIG. 8 Percentages of correct choices on test trials of a Moss–Harlow design after a single reinforced trial (positive demonstration trial) and after a single nonreinforced trial (negative demonstration trial). Low MA performances are plotted in the left panel over the course of 60 different problems. Corresponding plots for high MA subjects appear at the right. (Data from Greenfield, 1975.)

negative stimulus demonstration condition, starting as they did with strong preference for novelty, had little room left for improvement in the use of this cue.

The high MA group was expected to start with a familiarity preference, but the average MA of this group at about $5\frac{1}{2}$ years was apparently not high enough to produce the effect. The data indicate that they started with neutral preferences for novelty and familiarity and learned to prefer one or the other of these cues in the two conditions of the experiment.

The point of major interest for my arguments, deriving from these data, is this: the young subjects in the positive cue demonstration condition entered the experiment with a strong novelty preference, but ended the experiment with a correspondingly strong familiarity preference.

It must be admitted that the fact that training can replace novelty preferences with familiarity preferences does not mean that there is no native or maturational basis for novelty preferences in the first place. But it certainly raises the suspicion that older subjects may also natively prefer novelty, but have through training and experience developed a preference for familiarity in those tasks in which familiarity preferences pay off.

In what tasks do familiarity preferences pay off? The answer is: almost any discriminative task in which the Law of Effect plays some role. Correct stimuli are generally familiar. For us to know they are correct they must have had a history of reinforcement. Novel stimuli have unknown histories.

If familiarity preferences facilitate the operation of the Law of Effect then world-wise subjects will likely learn generalized strategies of approach to familiar stimuli in those tasks in which reward is likely to be found. Older subjects, of course, are more world wise, and have had more opportunity to learn generalized familiarity preferences in reward situations.

An experiment that gives more than a little comfort to this interpretation was done in our laboratory by Dr. Barbara Losty (1971). She used a Moss–Harlow design in which the usual reinforcement–nonreinforcement conditions obtained. At the right side of Figure 9, we see that the lower-MA subjects were novelty preferrers and the older children were familiarity preferrers. The transition age was slightly higher than usual, but the pattern of age changes is certainly familiar enough to the reader by now.

In Figure 9, the panel at left represents a slight variation in the Moss–Harlow design. The subjects were shown a single demonstration stimulus, as is typically

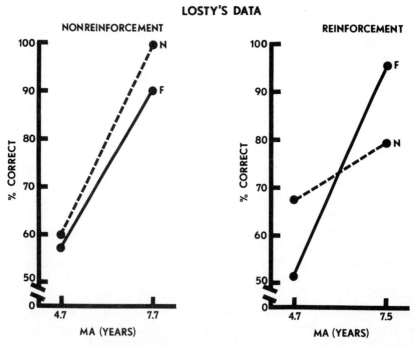

FIG. 9   Test trial performances with a Moss–Harlow design at two levels of mental age. The panel at left represents a condition in which no candy reward was involved, in contrast to the panel at right in which candy was given for correct responses. The letters N and F indicate that the novel or familiar stimulus was correct, respectively. (Data from Losty, 1971.)

done in this design, and told that on the next trial (when two stimulus cards are shown), they would have to choose either the old or the new stimulus. No candy was involved during the training. The line marked N at the left of the figure represents performances when the subjects were asked to choose the *new* stimulus. The line labeled F indicates the problems requiring choice of the old or familiar stimulus. The stimuli used in this experiment were not as highly discriminable as those we usually use in this type of research and the younger subjects had very low performance levels, and an unexpected absence of novelty preference in the nonreinforcement condition, but the significant feature of the results lies in the performance of the older subjects. They did better when selecting a new stimulus rather than a familiar stimulus.

More than one interpretation can be made of these results, but the one I like is this: taking out the differential reinforcement in the demonstration trials allows the native attractiveness of novelty to shine through, overcoming learned preference for familiarity generally characteristic of older children. They reserve familiarity preferences for reward situations.

A great deal of evidence can be cited from at least four sources showing that older subjects manifest intrinsic novelty preferences in situations *without* extrinsic rewards.

When adults are asked to rate the hedonic value of stimuli, they show marked novelty preferences. Researchers such as Berlyne and others have demonstrated this many times in experiments where there are no correct or incorrect responses.

In other situations with no obvious extrinsic rewards such as reaction—time experiments, Cantor and others have published many studies showing that novel stimuli give rise to faster RT's than familiar stimuli. This "stimulus familiarization effect" has been observed in both younger and older subjects.

Orienting responses are generally measured in tasks not involving differential reinforcement, and the attractiveness of novelty to sneak-peeks is too well-known to document here. Covert correlates of orienting responses, such as heart-rate and GSR and EEG changes also reflect the salience of novel stimuli.

Habituation—dishabituation effects, which involve differential response to novel and familiar stimuli, have been observed at all developmental levels, typically in situations without extrinsic reinforcement.

The idea promulgated here can be summarized graphically as shown in Figure 10. Unlearned or intrinsic novelty preference is assumed constant throughout life (after two or three months). A generalized tendency to prefer familiarity in reward situations is assumed to grow with age. Somewhere in the age neighborhood of four to five years, the two preferences are about equal in strength. This would be the point of indifference in a novelty—familiarity choice situation featuring rewards. In nonreward situations, the only preference operating is assumed to be the developmentally constant novelty preference.

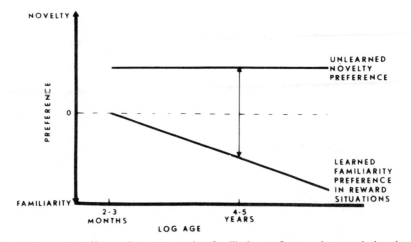

FIG. 10 Assumed effects of age on novelty–familiarity preferences in reward situations (lower function) and in all situations (upper function). The double-headed arrow indicates that in early childhood the two competing preferences become equal and neutralize each other.

The two functions have been plotted to begin at two to three months, since almost all studies of infants above this age report reliable habituation–dishabituation effects, while before this age some investigators fail to get these effects or report weaker degrees of habituation–dishabituation (see Jeffrey & Cohen, 1971, for a literature review; also see Clifton & Nelson, Chapter 5, and Cohen, Chapter 6, in this volume). What do the functions of Figure 10 look like earlier? I have no hesitation in extrapolating the bottom function to the zero point, but the extrapolation backward of the novelty–preference function is a bit stickier.

Since, in general, the probability of getting habituation effects in these early months increases (along with the rate and magnitude of effects), it might be postulated that novelty preference is increasing. Extrapolating the novelty–preference curve back to zero at birth would provide an account of this age trend, but this is not the usual postulate. Theorists in this area appeal not to a preference factor but to learning or memory factors to account for early developmental differences (or phylogenetic differences). In order for a subject to prefer novelty there must be *knowledge* or recognition that some competing stimulus is familiar. The assumption of developmental differences in rate of acquisition or retention of the knowledge of familiarity offers an alternative explanation to the novelty preference hypothesis.

A third possibility accounting for early developmental changes in habituation effects may appeal to affective factors. Fear or wariness changes novelty preference to familiarity preference. This has been well established in the literature on lower animals, but there is some baby-watching evidence suggesting the same thing.

Figure 11 graphically depicts the theoretical assumptions I have been describing. The wariness idea does not lend itself ideally to a developmental progression of habituability, without some additional assumptions, but it might account for a few stray facts in the baby literature in which familiarity preferences have been reported in the early months of life (Greenberg, Uzgiris, & Hunt, 1970; Hunt, 1970).

I have nothing to contribute to any controversy about the proper explanation of developmental differences in habituability early in life. The evidence I have presented is primarily supportive of a theory about later developmental differences in novelty–familiarity preferences. For this reason, I have not extrapolated back to birth the two theoretical age functions shown in Figure 10. Figure 10, then, as drawn is a final graphical statement of my theoretical position. If it were to be described in more literary terms, I would say: *Novelty is intrinsically good all your life, but as you get older, you learn that familiarity is extrinsically good in reward situations, because rewarded things are usually familiar.*

An alternative statement might be: *The Law of Effect competes with novelty preferences in the young, but less so in the older because they have learned when to overcome their novelty preference.*

With these summary statements I approach the end of this contribution. My research has now reached the stage where novelty–familiarity effects no longer creep into our laboratory uninvited, to be discovered after the fact and serendipitously. Instead we now use what we know of these *N–F* dynamics to predict

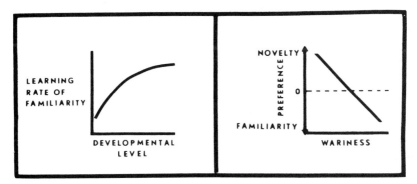

FIG. 11 Two hypothetical functions that may account for differences in novelty and familiarity preferences during the first few months of infancy. The figure at left shows a hypothetical growth of learning ability during early months. The ordinate could alternatively be labeled retention ability. The figure at right shows a hypothesized change from novelty to familiarity preference with increase in wariness. Difficulties in control of the subjective factor of wariness could possibly account for the occasional report of familiarity preference in very young infants.

otherwise contraintuitive effects and to achieve great facilitation of discrimination learning. I will conclude with two representative studies, sketched briefly to buttress these claims.

First to be presented are some predictions in the domain of relational learning of the oddity or matching concept. Without a consideration of novelty–familiarity dynamics, these predictions would appear contraintuitive. The simplest experimental tests of oddity or matching require the presentation of three stimuli, a sample stimulus A and two choice–stimuli, A and B. In a matching problem choice A is correct since it matches the sample A. In an oddity problem choice B is, of course, correct. Different stimuli are used in every problem to prevent specific-cue learning rather than the desired conceptual learning of same–difference (or matching–oddity).

Two procedures can be used to present these problems: (1) a simultaneous array of three stimuli with the middle or sample stimulus unavailable for choice:

Choice	Sample	Choice
A	A	B

or (2) a delayed array of choices, in which the sample stimulus is separated from the choices by a time delay:

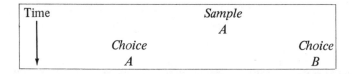

It might reasonably be expected that delayed oddity–matching would be the more difficult in that it puts some burden on memory: the subject must remember what the sample stimulus was in the subsequent choice of the odd or matching stimulus. Our intuitions, shaped as they were by our particular research history, were different. Observe first that the delayed oddity–matching paradigm is Moss–Harlow. The choice of stimuli on the oddity–matching dimension is confounded with the novelty–familiarity dimension. Therefore, in the delayed condition, the subject would have two redundant dimensions on which to base a choice: same–difference or novelty–familiarity. Our expectations therefore were that the delayed condition would be easier than the simultaneous condition. Following from this analysis is another not so intuitive prediction: young children (with their strong novelty preferences) should do better on delayed oddity problems than on delayed matching, while older children should show the reverse ordering of problem difficulty, because of their familiarity preferences.

These predictions were put to test by Greenfield (1975) in a doctoral dissertation. The relevant portions of his findings are shown in Figure 12. Retarded

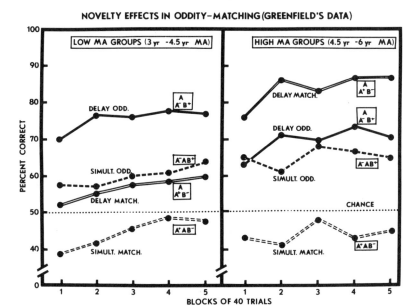

FIG. 12 Performances of low MA and high MA retardates on oddity and matching problems presented with delayed or simultaneous procedure. Each of the 8 groups of subjects received 200 problems. Stimulus arrangements are symbolized at the right of each function. (Data from Greenfield, 1975.)

children with mental ages between 3 and $4\frac{1}{2}$ years were compared with those of MAs of $4\frac{1}{2}$–6 years. Each subject was tested repeatedly on just one of the 4 types of problems representing the combinations of oddity or matching, simultaneous or delayed. Both theoretical predictions were borne out by the data. Delayed oddity and delayed matching were easier than their simultaneous counterparts for both high and low MA subjects. Also, delayed oddity was reliably easier than delayed matching for the low MA children, while the ordering was reversed for the high MAs.

One surprising aspect of the data did emerge. The subjects in both high and low MA Groups showed a preference for the odd stimulus in the Simultaneous array $(A\ A\ B)$. This is inferred not only from the superiority of simultaneous oddity performance over simultaneous matching, but more strongly from the consistently subchance performance of the Simultaneous Matching Group. This finding supports the notion that oddity–matching is a different dimension than novelty–familiarity, since stimulus preferences follow a different developmental course for the two dimensions, that is, both young and old children prefer the odd stimulus (B) in an AAB array, while in an

$$A$$
$$A \qquad B$$

array younger children prefer the novel stimulus (B) and older children prefer the familiar stimulus (A). It can easily be seen from these data and analyses that without an understanding of novelty–familiarity dynamics and other stimulus preferences, not much sense can be made of developmental comparisons of the conceptual or relational learning represented by these task performances.

The final study to be presented demonstrates the remarkable facilitation of discriminative learning that can be obtained by harnessing N–F dynamics. In a doctoral dissertation by Martin (1970) retarded children with MAs averaging 7.8 years were given the task of learning a set of concurrent discriminative problems. As an example of such a set, let A, B, C, X, Y, Z be six discriminable stimuli, and the symbols "+" and "–" designate positive and negative stimuli. Using these stimuli a list of three theoretical problems could be arranged to run in sequential order. On the first list trial the order might be

$$A+ \quad X-$$
$$B+ \quad Y-$$
$$C+ \quad Z-$$

On the next list trial, the same three concurrent problems would appear but in different sequence. The paradigm resembles closely that of paired-associates list learning. Trials continue and learning is measured by improvement in overall percentage of correct responses. In general the larger the set size the slower the learning.

To facilitate the learning of concurrent problems with retarded children, Martin (1970) used a single-prefamiliarization operation. The positive stimuli of all problems were initially presented to the subjects one at a time for their inspection. Following this single familiarization the children were presented pairs of stimuli with the familiar stimulus positive and the negative stimulus novel. The subjects were told that the candy reward was hidden under the "old one" (the stimulus they had seen before). It was expected that this simple prefamiliarization (or demonstration) trial would facilitate the learning of the concurrent problems, since the relatively high MA of these subjects would give them strong preference for familiar stimuli. For comparison purposes two other, equated groups of retardates were run, one without the prefamiliarization operation, and another without the differential candy reinforcement. The design is summarized in Figure 13.

The 3 conditions of Martin's design were run with different groups given either 5, 10, or 20 concurrent problems. The results are shown in Figure 14. The effects of a single prefamiliarization trial on discrimination learning are shown by the very large performance differences between the learning and learning–plus–familiarization functions.

I have been doing research for over 20 years in retardate discrimination learning but if 10 years ago someone were to ask me how to get moderately retarded children to learn a set of 20 concurrent discriminative problems in a

MARTIN'S DESIGN

	FAMILIAR-IZATION (F)		LEARNING (L)		F + L	
DEMON-STRATION	A B C				A B C	
TRAINING	A B C	X Y Z	A⁺ B⁺ C⁺	X⁻ Y⁻ Z⁻	A⁺ B⁺ C⁺	X⁻ Y⁻ Z⁻

FIG. 13 Stimulus arrangements for three conditions of Martin's (1970) study. Under the familiarization condition (*F*) the positive stimuli are demonstrated one at a time followed by recognition test trials with one old and one new stimulus. Subjects are instructed to choose the "old" stimulus. Under the learning condition (*L*) subjects are given standard discriminative training with positive stimuli rewarded. The familiarization-plus-learning condition (*F* + *L*) combines the features of both F and L conditions.

MARTIN'S DATA

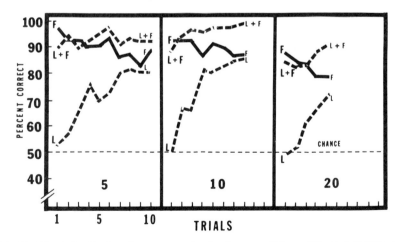

FIG. 14 Discriminative learning curves under the three conditions of Martin's (1970) study with lists of 5, 10, and 20 concurrent problems. The symbols *L*, *F*, and *L* + *F* represent the learning, familiarization, and learning-plus-familiarization conditions.

few trials I would not have known how. Now we are more sophisticated in our laboratory. We harness the force that confounded so many of our earlier experiments.

REFERENCES

Cross, H. A., & Vaughter, R. M. The Moss–Harlow effect in preschool children as a function of age. *Journal of Experimental Child Psychology,* 1966, *4,* 280–284.

Dember, W. N., & Fowler, H. Spontaneous alternation behavior. *Psychological Bulletin,* 1958, *55,* 412–428.

Ekstrand, B. R., Wallace, W. P., & Underwood, B. J. A frequency theory of verbal-discriminative learning. *Psychological Review,* 1966, *73,* 566–578.

Fisher, M. A., Sperber, R., & Zeaman, D. Theory and data on developmental changes in novelty preference. *Journal of Experimental Child Psychology,* 1973, *3,* 509–520.

Fowler, H. *Curiosity and exploratory behavior.* New York: Macmillan, 1965.

Grabbe, W., & Campione, J. C. A novelty interpretation of the Moss–Harlow effect in preschool children. *Child Development,* 1969, *40,* 1077–1084.

Greenberg, D., Uzgiris, I. C., & Hunt, J. McV. Attentional preferences and experience: III. Visual familiarity and looking time. *Journal of Genetic Psychology,* 1970, *117,* 123–135.

Greenfield, D. Novelty and familiarity as redundant cues in retardate discrimination learning. Unpublished Masters thesis, University of Connecticut, 1975.

Greenfield, D. Relational learning in retardates: Facilitative effects of novelty and familiarity in identity and difference learning. Unpublished doctoral dissertation, University of Connecticut, 1975.

House, B. J., Orlando, R., & Zeaman, D. Role of positive and negative cues in the discrimination learning of mental defectives. *Perceptual and Motor Skills,* 1957, *7,* 73–79.

House, B. J., & Zeaman, D. Reward and nonreward in the discrimination learning of imbeciles. *Journal of Comparative and Physiological Psychology,* 1958, *51,* 614–618.

Hunt, J. McV. Attentional preferences and experience: I. Introduction. *Journal of Genetic Psychology,* 1970, *117,* 99–107.

Jeffrey, W. E., & Cohen, L. B. Habituation in the human infant. In H. W. Reese (Ed.), *Advances in child development and behavior* (Vol. 6). New York: Academic Press, 1971.

Kaess, W., & Zeaman, D. Positive and negative knowledge of results on a Pressey-type punchboard. *Journal of Experimental Psychology,* 1960, *60,* 12–17.

Losty, B. P. Stimulus integration and novelty as factors in the discriminative learning of retarded children. Unpublished doctoral dissertation, University of Connecticut, 1971.

Martin, A. S. The effect of the novelty–familiarity dimension on discrimination learning by mental retardates. Unpublished doctoral dissertation, University of Connecticut, 1970.

Moss, E., & Harlow, H. The role of reward in the discrimination learning of imbeciles. *Journal of Comparative and Physiological Psychology,* 1947, *40,* 333–342.

Zeaman, D., & House, B. J. The growth and decay of reactive inhibition as measured by alternation behavior. *Journal of Experimental Psychology,* 1951, *41,* 177–186.

Zeaman, D., House, B. J., & Orlando, R. Use of special training conditions in visual discrimination learning with imbeciles. *American Journal of Mental Deficiency,* 1958, *63,* 453–459.

10

Comparisons between Habituation Research at the Developmental and Animal-Neurophysiological Levels

R. N. Leaton
T. J. Tighe

Dartmouth College

In this chapter we shall try to identify the significant points of contact between research in habituation at the animal-neurophysiological level and the developmental level. Of course, generalization from animal behavior and simplified preparations to the behavior of intact humans has always been problematic. However, we might gain hope for this enterprise from the work of Thompson and his associates (Thompson & Glanzman, Chapter 2, this volume) and Kandel and his associates (Castellucci & Kandel, Chapter 1, this volume) and others who have been strikingly successful in delineating parallels between the behavior of neurons and the behavior of the intact organism. One might suppose that the distance along the generalization continuum from neuron to intact rat or cat is at least as great as the distance from rat or cat to man. Given this perspective, there is good reason to expect that comparison of habituation research on children and habituation research on infrahumans can yield significant returns for both endeavors, particularly in view of the relative simplicity of the behavioral process at issue. The procedures used at the two levels are at least superficially similar; a stimulus is repeatedly presented and a decrement in response is recorded. Although parallels at these two levels of analysis are not sufficient to establish similarities in underlying mechanisms, each approach may be instructive to the other. On the one hand, the detailed analysis available to the animal-neurophysiological researcher enables a theoretical and parametric framework that is difficult to attain at the human developmental level. On the other hand, the research of the developmentalists should impress the animal-neurophysiologists with the behavior complexities their molecular analyses must ultimately handle.

These, of course, are among the considerations that motivated the conference from which this volume stems.

What the conference made clear was that its participants, whether working at the level of neural, animal, or child behavior, have many interests and problems in common. We are not, and the field is not, prepared to integrate the data and theories that have stemmed from these diverse efforts. However, we would like, in these closing paragraphs, to take an overview of the procedures and outcomes represented in this book to see where lie the most obvious parallels, the most obvious differences, and the most obvious lack of data.

Any comparison of the developmental and animal-neurophysiological research on habituation must begin with the consideration that investigators in these areas have approached habituation for different reasons. The animal-neurophysiological researcher has been interested in habituation as a model form of simple behavioral plasticity, while the developmental psychologist has been attracted to habituation because it provides an indexing response in organisms that can make few such responses. The researcher at the animal-neurophysiological level, then, has been interested in habituation per se while the developmental investigator has been interested for the most part in using habituation to study other processes.

The general character of the research in each area follows directly from these orientations. Habituation research with infrahumans has sought full description of the habituation process at the behavioral and neural levels by means of parametric investigation of simple, standard preparations. Perhaps the best exemplar of this approach is the work of Kandel and his associates who have achieved virtually complete description of the cellular architecture and neurophysiology underlying habituation of gill withdrawal in *Aplysia*. In contrast, developmental research has been primarily concerned either with demonstrating habituation at various periods of development or with using habituation as a tool to measure perceptual and cognitive processes. It is hardly surprising, therefore, that the bulk of our empirical knowledge and parametric understanding of the habituation process has come from the animal-neurophysiological rather than the developmental area. The developmental work, on the other hand, has indicated the rich and varied role that habituation may play in complex behavioral processes.

In addition to these differences in the broad concerns of each investigative level, the animal and child research groups in this text differ notably with respect to the complexity of the stimulus–response relations under study. Researchers in the child area have focused on visual orienting and heart rate responses, and in the usual experiment these behaviors are measures throughout presentation of long duration, frequently complex stimuli under conditions that afford opportunities for the subject to attenuate the input by peripheral or perhaps central attending responses. For example, visual fixation of a multidimensional pattern may be measured throughout successive 1-min presentations of the pattern with the child free to attend or not attend to the stimulus. In contrast, the animal research is characterized by short-term, discrete stimulus—response events with stimulus input controlled primarily if not exclusively by the experimenter, for example, muscle twitch to a 100-msec nerve shock, gill withdrawal to a 500-msec jet of water, or startle response to a 50-msec tone. While complex behaviors have been included in animal habituation experiments, particularly in work conducted within the ethological framework (Hinde, 1970), it is nevertheless true that the major theoretical conceptions of habituation in animals stem chiefly from the study of simpler reflexes.

As a broad gauge of the differences between the animal and child habituation research areas, it might be noted that the tradition of work on animal exploratory behavior appears to occupy a position intermediate to these efforts. While animal researchers working within the paradigm of exploratory behavior are dealing with a level of organismic complexity similar to that dealt with by animal researchers working within the habituation paradigm, procedurally the exploratory paradigm is quite similar to much of the habituation research with children, particularly to that on visual orienting behavior. For example, the typical animal exploratory experiment measures voluntary response processes (for example, approach or choice behavior) throughout extended exposures to a novel stimulus that is often quite complex. It has been generally assumed that exploratory behavior can be understood within the framework of habituation research on simple reflexes (e.g., Thompson & Spencer, 1966), but there has been little effort to relate these research areas in a systematic or comprehensive fashion, and some recent data (Williams, Hamilton, & Carlton, 1974, 1975) suggest the involvement of different underlying mechanisms. We suspect that significant gains in our basic understanding of habituation would follow both from a systematic extension to exploratory behavior of the theories and parametric relationships derived from animal habituation research and from detailed comparisons of child development research to animal exploratory research.

In the light of these considerations, the absence of representatives of the exploratory research tradition at this conference is seen as a significant omission, and one that should be rectified in future study groups of this nature. In the comparisons we make throughout this chapter between animal-neurophysiological and child development research we will be using the habituation paradigm as our standard rather than the exploratory paradigm. However, many of the similarities and differences we will identify between these two fields would, in fact, appear in the same form if our comparisons were made between the habituation and exploratory paradigms within animal research alone.

At present, the best guide to evaluation of the similarities and differences between the developmental and animal-neurophysiological areas are the nine parametric characteristics of habituation outlined by Thompson and Spencer (1966). These criteria have been very influential in shaping conceptions of habituation at both the animal-neurophysiological and child development levels

(Jeffrey & Cohen, 1971), and throughout the conference we depended heavily on these criteria as our definition of habituation. We shall use these nine criteria as an organizational framework to compare the data and experimental procedures from the two research areas and to discuss some general concerns that were expressed during the conference. Following our consideration of the parametric characteristics of habituation we will briefly discuss several additional issues which were raised in various forms during the conference from which this volume stems.

PARAMETRIC CHARACTERISTICS OF HABITUATION

The nine criteria (quoted from Thompson & Spencer, 1966) are used here simply to facilitate comparison of the developmental and animal-neurophysiological research on pertinent points of data and procedure. Our discussion in this section is intended neither as a critique of the nine criteria (see Hinde, 1970; Graham, 1973) nor as a review of the empirical support for the criteria (see Groves & Thompson, 1970; Groves & Thompson, 1973; Thompson & Glanzman, Chapter 2, this volume; Thompson, Groves, Teyler, & Roemer, 1973).

   1. *"Given that a particular stimulus elicits a response, repeated applications of the stimulus result in decreased response (habituation). The decrease is usually a negative exponential function of the number of stimulus presentations"* *(Thompson & Spencer, 1966, p. 18).*

   In part this is simply a statement of the primary operational definition of habituation, response decrement resulting from repeated stimulation. Habituation in this sense has been well documented in research preparations ranging from single neurons to normal human infants. Decremental curves of negative exponential shape can also be easily documented both in the developmental and animal-neurophysiological literature. Of course, depending upon the exact defining equation, almost any monotonically decreasing function, however rapid or gradual the decrease, can be considered a negative exponential. However, curves are found within both areas of research that cannot be characterized as negative exponential functions. For example, many "habituation curves" show an increase in responsiveness over the initial periods of stimulation (Groves & Thompson, 1970). Therefore, we must assume that the negative exponential function refers to an underlying theoretical construct, and that the shape of the actual empirical curve may vary with many parametric features of the experimental situation. Some confusion is created even at this basic definitional level if we do not clearly specify whether we are speaking in empirical or theoretical terms. (See the discussion of Type I and Type II definitions of habituation in Thompson *et al.,* 1973.)

Given that empirical habituation curves may take a number of forms, comparisons of the shapes of habituation curves are meaningful only in the light of some clear theoretical expectations. The dual process theory, for example, attaches theoretical significance to initially increasing curves and makes predictions about the operation of a number of variables on the overall shape of the empirical curve (Groves & Thompson, 1970). Cohen (Chapter 6, this volume) has suggested an all-or-none like underlying process for habituation in human infants and presents "backward habituation curves" in support of this position. Such a theoretical position, contrasted with, say, a negative exponential hypothesis, also makes a comparison of the shapes of the habituation curves potentially meaningful. In such comparisons, of course, we must keep in mind the possibility that procedural differences, rather than process differences, may underlie different empirical curves of habituation. Cohen's procedure, for example, is not unlike a preference test in which the habituatory stimulus competes for the child's attention with other features of the experimental environment. From this viewpoint, once the attractiveness of the stimulus has been reduced, through habituation, to a level comparable to other available stimuli, the child will suddenly reach the habituation criterion. For the proponent of a negative exponential hypothesis the suddenness of the decrease would depend upon the size of the exponent. Thus, one-trial habituation in this paradigm may be similar to demonstrations of one-trial learning in simple two-choice situations. One might suppose that if multiple response measures were taken in Cohen's paradigm, some response decrements might appear that would more nearly suggest a negative exponential function.

Our purpose here is not to argue for one preferred form of the habituation curve. Rather, the foregoing considerations are advanced to underscore the point that if we are to arrive at meaningful conceptualizations of habituation we must be careful to make a distinction similar to the learning–performance distinction we long ago learned to make in learning theory. That is, we must distinguish between particular measures of behavior under given conditions of repeated stimulation and the hypothetical underlying process of habituation. Clarity on this dimension is particularly critical when we try to bridge the gap between research traditions relying upon different experimental procedures. Discussions of this empirical–theoretical distinction came up repeatedly at the conference and misunderstandings and confusion not infrequently revolved around our failures to clearly specify whether we were talking the language of data or the language of theory.

2. "If the stimulus is withheld, the response tends to recover over time (spontaneous recovery)" (Thompson & Spencer, 1966, p. 18).

Two statements are really embodied here. One, that habituation is retained for some interval of time and two, that retention is not forever. Whether one speaks of spontaneous recovery or retention seems to depend upon whether one wants to emphasize the relatively permanent or the relatively transient properties of habituation. There is no clear distinction between the time course of recovery found in developmental and in animal-neurophysiological research, although the more cognitive theories in the developmental tradition seem to *imply* a more permanent effect. Long-term retention of habituation has been reported for many species with no obvious systematic differences between species. Retention of habituation has been demonstrated for up to 21 days in *Aplysia* (Carew, Pinsker & Kandel, 1972; Castellucci & Kandel, Chapter 1, this volume), for up to 4 days in the earthworm (Gardner, 1968), for up to 42 days in the rat (Leaton, 1974), and for up to a week in man (Harding & Rundle, 1969). There is no reason to assume that these data represent the limits of retention for these species.

Short-term habituation, with apparently full recovery occurring within minutes, is often reported at the animal-neurophysiological level but the experimental paradigms typically used in developmental research rarely permit the evaluation of these very short-term processes. Given the paradigmatic differences between the two research areas, particularly in terms of frequency of stimulation and duration of both the stimulus and the response, we can in no way distinguish animal-neurophysiological data from child-developmental data on the basis of the spontaneous recovery or retention of habituation. We simply do not have the appropriate data.

Within any level of analysis, response systems that apparently show only short-term habituation may have significant long-term components that the experimental paradigms do not detect. For example, startle response habituation in the rat has been typically characterized as a rapidly recovering system (e.g., Prosser & Hunter, 1936) yet more recent data have shown retention within that response system for up to a week (e.g., Davis, 1972; Moyer, 1963). On the other hand, short-term, rapidly recovering processes may go undetected in experiments designed primarily to research long-term processes. These considerations should make us hesitate in characterizing a species or a response system in terms of recovery time, and should encourage us to consider the operation of both long- and short-term processes within every response system studied.

In general, there has been little effort to categorize habituation in terms of retention or recovery time. The basic assumption of many researchers seems to be that whatever the recovery time, recovery does occur and the same basic mechanisms underlie both long- and short-term processes. Although several investigators have suggested a basic distinction between long- and short-term habituation, little effort, either theoretically or empirically, has been made to examine this distinction in detail. Indeed, there has been little investigation of the possible mechanisms underlying retention of habituation or of the variables that may affect the length of the retention interval. Wagner's theoretical position (Chapter 3, this volume) is one of the few attempts to conceptualize the differences between short- and long-term habituation and to make clear predictions concerning manipulations affecting retention. Castellucci and Kandel (Chapter 1, this volume) describe some of their initial efforts to study possible differences between short- and long-term habituation at the cellular level.

In spite of the general reluctance to conceptualize habituation in terms of the length of retention, a length-of-retention criterion is often used, at least implicitly, to rule out two processes that one always hopes to exclude from the definition of habituation: receptor adaptation and effector fatigue. It is usually assumed that adaptation and fatigue are short-term processes, but no one is in a position to make a general statement about the duration of such effects and no one is able to predict how long a response decrement must be retained before it can be considered habituation. In addition, short-term decremental processes that are apparently distinct from adaptation and fatigue have been noted, for example, prepulse inhibition (Ison & Hammond, 1971) and response refractoriness (Wilson & Groves, 1973), and apparently "true" habituation may have a relatively short time course (Wagner, Chapter 3, this volume). Certainly some experiments include controls that seem to rule out decremental processes other than habituation, but these controls presuppose some theoretical assumptions (often implicit) about the nature and persistence of habituation. It is obvious that retention alone is not an adequate criterion for habituation. We need specific theoretical guidance before we can say which of many possible decremental processes can be considered habituation.

3. *"If repeated series of habituation training and spontaneous recovery are given, habituation becomes successively more rapid" (Thompson & Spencer, 1966, p. 18).*

This characteristic of habituation suggests a specific way that retention of habituation may be indexed, comparable to a savings score following relearning in traditional learning paradigms. As with relearning measures, rehabituation is potentially a very sensitive measure of retention. Indeed, rehabituation might show retention of habituation even when initial responsiveness on retest indicates complete spontaneous recovery, and differences between these two indices of retention might provide some insights into underlying mechanisms. Also, one might assume that long-term, even permanent, effects of habituation would be commonly found following an extended series of habituation and spontaneous recovery sessions.

This characteristic of habituation has been demonstrated several times at the animal-neurophysiological level but has seldom, if ever, been looked for in developmental studies. One might expect it to be a particularly useful index of enduring effects of habituation in developmental research.

4. *"Other things being equal, the more rapid the frequency of stimulation, the more rapid and/or more pronounced is habituation" (Thompson & Spencer, 1966, p. 18).*

As Thompson *et al.* (1973) have pointed out, the relationship between frequency of stimulation and habituation is very complex. Under certain conditions, for example, habituation seems to be independent of frequency, depending only on the number of stimulus presentations. A direct relation between frequency of stimulation and degree of habituation is most clearly documented for rapid frequencies, one stimulus every few seconds or so. These relationships have been documented at the animal-neurophysiological level but have not been systematically examined in the developmental literature. Developmental research typically does not employ the rapid frequencies of stimulation that seem to be necessary to produce a clear relationship between frequency and habituation.

We should also note that when a direct relation between frequency of stimulation and habituation is shown, the relationship refers to what may be called "relative habituation" (see Thompson & Glanzman, Chapter 2, this volume), that is, response decrement measured under unchanging stimulus conditions, in this case repeated application of the same stimulus at a constant frequency. There are data (Wagner, Chapter 3, this volume) that show an inverse relationship between habituation and frequency of stimulation when habituation is indexed by retention over intervals that are relatively long compared to the interstimulus intervals used during training. Such data suggest that at least under some conditions massed versus spaced training produces effects in habituation paradigms similar to the effects produced in conventional learning paradigms.

Obviously, the whole question of the effects of frequency of stimulation on habituation is a complex problem that has not yet been completely solved within any area of research. Comparisons between animal-neurophysiological and developmental research are particularly difficult on this dimension because the range of frequencies of stimulation used in the two research areas are so vastly different. The situation is further complicated when we consider the possibility, discussed above, that stimulation over short interstimulus intervals produces decremental processes other than habituation. Developmental researchers simply have not dealt with a range of frequencies of stimulation which may yield unique habituation effects and which may produce decremental processes distinct from habituation. This is one of the empirical gaps that must be filled if we are going to make meaningful generalizations between the two areas of research.

5. *"The weaker the stimulus, the more rapid and more pronounced is habituation. Strong stimuli may yield no significant habituation" (Thompson & Spencer, 1966, p. 19).*

Stimulus intensity, like stimulus frequency, is a complex variable and one of considerable theoretical significance. The stated inverse relationship between stimulus intensity and habituation refers to "relative habituation," that is, response decrement with repeated application of the same constant intensity stimulus (Thompson & Glanzman, Chapter 2, this volume). As noted elsewhere in this volume (Thompson & Glanzman, Wagner) when different stimulus intensities are used for training and testing the situation becomes more complex. Under certain conditions, if amount of habituation is indexed by responsiveness to a given intensity stimulus, that responsiveness will be less following habituation training to a stronger stimulus than following training to a weaker stimulus. Thus, if we are to make meaningful generalizations about the intensity variable, we must keep in mind the specific testing procedures used, and we must clearly specify whether we are referring to habituation in empirical or theoretical terms. The situation is further complicated by the possibility that the application of a stimulus, aside from producing an increment in habituation which may be related to stimulus intensity, may also produce a second, independent process, sensitization, which varies directly with stimulus intensity (Groves & Thompson, 1970; Thompson & Glanzman, Chapter 2, this volume). The basic relationship between stimulus intensity and the underlying mechanisms of habituation and sensitization are not completely understood.

Given the potential for stimulus intensity to affect the outcome of habituation research, any systematic differences in this variable could seriously complicate comparisons between animal-neurophysiological and developmental research. Just such systematic, yet unintentionally systematic, differences seem to exist. Very few developmental studies of habituation deal in a direct way with intensity as a variable, and for obvious reasons the typical experiment with human infants uses relatively weak stimuli. The range of stimulus intensities used in the two research areas hardly overlap. The "strong" stimulus in developmental study is often comparable to the "weak" stimulus in animal-neurophysiological study.

Therefore, since sensitization is assumed to vary directly with stimulus intensity, systematic differences in both the presence and degree of sensitization may arise between the research areas. Certainly, in the developmental literature as a whole, sensitization is not a conspicuous phenomenon, in striking contrast to the empirical and theoretical prominence it has in the animal-neurophysiological literature. One might expect to find sensitization effects in studies of infant heart rate habituation since these studies generally employ relatively intense auditory stimuli. The characteristic heart rate response of the neonate to auditory stimuli is a monophasic acceleratory pattern that may persist throughout repeated stimulation (Graham & Jackson, 1970). Although this response pattern is an incrementing process, its relationship to the conceptualization of sensitization by Thompson and his associates (Groves & Thompson, 1970; Thompson & Glanzman, Chapter 2, this volume; Thompson et al., 1973) is debatable (Graham, 1973).

One should note that in many instances the stimuli used in developmental studies, such as visual patterns, cannot be unambiguously scaled along an intensity dimension. It is possible that the complexity dimension that is often manipulated in developmental studies may be, at least in part, an intensity dimension. It would be illuminating to see whether or not characteristics of habituation that vary with the intensity of the stimulus might not also vary in similar ways with stimulus complexity. For example, Cohen's "backward habituation curves" (Chapter 6, this volume) show a sensitization-like increased responsiveness just before the habituation criterion is reached for complex (strong?) stimuli but not for simple (weak?) stimuli. Jeffrey and Cohen (1971) have suggested a similar relationship between complexity and rate of habituation. Perhaps these are only superficial similarities, perhaps not.

Duration of the habituatory stimulus is a variable that may have certain properties in common with stimulus intensity, or may interact in significant ways with intensity, but it has not been a well-researched variable at either the animal-neurophysiological or developmental levels. However, it is a variable, like intensity, that tends to systematically differentiate the procedures in the two areas. In the typical animal-neurophysiological experiment the duration of the habituatory stimulus is often a few hundred milliseconds or less and a stimulus of 1 or 2 sec is a "long" duration stimulus. In human developmental research habituatory stimuli of 30 sec or more in duration are not uncommon and a "short" duration stimulus in developmental research is comparable to a "long" duration stimulus in animal-neurophysiological research. Here, as with stimulus intensity, the range of the variable used in the two research areas rarely overlaps. Systematic differences in these basic stimulus variables could lead to erroneous assumptions of process differences, and we can only avoid these potentially significant complications if researchers in both areas extend the range of their variables.

6. *"The effects of habituation training may proceed beyond the zero or asymptotic response level" (Thompson & Spencer, 1966, p. 19).*

There have been very few direct tests of this characteristic of habituation with any preparation, and we know of no systematic attempt to study it in the developmental literature. As Thompson and Spencer pointed out, this characteristic is basically a further statement of the relationship between number of trials and degree of habituation. It further implies that habituation may proceed without changes in the elicited response or even without direct elicitation of the response. It thus comes to involve the complex issue of response definition. What is or is not "below zero" depends upon the level and the sensitivity of the response measure. It may be assumed that, other things equal, the more molecular and/or more sensitive the response measure the less likely one is to find "below zero" effects.

Sensitivity of the response measure is a critical consideration when comparing different habituation studies, particularly when comparisons are made along such dimensions as specificity, generalization, rate of habituation, and speed or degree of spontaneous recovery. A response measure sensitive only to the relatively large initial decrements in an habituation series might show an asymptotic level after very few stimulus presentations, there would be relatively little habituation at asymptote, and complete spontaneous recovery might appear to be relatively rapid. In contrast, with a measure sensitive to a wider range of decrements, an asymptotic response level would be reached more slowly, the degree of habituation at asymptote would be greater, and complete recovery would be relatively slow. Thus, two measures that might be tapping the same basic response system would suggest different functions for rate of habituation and spontaneous recovery. Similar considerations apply to differences in the way data from any single response measure are treated. For example, one might analyze data from a single response measure in terms of absolute response decrements, percentage of response decrement, or changes in response frequency, and these different treatments of the data might yield different conclusions (Hinde, 1970). If systematic differences do exist in the sensitivity of the response measures (or in the techniques of data treatment) used in animal-neurophysiological and developmental research, still another condition would exist which could produce inappropriate conclusions concerning differences in habituation.

7. *"Habituation of response to a given stimulus exhibits stimulus generalization to other stimuli" (Thompson & Spencer, 1966, p. 19).*

This is basically a straightforward characteristic of habituation. When response decrements occur to one stimulus the response to other, "similar" stimuli will be at least partially decremented. The implied half of this characteristic is that generalization is not complete; that is, habituation is stimulus specific.

However, confusion is often generated here because of inconsistent use of terminology. It is certainly true that terminology problems occur within both animal-neurophysiological and developmental research, but the problem becomes seriously compounded when we try to bridge between the fields. Some investigators, particularly within the developmental area, refer to the reappearance of a response to a changed stimulus as "dishabituation" or "recovery." We believe that for the sake of clarity both of these terms should be used to refer only to the response to the original habituatory stimulus and not to the response to a new stimulus. *Dishabituation,* which will be discussed further below, should refer specifically to increased responding to the original habituatory stimulus following the presentation of another stimulus. We should restrict the use of the terms generalization and specificity to descriptions of the response to a stimulus other than that used in the original habituation training. *Generalization* should be indexed by the difference between the response to stimulus X following habituation training with a different stimulus and the response to stimulus X without prior habituation training. *Specificity* should be indexed by the difference between the response elicited by a new stimulus and the final response level attained to the original habituatory stimulus. This volume would be of significant value if it did no more than lead to consistent use of terminology both within and between fields. (For further comments on these terminology problems, see Clifton, & Nelson, Chapter 5, and Jeffrey, Chapter 8, this volume.)

Demonstrations of generalization and specificity can be found within both animal-neurophysiological and developmental research although these demonstrations are rarely systematic enough to indicate the extent of the effects.

Possible differences in intensity between the original stimulus and the new stimulus must be carefully controlled if meaningful generalization and specificity data are to be gained. And, of course, the balance between generalization and specificity will depend upon details of the experimental situation and the particular stimuli used.

Tests for stimulus specificity are among the most significant control procedures in distinguishing between habituation and other possible decremental processes, like fatigue. These tests are particularly important and frequently used with young infants because of the very real possibility of changes in state variables over the course of the experimental session (see Clifton & Nelson, Chapter 5, this volume). It should be understood that a demonstration of stimulus specificity is inconclusive unless we can be convinced that the changed stimulus is no more intense than the original habituatory stimulus.

8. *"Presentation of another (usually strong) stimulus results in recovery of the habituated response (dishabituation)" (Thompson & Spencer, 1966, p. 19).*

Embedded in this characteristic of habituation are a whole series of procedural, empirical and theoretical questions. At the procedural level, we have already noted the terminology problems. As detailed above, the term dishabituation should only be used to refer to increased responsiveness to the *original* habituatory stimulus following the presentation of a different stimulus, the dishabituatory stimulus. Considered only in this operational form, dishabituation has been frequently demonstrated in the animal-neurophysiological literature. Dishabituation is often considered one of the primary defining characteristics of habituation, and tests for dishabituation have been used to distinguish between habituation and other forms of response decrements. Indeed, dishabituation is one of the few behavioral controls for distinguishing between response decrements resulting from sensory adaptation and response decrements resulting from habituation. In spite of the significance that has been attached to this characteristic of habituation, it has rarely been researched in the human developmental literature (see Jeffrey, Chapter 8, this volume). Whether or not it would appear as ubiquitously there as it does in the animal-neurophysiological literature remains to be seen.

At the theoretical level dishabituation has usually been conceptualized, as the term implies, as a disruption of the basic habituation process, a disinhibition. However, Thompson and his associates (Thompson & Glanzman, Chapter 2, this volume; Groves & Thompson, 1970; Thompson, Groves, Teyler & Roemer, 1973; Thompson & Spencer, 1966) have argued persuasively in the context of their dual-process theory that demonstrations of "dishabituation" do not represent basic disruptions of the habituation process, but rather, are produced by the action of a more generalized superimposed independent excitatory process, sensitization. There is a great deal of empirical support for this position, and a mechanism of sensitization has many significant empirical and theoretical implications for research in habituation. One implication in the context of our discussion here is that if demonstrations of dishabituation represent increased responsiveness resulting from a generalized increase in excitability, the basic logic of dishabituation as a control to distinguish habituation from sensory adaptation and fatigue is destroyed.

However pervasive the action of sensitization, the possibility still exists for the operation of "true" dishabituation, that is actual disruption of the basic habituation process. Whether or not dishabituation in this sense exists is an important theoretical issue because it would impose certain significant restrictions on the underlying mechanisms of habituation. For example, its existence would require some fundamental modification of current synaptic depression models of habituation (Castellucci & Kandel, Chapter 1, and Thompson & Glanzman, Chapter 2, this volume). Wagner's theoretical position (Chapter 3, this volume) offers a mechanism for the operation of "true" dishabituation, and data reported in his chapter support the possibility of the operation of dishabituation apart from sensitization. To our knowledge this is the only report of dishabituation that cannot be readily handled by postulating the independent action of sensitization. We must await further research on this important issue and further theoretical clarification on the degree of generality and specificity of sensitization. There is perhaps no issue more critical to our understanding of habituation and behavioral plasticity generally.

9. *"Upon repeated application of the dishabituatory stimulus, the amount of dishabituation produced habituates (this might be called habituation of dishabituation" (Thompson & Spencer, 1966, p. 19).*

This characteristic is simply a restatement of the fact that responses to stimuli habituate. That the dishabituatory effects of a stimulus habituate has been demonstrated in the animal literature almost as frequently as dishabituation itself. Of course, any characteristic of dishabituation must involve the same theoretical complications discussed above. For example, does this characteristic apply to dishabituation as a disruption of the basic process of habituation as well as to dishabituation as sensitization? Are there ways to vary sensitization independent of variations in the specific dishabituatory stimulus (general arousal, deprivation, basic state changes, etc.) and if so what is the relationship between intrinsic and extrinsic sensitization? We should also note here that a sensitization process that does not decay with repeated stimulation has been hypothesized (Graham, 1973). One may wonder whether there are two or more incrementing processes that may interact in any habituation paradigm. These questions carry us well beyond the limit of this characteristic of habituation and well beyond the scope of this chapter.

ORGANISMIC STATE VARIABLES

In addition to the variables discussed above, animal-neurophysiological and developmental research can be distinguished on the basis of the concern shown for changes in the state of the organism over the course of habituation experiments. As Clifton and Nelson so clearly establish in this volume, meaningful interpretation of habituation measures on infants requires control and measurement of the subject's state throughout the experiment. In contrast, state changes have been viewed generally as a negligible source of variance in animal habituation research. But while state changes may operate in a more obvious fashion in infant research than in animal research, it is nevertheless a potentially significant problem in research at all phylogenetic levels. For example, Roldán, Weiss, and Fifková (1963) showed that what appeared to be habituation of the arousal response in rats was, in fact, no more than a reflection of excitability changes during the sleep cycle. However, when care is taken to control for such excitability (state) changes, habituation of the arousal response in rats can be unambiguously demonstrated (Leaton & Buck, 1971). The possible operation of state variables is also suggested by data showing that both increments (Davis, 1974) and decrements (Korn & Moyer, 1966) in startle response can be related to time spent in the test environment.

Observations such as these suggest that state variables may play just as significant a role in animal research as in research with human infants. We should be encouraged to expand these observations at the animal-neurophysiological level. Within both research areas there is a need to regard state as more than simply a nuisance variable to be avoided or at least minimized in the measurement process. The interaction between state changes and habituation may be more fundamental to our understanding of the habituation process than we seem usually to assume. Groves and Thompson (1970) assumed that sensitization operates through a "state system" that has tonic nonspecific and motivation properties, but the explicit relationship between state and the sensitization produced by repetitive stimulation has not been worked out. There seems to be a promising area for further research here, one that could yield significant insights into the habituation process and behavioral plasticity generally, and one that could produce some interesting parallels between animal-neurophysiological and developmental research.

THEORY

We have already noted several points at which additional theoretical clarification might yield significant gains in our basic understanding of habituation. Such points can be identified because current theories of habituation have reached a level of sophistication that allows data to be related to theory in sufficiently specific ways to reveal needed modifications, elaborations, or clarifications. We thus may be on the threshold of rapid and significant theoretical progress in habituation. Such imminent progress is also suggested by the appearance of a theory (Wagner, Chapter 3, this volume) which brings habituation within the scope of the major theories of animal learning. At the developmental level Cohen and Olson (Chapters 6 and 7, this volume) attempt to relate the concepts of cognitive psychology to habituation. The need for such theoretical integrations is underscored by Zeaman's demonstrations (Chapter 9, this volume) of the close interrelationships between habituation and developmental phenomena of learning.

Here we would like to focus briefly on the general character or flavor of the theoretical differences separating the animal-neurophysiological and developmental areas. The typical working hypothesis in much of animal-neurophysiological research, whether elaborated into a systematic theory or not, is a common elements model based upon an underlying mechanism of synaptic depression. On the other hand developmental researchers are naturally predisposed to more cognitive and complex hypotheses which are often based more or less loosely on Sokolov's theory (1963). As Thompson and Glanzman suggest (Chapter 2, this volume), the differences between Sokolov's hypothesis of a neuronal model of the stimulus and a synaptic depression hypothesis may be much less than the degree of difference implied by the cognitive language on the one hand and the neurophysiological language on the other. Indeed, Jeffrey (Chapter 8, this volume) has warned against the uncritical adoption of complex cognitive language. These is no question that "stimulus models" can be formed through the action of synaptic depression. Horn (1970), for example, presents several hypothetical neural circuits which will show a variety of rather complex habituation phenomena with the response decrements mediated solely by synaptic depression resulting from repeated stimulation. One such hypothetical circuit would show pattern specific habituation, that is, habituation to a compound of two stimuli but recovery to either element of the compound alone. It is obviously overzealous to suggest that all of the phenomena of habituation in human infants can be reduced to an underlying mechanism of synaptic depression. However, it could be very instructive to see how far such a mechanism can take us. It should be apparent that an underlying mechanism of synaptic depression within neural circuits cannot be dismissed as too simple a mechanism to account for the complexities of infant habituation.

DEVELOPMENTAL ASPECTS

Developmental aspects of habituation can be discussed along several dimensions. First, there is the matter of possible developmental differences in habituation itself. Second, there is the question of how habituation might contribute to developmental differences in other behaviors. Third, there is the general issue of the importance of habituation in development.

In regard to the first of these dimensions, we know very little about the relation between age and habituation. In contrast, Campbell and Coulter (Chapter 4, this volume) have marshalled considerable support for the conclusion that young organisms accomplish a wide variety of standard learning tasks as readily as adults but have much poorer retention for that learning than do adults. This body of empirical work, together with their analysis of possible psychological and neural causes of the observed developmental pattern, provides a useful framework for ontogenetic study of habituation. If habituation is on a continuum with the simple learning tasks reviewed by Campbell and Coulter, we can expect similar developmental patterns across these paradigms

In regard to retention of habituation, a recent study by Parsons, Fagan, and Spear (1973) has shown that infant rats show poorer retention of habituation of exploratory behavior than adults. While there are few data comparing retention of habituation as a function of age at the human level, Olson (Chapter 7, this volume) does suggest the provocative hypothesis, supported by data from his own and other laboratories, that recognition memory for visual stimuli is developmentally invariant.

While Campbell and Coulter's review did not find a relation between age and acquisition for most learning tasks, the few existing developmental studies of rate of habituation in animals suggest that rate may vary with age. Three studies have observed an abrupt transition from a pattern of little or no habituation of exploratory behavior in 15-day-old rats to a pattern of adult-like habituation in rats 18 to 25 days old (Feigley, Parsons, Hamilton, & Spear, 1972; Parsons, Fagan, & Spear, 1973; Bronstein, Neiman, Wolkoff, & Levine, 1974). Williams, Hamilton, and Carlton (1975) found a similar age difference in habituation of exploratory behavior in rats but also found that the rate of decrement of startle reflex was *not* clearly differentiated as a function of age. This ontogenetic dissociation of the two instances of response decrement parallels (and was suggested by) observation of a pharmacological dissociation of these behaviors (Williams, Hamilton, & Carlton, 1974), the entire pattern suggesting that the different instances of response decrement are dependent on different biochemical substrates (Williams, Hamilton, & Carlton, 1975). At the anatomical level, the hippocampus, which has often been associated with habituation of exploratory behavior (e.g., Douglas, 1967), is poorly developed in immature organisms (Altman & Bayer, 1975). The suggested relationships between habituation and ontogenetic, pharmacological, and anatomical variables within these studies suggest that programmatic study of the development of habituation in infrahumans would richly benefit several areas of research.

At the human level, general conclusions concerning the relation between age and rate of habituation are still not possible despite considerable study of habituation at different points within the first year of life. The well-known difficulty of obtaining habituation in the neonate in contrast to the relative ease of establishing habituation in children beyond 2 months of age (Jeffrey & Cohen, 1971) is indirect evidence for a developmental difference in habituation. However, it has been argued that the failures to demonstrate habituation in the neonate reflect stimulus and procedural limitations rather than any inherent inability of the young organism (e.g., Horowitz, 1975; Hunter & Ames, 1975). This view is supported by a number of recent experiments (cf Cohen in this volume). In addition, there have been a number of observations of both age and individual differences in rate of habituation in children (e.g., Friedman, 1975; McCall & Kagan, 1970), as well as intriguing observations of correlations between rate of infant habituation and behavioral and neurological indices of development (e.g., Lewis, Bartels, Campbell, & Goldberg, 1967). While such observations point to ontogenetic factors in habituation, there are truly formidable problems in the way of isolating and fully understanding such factors. Clifton and Nelson (Chapter 5, this volume) have thoroughly reviewed the many difficulties besetting developmental comparisons of response decrement. In the light of their review, it appears that a good deal of methodologically oriented work remains to be done if we are to have accurate and meaningful conclusions regarding the ontogeny of habituation. In particular, Clifton and Nelson make a persuasive case for conducting developmental comparisons in the context of systematic variation of several major parameters of habituation.

The chapters by both Jeffrey and Zeaman in this volume provide prime examples of how the study of habituation might aid analysis of other developmental processes. Jeffrey sees habituation as a mechanism whereby stimulus experience is organized into percepts or schemas of progressively more abstract character, and he has detailed how the development of schemas through habituation might underlie known developmental differences in a variety of problem-solving behaviors (Jeffrey, 1968). Zeaman's analysis establishes that the Law of Effect often conflicts with a Law of Habituation and that the outcome of that conflict varies with development of the organism. To put the matter in somewhat more specific terms, Zeaman shows how age differences in preferences for stimulus novelty and familiarity account for age differences in performance within standard learning tasks, differences heretofore ascribed to ontogenetic difference in the operation of traditional learning variables. These and other possible links between habituation and developmental differences in behavior (e.g., Sameroff, 1972; Tighe & Tighe, 1968) suggest the potential value of habituation as an empirical and conceptual tool in the study of development.

In regard to the general significance of habituation in development, it can be argued that habituation plays a much more important role than generally credited. The strong response–reinforcement bias that has prevailed since Watson has led students of behavior to ignore or minimize the possible contributions to behavior from nonreinforced stimulus exposures. Then, too, the effects of stimulus exposures are easily overlooked as compared to the specific, targeted changes brought about by traditional conditioning procedures. The habituation paradigm is now proving itself a powerful tool for studying the changes induced by stimulus exposures at many levels of organismic processing, and it is already clear that a few presentations of a new stimulus may have very significant effects upon the organism. As the chapters in this volume make clear, habituation may prepare the organism for other forms of behavior plasticity, modify attention and other stimulus selection processes, build representations of stimuli, and produce expectancies concerning the relationship between environmental events. These are surely critical effects at any age, but the special significance of habituation for development is given by the consideration that exposure to new stimulation doubtless comprises a greater proportion of experience in the younger organism.

ACKNOWLEDGMENTS

Preparation of this chapter was supported in part by Grant HD-04199-06 to R. N. Leaton from the National Institute of Child Health and Human Development and by Research Career Development Award KO4-HD-43,859 to T. J. Tighe from the National Institute of Child Health and Human Development.

REFERENCES

Altman, J., & Bayer, S. Postnatal development of the hippocampal dentate gyrus under normal and experimental conditions. In R. L. Isaacson & K. H. Pribram (Eds.), *The hippocampus.* Vol. 1: *Structure and development.* New York: Plenum Press, 1975.

Bronstein, P. M., Neiman, H., Wolkoff, F. D., & Levine, M. J. The development of habituation in the rat. *Animal Learning & Behavior, 1974, 2,* 92–96.

Carew, T. J., Pinsker, H. M., & Kandel, E. R. Long–term habituation of a defensive withdrawal reflex in *Aplysia. Science, 1972, 175,* 451–454.

Davis, M. Differential retention of sensitization and habituation of the startle response in the rat. *Journal of Comparative and Physiological Psychology, 1972, 78,* 260–267.

Davis, M. Sensitization of the rat startle response by noise. *Journal of Comparative and Physiological Psychology, 1974, 87,* 571–581.

Douglas, R. J. The hippocampus and behavior. *Psychological Bulletin, 1967, 67,* 416–442.

Feigley, D. A., Parsons, P. J., Hamilton, L. W., & Spear, N. E. Development of habituation to novel environments in the rat. *Journal of Comparative and Physiological Psychology, 1972, 79,* 443–452.

Friedman, S. Infant habituation: Process, problems and possibilities. In Ellis, N. R. (Ed.), *Aberrant development in infancy.* Hillsdale, N. J.: Lawrence Erlbaum Assoc., 1975.

Gardner, L. E. Retention and overhabituation of a dual-component response in *Lumbricus terrestris. Journal of Comparative and Physiological Psychology, 1968, 66,* 315–318.

Graham, F. K. Habituation and dishabituation of responses innervated by the autonomic nervous system. In H. V. S. Peeke & M. J. Herz (Eds.), *Habituation.* Vol. 1: *Behavioral studies.* New York: Academic Press, 1973.

Graham, F. K., & Jackson, J. C. Arousal systems and infant heart rate responses. In H. W. Reese (Ed.), *Advances in Child Development and Behavior* (Vol. 5). New York: Academic Press, 1970.

Groves, P. M., & Thompson, R. F. Habituation: A Dual-process theory. *Psychological Review, 1970, 77,* 419–450.

Groves, P. M., & Thompson, R. F. A dual-process theory of habituation: Neural mechanisms. In H. V. S. Peeke & M. J. Herz (Eds.), *Habituation.* Vol. 2: *Physiological substrates.* New York: Academic Press, 1973.

Harding, G. B., & Rundle, G. R. Long-term retention of modality- and nonmodality-specific habituation of the GSR. *Journal of Experimental Psychology*, 1969, *82*, 390–392.

Hinde, R. A. Behavioral habituation. In G. Horn & R. A. Hinde (Eds.), *Short-term changes in neural activity and behavior.* Cambridge, England: Cambridge University Press, 1970.

Horn, G. Changes in neuronal activity and their relationship to behavior. In G. Horn & R. A. Hinde (Eds.), *Short-term changes in neural activity and behavior.* Cambridge, England: Cambridge University Press, 1970.

Horowitz, F. D. (Ed.), Visual attention, auditory stimulation, and language discrimination in young infants. *Monographs of the Society for Research in Child Development,* 1975, *39,* Nos. 5–6.

Hunter, M. A., & Ames, E. W. Visual habituation and preference for novelty in five-week-old infants. Paper presented at meeting of the Society for Research in Child Development, Denver, 1975.

Ison, J. R., & Hammond, G. R. Modification of the startle reflex in the rat by changes in the auditory and visual environments. *Journal of Comparative and Physiological Psychology,* 1971, *75,* 435–452.

Jeffrey, W. E. The orienting reflex and attention in cognitive development. *Psychological Review,* 1968, *75,* 323–334.

Jeffrey, W. E., & Cohen, L. B. Habituation in the human infant. In H. W. Reese (Ed.), *Advances in child development and behavior* (Vol. 6). New York: Academic Press, 1971.

Korn, J. H., & Moyer, K. E. Habituation of the startle response and of heart rate in the rat. *Canadian Journal of Psychology,* 1966, *20,* 183–190.

Leaton, R. N. Long-term retention of the habituation of lick suppression in rats. *Journal of Comparative and Physiological Psychology,* 1974, *87,* 1157–1164.

Leaton, R. N., & Buck, R. L. Habituation of the arousal response in rats. *Journal of Comparative and Physiological Psychology,* 1971, *75,* 430–434.

Lewis, M., Bartels, B., Campbell, H., & Goldberg, S. Individual differences in attention: The relation between infants' condition at birth and attention distribution within the first year. *American Journal of Diseases of Children,* 1967, *113,* 461–465.

McCall, R. B., & Kagan, J. Individual differences in the infant's distribution of attention to stimulus discrepancy. *Developmental Psychology,* 1970, *2,* 90–98.

Moyer, K. E. Startle response: Habituation over trials and days, and sex and strain differences. *Journal of Comparative and Physiological Psychology,* 1963, *56,* 863–865.

Parsons, J. P., Fagan, T., & Spear, N. E. Short-term retention of habituation in the rat: A developmental study from infancy to old age. *Journal of Comparative and Physiological Psychology,* 1973, *84,* 545–553.

Prosser, C. L., & Hunter, W. S. The extinction of startle responses and spinal reflexes in the white rat. *American Journal of Physiology,* 1936, *117,* 609–618.

Roldán, E., Weiss, T., & Fifková, E. Excitability changes during the sleep cycle of the rat. *Electroencephalography and Clinical Neurophysiology,* 1963, *15,* 775–785.

Sameroff, A. J. Learning and adaptation in infancy: A comparison of models. In H. W. Reese (Ed.), *Advances in child development and behavior* (Vol. 7). New York: Academic Press, 1972.

Sokolov, E. N. *Perception and the conditioned reflex.* Oxford: Pergamon Press, 1963.

Thompson, R. F., Groves, P. M., Teyler, T. J., & Roemer, R. A. A dual-process theory of habituation: Theory and behavior. In H. V. S. Peeke & M. J. Herz (Eds.), *Habituation.* Vol. 1: *Behavioral studies.* New York: Academic Press, 1973.

Thompson, R. F., & Spencer, W. A. Habituation: A model phenomenon for the study of neuronal substrates of behavior. *Psychological Review,* 1966, *73,* 16–43.

Tighe, T. J., & Tighe, L. S. Perceptual learning in the discrimination processes of children:

An analysis of five variables in perceptual pretraining. *Journal of Experimental Psychology*, 1968, *77*, 125–134.

Williams, J. M. Hamilton, L. W., & Carlton, P. L. Pharmacological and anatomical dissociation of two types of habituation. *Journal of Comparative and Physiological Psychology*, 1974, *87*, 724–732.

Williams, J. M., Hamilton, L, W., & Carlton, P. L. Ontogenetic dissociation of two classes of habituation. *Journal of Comparative and Physiological Psychology*, 1975, *89*, 733–737.

Wilson, C. J., & Groves, P. M. Refractory period and habituation of acoustic startle response in rats. *Journal of Comparative and Physiological Psychology*, 1973, *83*, 492–498.

Author Index

Numbers in *italics* refer to pages on which the complete references are listed.

Kagan, J., 159, 163, 164, 165, 166, 167, *198, 199, 200,* 211, *238,* 337, *339*
Kail, R. V., Jr., 247, 248, 249, *274*
Kalafat, J., 166, *200*
Kamenetskaya, A. G., 159, 161, 187, *195*
Kamin, L. J., 96, 97, 99, 100, *127,* 105, *155*
Kandel, E. R., 1, 3, 4, 5, 7, 8, 9, 10, 11, 12, 13, 14, 15, 16, 17, 19, 20, 21, 23, 24, 25, 27, 29, 30, 31, 33, 34, 35, 36, 38, 40, 42, 44, *45, 46, 47,* 50, 52, 71, *90, 92, 93,* 259, *272,* 326, *338*
Kane, J., 187, 191, *195*
Kantowitz, S. R., 168, 184, 185, *197, 198*
Kapuniai, L. E., 173, *196*
Karlin, M. B., 246, *272*
Katz, B., 26, 29, *45,* 79, 82, *92*
Kay, H., 134, *155*
Kaye, H., 162, 173, 174, 182, 184, 188, *197, 199*
Kearsley, R. B., 168, 173, 185, *199*
Keen, R., 161, 162, 171, 184, 188, *199*
Kehoe, J., 4, 5, *45*
Kennedy, D., 40, *45,* 52, *91*
Kerr, J., 188, *203*
Kessen, W., 185, 186, *199, 203,* 251, *274*
Kety, S. S., 169, *199*
Khachaturian, Z., 188, *203*
Kimble, D. P., 292, *295*
Kimble, G. A., 119, *127*
Kimmel, H. D., 119, *127*
Kintsch, W., 118, *127,* 259, *274*
Kirby, R. H., 133, 137, *155*
Klein, S. B., 133, *155*
Kleitman, N., 168, 169, 174, *194, 199*
Kline, N. J., 133, *153*
Kling, J. W., 43, *45,* 95, *127*
Koch, J., 181, *199*
Koenigsberg, L. A., 133, 138, *157*
Koester, J., 3, 4, 5, 17, 20, *44, 45, 46*
Koike, H., 4, *45, 46*
Konorski, J., 103, *127,* 290, *295*
Kopp, C. B., 184, *203*
Korn, J. H., 334, *339*
Korner, A. F., 169, 174, 178, *199*
Kotses, H., 63, 64, *93*
Krasne, F. B., 40, *46*
Kremer, E. F., 120, *127*
Kreutzer, M. A., 247, *274*
Kruger, R., 188, *203*
Kuno, M., 78, 79, *92*

Kupfermann, I., 1, 3, 5, 7, 8, 11, 13, 14, 15, 16, 20, 21, 23, 25, *44, 45, 46,* 52, 71, *90, 92, 93*

L

Lacey, B. C., 167, *199*
Lacey, J. I., 167, *199*
Lackenmayer, L., 89, *90*
Lacote, D., 144, 151, *155*
Lantz, A., 125, *127*
Lapáčková, V., 180, *196*
Latz, E., 235, *238*
Lawicka, W., 103, *127*
Lazar, M. A., 214, 227, *237,* 254, *273*
Leaton, R. N., 120, *127,* 152, *155,* 326, 334, *339*
Lecours, A., 150, *157*
Lee, D., 54, *91*
Lee, J. C. M., 172, *201*
Lee, Y. H., 172, *201*
Lehner, G. F. J., 116, *127*
Lenard, H. G., 169, 172, 173, 174, 175, 182, 184, 185, *198*
Leonard, C., 247, *274*
Leply, W. M., 209, *238*
Leuba, C., 209, *238*
Levanthal, A. S., 188, *199*
Levin, G. R., 174, 184, *199*
Levine, J., 163, 165, *198*
Levine, M. J., 336, *338*
Levine, S., 86, *91,* 130, *157*
Levinson, L. V., 79, *93*
Levy, E. I., 244, 245, *276*
Levy, H., 185, *203*
Levy, N., 173, *200*
Levy, W. B., 86, *92*
Lewis, M., 159, 163, 165, 166, 167, 173, 179, 182, 192, 193, *198, 199, 200,* 211, *238,* 337, *339*
Liebeswar, G., 5, *46*
Lindsay, P. H., 239, *274*
Lipsitt, L. P., 130, 135, *155,* 162, 173, 182, 184, 187, 188, *197, 199, 200, 203*
Lipton, E. L., 173, *200*
Lockhart, R. S., 242, 243, *273*
Lodge, A., 175, *200*
Loftus, G. R., 244, 245, 246, *274, 275*
Losty, B. P., 312, *320*
Lubow, R. E., 125, 126, *127*

Subject Index